Mimesis

Mimesis

Culture—Art—Society

Gunter Gebauer
Christoph Wulf

Translated by Don Reneau

UNIVERSITY OF CALIFORNIA PRESS
Berkeley / Los Angeles / London

Originally published under the title *Mimesis*
Copyright © 1992 by Rowohlt Taschenbuch
Verlag GmbH, Reinbek bei Hamburg

University of California Press
Berkeley and Los Angeles, California

University of California Press
London, England

Copyright © 1995 by The Regents of
the University of California

Library of Congress Cataloging-in-Publication Data
Gebauer, Gunter.
    [Mimesis. English]
    Mimesis : culture, art, society / Gunter Gebauer,
  Christoph Wulf ; translated by Don Reneau.
        p.   cm.
    Includes bibliographical references and index.
    ISBN 0-520-08458-6 (cloth : alk. paper). —
  ISBN 0-520-08459-4 (pbk. : alk. paper)
    1. Mimesis in literature. 2. Literature—
  Aesthetics. 3. Aesthetics, Modern—20th century.
  I. Wulf, Christoph, 1944–   . II. Title.
  PN45.G3813 1995   95-36928
  801'.93—dc20   CIP

Printed in the United States of America

1   2   3   4   5   6   7   8   9

The paper used in this publication meets the minimum
requirements of American National Standard for
Information Sciences—Permanence of Paper for
Printed Library Materials, ANSI Z39.48-1984

Contents

Acknowledgments

We owe our thanks to our collaborators, Brigitte Akkoyunlu, Rita Beetz, Regina Bornmann, and Tanja Neumann, to the students in the seminar we offered together, and to the Volkswagen-Stiftung for its financial support to Gunter Gebauer.

Gunter Gebauer and Christoph Wulf

Introduction

Conventional understandings of mimesis fall short of the complexity and significance of the concept. It is restricted in some cases to aesthetics, in others to imitation. These definitions reveal neither the anthropological dimension of mimesis nor the variety of meanings that can be and have been attached to the term. And this is the case even though mimesis plays a critical role in nearly all areas of human thought and action, in our ideas, speech, writing, and reading. Mimesis is a *conditio humana* at the same that it is responsible for variations among individual human beings. A spectrum of meanings of mimesis has unfolded over the course of its historical development, including the act of resembling, of presenting the self, and expression as well as mimicry, *imitatio,* representation, and nonsensuous similarity. The accent may lie on similarity in sensuous terms, on a nonsensuous correspondence, or on an intentional construction of a correlation. Some writers have emphasized the intermediary character of mimesis; they locate it in medial images, which occupy the space between the inner and the outer worlds. Depending on developments in the larger aesthetic, philosophical, or social context, the meaning of mimesis changes, betraying a hitherto scarcely noted richness in the concept.

On the basis of selected examples, we have undertaken a historical reconstruction of important phases in the development of mimesis, which has allowed us to identify continuities and breaks in the usage of the term. An effort such as ours necessarily confronts considerable difficulties. In too many cases we have not been able to consider whole spheres, like music and architecture, that are critical to a complex understanding of mimesis, and we have devoted insufficient attention to others. Nevertheless, the insights we have gained warrant, in our judgment, a view of mimesis as belonging among those

1

concepts that are central to the human sciences. Mimesis has fascinated such writers as Walter Benjamin, Theodor Adorno, and Jacques Derrida, stimulating their reflections. With these writers the vagueness of the concept, rather than interfere with its precise application, has been turned to advantage.

It is not arbitrariness that has characterized the use of the concept, but a peculiar intuition, which often appears in the form of an adaptation to broader historical changes. There is less a lack of conceptual discipline in the history of mimesis than a resistance to theory building. As a concept, mimesis betrays a distrust of the instrumentalities and procedures of theory kept ''pure'' of the contamination of human practice. The artificiality, precision, and immobility characteristic of conventional definitions in scientific thought are hostile to mimesis, which tends toward action and is bound to time's passage and human productive activity. It would be more accurate to say that that bond, which comes to light in the form of insufficient technical rigor, has stood in the way of a clear explication of the concept.

Mimesis is not concerned with boundaries drawn between art, science, and life. It causes accepted differentiations to lose their power to distinguish and strips definitions of their conventional meanings. New connections, distinctions, and orders of thought come into being. Hitherto overlooked mimetic processes come into view; they appear in the entanglements of art and literature, aesthetics and science. The productive side of mimesis lies in the new connections it forges among art, philosophy, and science.

Mimetic processes are not unequivocal; they are better understood as ambivalent. Mimesis leads one to adapt to destroyed environments and petrified social relations; it has a part in our symbolization of the world and in processes of simulation. The aestheticization of the world is continued in the images of the mass media, which are related mimetically to presupposed realities. They create ostensible or constructed realities, change and absorb them; images are miniaturized and accelerated in video form; they become a surrogate experience of reality. Realities are not becoming images here, but images are becoming realities; a plurality of image-realities come into being. Distinctions between realities, images, and fictions break down. The world appears subject to a making in images. Images come into mimetic relation with other images. Floods of images drown the imagination and cancel the inaccessibility and oppositionality of the Other.

Mimesis resists a clear-cut split between subject and object; it resists any unequivocal distinction between what is and what should be. While it does indeed contain rational elements, they themselves evade instrumental interventions in and approaches to the world. The individual ''assimilates'' himself or herself to the world via mimetic processes. Mimesis makes it possible for individuals to step out of themselves, to draw the outer world into their inner world, and to lend expression to their interiority. It produces an otherwise unattainable proximity to objects and is thus a necessary condition of understanding.

In what contexts does mimesis appear? It is felt in discussions of how others are to be described physically, in statements about dance, music, and theater; it stimulates the imagination through writing and artistic representation. The often unconscious blend of doing and knowing found in mimesis designates a particular type of thinking or a faculty, which fuses the practical and technical skills we gain through experience and our theoretical abilities to recognize and evaluate. In this interpretation, mimesis characterizes the act of producing a symbolic world, which encompasses both practical and theoretical elements. The capacity and the procedure of representing on stage a person whose role is laid down in a text is a characteristic example of this. The concept of mimesis implies a resistance to splitting the human spheres of experience, action, and symbolic production into two parts, one practical and the other theoretical; it opposes analysis so definitive as to render mediation senseless. The history of mimesis as a whole makes reference to the mutual interpenetration of spheres, to a nonrecognition of the split, to symbolically constituted worlds.

Characterized in this way, it becomes evident that the concept of mimesis necessarily loses its intellectual centrality with the rise of rational thought. The field of art, which comes to be regarded in the process as autonomous, undergoes a complete and fundamental restructuring. The change itself allows us to recognize a second characteristic of mimesis: while modern rational thought refers to the single isolated cognitive subject, mimesis is always concerned with a relational network of more than one person; the mimetic production of a symbolic world refers to other worlds and to their creators and draws other persons into one's own world. As is apparent in this constellation, mimesis implies the recognition of mediation between worlds and people; it does not designate a subjection to received models, but rather an acceptance of traditions and the work of predecessors. It also implies a recognition of power: the inclusion of others introduces power, if only in symbolic terms, into one's own personal world, into the interpretive and perspectival modes developed there. The history of mimesis is a history of disputes over the power to make symbolic worlds, that is, the power to represent the self and others and interpret the world. To this extent mimesis possesses a political dimension and is part of the history of power relations.

An "impure" concept in the sense of rational thought, a concept immersed in practice and shot with traces of tradition and power, a variable of history and social relations and therefore not subject to formalization (thus compromised in modern terms), the rediscovery of mimesis takes place in a time in which the ideal of solipsistic cognition, a sharp distinction between theory and practice, and the ideology of the autonomous self, glorified as a creative ego, are all losing their universally obligatory character for scientific thought. Reference to others, the practice of thinking in terms of context and established customs and games, the turn toward action, the externalization of the self—all of these represent aspects of various endeavors to complete modernity in the sense of improving or, as the case may be, overcoming it.

Erich Auerbach, a German romance scholar living between cultures in exile in Istanbul when he wrote his major work on mimesis as a central element in the history of European ideas, began the contemporary retrieval of the concept of mimesis. We shall therefore begin with Auerbach and, through a discussion of the manner of his investigations, develop a terminology for our observations that is as adaptable and as flexible as possible. That our aim is not theory formation, with exact definitions, explications, and allegedly faithful reconstructions, should be evident by now. Just as little can it be disputed that our intention is a theoretical one. Our object requires us to confront processes of historical transformation; it calls for a specific kind of intellectual recapitulation of historical movement. But our undertaking only makes sense given a minimum degree of comparability among the various usages of the concept; we will introduce frame concepts to this end. The only concepts suitable for such a purpose are ones that have themselves been part of the historical processes, as the intellectual product of the persons involved. We shall develop our frame of conceptual reference out of the history of mimesis, which means precisely that historical reflection serves to establish the frame of reference without which the reflections would not be possible.

Mimesis in reference to others represents a productive intervention into modes of thinking and speaking that are other than one's own. An important question is whether this process gives rise to new modes of thinking and speaking, or whether all that results are variations of old ones. For us, however, it is a matter of gradual movement along a continuum; it is not here that the question of whether an author acquires the quality of an autonomous voice is decided. The influence of the ideology of original genius is evident here, but the more important question is the extent to which an author is able to resist social pressure, able to produce a counterpressure of his or her own, whether, that is, a particular strategy adopted in relation to the medium of expression generates a system of codification through which an author gains symbolic power.

With his concept of mimesis, Plato forged the intellectual tool that would introduce the decisive turn into the history of mimesis. His concept unifies certain linguistic customs while excluding others; he constructs wholly abstract typologies, applying the linguistic label ''mimesis'' to specific extracts of social, artistic, and practical action. He makes of a vague, nonspecific expression with diffuse usages a verbal label, one that is clearly determined by broader theoretical interests, which he then uses to characterize a specific subject matter. In our attempt to do justice to the breadth of the concept, we shall begin by pursuing the opposite approach; by considering all of the most important qualities attributed to mimesis over the course of its history, we shall attempt to restore to the concept the full spectrum of its meanings.

1.   In many usages mimesis entails an *identification* of one person with another. People identify themselves by means of their mimetic abilities when they see themselves in the Other and perceive a state of mutual equality. In this sense mimesis is distinct from mimicry, which implies only a physical and no mental relation. There is a complementarity of perspectives in mimesis: a person regards the Other as equal and assumes the Other to be doing the same in reverse. Such an act of complementary seeing produces a correspondence between people. Complementarity is manifest in physical form when one person clings to another; it is a sensuous, bodily act, but it is already penetrated by order; the Other is assimilated to the world of the person who is clinging. An affective moment, which is inherent in mimesis, is also expressed in this metaphor.

2.   Mimesis includes both an *active* and a *cognitive* component. The two cannot be sharply distinguished. Pierre Bourdieu, with the term *sens pratique,* designates this particular type of knowledge of practical action.

3.   Mimesis originally denoted a *physical action* and developed first in oral cultures. It has an indicative character, with attention turning repeatedly to the gestural over the history of the concept. Even as purely linguistic mimesis, it remains an "indicative speaking." The pointing is perceived by the recipient such that he or she is called on to see certain things or procedures as something. In this reciprocity lies one component of mimesis, one that renders into a spectacle that which is indicated or represented.

4.   Associated with the physical aspect of mimesis is its *performative* aspect, as an actualization, a presentation of what has been mimetically indicated. Thus is mimesis often combined with an action-oriented speaking. The action character of mimesis is even taken over into its written form. In other modes mimesis tends toward condensed symbols, for example, toward rituals and images.

We use the term "mimesis" as a verbal label for manifold social processes summarized conceptually. But here another problem arises: we have access to the original mimetic processes of practice only as verbal constructs and usually in written form. But mimesis moves with history, coming to expression in forms appropriate to respective historical periods. Our method is also constructive; it is designed to serve the purpose of introducing into thought an order that encompasses as much about what we know about mimetic processes as possible. By reconstructing variations on the concept of mimesis in historical context, we attempt to transcend the kind of thought that deals excessively in conceptual labels. Admittedly, the question remains unanswerable as to whether our way of ordering the world corresponds to this or that historical figure, or is even appropriate to his or her time. Yet this problem is not that of historical representation alone but one of intersubjectivity as such.

We have no language with which to illustrate original mimetic processes. Other aspects as well, however, of historical changes in mimesis can be understood only by means of subsequent construction. Alongside the concept of the individual, the way in which others enter into mimetic processes and what references are made to them also change. The involvement of an individual's interiority, the role of inner images, and the imagination itself change over time. Of critical significance to us are the historical transformations of literary genres, thus the relationship of epic, novel, and story to each other and their relationships to drama; the epic represents differently than the novel, which was able to distance itself from mimesis. A negative view of mimesis runs all the way through the history of the concept. Certain writers distance themselves from its various components: the role of the body, reference to others, practical action, the affective content of mimesis, the influence of the medial.

Our investigation begins with Greek antiquity, where the concept arose and where its first meanings evolved. Here a distinction is to be made between a pre-Platonic usage of the term oriented toward everyday meanings and Plato's "discovery" of mimesis and Aristotle's condensed use of the concept in his aesthetics. In Plato, mimesis is bound to the transition from oral to literary culture. His assessment, in that context, is ambivalent: on the one hand, he recognizes its significance; on the other, he fears its power, which is difficult to calculate. In any case, the widespread notion that Plato developed only a critical view of mimesis attends too narrowly to the facts. In his conception, mimesis is also the force that creates images and therefore underlies aesthetics. Plato sometimes designates even the works of philosophers as mimetic and calls for the creation of a society related mimetically to the eternal world of the Ideas. Even his relation to Socrates and the representation of Socratic philosophy in dialogues is mimetic. The prevailing view into the present, however, derives from the subsequent Aristotelian restriction of mimesis to aesthetics.

There has been no truly stationary period in the history of the concept of mimesis. New usages produce new contexts in which the concept—sometimes nearly imperceptibly—is changed. Mimesis is deeply entangled in society. Its respective historical positions are defined by authors, painters, musicians, architects, historians, and philosophers; they offer designs of how it might be possible, under the conditions of their time, to make artistic and other worlds. How can one create other worlds supplemental to the existing one? With what intention? What relationships should these other worlds have to the one that is taken at the time as the prior one?

The historical succession of such positions is most often conceived in terms of a model, as the progressive approximation of an empirically given social world, for example, or as growth or a collection of historical deposits around a conceptual core, as a dialectical ascendance or a spiral. There is no essential core of mimesis removed from history. Where would any such thing be located? Considering only antiquity, would it be in the pre-Platonic conception of musical theory? In the third or tenth book of the *Republic?* In Aristotle's *Poetics?* Or in Horace's conception of imitatio? To the notion of an augmentation of a conceptual core we can oppose the complex and multilayered meanings of mimesis in Plato, whereby it is difficult to imagine the concept being rendered any more complex later in its history. It is not possible to discern a general dialectic in the history of mimesis. Nor is a continuous ascendancy, also expressed in the image of the spiral, an appropriate metaphor, because a conceptual level once attained (as in Greek antiquity or in the eighteenth century) can be lost once again in a subsequent period.

Concepts cannot be referred back onto essences, and, in our view, the imposition of a specific course on history by means of structural theories is not tenable. Nevertheless, there are links among the various historical positions of mimesis, so that it is finally possible to conceive them as related to each other: later positions derive from earlier ones and are similar to them, just as they are related among themselves on the basis of a common derivation. Overlapping and crosscutting similarities are to be found among variations on the concept, without this meaning that they all share any one characteristic in common. The red thread we attempt to follow in this work is woven of such "family resemblances" (Wittgenstein). To this extent, our study has no central thesis to be imposed on the body of texts under consideration. Our intention, expressed in our recapitulation of the historical changes mimesis has undergone, is to expose the buried dimensions of the term and to correct and move beyond reductions, beyond the kind of unwarranted precision that results in an impoverishment of the concept.

What is remarkable in the history of mimesis is that it was already a theoretical problem very early on in the European tradition, that throughout the whole of its history it has always been the simultaneous object of theoretical reflection and aesthetic and social application. Mimesis as a concept of practice has prompted theorization in every epoch since its initial formulation. Rather than being accepted simply as representation, imitation, or whatever else it might be taken to mean, it has always been understood as a problem; mimesis, by virtue of the changes it effects, makes of one thing something Other. It is and has been regarded as an anthropological, epistemological, social, and political problem that demands reflection. Various solutions to the problem have been offered in the various historical epochs since antiquity; they are to be found not only in theoretical texts but also, in explicit or implicit form, in literature. We shall therefore include literary as well as theoretical texts in our investigation, concentrating primarily on explicit theory only in epochs in which mimesis became an explicit object of lasting theoretical treatment. It is important for our purpose that we convey an impression of the sheer multitude of reflective approaches to mimesis. We have therefore found it necessary, even at the risk of occasional cursory treatment, to provide an overview of entire epochs. Since mimesis is more than a procedure by which works of art are produced, it has been equally necessary for us to expand our field of vision beyond art and to introduce into the discussion a number of nonaesthetic aspects.

1

Point of Departure

Reflecting back on his history of mimesis, Auerbach had this to say to his critics: "The book is not a system; it strives to present a way of viewing its object, and the very elastic thoughts or ideas that hold it together cannot be taken as individual, isolated statements and refuted."[1] Auerbach's work offers the reader an implicit but nonetheless fundamental understanding of the relation of art to reality: artistic mimesis signals a turn toward social reality. But the latter is in no sense given once and for all; it takes on different forms through various historical epochs. It is therefore not enough simply to define the concept; we must follow its historical movement. The changes in "mimesis" express mutations in social reality. It is necessary, in a historical examination of the concept, to give precedence to the historical movement itself.

Auerbach's *Mimesis* has a strongly intuitive character. He overlooks the question of power in history and thus fails to recognize the potential inherent in having at one's disposal the means of symbolic expression, which entails the power of interpreting social reality and in that way endowing it with form and meaning. Auerbach does not take into account that mimesis in general is a turn toward a world that is by no means identical with empirical reality.

Our detailed discussion of Auerbach's book will indicate in which regards his concept of mimesis is too narrow and thus serve as a point of departure for a new methodological orientation.

On Auerbach's History of Mimesis

Auerbach's book is the first comprehensive work on the history of mimesis and probably the best known. Composed of a series of independent studies, the book has little to say about itself. Which aesthetic, literary critical, and philosophical interests does it pursue? On a cursory reading, it scarcely discloses the theme of mimesis itself. The book, which has no introduction, launches into the reading of texts: first Homer, then, juxtaposed comparatively to him, the Old Testament, then a succession of textual analyses. There is no explication of the concept of mimesis, no justification of the selection of authors; instead, we encounter a continual change of analytical objects. The only constants running through the book as a whole are Auerbach's fundamental concepts, "reality," "history of style," and "realism." In current aesthetic and literary critical discussions, these concepts no longer play an essential role.[2]

Despite what we might term its obsolete conceptual instrumentality, Auerbach's work is palpably contemporary—though this is a difficult fact to explain. His guiding interest is the interpretation of the real by way of literary representation. But the real makes no appearance in the book; social history is touched on in passing remarks but scarcely integrated into the discussion. Auerbach does not investigate mimesis in terms of its constructed character; the ways in which a world is made out of its fictional and imaginary aspects escapes analysis. He represents neither the constitutive principles of literary worlds nor the interaction or opposition between worldly domination and authorial power. The point for Auerbach is human being in the general sense and the style in which it is spoken about.

Auerbach devotes the first half of the book, in fact, to a treatment of the doctrine of distinct levels of style in literary representation. The investigation identifies several fundamental turning points in the history of "mimesis," in particular, the New Testament, which is "written . . . directly for everyman,"[3] and the *Divine Comedy*. With Dante another shift occurs: the representation of reality assumes the place of figural interpretation.[4] The shift is prepared by the emergence of a "sensory reality," the development of "a language . . . which is used to deal with everyday reality."[5] The figure becomes autonomous; an ontogenetic history, "the history of an individual's personal growth," becomes possible.[6] Dante "was the first to lay open the panorama of the common and multiplex world of human reality."[7] This break exhausts Auerbach's hypothesis regarding the mixture of styles. He does indeed illustrate the critical processes of modernity on the level of style, but the essential forces are different ones: forces that work their effects inside of literature and, in turn, issue from it and that derive from the pressure of society and the counterpressure exerted by authors. Once past the Renaissance, Auerbach devotes his investigation primarily to crisis models, in which authors oppose their own conceptions of social reality to the one prevailing at the time.

The French realistic novel, Auerbach's central thematic concern in the second half of the book, breaks with "the classical rule of distinct levels of style, for according to this rule, everyday practical reality could find a place in literature only within the frame of a low or intermediate kind of style, that is to say, as either grotesquely comic or pleasant, light, colorful, and elegant entertainment."[8] But the question of the conditions under which this distinction of styles was abandoned is not one to which Auerbach gives an answer. We do gain the insight that that answer might concern a historical sequence in the course of which, from late antiquity through the Middle Ages and the Renaissance and into modernity, realistic representation repeatedly violated the canon of poetic and rhetorical rules developed in the respective periods. Auerbach is quick to discover a whole series of "realisms." But what can be meant by this term in the plural? Auerbach's answer: moments of violation of traditional forms, the new formulation of alternative principles, a new beginning, personal speech, a change in literary objects. What comes of this is a new view of "the common and multiplex world of human reality"[9] and a new tone: "In modern literature the technique of imitation can evolve a serious, problematic, and tragic conception of any character, regardless of type and social standing."[10]

The "breakthroughs of realism" provide the turning points and pivots of Auerbach's book. It is obvious that a specific systematic can be attributed to them. But which one? Auerbach's concern is continually the way in which the individual is represented, whether as serious, problematic, or tragic. This is not only a question of style but also of context, in the broadest sense. If it is correct that the story of Christ, "with its ruthless mixture of everyday reality and the highest, most sublime tragedy,"[11] is responsible for the first historical triumph of realism, then the reasons for it were by no means merely stylistic, which is the basis Auerbach would like to use to explain the literary change. His realism thesis proves incapable of ordering the subtly interpreted literary historical material. The history of mimesis outlined by Auerbach as the representation of reality has, if only for that reason, neither structure nor an actual course, because he restricts it to the problematic of representation and attempts to comprehend that solely on the level of style.[12]

For Auerbach, the central point is the historically changing relation between the Western individual and his or her respective historical situation. Intellectual dispositions find expression in the literary language and are articulated in forms specific to each epoch. Auerbach sees language and historical situation in their capacity as intellectual forces realized and expressed in narrative, not, that is, in the terms of their materiality. The "construction consummated in language" is mimesis.[13] Mimesis is thus not imitation; rather, it constitutes itself in "reciprocal relations between fateful events and the reference made to them by individuals."[14] "The unity of Western culture"[15] is manifest in the metamorphoses of linguistic formations.

Auerbach's investigations presuppose two entities, the conceptual uniformity of which he assumes from the outset—language and the individual. We would raise in opposition to this speculative assumption evidence of profound historical changes in the conception of the individual as well as fundamental changes in language, which in both cases forbids a philosophically essentialist point of view. We shall therefore take up the threads of Auerbach's investigation from the beginning so as to consider how his method requires expansion or revision.

Auerbach offers the following as the basic tendencies of Homeric "realism": "fully externalized description, uniform illumination, uninterrupted connection, free expression, all events in the foreground, displaying unmistakable meanings, and few elements of historical development and of psychological perspective."[16] "A continuous, rhythmic procession of phenomena passes by," with "never a lacuna, never a gap."[17] The Homeric style has no perspectival method to separate foreground and background; it leaves "nothing which it mentions half in darkness and unexternalized."[18]

The story of Isaac's sacrifice in the Old Testament is completely different; its stylistic characteristics have "certain parts brought into high relief, others left obscure, abruptness, suggestive influence of the unexpressed, 'background' quality, multiplicity of meanings and the need for interpretation."[19] There is tremendous suspense in representation such as this, which, while "directed toward a single goal (and to that extent far more of a unity), remains mysterious and 'fraught with background,'"[20] The biblical narrator raises an objective claim to the truth of his report. The stories of the Old Testament "seek to subject us," for they "are not, like Homer's, simply narrated 'reality.'" The biblical narrative "seeks to overcome our reality: we are to fit our own life into its world."[21] It is simultaneously reinterpretation in a specific sense: "the new and strange world which now comes into view" must be reinterpreted to make it fit into the Jewish religious frame.[22] In the process, however, the multiplex nature of what happens internally and externally is maintained.

Auerbach takes both narrative modes, the Homeric and that of the Old Testament, to be fundamental types of "realistic" representation, each in its own way. In the New Testament the Jewish tradition undergoes a further development, assuming a sharply oppositional stance toward the rhetoric of antiquity.

> The spirit of the rhetoric—a spirit which classified subjects in *genera,* and invested every subject with a specific form of style as the one garment becoming it in virtue of its nature—could not extend its dominion to [the New Testament texts] for the simple reason that their subject would not fit into any of the known genres. A scene like Peter's denial fits into no antique genre. It is too serious for comedy, too contemporary and everyday for tragedy, politically too insignificant for history—and the form which was given it is one of such immediacy that its like does not exist in the literature of antiquity.[23]

What Auerbach fails to consider is *this* sense in which texts are produced, as verbal encounters with social reality, as a kind of textual "engagement" in the world to which the narrator himself or herself belongs. The reader is able to perceive the production of texts in the specific ways in which a literary work can be organized, a verbal world made. Indeed we cannot know from the texts themselves whether they offer a likeness of social reality in its essential features; the "realism" that Auerbach means makes reference to a social practice. Requiring explanation is the way in which this is supposed to take place.

Thus far we have offered a cautious reformulation of Auerbach's straightforward and unbiased approach to the question of the relationship between literature and reality, which he expresses as the simple relations of the production of likeness, and distanced his concept of mimesis from notions of imitation. We have used other terms, which, though provisional at this point, will acquire greater rigor as the discussion proceeds: "the textual production of worlds"; "confrontation with reality"; "reference to social practice." We have conjectured that the "breakthroughs of realism" Auerbach examines— direct speech, the mixing of styles, the seriousness of representation, the literary consequence of the isolated individual—cannot be explained solely by reference to devices exemplified in the history of style. We conclude that it is necessary to supplement the ways we have of viewing the object. The meaning of styles can only be discovered in its location within a more complex, more comprehensive context, which includes a number of major developments outside the sphere of style. This can be demonstrated in reference to Auerbach's juxtaposition of rhetorical tradition, on the one hand, and Homeric Old and New Testament "realisms," on the other.

The stylistic peculiarities of the Homeric text, for Auerbach, work to mark out a specific bearing toward the world. Stylistic characteristics have their cause in an interpretation of the world. Auerbach bases this claim on a simple relation of conditions: from within an interpretation of the world a style is chosen, and by way of the style a likeness is made of a pregiven reality. And vice versa: from the style we infer an interpretation of the world, on the one hand, and the presupposed reality, on the other. Things are obviously more complex. An interpretation of the world is not independent of the ways in which it is expressed; to this extent it cannot simply determine style. The interpretation can be represented in many different ways, for example, in bodily rituals, in cave paintings, in stone architecture, in expository speech or written descriptions, whereby further distinctions are required according to the various alphabetic systems, to whether the letters are carved in stone, written on paper, or printed, to whether pictographs are used, or a phonetic alphabet, and so on.

Homeric poetry itself is an example of how the representational medium influences what it represents and the worldview it expresses. Without raising controversial questions regarding the *Iliad*—whether it was a purely oral poem, that is, one associated exclusively with spoken delivery, passed on by the same means, and only later written down; whether it was developed with the aid of notes or under the influence of a still earlier written culture—we can say that it contains a multitude of qualities characteristic of oral poetry, suggesting that it was not yet fully affected by the "consequences of literacy,"[24] that its style can be recognized in the strong influence of spoken delivery and transmission. The written texts of Homeric poetry codify a style of speech that is essentially typical of spoken language; they possess clear features of orality and, vice versa, give little indication of the influence on speech and thought attributed to the phonetic alphabet.[25] The directness, the uniform externalization and illumination, the restriction to becoming—all of that which appears to us today as foreground—belongs predominantly to an oral stage, prior to the literate stage, of human speech and simply cannot be regarded as the consequence of the poet's worldview and his stylistic accomplishments.

The stylistic characteristics of the *Iliad* that Auerbach mentions can be interpreted as having arisen in the transition from an oral to a literate culture: the performance of the poem by a singer before a public favors a spontaneous and direct manner of speaking influenced by the physical; formulaic turns of phrase and rhythmical devices, the uniform and schematic procession of the events and circumstances described, help the memory retain long poetic speeches. It is therefore the *conditions of the medium* of spoken language that influence the mode of representation. They demand or favor specific types of speech; these may be simultaneously action oriented, ritualistic, and formulaic and make more difficult—or even exclude entirely—the development of other themes and representational modes. An example is precisely that which Auerbach stresses about Old Testament representation: the intensity of the personal story and "everything unresolved, truncated, and uncertain, which confuses the clear progress of the action and the simple orientation of the actors," have disappeared.[26] If an oral medium (or a culture still bound to the conditions of orality) can represent such substance only with difficulty or not at all, its view of the world will be restricted in the sense that it will not be able to elaborate differentiated interpretations of events and valuations.[27]

Auerbach attributed to "the view of the world," that is, the sum of philosophical or religious conceptions of reality, something that should be seen in part as belonging to the technical effects of the medium. If the medial aspect of language sets limiting conditions on the conceptions making up a view of the world and influences which elements are and which are not codifiable, expressible, and transmittable to posterity, then its role in the history of the representation of reality will be a major one. The concept of mimesis must be examined against the background of the slow development of the phonetic alphabet and the possibilities it opened up, as well as whatever external conditions exercise an effect on the medium. Stylistic changes, from this point of view, could be *indicators* of historical changes in the medium and the conceptions making up the worldview. From such a broadened perspective, it becomes possible to see the effects of changes in the medium and stylistic developments on the worldview.[28] Our approach therefore differs considerably from Auerbach's. We assume that style, conceptions making up a worldview, and the various media, each with its respective technical history, are all interdependent, so that *each* of these areas is involved in historical change.[29]

Biblical texts suggest additional reasons for objection to Auerbach. Obviously they release tremendous energies running directly counter to the social pressures weighing on the medium of poetic speech: "The biblical narrator, the Elohist, had to believe in the objective truth of the story of Abraham's sacrifice." He juxtaposed to the old order a new one in which he passionately believed.

> The Bible's claim to truth is not only far more urgent than Homer's, it is tyrannical—it excludes all other claims. . . . All other scenes, issues, and ordinances have no right to appear independently of it, and it is promised that all of them, the history of all mankind, will be given their due place within its frame, will be subordinated to it. The Scripture stories do not, like Homer's, court our favor . . . —they seek to subject us . . . ; because the stories are not, like Homer's, simply narrated 'reality.' Doctrine and promise are incarnate in them.[30]

The world is reordered in biblical texts; that is, it is not simply that a likeness is produced, but that the narration produces a new world.

The medium of representational language is the focus of an interplay between pressures exerted by society and counterpressure exerted by authors. As a rule, external pressures are strong enough to compel use of the medium in the spirit of prevailing social norms. In Auerbach's example of the New Testament, the counterpressure comes from a historical movement borne by an increasing number of people characterized by a new orientation toward the world and visions and ideas of redemption. But there are also other constellations in which an individual in a particular historical situation rebels against unstable institutions, begins to speak his or her own language and in this way refashions the medium. Such movements of successful counterpressure develop a self-authorized mode of writing that takes a stand opposed to established social forces and institutions. Examples of this are Luther and Shakespeare,[31] Montaigne,[32] Descartes,[33] and Rousseau. In the history of mimesis, authors making their own world by means of the medium come to play an increasingly prominent role.

Worldmaking and Social Pressure

On the basis of what we have said thus far, we find Auerbach's history of mimesis situated in a new problem context, in that of the power of the individual literary figure and his or her reaction to social pressure. How can the constellation of power, style, medium, and worldview be conceived? Social pressure and political pressure do not generally exercise their effects directly. But they can compel authors to express a specific worldview,[34] put them under pressure to conform, and supervise their observance of official demands in their verbal productions. It is this idea that we would like to develop now.

Let us examine a case in which social pressure on language is so strong that it is involved in the formation of the literary language. A "higher style," a "legitimate" literary language, takes form which is absolutely obligatory for the cultivated stratum of society. Examples are the rhetorical tradition and the court society of Versailles. Literature is required to create a kind of verbal code, which then becomes the obligatory form of high speech in society in general, that is, also for nonliterary speech. All-encompassing social pressure minimizes the difference in linguistic elevation between literary and nonliterary language for the elite group in society.[35] In these circumstances, not only a specific style is compulsory but above all the specific ways in which thought, experience, and emotion are verbally codified. Fundamental to any empirical society are several distinct, socially stratified principles of codification that predetermine rules governing speech and writing. A few of the elements of verbal codes identified by sociolinguistics can also be found in codifications in general: syntactical planning, alternative verbal expressions, orientation to specific social, intellectual, and emotional reference objects.[36]

Mary Douglas works fruitfully with these principles in reference to the Durkheim-Mauss hypothesis of classification. Her assumption is that these principles, which are used by various speakers and authors, form various "classification grids" that organize named or described objects into specific groups. The relevant criteria are clarity and specificity of the categories; differentiation of the distinctions; association of the entire differential system to social customs; connections within the system; its articulation as a whole; degree of verbal articulation of the categories; and organizational coherence. In Douglas's judgment, the classification grids achieve their specific form under the influence of social pressure, which is intensified by control. We will take up these ideas in order to pursue the question of the codification system on our own. In archaic societies like Homer's, the speaker exerts powerful pressure on the codification system; the singer possesses "a degree of cultural control over his community which is scarcely imaginable under modern literate conditions."[37] The codification system is rather formulaic and relatively undifferentiated. In the language of court society at Versailles, in contrast, codification is extremely elaborate, which implies a high degree of social pressure on both speakers and authors.[38]

Our intention is to introduce these considerations into a broader and more flexible conception of the interrelations among codification systems, social pressure, and worldview. We also adopt Nelson Goodman's conception of the way verbal representations not only perform classificatory functions but also, taken all together, construct an entire world.[39] Constructive, fictional, and ordering factors also contribute to the process, whereby a world comes into existence which is dependent on a codification system and cannot escape the influence of the system's essential features. Following is a brief depiction of Goodman's conception of worldmaking, the point of which for us is to elucidate the interrelation between a codification system and a view of the world.

Goodman shares with many contemporary philosophers the assumption that facts do not exist independently of description. He expands and refines the idea, arriving eventually at a new and original perspective. The dependent status of our knowledge of the world suggests that the latter should be regarded as a symbolic construction. Verbal representations are valid only within a frame of reference. The statements "The sun never moves" and "The sun is always moving" can both lay claim to truth depending on the frame of reference, that of personal experience or that of physics, in which they are placed. Truth, pertinence, and correctness can only be established in terms of respective reference frames. The critical point, however, is that the latter has no extra-linguistic existence either; it also belongs to the codification system (in Goodman's terms, "descriptive system"). Nothing is prior to the "constructional system." All the symbolic moments adding up to description of a world—codification system, frame of reference, language, and order—are subject to change: there exists not a single world, but many different worlds. "We are not speaking with concepts of multiple possible alternatives to a single actual world, but of multiple actual worlds."[40] The world is something that is described in individual representations, in its "versions." The versions contain the entirety of our knowledge concerning a world. Goodman's philosophy develops a constructive point of view according to which a world is produced in all the correct versions of it that exist.

Knowing in terms of this model is a matter of invention: modes of organization "are not 'found in the world,' but *built into a world.*"[41] Understanding is creative. With the aid of Goodman's theory of worldmaking, mimesis can be rehabilitated in opposition to a tradition that rigidly deprived it of the creative element—and that itself rests on false presuppositions: on the isolated object of knowledge, the assumption of a world existing outside codification systems, the idea that truth is the correspondence between statements and an extralinguistic world, the postulate that thought can be traced back to an origin. Nothing of this theory remains intact after Goodman's critique: worlds are made "*from other worlds.*" "Worldmaking as we know it always starts from worlds already in hand; the making is a remaking."[42]

The object of philosophy in Goodman's sense is these versions, rather than the world itself. For him, the critical thing is to investigate the various ways in which worlds are produced; mimetic processes and procedures are also part of this. Artworks reorganize and remodel the world.[43] Differences of style express distinctions as to the weighting of factors—often without a single element being newly introduced or left out—and are capable in this way of generating two different worlds. In this interpretation, "the arts must be taken no less seriously than the sciences as modes of discovery, creation, and enlargement of knowledge in the broad sense of advancement of the understanding, and thus . . . the philosophy of art should be conceived as an integral part of metaphysics and epistemology.''[44]

Such an interpretation renders problematic certain concepts, such as identification, similarity, repetition, imitation, and mimicry, that were used without question in earlier philosophy. The identical, the same, the similar—these relations are not givens but can be known only in relationship to symbolic organization.[45] Mimetic processes in whatever form, even as simple imitation, presuppose the interactive influence of both symbolic organization and the apprehension of similarity. Mimetic processes imply simultaneous versions of the same world; they produce the same order and lend emphatic expression to the latter. They contain a form of knowledge and understanding possessed of creative qualities—when, for example, they emphasize particular aspects of the symbolic order, as in a sketch or caricature. Variations on a world can considerably expand our knowledge of it; Goodman himself has analyzed a compelling example, Picasso's variation on Velázquez's *Las Meninas*.[46]

Our discussion of Goodman has allowed us to examine the systematic nature of the relationship among codification systems, mimesis, and worldmaking. We have provisionally set aside the social aspect of mimesis, namely, the pressure exerted by society on the codification system, which Goodman's analytical philosophy does not take into account. Yet we began with Douglas for precisely that reason, because she shows how codification systems and social pressure *together* exercise an effect on worldmaking.

At what points does social pressure make itself felt in literature? It obligates authors to a specific worldview (for example, the poets of the Roman Empire or those of the French court in the seventeenth century). It has effects through its *control* of literary products. Censors can supervise the ideological content of what is written and said or exercise other indirect supervisory procedures. This applies equally to other, nonliterary areas, for we are not dealing with a pressure applied exclusively to literature. The pressure comes to bear on the level of style, on the level of the available syntactical and lexical alternatives, the representational objects, and formal characteristics selected by the author. Codification principles can be recognized in style; they are what forms a connection between speaking or writing and a worldview. There therefore exists a close connection between worldview and the supervisory system: when social control is strong enough to repress certain stylistic tendencies that are essential to the codification of a certain worldview so that it can be expressed, that worldview has no chance to develop. Such a development does, however, occur when stylistic possibilities are surrendered to a new worldview, or when a new worldview prevails in its opposition to established powers. The rhetorical tradition, undergirded by political pressure, was able to control literary speech and writing for centuries. The further development of literature in these epochs consisted in withstanding social pressure and, in periods of relatively liberated personal expression, pushing it back by means of another language.

Among the Russian formalists, in particular, in their conception of the "difference quality,"[47] we find such a conception of literary history, according to which what drives the ongoing development of literature is the rise of new codification systems that distinguish themselves from established literary language. There is, in other words, a historical movement of literary mimesis, even if that movement is not to be understood in terms of the principle of progress, but rather as a permanent preoccupation with the problem of codification. Clearly the development of mimesis involves a confrontation not only with reality but also with established codification systems. Social pressure can be applied to literary works in manifold ways. It can be the direct pressure of social institutions or persons holding power; this case appears most clearly among the court poets. It can come from a group that has split itself off from society and stands in opposition to it, the opposition manifest in antitraditional codifications and stylistic forms. An example of this sort is early Christianity with its principle of the mixture of styles. Yet all authors respond to social pressure. They either take it up in conformist behavior or they adopt an oppositional stance and produce a counterpressure; or they seek a middle way between the two alternatives. From this perspective, literary mimesis consists of a confrontation with the power of social institutions and the holders of power, with traditional codification systems, stylistic models, and the worldviews that come to expression through them.

Douglas represents social control such that it becomes increasingly externalized in two opposing directions. We have already seen how control over language can be exercised from various sides. From one side it can affect literature like an alien pressure. Such control can originate equally in impersonal social institutions and in classes and groups, and ultimately the individual, who exerts an internalized social control against himself or herself. Inversely, individuals or groups can manage to bring their production of texts under their own control. This tendency is particularly well characterized historically by the modern avant-grade. The points we have made so far describe the objective side of the process, but it also has a subjective side: the codification system that is "permitted," or that takes shape under pressure, works simultaneously to form the real-life relationships of those employing it after its own image. For writers of literature, this means that their relation to the *literary* world of their own making is also formed under the influence of such pressure.[48]

There are multiple causes for the counterpressure authors exert against society. In one instance the authority of social institutions decays, allowing a single author to break through the "legitimate" codification system. A second possibility is that an individual self-authorizes and self-legitimates his or her articulation of a new perspective against pressure-bearing social institutions.[49] This possibility depends on the author's stylistic mastery and philosophical principles and worldview, by means of which the author formulates a response to the problems of his or her historical period. Thus did Descartes outfit the skeptical ego with the power to call the socially sanctioned scientific knowledge of his time, including theology, radically into question and to reorder it fundamentally according to its own principles. He overwhelmed the theological and scientific institutions of his time with an enormous intellectual energy, which all but swept aside the established styles of thought and writing, including the entire mimetic tradition.

A further case of counterpressure occurs in situations in which control models are no longer stable enough to support a society's legitimate codification system and an author prevails against it with a more powerful and persuasive system. In Auerbach's work this case is exemplified by the texts of Augustine, with their "dramatization of an inner event, an inner about-face." The inner action is "imbedded in concrete contemporary reality."[50] The embeddedness is directly manifest in style: instead of a style "which carefully interrelated the elements of history, which respected temporal and causal sequence [and] remained within the domain of the earthly foreground," a new style takes hold, one of a "fragmentary, discrete presentation, constantly seeking an interpretation from above."[51]

In another of Auerbach's examples new objects are discovered for literature, but no real counterpressure is exerted against social power, which gradually disintegrates. This is the case with French literature of the fifteenth century. Thus Villon, with his "utmost perfection of a creatural realism which remains completely within the sensory and, for all its radicalism of emotion and expression, shows no trace of intellectually categorizing power, or even of revolutionary power, shows indeed no will whatever to make this world any different from what it is."[52] The "creaturality" of the writing is necessarily conservative in its bearing and does not work to establish a new order.

The last case is that of the modern author. The social power that brings pressure to bear on writing and speaking has meanwhile undergone fundamental transformations. It is now relatively decentralized; it has constructed a sophisticated supervisory apparatus; its reach has extended inside the individual. There is no longer any absolutely obligatory and legitimate codification system, and to this extent the role of literary authors has also changed: their counterpressure no longer violates social convention at a central point; their dissident speech, given their social role, is much more part of what is expected of them. No one anymore regards literary codification systems as the instrument of "a will to power"; instead, we have the image of preexisting material with which one works. So, for Flaubert, the only remaining desire is "dire à la fois simplement et proprement des choses vulgaire" (to say vulgar things in a way that is both simple and ordered at once).[53] In *Madame Bovary* his opinion of the events and persons treated there goes unspoken; he merely selects the events and formulates them verbally "in the conviction that every event, if one is able to express it purely and completely, interprets itself and the persons involved in it far better and more completely than any opinion or judgment appended to it could do.''[54]

Literary and Social Mimesis

Representation, contrary to Auerbach's conviction, is not the act of an autonomous mind but the product of a practice: the practice of the hands in the formation of materials, painting, or writing; of the face, the mouth, the whole body; of the collective activities of a linguistic community. We are concerned here with the ways in which symbolic worlds are made through a practice. We begin our considerations with the observations that mimesis has also a practical side, or that it at least contains within it the traces of a practice; that it is an interpersonal activity, which is to say that others are always included in it; and that it makes use of a material medium and occurs in situations that can be interpreted in material terms. From this perspective no sharp line can be drawn between artistic and other, extraartistic representations. This point applies in equal force to our own representation of mimesis. The fact that mimesis cannot be represented without the use of mimetic processes poses the fundamental problem of theory formation in reference to our object. We talk about the ways in which symbolic worlds are made by producing a symbolic world of our own. What is the relationship between the representational and the represented world? Is the representation of representation structurally equivalent to simple representation? A *conceptual representation* of mimesis is not a priori superior to simple mimesis; it too contains a mimetic representational component. Even granting that it has at its disposal a few general analytical concepts, it still possesses, in principle, no better representational instrument than representational mimesis. This fact is itself one reason that we prefer to place our initial trust in mimetic representation, rather than displacing it by a theoretical reconstruction. We shall therefore attend first of all to representations of mimesis found in the texts best selected for that purpose and only afterward begin to offer considerations of a more generalizing nature.

We made an initial, preliminary decision to do away with any sharp distinction between artistic and nonartistic mimesis, which would include the distinction between literary and extraliterary texts that divides literature from sociology. It is more reasonable, however, simply to maintain that the codifications specific to literature have a close relationship to other verbal means by which worlds are made by social practice. Literary texts are always working with verbal material, modes of codification, interpretations of the world and worldviews, which authors find already existing in their societies and with which they are familiar. Thus mimesis not only supplies literary writing with principles of representation but also becomes a literary theme. Literary characters are themselves authors. That is, they are originators of frequently very personal but still socially representative representations; they make their own worlds. In both literature and in our conceptual representation, there are therefore two types of mimesis: *representational and represented.* As we shall see, the novel emphasizes the mimetic aspect of the social action of the characters it describes; the author is thereby bound to his or her fictional characters. What goes on inside the characters—they perceive and interpret and order the world and what the author is doing, arranging, emphasizing, and developing perceptual modes—is in many respects equivalent. "Mimesis," in this interpretation, becomes a metaliterary *anthropological* concept designating a specifically human ability, which is characteristic of action in the world, of observations and representations of the world, whether the activity takes place in empirical life or in a fiction.

Representation takes place on three levels. The empirical author narrates, and within the literary work a fictional author also narrates, whether or not this fictional author is named. The fictional characters described in the narration are themselves observers; they perceive other people and describe them. The same is true of the reader, who exists first of all as an empirical reader decoding the text. Decoding is possible because there exists within the text a fictional or "implicit" reader;[55] the text provides keys to its understanding in reference to this nonempirical reader. Finally, the fictional characters are also readers of texts, interpreters of persons and events. Seen from this angle, the empirical persons involved in literature—the author and the reader—have fictional pendants or "outposts" in the texts, once on the level of textual organization and again in the collection of the fictional events themselves.

It should occasion no surprise that many authors take the codification process as the actual theme of their writing, that they represent certain aspects of it, ones they regard as characteristic for worldmaking, for the worldview of an epoch, or a character type that plays an important role in the story. Of interest to these authors is the question of how concrete individuals make their world and the role played in this making by the medium of language and the underlying relations of pressure and supervision. The genre of the novel has been typified by this interest from the beginning. Our investigation of mimesis, in these terms, is not focused on some kind of prior reality but on a comparison of various codification and worldmaking mechanisms. We cannot draw a sharp distinction between the two types of mimesis. If we want to investigate the one, we have to take the other into consideration.

We gain access to the problematic of mimesis through the literature. The concept was first subjected to discussion in a literary and philosophical context, at least in its classical formulation, by Plato and Aristotle. Literary texts offer us a reflection of the principles of mimetic action, while mimesis itself is inseparable from practical action, from an interplay among perception, evaluation, and interpretation between fictional elements and active interventions in worldly events. Mimesis is thus composed of practical knowledge, imaginative power, and theory. The individual engaged in practical action is not conscious of the mimetic side of his or her action; it remains hidden. Scientific thought, because it takes the path of conceptual construction, is also unconscious of mimesis. The literary genres of the drama, the novel, and the story, in contrast, take worldmaking itself as a theme. Action is *shown;* this induces the reader to an act of seeing: he or she sees how unknown persons create order, how they interpret their lives, society, and their environment, and how they express all of these arrangements in symbolic terms.

Without the practical mimesis of daily life, literary mimesis would bear no reference to the world. It does not matter how far literature diverges from the daily practice of its time or how closely it embraces it: even the extreme cases of distancing maintain a thread of connection to the modes of worldmaking inherent in social practice. The meanings of verbal expressions in literary texts have no practical context; they are ultimately citations of social practice. Literature cannot detach itself from its linguistic anthropological foundations. Experiences, thought, and knowledge are always referred back to the codifications preestablished in social practice; they might distance themselves considerably from these codifications, but they cannot definitively transcend the connection. Inversely, literary mimesis can intervene in the mimetic processes of social practice. It can provide models for the latter and influence the way in which social behavior is undertaken, alter codifications, or create new ones; it can persuade empirical persons of their ability to experience the world similarly to models found in literature, if they adopt the codification modes they find there. In short, literary mimesis can itself flow back into social practice. That literature can devise influential ways of seeing (potentially, even possibilities of action) is to be understood in terms of this double movement: literature works with mimetic material; literature can become mimetic material.

Literary mimesis depicts a world as a specific reality. It is one type of symbolic worldmaking. The daily actions of people in society are filled with encounters with the instances of power that establish the symbolic constitution of social reality. Whether literature actually takes on the qualities of a demiurge is a question of the "will to power" and whether literature can prevail against other instances of power. Literature does not possess a similarity to the empirical world; such a thought would render it harmless. Rather, it either supports dominant symbolic power, engages it in a rivalry, or avoids establishing relations altogether by withdrawing. Some areas of rivalry are more central than others: the symbolic codification of society and its history; the interpretation of the individual; the relation of speaker to speech; the attitude toward the medium being used; and so on.

Mimesis referred to other persons amounts to a productive intervention in other modes of codification. The question of whether new codificational modes arise in the process, or whether there are only variations on old modes, is certainly an important one. But it is a matter of gradations. Our concern is not with deciding whether or when an author can achieve independence. The question, for us, is the extent to which the author resists social pressure and produces a counterpressure, whether the author's strategy in relation to the medium generates a codification system through which he or she gains symbolic power.

Part I

Mimesis as Imitation, the Production of Appearances, and Fiction

There was already great complexity to the concept of mimesis in classical Greece. Three central significatory dimensions in pre-Platonic times—"imitation," "representation," and "expression"—can be identified, and they underwent further differentiation over the course of their development. Initially the concept referred not only to art, poetry, and music but also to the extraaesthetic realm; in its development from Plato to Aristotle it became restricted to literature, art, and music.

In Plato's works mimesis has numerous heterogenous meanings: in addition to imitation, representation, and expression, there is also emulation, transformation, the creation of similarity, the production of appearances, and illusion. Plato did not manage to elaborate a unified concept of mimesis but applied and evaluated it variously depending on context. The *Republic* stresses as the preeminent meaning of mimesis its role in education, which is accomplished largely through the emulation of models. A young person strives to become similar to the model and in the process undergoes development. The representation of bad models poses the danger of spoiling youth. That is why Plato insists on the supervision of poetry and the models contained in it. Since literary representations stimulate mimetic capacities, they initiate transformations and changes; which does not mean, however, that literary representations are easily subordinated to pedagogical and social objectives. There is always an uncontrolled moment in their profusion, and they therefore lead to undesired side effects.

The central meaning of mimesis for art, literature, and music is already apparent in Plato's works. He attributed to it the capacity of producing a world of appearances. He understood imitation as the capacity not for producing things but for producing images. Definitive of these images is the relation of similarity they bear to things and objects, in which the real and the imaginary come into combination. If images are defined by similarity, they belong to the world of appearances; they make something visible which they themselves are not. They have an intermediary status between being and nonbeing.

Plato's works contain far-reaching and contradictory notions of mimesis, but scarcely less important is Plato's critique of mimesis, which is derived from the truth criteria of his philosophy. In our approach, Plato's ideas on mimesis and his critique of the concept relate to the larger social transition from orality to literacy. It is possible, in particular, to understand Plato's critique against the backdrop of the slow spread of literacy, since some of the things by which it is fundamentally characterized become possible only after this occurred. Seen in this way, Plato's critique of mimesis is closely related to his effort to replace an image-based discourse, with its major tie to orality, with a conceptual one. The tension between these two discourses, in which is manifest a transformation of language and thought, remains ever-characteristic of Plato. Certain mimetic qualities that are specific to oral culture lose significance with the spread of writing and reading. Others, those associated more with writing and reading, move into the foreground. Aristotle's analysis of mimesis in terms of the categories poetry, art, and music can likely be understood only in the context of his ''literate'' style of philosophizing.

Aristotle develops two aspects of the concept of mimesis in the *Poetics*. First he takes up where Plato left off, emphasizing the significance of mimesis in the production of images. He then develops his own conception of literary mimesis. According to Aristotle, mimesis embraces not solely the re-creation of existing objects but also changes that were introduced in the process of re-creation—embellishment, improvement, and the generalization of individual qualities. In literature, the possible and the general are products of mimesis. Mimesis, according to the *Poetics,* leads to the construction of the ''fable'' or the ''plot.'' In tragedy, it is directed toward the dramatization and embodiment of speaking and acting individuals. It can be understood as the capacity for literary representation, which is expressed in the verbal and imaginary sketching of actions. Mimesis creates fictional worlds in which there exists no nonmediated reference to reality. The cathartic effects of tragedy are produced less via the individual elements of action than by way of artistic organization. In distinction to Plato, who feared the consequences of negative models, Aristotle sees precisely in their mimetic recapitulation a possibility of lessening their effects. It is therefore not the avoidance of models but a confrontation with them that Aristotle calls for.

The respective positions of Plato and Aristotle mark the horizons of possible meanings of mimesis, to which discussions up to the present continue to make reference. The complexity of the concept and its meaning for the human sciences and for aesthetics are visible in ever-new interpretations and elaborations of their ideas.

2

On the Origins
of the Concept

It is possible to identify mimetic behavior in the earliest cultures. The concept of mimesis most familiar to us, however, appears first in the Greek world, in the fifth and then more widely in the fourth century B.C. It has attracted the attention of linguistic historians, on the assumption that study would help decipher its enigmatic character. Hermann Koller, Gerald Else, and Goran Sörbom[1] have all attempted to clarify the linguistic and cultural historical background of mimesis.[2] Linguistically, the root word is *mimos;* derived from it are *mimeisthai, mimesis, mimema, mimetes,* and *mimetikos.* "Mimeisthai" denotes imitation, representation, or portrayal. "Mimos" and "mimetes" designate the persons who imitate or represent, whereby "mimos" also refers to the context of the dramatic action. "Mimema" is the result of mimetic action, and "mimesis" the action itself. "Mimetikos" refers to something capable of imitation or to that which is subject to imitation.

The cultural historical background of the word family *mimesis* is a matter of dispute. Koller operates on the assumption that the word *mimesis,* unknown to Homer and Hesiod, makes its first extant appearance in the Delian hymn, where it is used in the context of dance; a fragment from Pindar and a passage from the work of Aeschylus can be adduced as evidence for a definition of mimesis as "to represent through dance." Its core signification having to do with dance, its historical origins are located in the Dionysian cult drama. Mimesis is understood in reference to the musical theory of Damon as "representation, expression by means of sound and gesture,"[3] or in music by means of tones and dancing figures.[4] In this context mimesis is defined as "imitation," "representation," and "expression," and its range of meanings are thus expanded. Koller regards "representation" as the original meaning of the concept of mimesis. At the same time, he endeavors to prove that Plato and his successor Aristotle, with momentous consequences, restrict the concept to "imitation" in the aesthetic sphere and that Plato consciously "falsifies" the concept in this sense in the tenth book of the *Republic*.

Koller's interpretation, which casts the origins of mimesis in a new light, unleashed intense discussion when it appeared and seems scarcely tenable today. Before moving on to Else's comprehensive critique, however, we must mention a fundamental problem with Koller's method. There is something to the claim that the meaning of the concepts belonging to the word family mimesis can be inferred from usage; yet mistakes can easily slip into such a procedure. Even if the word family Koller examines frequently appears in the context of music and dance, it cannot be summarily concluded that it means "representation" (or "expression") by means of music and dance.

Else, in particular, has taken exception to Koller's location of the origins of mimesis in dance. Having analyzed all the passages that mention mimesis (still not a large number in the fifth century), he rejects Koller's claim as to the central meaning in the concept of mimesis of Damonist music theory, replacing it with three definitional points of emphasis derived from his own analysis:

1. "Miming": direct representation of the looks, actions, and/or utterances of animals or men through speech, song, and/or dancing. . . .
2. "Imitation" of the actions of one person by another, in a general sense. . . .
3. "Replication": an image or effigy of a person or thing in material form.[5]

The general meaning stipulating imitation of the expressions of animals and humans (1) thus has two further specifications: the imitation of a person by another without direct physical mimicry (2); and the imitation of persons or things in an inanimate medium (3). Both of these variants can be found in the fifth century. There is not yet at this time, however, any theory of mimesis; scholars find instead a few similar usages of the term, meaning that Else's differentiation is of heuristic value only. Often, though not exclusively, the concept of mimesis is used in the context of dance and music. What is distinctive in those cases is the element of re-creating characteristics by human means. It is likely that this usage, found in Doric Sicily, which is the home of miming, spread only gradually in the Ionic-Attic region. In any case, the three dimensions of mimesis listed above can be assumed to have been known as early as the time of Plato and Aristotle.[6]

The origin of the *mimeisthai* group lies in the word *mimos* (mime), which first appears in the Doric sphere of influence in Sicily. It designates either a *recitation* with several parts delivered by one person or a dramatic *performance* by two or more persons. The mime probably appeared not at religious festivals but more likely at banquets given by wealthy men. The themes and objects of the presentation often came from the world of commoners and not from the world of the aristocracy. The mime depicted human life "as it is." That is, his presentations are distinct in terms of content from tragedies and comedies, which drive events represented in one or another direction. Instead, the mime represents daily life; he simplifies, emphasizes, and caricatures. As far as is known, the mime's show tended to be devoted more to universal phenomena and character traits than to individuals, though the representation no doubt included more personalized traits as well. The distinction between the two becomes clear in an attempt, for example, to represent a coward. To portray a coward persuasively, the mime must know how a coward behaves and what the characteristic qualities of a coward are, for that is what must determine his representation. What matters, in other words, is that the relations of similarity he establishes be correct: the character traits represented in the coward must correspond to the qualities typical of a coward. Such performances were often accompanied by music and rhythmic movement.

According to Sörbom's study, there are sixty-three textual passages preserved from the fifth century containing one of the words from the *mimeisthai* group, of which only nineteen appear in the context of aesthetics.[7] Variants in the word family in the fifth century thus occur most often in nonaesthetic contexts. Already characteristic, however, is the claim of similarity between the result of the mimetic process and the result of another process; the mimetic process refers to the other one and in the course of making reference produces the similarity. Present this early, then, is the definition of "imitate" as "to make oneself similar" to a person or thing. Often there are two meanings when "mimos" occurs in a passage: the first is a specific form of action or performance; the second involves the representation of a person behaving appropriately to his or her type. There are thus also two meanings of the verb: to perform a play called "mimos" and to behave like a mime, which is to say, to behave like persons involved in a kind of playing called "mimos." While the first meaning slowly declines in importance, the second rises. Koller, Else, and Sörbom all agree that the concept's range of applicability expands, with the meaning eventually including "representing something animate and concrete with characteristics that are similar to the characteristics of other phenomena." The meaning of the concept had expanded this far toward the end of the fifth century and has remained valid to this day. This may also locate the original context of the negative associations so evident in Plato. In the last analysis, neither was the "mimos" a show with much social prestige nor was the mime very highly valued. A reference to someone "behaving like a mime" could have retained a negative flavor for a long time, which is also suggested by the use of the expression in the sense of fooling someone—as a mime fools his public.

So it is not possible to identify any clear aesthetic usage of members of this word group prior to Xenophon and Plato. A study of nineteen extant passages in which a variant appears in the context of an artwork proves that the relevant word combinations are used no differently here than in the other forty-four known passages. Artworks are generally not termed mimetic or explained with reference to mimesis. As in the extraaesthetic sphere, the concept serves solely to designate individual situations or traits, meaning that mimesis has not yet become an aesthetic category.

A change first appears with Xenophon: in the *Memorabilia,* he terms mimesis a general ability to make sculptures.[8] Though Xenophon's conception of mimesis is rendered in less detail than Plato's, there are similarities to be found in the ideas of the two thinkers. Like other objects, artworks are perceived by the eyes. Similarity, referring to a type of perception, is thus a characteristic artworks and other objects have in common. Since Greek artists of the time used no actual models to create their works, similarity does not refer to the relation between model and work. Rather, the idea was that artworks rest on other things in reference to which the similarity of the artwork is produced. What was needed to select and order more appropriately the relevant characteristics for the artwork was a more general ''mental image''—one that also encompassed concrete traits. The similarity between this ''mental image'' and the Platonic Idea is obvious.

Two further innovations appear in the fifth century.[9] Works like the *Calf Bearer* convey more than a concrete universal. There appears now in artworks something ''animate''; they begin to depict particular moments of organic life. And feelings of various kinds gradually come to expression, are made visible to the eye, in sculpture.

3

Imitation, Illusion, Image (Plato)

A new chapter in the history of mimesis begins with the works of Plato. For one thing, there are in the dialogues a large number of differentiated contributions to the definition of mimesis. For another, Plato's dialogues themselves are an example of mimetic behavior. They depict Socrates in philosophical conversation with other people. This Platonic representation can be understood as a mimesis of the philosophizing Socrates. What we have to examine now, therefore, are Plato's substantive claims in reference to mimesis. We shall also explore the implicit definitions of mimesis given in the form of the dialogues, as well as the question of how well Plato's critique of writing in the *Republic* coheres with the development of mimetic philosophical writing in the dialogues. There is an element of contradiction in the fact that Plato criticizes art as mimesis in principle but at the same time works mimetically in producing dialogues in which artistic elements are present. In the early dialogues, writing is not yet understood as mimesis and mimesis has not yet been restricted to questions of art. Initially Plato uses the concept more in the general sense of imitation. Only in the *Republic* does a change occur, whereby it is a matter of dispute whether and to what extent there is a break in the concept of mimesis between the first and the tenth books. In any case, Plato formulates there a new concept of mimesis as constitutive of the *aesthetic* sphere.[1]

Part of any attempt to systematize Plato's use of the concept of mimesis prior to the *Republic* would be the following three differentiations.

I. Mimesis as the imitation of a concrete action. Mimesis designates the process in which someone is imitated in regard to something;

there is a representative, an occasion, and a point of view for the mimetic action; often a motive can also be identified.

2. Mimesis as imitation or emulation. Presupposed here is that the person or object being imitated is worthy of being imitated. This valuation involves an ethical point of view. Persons imitated exist as models, for example, the "excellent men of earlier times." Their abilities are worthy of becoming common knowledge. The imitation of their actions and ways of behaving will cause something of value to be gained by the imitators.

3. Mimesis as metaphor. Something is designated imitation which was not necessarily meant to be. "Imitation" designates here the interpretation of a speaker. When one speaks of woman imitating the earth, it is an example of metaphorical usage. "The distinction between the object of imitation in a broader sense and the respect in which it is imitated is entirely absent, and the object becomes a simple one."[2] Plato's representation of Socrates can likewise be understood as a figuration that allows Plato's presentation and the self-representation of Socrates to coincide.

These differentiations remain inadequate and must be supplemented by further distinctions. A heterogenous usage of the mimesis concept is found in Plato's works as a whole, many passages by no means stamped by the negative assessment known from the *Republic.* Thus Plato uses the concept of mimesis in a thoroughly metaphysical sense. Initially he takes over this understanding of mimesis from the Pythagoreans; later he transposes mimesis into the concept of *methexis* (participation). The following definition of mimesis, which will be surprising to readers familiar only with the *Republic,* is found in the seventh book of the *Laws.* "We are ourselves authors of a tragedy, and that the finest and best we know how to make. In fact, our whole polity has been constructed as a dramatization [mimesis] of a noble and perfect life; that is what *we* hold to be in truth the most real of tragedies."[3] This is the response of the organizers of the ideal state to the writers of tragedies, who are demanding access to the state. Here Plato formulates the concept of mimesis positively; he designates as the ideal state a mimesis of the "noble and perfect life."

The conflict between writers and philosophers, which consists in a rivalry between perspectives on life and the divine, can scarcely be expressed more clearly. The philosophers claim themselves capable of mimesis of the noble and perfect life—the same ability they disdain in other passages. Here, as also in the *Timaeus,* the assessment of the value of mimesis depends on the value of the model to which mimesis refers. As stated expressly in the *Timaeus,* the earthly world, "by imitation [mimesis] of [the] eternal nature" of the heavenly world, might come to approximate it as nearly as possible.[4] All of the objects of this world are said to be ''mimemata'' of a few objects; time is mimesis of eternity;[5] the demiurge appears as the divine poet. Mimesis refers to correspondences between mimetic subjects and the objects of the world. It is what makes the eternal capable of producing the world and the means by which people achieve knowledge of the world.

Socrates compares himself in the *Timaeus,* because he is unable to design the ideal state, to the poets;[6] and Timaeus himself speaks on the assumption that his reasoning refers mimetically to the perceivable world.[7] The philosopher, in order to know the world, has to behave mimetically. This point is also made in the *Crito:* all statements about the world are mimetic and inseparable from the production of images.[8] Plato regards it as self-evident that the philosopher's mimetic abilities are an inferior version of abilities attributed to God. Thus in many places, in metaphorical passages in particular, Plato offers a more neutral, not to say positive, assessment of mimesis, one that clearly contradicts his later critical position in the *Republic*. It is to the reasoning in the *Republic* that we now wish to turn.[9]

Similarity, Imitation, Education

In the third book of the *Republic,* Plato provides further definitions of mimesis, centering on the relation between mimesis and poetry, mimesis and education, and poetry and education. At issue is the education of members of the guardian class, with the goal of making them capable of fulfilling the duties they will be assigned by the state. Since young people learn essentially through imitation, one of the most important tasks of education is the selection of objects to which they will be exposed. Plato does not share the assumption that young people can become stronger by confronting negative models; his conception of mimesis suggests more that the effect would be unfavorable, leaving them weaker than before. For that reason young people should be shielded from everything that might interfere with their ability to fulfill tasks later entrusted to them by the state.

Plato regards youth's fascination with models and examples of all sorts as irresistible. Poetry, which plays a major role in education, is one important source of youth's experience with examples and models. If, therefore, the world of models and examples ought to be controlled in the interest of education, then poetry, a primary source of these models and examples, must likewise be subject to control. Caution is all the more necessary because, in Plato's view of developments so far, poetry has inadequately fulfilled its pedagogical task in relation to young people. The extensive and powerful representation of the terrors of the underworld and the lamentations of heroes over the death of a friend often found in poetry do not educate the guardians in courage, gallantry, and strength. If poetry represents the great men of Greek history as unrestrained, avaricious, and wanton, or if it even asserts that heroes and gods have committed wicked deeds, that not even Zeus is free of deficiencies, then it squanders its opportunity to make a constructive contribution to education. Because, by occasioning mimesis, these negative representations exert power over youth, poetry in the ideal state would not be allowed to represent the negative. It is necessary to ban negative representations anyway, in Plato's view, especially since doubts are in order as to whether negative representations of gods and heroes can be called truth. For poetry to make the constructive contribution to the education of youth of which it is capable, it must be subjected to ethical criteria of selection. Mimesis is thus defined as *the imitation of role models,* whereby the goal is to become like the models.

A further elaboration of the meaning of mimesis quickly follows the first. The extent to which a text is mimetic becomes the central characteristic distinguishing the various types of writing. Plato defines mimesis as "likening oneself to another in speech or bodily bearing," which is to say imitating "him to whom one likens oneself."[10] He designates tragedy and comedy mimetic poetry, and he sees the epic as a mixed form and the dithyramb as the pure narration of the poet.[11] He takes this distinction from the beginning of the *Iliad,* where Homer has Chryses bid Agamemnon to release his daughter, allowing Chryses to speak and represent himself. In comparison, simple narration devoted solely to a report of the substance of the matter is clearly a distinct form. Consonant with Plato's conviction that mimetic poetry in particular has a great power to prompt mimesis in the hearer and reader, such poetry acquires special significance for education in the ideal state. Especially to be feared is its seductive power to exercise a negative effect on the younger generation. Plato even poses the question of whether this form of poetry ought to be forbidden and whether, therefore, the form of representation is an issue that may be left to the poets, the more so if the content of poetry is to be controlled. Here Plato develops a second definitional variant of the concept of mimesis, this one in the sense of representation, of representing something in poetry.[12]

Poets are not capable of "imitating many things,"[13] nor are the guardians able to perform many things that would be for the good of the state. Some kind of limitation is necessary in both cases. The poets must limit themselves to a single representational form, the guardians to their duties for the state. Only a willingness to divide labor and concentrate on their specific obligations can enable them to fulfill the latter optimally. For that reason they should have nothing to do with anything outside the sphere of their assigned tasks. From early childhood on they should imitate only what will help them fulfill their tasks; everything else they should leave aside. They should imitate only brave, sober, pious, and noble men, not weaklings and insane and bad men. While imitation of men of the first sort will increase their strength for performing their state tasks, imitation of the latter sort will infect them with weaknesses and hinder them in the optimal fulfillment of their duties. In any case, imitation in early childhood habituates one either to good or to bad, leaving one or the other to influence behavioral dispositions in the adult.[14]

Because of the lasting nature of the effects of representational poetry, it should create only the exemplary and report the bad—if at all—only in a distancing fashion. In any case, Plato subjects both the content and the representational forms of poetry to supervision and control in the ideal state. He would ban representations of the "multifarious," leaving room only for treatments of that which is useful to the state; he persists in the claim, even given the possibility that the poets and actors willing and able to accomplish such treatments are of inferior quality. Poetry, its representational forms, and its performers are subordinate to an ethical principle, which derives its justification from the nature of the adult tasks to be assigned to youth being educated in the state.

In the name of these tasks, the types of musical modes and instruments should also be restricted. Only that should be allowed which benefits education in the sense sketched above. Correspondingly, the only rhythms that should be performed are those it is assumed will contribute to the "seemliness" of the soul. Thus are the Dorian and Phrygian musical modes, the lyre and cithara, and the "seemly" rhythms allowed and other modes, instruments, and rhythms prohibited. The contents, forms, and representational modes of poetry and music, which have always played an important role in education, should, because of the effects they exercise through mimetic processes, be made subject to control in the ideal state, a state based on an ethical principle derived from the collective goals of the community. The goal of education is the "beautiful disposition of the soul," which is developed by means of mimesis.

The definitions of mimesis found in the third book of the *Republic* may be summarized in the form of the following theses.

1. Major portions of traditional poetry violate the principles of mimesis in the sense of the production of *similarity*. This is true, for example, of the representation of injustice among the gods, the assertion that the gods were responsible for unhappiness among people, and the representation of the weaknesses of the heroes of early times. Since in the Platonic conception, gods cannot be bad and heroes cannot be weak, the criterion of similarity between what is represented, that is, the gods and heroes, and the representation is violated. The poets' mimetic representation thus transgresses against the truth. When poets violate ethical postulates in regard to the representation of truth, they become subject to criticism. For transgressions against the truth and the representation of deficient gods and heroes have a negative effect on the community, in particular, on the education of youth.

2. Mimesis designates the representation of something on the assumption that the latter is similar to the true, without this assumption being subject to verification. If we, for example, conceive ideas of a past time about the reality of which we know nothing and nevertheless endeavor to assimilate our ideas to the "truth" of this unknown reality, then we have such a situation. It is not possible to draw a substantive distinction

between mimetic representation and truth. Yet such representations, which refer to the production of images or, as the case may be, ideas, are necessary and useful. In this case the ideas and images are not copies; rather, they stand as *mentally constructed images* of something to which it is assumed they are similar.

3. Mimesis is introduced as a *transformative* capacity. Implied in the mimesis of specific behavior is a change on the part of the imitator; the intention is to emulate a model and appropriate its abilities and to do this in the name of self-improvement. Mimesis in this case means to aspire to or to emulate.

4. Occasionally mimesis takes on the meaning of *simulation;* something is represented of which it is known that it does not correspond to the truth because it is in some sense advantageous to do so. Thus do poets gain the interest and appreciation of the masses by representing something with popular appeal, without having posed the question of whether it satisfies the demand for similarity, which is to say, truth. This sense of "simulating" something is preserved in the present-day usage of "to mimic."

5. The individual, by way of his or her mimetic abilities, is infected by poetry; the result is that powerful influences—sometimes against the individual's will—are exercised. Since poetry often takes as its theme emotion and human frailty, it threatens to disturb the balance and rational disposition of the individual. To the extent, however, that balance and rationality are requisite to the maintenance of community, their development should not be left vulnerable to the disadvantageous effects of mimetic processes.

6. Mimesis also refers to the *form* of representation, to the voice and gestures,[15] with which something is represented. The focus here is on the formal aspect, which is an indicator of how something is represented by means of mimos. Mimesis, through speech and gesture, objectivizes content. Since no one representation is equivalent to another, a new element goes into the manner of each respective representation. In any case, the manner and mode of representation determines how the "infection process" proceeds.

7. Mimetic processes operate independently of ethical approbation or disdain. Mimesis is preethical or extraethical. This is the justification for Plato's attempt to introduce a secondary control over mimesis into his theory of community.

8. Mimesis is not subject to internal restraint. The characteristic of mimetic creativity is that it disposes over a wide variety of divergent effects. The unrestrained juxtaposition of "good" and "evil" as if they were equal should be restricted in the interest of the community.

By subordinating mimesis to the principles of the division of labor and the unity of the object, that which is imitated would no longer be a variety of things, but exclusively that which is important for the community. At issue here are Plato's philosophical conversations with Socrates, in which the latter, as a model of the type of man needed for the leadership of the community, is imitated.

9. Mimesis is always to be permitted when it is certain that mimetic processes will produce no unwanted side effects and the effects of mimesis promote the aims of the polity and education. Thus the guardians are not to indulge in effeminate behavior, are not to pursue any extraneous crafts, and are not to make any noises as found in nature, but should take part—represent or imitate—solely those activities that are important for the practice of their profession.

10. Those who do not limit themselves and who imitate many things instead of the one thing required of them should be kept apart from the community. This practice would lead to the exclusion of unwanted musical modes, instruments, and people, thereby "purifying" art and education. Education should foster love for music as the love of the beautiful and as a method, through mimesis of the music, to develop a sense for the ordered and the beautiful and thereby also for philosophy, which Plato characterizes as the "greatest music."

Appearance and Illusion

We want now to pursue somewhat more pointedly the critique of mimesis offered thus far. The import of the positions we shall develop here for Plato's understanding of mimesis remains in dispute, despite numerous attempts in the scholarship to clarify the issues.[16] Plato denies that painting and poetry are capable of imitating the Ideas. In his understanding, they produce only the phenomenal form of things. Since representational poetry appeals to the "lower parts of the soul," it should not be allowed at all in the state. For, he claims, from Homer on all poets have been "imitators of the shadow images of virtue" and have had no contact with the truth. The apprehension of truth is the task of the highest part of the soul; the path to truth is philosophy. Philosophy then takes over the significance for education that poetry had long possessed.

Plato offers a first definition of mimesis from an ontological point of view. This yields a hierarchy running from the Idea of the object to a copy of the object, which corresponds to the sequence God, demiurge, painter or poet. God creates the Idea; by beholding the Idea, the demiurge produces objects; his ability is exhausted in the imitation of an Idea. The painter, however, creates his pictures neither by seeing the Idea nor from a more precise substantive knowledge of the object. For he produces nothing but phenomena—as they can be produced easily and quickly, on the basis of no substantive knowledge, by someone holding a mirror. In the painter's ability to make many different pictures without precise knowledge of the things underlying each one, he is equivalent to the poet as the latter is represented in the third book of the *Republic;* capable of imitating much, the poet, should he wish access to the state, will have to restrict himself to the one.

For the painter, this restriction makes no sense; for what he can produce has always been part of the world of appearance and phenomena. It has no reference to the world of the Ideas and has nothing to express about them; given its lesser ontological status, painting is devoid of the sort of expression required by knowledge of the truth. The painter is in this respect equivalent to the Sophist, who, likewise captive to the world of appearance, is uninterested in the question of truth. Plato designates the production of appearance by painters and poets doing or creating (*poiein*). Although the same word is used for the activities of the craftsman and the painter, the two are distinguished here and the sphere of artistic creation is delimited from that of creation by a craftsman. Implicit in this delimitation is an important precondition for the rise of an independent aesthetic sphere. The artist produces appearance; his work is to make available a phenomenon. When the painter represents a bed, it is not the same as when the craftsman manufactures a utility object; painting, rather, is a matter of bringing forth a bed "in a certain way," namely, as a phenomenon, which does not take on being. Such phenomena are not welcome in the state because they have no reference to the Ideas brought forth by God. God is understood as the real creator (*phytourgos*), whom the craftsman, as demiurge, merely imitates; the work of the craftsman, in turn, becomes an object of imitation for the painter.

This ontological degradation of the artwork makes it possible to conceive the world of appearance, of phenomena, as a world produced by human beings, which is not created by God and which does not share in the nature of the Ideas. In this definition of the world of phenomena lies the possibility of art. Insofar as divine creation brought forth all being, the artist imitates God in the production of the world of appearance. The artist, like God, creates; only he creates no being, but solely a world of phenomena, of images. What he can do, however, is create phenomena of many different things, for which he, in contrast to the craftsman, who requires for the manufacture of an object a precisely defined ability, needs no special technical competence beyond the general power to create. Painters and poets, in distinction to specialized craftsmen, are therefore in the position of creating and giving form to manifold things. In this they are more similar to God than to the craftsman. Mimesis means the *production of an appearance.* Artistic representation, however, is not the appearance of that which is or really exists but the appearance of something phenomenal.[17]

This argument constitutes art and aesthetics as independent spheres in which the artist is the master. Art and poetry produce only phenomena, so they are comprised only of the phenomenal aspect, not reality. Herein lie both the potential and the limits of art and poetry. Mimesis is directed not at the production of a real thing and not at the production of an appearance of the Idea. It aims at the representation of appearance, at the production of phenomena, which have a relation to the world of the real. "Similarity" here, as a criterion of mimesis, no longer has the meaning it did in the third book in regard to the representation of gods and heroes.

What is understood as mimesis depends on a prior understanding of art and poetry. If we take artistic and poetic productions to be representations of reality, then we commit ourselves to postulates of similarity and truth in terms of correspondence; if, however, we understand art as the appearance in phenomenal form of the phenomenal, we relativize the meaning of representations. As phenomena they need not come into conflict in the same way with the postulates of the ideal state regarding the education of its members and their fulfillment of their duties. The situation is different if we conceive the representations of painting and poetry as copies of reality and make them subject to the truth postulate. Yet it is not likely that any such understanding of art and poetry was current at the time; artistic and poetic statements were much more likely to be understood as statements of the truth. This is evident, for example, in the fact that Homer's poetry was drawn on for educational purposes as a collection of knowledge and wisdom, rather than regarded as poetry and thus part of a world of appearance. As long as art and poetry are conceived as a source of knowledge and wisdom, they enter into competition with philosophy and are therefore to be excluded from the ideal state. Consequently, Homer should no longer be accepted as the mentor of the Greeks. As a poet he is only a copier of phenomenal things and thus connected solely to the world of opinion (*doxa*). While painters and poets are "imitators of the manifold," the philosopher is able to concentrate on the Idea.

The suggestion that the poet, by representing human passions and deficiencies that interest the audience, also endangers those who have managed to remain reasonable and exemplary by controlling their feelings and desires radicalizes Plato's critique of poetry. Only too often do individuals fall under the mastery of the part of the soul that should be mastered. Poets are often praised for representing certain kinds of behavior when what is necessary is for that behavior to be overcome. Poetry, especially if its phenomenal character is not understood, must therefore be kept away from the state for the sake of the advancement of logos. Its place should be taken by a philosophy on the model of Socrates, defined as love for the good, the beautiful, and the true, which the philosopher attempts to approximate.

It is not finally possible to determine the extent to which the process of approximation achieves its goal. For mimesis means here the imitation of something that is not known, yet that is so important for human life that it is not possible to manage without more precise definitions of its substantive content. This concept of mimesis is metaphorical. There is no subject-object relation implicit in it; it suggests rather a *self-referentiality* that will gain in importance over the course of the history of mimesis. It is not possible to adduce proof that the good, the beautiful, and the true can be grasped by undertaking a specific epistemological movement; nevertheless, it is necessary to hold on to the sense and utility of such movements. We can clarify this definition of mimesis in reference to a painter: if a painter paints the most beautiful person conceivable, the quality of his painting will not be diminished by the fact that this person does not exist in reality. A corresponding point applies to poetry; often the models for the likenesses created by poetry cannot be named. Thus are the descriptions produced by poetry phenomena that refer to something that is itself inaccessible.

Images as Appearances with the Character of Similarity

In the course of the further development of the concept of mimesis, the relationship between mimesis and image takes on a particular significance, a suggestion of which already appears in Plato's works.[18] In the *Republic* mimesis is defined, among other things, as the capacity for making images; likewise in the *Sophist:*[19] "For imitation is surely a kind of production, though it be only a production of images, as we say, not of originals of every sort." With this definition, Plato surpasses Xenophon and the current usage of the *mimesis* word group at the time inasmuch as he sees in mimesis an element that all human figurative and representational activities share in common.[20] With this broadening of the meaning, Plato shifts attention from the relation between what is represented and the observer to the relation between image and representation. Mimesis now designates the ability to create expression and representation on the part of painters, poets, or actors. For example, the painter produces a relation between an image he himself created and the object that supplies the basis for the image. If this relation consists in the production of similarity, then there arises the question of where the similarity between image and object lies. Images do indeed make reference to real objects, but at the same time the relationship of similarity is just as unreal as the relationship of art to the world of objects. Just as the images of objects produced in a mirror are similar to real objects, without, however, themselves possessing reality on the level of the objects, so do mimetically produced images, figurations, representations, and expressive forms refer to real objects without themselves being real. Similarity is thus the determinative characteristic of the image, in which reference to the real is combined with the illusory; on the one hand, the image is a double, and on the other, it is mere illusion. In the *Sophist* we find a fitting definition of the image:[21]

> *Theaetetus:*   Well, sir, what could we say an image was, if not another
> thing of the same sort, copied from the real thing?

Stranger:	"Of the same sort"? Do you mean another real thing, or what does "of the same sort" signify?
Theaetetus:	Certainly not real, but like it.
Stranger:	Meaning by "real" a thing that really exists.
Theaetetus:	Yes.
Stranger:	And by "not real" the opposite of real?
Theaetetus:	Of course.
Stranger:	Then by what is "like" you mean what has not real existence, if you are going to call it "not real."
Theaetetus:	But it has some sort of existence.
Stranger:	Only not real existence, according to you.
Theaetetus:	No, except that it is really a likeness.
Stranger:	So, not having real existence, it really is what we call a likeness?

The human ability to produce images, such that what does not have real existence is dovetailed together with what does have real existence, Plato terms mimesis. Insofar as the image is defined by similarity, the production of the same, not of the other, is the characteristic of mimesis. On account of its character as image, the image never represents solely the same, but always at the same time something other as well. A double—according to the *Cratylus*—could only arise if God not only represented the form and color of Cratylus as a painter does but if he also created his internal being just like Cratylus. Then, however, the double would no longer be an image. For in order to define the essence of the image, "we must find some other principle of truth in images, and also in names, and not insist that an image is no longer an image when something is added or subtracted. Do you not perceive that images are very far from having qualities which are the exact counterpart of the realities which they represent?"[22] Images are therefore characterized by their lack of something, while, at the same time, something comes to expression in them which the objects themselves do not have. In the visibility of the images there appears something invisible, something between being and nonbeing, between true and false, between the same and the other—a fictional space.

According to Jean-Pierre Vernant's analysis, these Platonic ideas of the image are bound to archaic ideas from Homer's time, for which the characteristic factor is that something nonimagistic, something invisible, comes to expression in the image. Using the example of graveside colossi, it is possible to show that these statues are only doubles and not yet images. They represent a form that can assume the psyches of the dead, in which the latter, themselves invisible, become visible. Death shows itself to the living through the statues, referring at the same time to its own invisibility and absence. In the colossi, the inaccessibility, the mystery, and the otherness of death becomes visible. From the colossi and other idols of early times, also not yet images, the development to the image as a mimesis of phenomena is fully accomplished by the fifth century.[23] Since the image now stands in reference to external objects, without being their double, it belongs to the world of phenomena and appearance. If the business of the colossus was the representation of the beyond, what arises with the image are the artistic spaces of the fictive and imaginative. While colossi and other architectural idols are used ritually to express the invisible and acquire their meaning in this way, the image as such can arise only in the context of the city, the temple, and a new public sphere. The existence of the city, the statue of which is preserved in the temple, is mediated over the circumstance of its public visibility. "The statue is 'representation' in a new sense. Freed from ritual and put under the impersonal gaze of the city, the divine symbol is transformed into an 'image' of God."[24] With this change in religious rituals and ideas and with the rise of the "image" of God, it also became possible to discover the human body, which came to be of central significance for the development of the image and the plastic arts in Greece.[25] "In order for the image to acquire the psychological meaning of a copy, which imitates a model and gives the observer the illusion of reality, the human figure must cease giving expression to religious value; it must itself and for itself become the model of the representation in its phenomenal appearance."[26] As soon, therefore, as the human body loses its religious character, it can become an image and an object of art; once this happens references to the beyond get displaced by the expression of relationships of similarity to living bodies or to notions of bodily perfection.

The transition to this new conception of the image and of the power of mimesis to create images is not yet complete in Xenophon, but only in Plato. Insofar as images are characterized by similarity, they belong to the order of phenomena; "the image becomes visible as the phenomenon of something it is not."[27] To the extent that it expresses similarity, it is not real, but fictional. By means of mimesis similarity phantasms are produced in the image, the point of which is not an exact copy but the production of an illusion of similarity in the observer.[28] Artists working mimetically create phantasms, images, simu-lacra; they represent something, not as it is, but as it appears; in the process they produce something that would not exist but for their mimetic action, namely, images, which are located between being and nonbeing. What Plato is talking about here is a dream made for waking eyes.[29] Mimesis is not only capable of representing the perceptible characteristics of an object, according to the discussion in the *Cratylus,* but even its essence,[30] though this repre-sentation, to be sure, is still far from the truth.

While the manufacture of a bed is the work of a demiurge, the production of images of the bed is the result of the mimetic faculty, whereby the images belong to the world of "phenomena," of appearances, of illusion. Aristotle is responsible for first reducing the difference between the two activities by interpreting Plato's conception of mimesis in such a way that not only aesthetic production but all human action became "mimesis of nature." Plato extends to philosophy the distinction between making things and producing images. In distinction to Socrates, who works to gain knowledge of things, the Sophists operate mimetically. As painters paint pictures, so do the Sophists "paint" their works with words. As the painter, in Plato's understanding, does not copy a real bed and the author of a tragedy produces no real action, so does the Sophist fail to create any knowledge of the truth. He appears to Plato as one who paints with words, who works with "spoken images." We find similar notions in Simonides, who says that "the word is the image of the action" and is reported to have called painting "silent poetry" and poetry "painting that speaks."[31] The paramount issue for Plato, however, is his negative assessment of these processes; he regards painters, poets, and Sophists as makers of images, illusions, and appearance. The Sophist speaks without knowing anything about things; his competence consists in his ability to generate fraudulent worlds and phantasms. Sophistic thinking aims to produce images that the listener will regard as real, all of which takes place in the world of phenomena. Image, thought, and opinion combine into a world of appearance characterized by nonbeing, a phenomenal nature, and similarity. As long as illusion and reality are not distinguished, science, ignorance, and appearance all merge together. Only the delimitation of the spheres of philosophy, science, and art make epistemological progress possible.

In Plato's time the character of the image as well (due to the introduction and spread of writing) as the character of speaking and of language begin to undergo permanent change. In his involvement in both transformations, Plato both inherits and surpasses received traditions. With his conception of mimesis he creates an independent sphere of the *aesthetic*—consisting of appearance, image, and illusion—that he is careful to exclude from the domain of philosophy. He likewise develops a new kind of philosophizing in that he renders philosophical discourse written, integrating the effects of this transformation into thought. In Socrates, who did not write[32] but whom Plato, by writing down the dialogues, made into an enduring figure, the nature of the contemporary situation as transitional between orality and literacy comes to clear expression. If mimesis of life forms, rituals, and oral poetry constitutes the collective memory of Greek oral culture, this does not mean that a fundamental change follows immediately on the introduction of writing; nevertheless, writing entails the possibility of preserving written records for generations to come and therefore expands and consolidates a culture's collective memory.

Neither writing nor reading is conceivable without mimesis. And yet among the effects of reading and writing are changes in ideas of mimesis. The Platonic critique of mimesis goes hand in hand with an increase in the significance of writing and reading, and at the same time it transforms mimesis as a concept;

mimesis now becomes the independent sphere of production of doxa, appearances and images, art, poetry, and music. It comes to be subsumed under principles other than those generated by Plato's rendering of oral Socratic philosophy as written. A conception of mimesis emerges in which the image is separated from the real and which, at the same time, lends new significance to what is visible and the gaze. Insofar as the image has an intermediary status between being and nonbeing, it comes to occupy in reference to objects an intermediary position within the subject by making it possible for the external world to achieve phenomenal appearance. Without confusing the image with the original of which it is a copy, it remains true that the relation of the image to its objective referent exists, or, in other words, that the image assumes its phenomenal appearance in terms of the category of subjective perception. On the one hand, the image is the quintessence of the visibility of things; on the other, we find here again the assumption that, given the nature of human consciousness, it is impossible for anything other than images, other than phenomena with the character of similarity, to be apprehended.

For Plato, there are no phenomena without being, no images without reality, no mimesis without a model. Yet the models of the images are not part of reality; nor are they phenomena subject to reproduction through other phenomena. They belong to a different order of knowledge. As long as artists orient themselves according to the phenomenal being of things, they run the danger of concentrating solely on the latter and overlooking the breach between model and image, between the real and the fictional. If one does not want to be taken in by an illusionary mimesis purporting to imitate what it cannot possibly imitate, it is necessary to recognize this gap. Now, the extent to which the world of appearance in Plato can already be conceived as a product of human imagination is not clear. In Vernant's judgment, a clear distinction between mimesis and imagination can only be established in the second century A.D. in the works of Flavius Philostrate.[33] According to our investigation, however, there is much to be said for the view that not only the visible but also the invisible or the newly created has a place in Plato's constitution of a mimetically produced world of appearances and images.

4

The Break in the History of Mimesis

The Use of Writing

Plato occupies a key position in the history of mimesis. His is the first fully developed philosophical work that fully exploits the potential opened up to thought by the gradual introduction of writing over the preceding few centuries. Mimesis is, for Plato, an element of the prewritten, obsolete oral culture, now in the course of being overtaken by the new literate culture. Mimesis is organized in Platonic philosophy in terms of an intellectual schema that previously did not exist. Plato breaks down into a series of individual elements the complex of relationships according to which mimesis had been integrated into philosophy prior to his time. He subjects whatever individual elements run counter to theoretical, conceptual, and essentialist philosophical thought. It is not possible to understand the transformation Plato marks in the history of mimesis without an awareness of the changes wrought by the introduction of writing as a medium of thought. This chapter concerns the respects in which Platonic philosophy takes leave of the conception of language in oral culture and the consequences his reformulations entail. It will become evident that the entire complex of language, bodies, images, medium, and social control underwent a change from the ground up.

It is extraordinarily difficult for us to gain access to the conception of language and thought that existed in preliterate times. Solely by way of inferences, reconstructions, and hypotheses can we achieve an approximate idea of the specific qualities through which the earlier periods diverge from our familiar written culture. Eric Havelock's pathbreaking studies,[1] based essentially on the work of Milman Parry and Albert B. Lord,[2] have pointed out which of the elements of oral culture may reasonably be inferred. His reconstruction culminates in an attempt to explain important features of the Platonic philosophy of knowledge from the perspective of the effects in literate culture of the new conception of language. Plato excludes language from the knowledge of the true; the true is accessible only to direct observation. In pre-Platonic thought, language plays a much greater role, if not a reflected one. Knowing, representing, and speaking were not yet sharply distinguished from one another and not yet detached from action. Plato opposes knowing to all other activities and postulates as its object pure forms, the Ideas. There is no doubt that he also develops language further, so that it becomes capable of identifying definitions and the essence of concrete things, abstract nouns, and actions. Plato's position marks not only a new bearing toward language and knowledge but also a fundamental change in language itself. It is no longer the same language as the one employed in previous centuries. The written language he develops is a highly cultivated means of expression, a precision instrument that did not exist prior to his work.

Oral Poetry

Studies of the primary process by which an alphabet came to be adopted in Greece typically are guilty of two mistaken judgments.[3] It is assumed, for one, that the process was accomplished within a relatively short historical period.[4] And it is easy to underestimate the effects of the process by reserving consideration exclusively to material innovations. In Havelock's view, the process by which written language was developed and became sufficiently widespread to be in general use spans a period of several centuries. He is able to identify a transitional period in which Greek culture remains essentially oral while literate expressive forms are already being developed in which oral linguistic forms, especially the poetic, are being written down. A way of thinking forged by the demands of orality starts being conveyed in written forms; the first specifically written means of expression are found, and they still preserve the essential characteristics of oral culture. The most significant and perhaps oldest transcription of this sort is Homeric poetry.[5] This process by which oral poetry becomes codified as written literature is the focus of the work of Parry and Lord, whose conclusions are fundamental to Havelock's interpretation of Plato.

Oral cultures are limited by the circumstance that they have no techniques for preserving tradition, such as written symbols and texts, which can be stored like things and then retrieved and read later and passed on to successive generations. This is naturally not specific to Greek antiquity, but applies to all oral cultures and has become since the 1960s the object of ethnological, philological, and semiotic research.[6]

It is in the nature of cultural knowledge that it is not stored in personal memory. Developments that take place outside the mind of any particular individual determine what a culture manages to preserve. Cultural knowledge is stored in behavior, in customs, and in the many verbal acts that together compose a linguistic community: in a cultural memory. The research of Parry, Lord, and Havelock can be regarded as a response to the empirical question of how the poets of the preliterate oral culture of early Greece were able to memorize their poetry. The poets devised mnemonic techniques related to symbolic usage, which helped them make, perform, and pass down a poetic world, which comprises an important aspect of the mimesis problematic. Our literate culture is also rooted to a certain extent in orality; there continues to be a basic oral reserve of learning to which people resort after the acquisition of writing, for example, in the learning of new meanings, the understanding of foreigners, and the clarification of ambiguities. Literate cultures do indeed possess a highly developed store of standardized knowledge; it can be called upon to make internal references in the language, to designate other words and objects with words. Once difficulties of understanding arise, however, it becomes the case that literate speech is also firmly bound to practical situations.[7] In oral speech the role of context is incomparably more significant and extensive and is mediated more physically than in literate speech. Standardizations of meanings are accomplished on the level of physical movements, immediate impressions, and emotions in the form of "verbal motor" schemata,[8] in particular, as they relate to rhythm.

How is knowledge fixed in oral language? Through repetition and "formulaic expressions," which generate variations on the basis of the same rhythmic and narrative schema. Thus are thoughts and actions expressed with the assistance of rhythmic patterns, "as repetition or antithesis, alliteration and assonances, epithets." The speaker—in particular, the performing poet—puts himself physically into his performance. His presentation is therefore not so much the recitation of an "inner text"; it demands, on the contrary, a high level of psychological and physical involvement. When the audience takes up the rhythm of speech and representation responsively, it becomes involved in the recitation emotionally and physically.[9] The poet's representation amounts to a kind of physical pointing that grips and involves those present. Indicative behavior and emotional imitation combine as the two-sided mimetic process on the level of the events. People often describe the immediate physical effects of such an oral poetic presentation as a contagion—a series of elementary mimetic processes by which listeners achieve a sameness with one another and which spreads epidemically. The epidemic quality of mimesis in this sense was one of the reasons the concept was met with the skepticism Plato was the first to express. Spoken and heard sounds, rhythm, schema, melody, bodily movements, and shared participation together form a kind of dance, comparable to an intricately choreographed gymnastic exercise. Representational forms of this sort belonged to the higher education of Athenian youth selected for roles in the chorus in tragedies and comedies.[10] The origins of Greek gymnastics presumably lie in the teaching of rhythms designed to support speech.

The act of speaking in oral culture has the obvious character of an appeal. The kind of speech that comes into being in that circumstance remains largely bound to physical reenactment. Certain specific stylistic and formal characteristics are preferred: it privileges linear representation; it follows the events depicted through time; and it selects a narrative form based on action, expressed, for example, in the way the description of objects is resolved in representations of action.[11] Tradition is taught, not in reference to ideas and principles, but in actions and behavior. Homer's poetry offers the best examples of this: his description of Achilles' shield fascinated thinkers in classical times; in a time that returns its attention to antiquity, it serves as an exemplary model of action-oriented speech.

In a systematic overview of the area, Walter Ong lists the following as characteristics of oral poetry: it is additive rather than subordinative, aggregative rather than analytic; it is redundant or "copious," conservative or traditional; it is close to the human lifeworld, agonistically toned, empathetic and participatory rather than objectively distanced; it is situational rather than abstract; and it tends toward homeostasis by eliminating memories with no present relevance.[12] In oral cultures the transmission of knowledge has a representational, indicative, and performative character; every performance is unique and not reproducible.[13] This, however, is by no means merely a drawback; that representation must be performative gives rise to a sensuous, richly imaged, emotional, and dynamic language, which standardized writing is not capable of reproducing.

The Platonic dialogues preserve remnants, which may be perceived retrospectively, of the traditional oral orientation toward language. But it is also Plato who formulated the new orientation toward language with unsurpassable precision and rigor: he is the first to create a conceptual language constructed on the basis of definitions. He isolates individual words, in particular, substantive nouns and nominal adjectives, removes them from the context of speech, and, at the same time, views them as representatives of the abstract essences of the heavenly Ideas on earth. The degree to which writing is involved in the formation of Plato's essentialist philosophy can scarcely be estimated. Havelock attempts to find an unequivocal answer to the question, but the way he chooses to do so is methodologically suspect. We may, however, adopt one of his points, namely, that the material potential given in oral language for analysis, definition, abstraction, and systematic articulation does not even approach that of written language. Oral language standardizes and formalizes differently than written language; its structural forms are formulaic expression,[14] rhythm, repetition, gesture, and the relationship between the speaker and the listener. Oral language develops its objects in movement, in addressing, listening, responding.[15] It develops a succession in time; without temporal succession it is inconceivable. Oral language is thus tightly bound to a speech situation, so that it has scarcely any latitude over against the representational and represented action.

In the oral culture of Greece, language, precisely because it lives through its power to incorporate other people, fulfills a direct pedagogical function by declaring what should be done in a given situation. Poets constitute cultural memory; poetry displays ritual paradigms; it can be regarded as the "encyclopedia" of a social disposition, of customary rights and conventions prevailing in Greece at the time of its performance. In addition to fostering continuity, poetry also shapes identity; paradigms show the members of the community who they are and how they should behave.[16] In this view, poetry is a "cultural storehouse," a "preserved communication."[17]

Not only the epic but also the theater entertains and instructs; it is a means by which a "shared communication" is developed. It selects historically, ethically, and politically meaningful material for its object. Its mimesis is the representation of the "*nomos* and *ethos* of the *polis*."[18] The chorus of a Greek tragedy lends the clearest expression to this didactic function; Havelock characterizes it as "a continual rehearsal (mimesis) of the lawful side of Greek life," as a mimetic repetition of and training in the legalities of early Greek life.[19]

Between Oral and Literate Culture

Orality persisted in Greece essentially into the fifth century B.C. The use of written language had not yet led to changes in expressive techniques and had as yet posed no new tasks for literature; it adhered still to the traditional methods of oral instruction. By Plato's time the situation changed fundamentally: toward the middle of the fifth century, the "silent revolution had been accomplished" and the "cultivated Greek public had become a community of readers."[20] The paradigmatic and indicative content of oral communication, which, indeed, had already itself been standardized in characteristic fashion, is now codified by means of writing. The first thing that language loses in the process is its pictorial character.

Plato's position as the first representative of a new, text-oriented culture at the end of the period of orality is the key to understanding his judgments on mimesis. Even after 450 B.C. an important aspect of the meaning of mimesis remained " 'doing what somebody else does' or in effect 'becoming like him,'" which is a sympathetic behavior and not an abstract copying or imitation.[21] In the majority of cases, the behavior is physical, a matter of speech, gesture, gait, pose, and the like.[22] An appeal to the older usage of the term justifies the connection Plato sees between mimesis and psychological identification. His use of the concept designates "active personal identification" through which listeners sympathize with the performance. Mimesis is the name of a "submission to the spell";[23] but it is also "an act of composition which constitutes an act of creation."[24]

What is the substance of the innovation introduced by writing? The most immediate effect is that an acoustical medium of communication is transformed into a visible object. What is once set down can be read later. Facts acquire a new quality; they become quotable, verifiable; they begin to lead a life of their own. With the new language of facts there begins a new language of theory. In this situation mimesis becomes a concept characteristic of poetic speech and of the specific power the poet achieves through the use of his medium to represent reality. In contrast to the absolute certainties of the episteme, mimesis is capable of generating only relative or conditional statements. As we have seen, Plato cedes a place in discourse to mimetic knowledge, but only to consciously acquired knowledge[25]—and poetry has nothing to do with the latter.

Plato evaluates the legacy of knowledge based on mimesis in terms of the changed conditions of literate culture. Before he can treat mimesis in the medium of writing, he must first conceptualize the complex set of interrelations existing among the poet, the public, a sensuous medium, physical and emotional processes, and recited material. From the assortment of usages of ''mimesis,'' which in oral culture designated, on the one hand, an expressive act and a rerepresentation and, on the other, a theatrical performance using voice, gestures, costume, and action, Plato articulates a precisely delimited concept within the frame of a powerful philosophy operating under the material and intellectual conditions of the new literate culture. He extricates the concept of mimesis from the less specific old context of cultural actions and constructs it as the conceptual counterpart to theoretical knowledge, namely, Platonic epistemology and pedagogy.

''Platonism is at bottom an appeal to substitute a conceptual discourse for an imagistic one. As it becomes conceptual, the syntax changes, to connect abstractions in timeless relationships instead of counting up events in a time series.''[26] In the face of such a conceptual discourse, mimesis is relegated to an obscure region rooted in the past, to which is added the further disadvantage that it designates a second-class procedure in epistemological terms: mimesis is confined to doxa, opinion. It comprises a form of knowledge bound to practical experience; it has to do with ''happenings'' that, isolated into separate units, are ''pluralized'' and not susceptible to integration into systems of cause and effect.[27] Doxa, in Plato's definition, deals with becoming instead of being, with the many instead of the one, and with the visible instead of the invisible and intelligible.[28]

The oral poet exercised a form of cultural control over his community. His language ''constituted . . . a frame of reference and standard of expression to which in varying degree all members of the community were drawn.''[29] In Plato's eyes, this power over thought must have appeared all but monopolistic. His strategy for depriving mimesis of power is to relegate it to a sphere of its own, aesthetics, which yields only a qualified form of knowledge.

For Plato, the philosopher's activity is to contemplate reality, and this activity takes place in a mental situation that does not exist in oral culture. ''This new contemplation is to be serene, calm, and detached. . . . Plato has changed the character of the performance and has reduced us to silent spectators.''[30] He characterizes philosophers by contemplative passivity. He separates the thinking subject from the activity and experience of the poet. Knowledge becomes the object of an educational system.[31] Plato's treatment of the concept of mimesis demonstrates that the system of understanding, knowledge, aesthetics, representation, and education in which mimesis has a place undergoes a fundamental alteration by virtue of the fact that the medium of language by which it is constituted itself fundamentally changes. The mimetic elements of oral culture (e.g., rhythm, formulaic expression, verbal melody, etc.) lose their classificatory function in writing. On the one hand, literate language offers more freedom to creativity, to the *delectare,* and individual aesthetic codifications; it can distance itself from physicality and succession in time. On the other hand, social control is exercised largely by means of writing and is thus depersonalized.

Mimetic processes in oral culture are centered on the person of the reciter. Everyone present is included in the performance situation the reciter initiates. Oral codification systems tend to transcend individual differences on the basis of the mutual interaction of the singer and the public and the identification effects that thereby arise. A written text, in contrast, can be continually examined from many different perspectives and according to various aspects. It has, in distinction to the variations of oral poetry, a unified form behind which the person of the author can withdraw. At the same time, writing offers the poet the possibility of lending individual form to mimesis by wresting personal expression from language. With written culture begins the play of social versus individual control and the search for differentiated modes of expression.[32]

Oral culture in the European tradition subsequent to the introduction of writing is not simply reanimated; rather, it always remains, even following the electronic revolution of our own age, the legacy of written culture. Earlier types of mimesis are not completely lost; they can reappear at later times and in other fields under changed conditions.[33]

In the reconstruction and analysis of the transition from orality to literacy, reading, as the complement to writing in the spread of literacy, is accorded scarcely less significance than writing.[34] This insight is the more applicable since for a long time in Greece reading was also an oral process in that texts were read *aloud.* Writing serves as a step in the process by which tones are produced. The author prepares a text to which the reader in the moment of reading lends his voice. There occurs a process of mimesis between the reader's voice and the author's text, in which the text becomes a body of sounds. The author, who is absent in the text, is made present in the sounds made by the reader in reading. Every author needs the voice of a reader for his words to be heard and his fame to grow. Moreover, it is necessary to read aloud for letters to become an understandable text in which sound and sense come together in logos. The Greek concept of reading, *anagignoskein* (recognition), illustrates its mimetic character. For recognition signifies nothing other than an act of relating mimetically to a text, of lending it audible expression, and, by way of that reconstruction, understanding it.

Only when silent reading has become prevalent does writing become the representation of a voice. In reading aloud the written characters conduct the voice, which, in turn, transforms the text into a body of sounds. The present reader takes up the written traces of the absent author, who needs the reader in order to be present, to live on, and to spread his fame. Fame is thinkable only acoustically for the Greeks, namely, as spoken aloud by a voice. Reading becomes a question of power. For the reader in reading subordinates himself or herself to the author's text; the reader's only freedom consists in refusing to read.

5

Poetic Mimesis
(Aristotle)

Aristotle also uses the concept of mimesis in various senses. The question, to what extent he relies on Plato, which is to say, how much he develops a conceptual complex of his own, remains controversial; none of the arguments advanced so far are really satisfactory.[1] Our view is that Aristotle is influenced by Plato's idea of mimesis but that he gives it a new turn. He frequently uses the word *mimesis* in an aesthetic context and only in isolated instances outside the aesthetic sphere. Thus in the *Politics,* for example, he claims that it would be a good plan to imitate the Tarentines;[2] and, further, he contends that children's games are for the most part mimicries of the earnest occupations of later life.[3] Also, in the *Poetics,* he emphasizes the mimetic aptitude as an anthropological constant distinguishing human beings from other animals. It is innate and therefore manifest from early childhood on. The child begins learning through mimesis before becoming able to develop other forms of appropriating the world. The particular cast one's mimetic abilities assume depends on how and in terms of what substantive content they develop.[4]

Plato's use of the *mimesis* word group is more faceted and less precise than Aristotle's; in Plato, the meanings fluctuate and contradict each other. Although the concept is scarcely less important for Aristotle, he comments on it less extensively. He restricts mimesis to poetry, music, and the plastic arts and develops further the beginnings of a formulation of the independent aesthetic realm found in Plato.[5] Aristotle uses the concept of mimesis in the *Poetics* both in the sense of producing images and in the sense of creating a fable or a plot.[6] The first meaning takes up from Plato's considerations. With the second, Aristotle offers his own contribution to the theory of mimesis by exemplifying the concept through dramatic performance or the problem of indirect speech.

53

Visual and poetic mimesis are related for Aristotle; they are comparable, which is to say, similar to each other and different.

The point of departure in the *Poetics* is a distinction between the meanings of mimesis in the extraaesthetic and in the aesthetic realms. Painters and poets, Aristotle says, should not copy people just as they are but operate like good portrait painters: "They, while rendering the individual physique realistically, improve on their subject's beauty. Similarly, the poet, while portraying men who are irascible or lazy or who have other such faults, ought to give them, despite such traits, goodness of character."[7] Homer's portrayal of Achilles is the model here, since it depicts, on the one hand, his harsh character, and, on the other, his goodness. At the center of painting and poetry lies mimesis; but it does not imply the mere copying of the externalities of nature and the portrayal of individual features. Art and poetry aim much more at "beautifying" and "improving" individual features, at a *universalization.* Mimesis is thus copying and changing in one.

Aristotle further describes two types of errors frequently encountered in poetry: the one manifests itself in the substance of what is represented; the other in the way it is given artistic form. In the first case, error is confined to the representation of substantive fact. An example is a galloping horse with both right legs simultaneously extended forward. In the second case, the error lies in the artist's work, in the essence of the artwork itself; this is more serious than the former error, which remains external to the artwork. While the first is a mere matter of faulty copying, the second signals a shortcoming in the artistic process. Following from this distinction is also the difference between extraaesthetic and aesthetic mimesis. The function of painters and poets in the realm of art and poetry is not mere reproduction. Their concern is much more an "imaginative imitation" in which an artistic or poetic synthesis is created.

The function of poetry is not to portray what has happened but to portray what may have happened in accord with the "principle of probability or necessity."[8] Here as well it is clear that poetry is "more than the imitation of that which is." Since poetry aims at the portrayal of what may happen, Aristotle distinguishes the poet from the historian, whose task is merely to convey what has happened. Poetry is concerned with the horizon of the possible. In contrast to historical writing, which deals with particulars, it deals with universals and can therefore claim to be more "philosophical" and "serious." Mimesis thus comprehends, in the aesthetic realm, both the possible and the universal.

Mimesis is characterized as a capacity to produce resemblance through the artistic media of color, shape, and voice. It follows that mimesis is common to all the arts. Poets, painters, and musicians are producers of resemblances that are referred to the horizon of the universal and the possible. They fashion their products in terms of three dimensions: how things were or are; how men say or think things are; and how things should be. At the center of the poet's creative activity is the task of elaborating the story of human action. In tragedy and comedy the plot determines the action and is the soul of the drama. It can stick very close to what really happened, or, that is to say, to an interplay between probability and necessity. Plot, character, and thought make up the objects; spectacle represents the mode; style and lyric poetry are the media of mimesis. The composition of objects, the mode, and the media of mimesis determine the quality of the poetic work.

Once mimesis is understood as the capacity to produce "plot," "intrigue," or "fable," a definition of mimesis becomes available which is distinct from mimesis as the making of images. Aristotle elaborates this idea of poetic mimesis in reference to tragedy. Mimesis aims here at the individual in action; it designates an ability to dramatize and personify speech and action.

Despite some similarities, mimesis as the ability to make images is distinct from mimesis as the making of a plot. The making of images refers to a correspondence between the visual arts and their models. Poetic mimesis, while it also aims at situations in which actions are represented by other actions, has as its primary concern the creation of actions for which there are no immediate models in reality; the essence of poetic mimesis is therefore determined by its imaginary aspect, through which its products detach themselves from reality and achieve autonomy. Mimesis eventuates in a poetic representation of the world, which comes to expression in the imaginary sketch of actions put down in language, a definition that serves particularly well in reference to the writing of tragedies. Yet, to make a dramatic performance possible, a further mimetic interaction with the text is required. The actors must engage mimetically the sketch of the actions they are to perform, in the course of which both their responsibility and latitude in regard to the text are articulated.

With these considerations Aristotle definitively relieves mimesis of the demand that it refer to a given reality. He likewise gives up Plato's reproach, that mimesis, in the case of Homer, for example, leads to untruth and deception. For Aristotle, the critical point is that mimesis produces *fiction;* whatever reference to reality remains is shed entirely of immediacy. The poet creates something that previously did not exist and for which there are no available models. Even in dealing with historical material, the poet must fashion it in accord with his art, raising it to a "higher" level than is found in reality. The poet achieves his work by means of fiction, which universalizes the plot and marks the distinction between poetic writing and the writing of history. The elaboration of a universalizable plot thus becomes the core of mimesis in Aristotelian poetics.

Poetry, painting, and music must create their works as *nature* creates—thus a further stipulation of mimesis. What is intended here is not an imitation of nature, such that a work should be fashioned as the equivalent of nature. The goal is rather to achieve similarity in the processes of creation. Painters, musicians, and poets should produce by means of the same force as nature. Like nature, they are capable of creating matter and form. The creative force in nature lies in nature itself; in art, artists fashion material in terms of a function they have themselves contrived. This process through which a work comes to exist in the world is what defines art, poetry, and music.[9] The statement "Art imitates nature"[10] refers to the same process. Insofar as the origin of nature is nature itself and the origin of art is not art but the artist, the two must be distinguished from each other, and the distinction further reinforces the autonomy of the aesthetic realm. Its defining characteristic is the ability of the artist, painter, or poet to create as nature does. The specificity of art, poetry, and music lies in the processing of different elements into a consistent work of art. In poetry, the plot is the synthetic principle, the one that mediates between necessity and probability. Mimesis creates art. Its objects, devices, and representational forms serve goals conceived by the artist, rather than things existing external to artistic intention.

It is possible to distinguish two further definitional variants of mimesis in the *Poetics*. Mimesis designates the imitation and the manner in which, in art as in nature, creation takes place. Through this definition there arises a difference between nature and art, which allows art to exist as an autonomous aesthetic realm; in addition, the creative force appears as something that nature and human being possess in common.

Aristotle's concern in his poetics and his theory of tragedy is not only with imitation of a serious, self-contained, unitary plot but also with the suitable conveying of the "horrifying" and the "pitiful." According to Ingram Bywater's analysis of Aristotle, catharsis is achieved primarily through the organization of the tragic plot and the materials; the plot, not catharsis, is the core of tragedy and the axis of its aesthetic organization. Moreover, an important and often overlooked concern of tragedy is to offer the audience pleasure. This feeling arises from the spectators' reexperience of the tragic events, which broadens their range of experience, knowing all the while that they themselves are not entirely subject to what happens on stage. The pleasure taken in tragedy is linked to the desire to survive. In contrast to Plato, mimetic identification with the horror expressed in tragedy suggests to Aristotle precisely the promise of fortifying oneself against the "horrifying" and "pitiful." Mimetic reception of tragedy is not, as it is in Plato, a threat to the individual but the means by which he or she cultivates internal strength. Aristotle interprets the strengthening as the result of a "purification process" set in motion by tragedy, which offers a further explanation for the pleasure it releases.

Mimesis serves not only to distinguish the aesthetic from the extraaesthetic sphere. It also provides criteria for distinguishing the various arts. Music is attributed a strong pedagogical effect, since it directly influences the character and soul of the listener. In hearing music, the listener enters into a mimetic relation to it.[11] Music creates pleasure and pleasure creates strength of character and fosters correct behavior. In distinction to Plato, who also emphasizes the ethical content of music, Aristotle assumes that the tones themselves are mimetic representations of character. Here the tonal quality of music appears as distinct from qualities taken in through sight or touch. Neither visual nor tactical qualities are capable of directly expressing the ethical; solely the visual perception of a person acting ethically can produce the appropriate effects. Sculptures are thus not signs of the ethical but can acquire an ethical quality only as the representation of persons behaving morally. Sculptures are only the signs of signs of *ethos*, copies of its manifestations. Ethical behavior is mediated by mimesis, whereby Aristotle attributes particular significance to music and tragedy.[12]

What Plato, in our view, has already suggested in the tenth book of the *Republic*, namely, that the aesthetic is constituted as an independent sphere by means of mimesis, Aristotle makes explicit, and his position will remain determinative of aesthetics from now on. The social significance of mimesis moves into the background. Plato responded to the ambivalent character of mimesis with the demand that it be controlled, while Aristotle sees precisely in one's mimetic interaction with passions and desires a defense mechanism against the power of affect.

Paul Ricoeur has shown that is not tenable to restrict mimesis to the process by which a work's plot is originated,[13] during the course of which a new order is laid out and literary innovation accomplished. Scarcely less important are mimetic processes that take place prior to creation as the presupposition of the fiction and in the work's reception by the reader. Ricoeur designates these processes Mimesis$_1$ and Mimesis$_3$, which lie "upstream" and "downstream" from the center of aesthetic creation, designated Mimesis$_2$. By presuppositions Ricoeur means the way intellectual structures, symbolic devices, and the temporal structures of the action are opened up to the process of literary creation. On the side of reception, mimetic processes involve the transposition and metamorphosis of the work on the part of the reader. Circular processes, in which readers make reference to their own experience, are also indispensable if they are to experience the work as vital.

Every plot is based on a preexisting understanding of the world of action set in motion by the work. Insofar as this world is made up of a mimesis of actions, it presupposes a prior understanding of actions, which implies the ability to identify the structural qualities of the actions, to understand their semantics, follow their symbolic articulations, and see through their temporal character. An understanding of what action means *structurally* requires a conceptual frame of reference determined by the goals, motives, circumstances, and results of action. Familiarity in these areas occasions a practical understanding of action, which is presupposed by the elaboration of a plot. This order of action is, in turn, fundamentally distinct from the linguistic-discursive order. The linguistic representation of action requires access to the devices of *symbolic practice;* without them the field of practice remains "mute." Access to the symbolic structure of a practice is opened up in large part by implicit norms and rules, which supply people with ethical standards and thus influence their behavior. Finally, the elaboration of plot presupposes an understanding of the temporality of actions and courses of action, on which the configuration of the temporal aspect of the story can be based. What results is a process of exchange among different times, whereby linear succession represents only one form of the temporal structuring of plots.[14]

At the center of Aristotelian poetics lies poetic mimesis (Mimesis$_2$). It occupies a position between the presuppositions and the reception of a literary work, where, in a dynamic process leading to the formulation of the *mythos,* that is, poetic configuration, it mediates between structuring events and isolated incidents. Working with the arrangement of the various threads of action, poetic mimesis draws all the heterogenous elements—the goals, means, and circumstances of the action—together. In plot, diverse temporal structures come together into a "synthesis of the heterogenous," by which is meant a meaningful totality raising universal claims. At the same time, plot manifests the critical aspect of distancing and delimiting, without which innovations would not be possible.

Central to the process of Mimesis$_2$ is the literary generation of innovation. Imitation and representation as well as expression and creative modification are all active in the process, through which the "what," the "whereby," and the "how" of the plot are given form. The specificity of the mimetic fashioning of the literary configuration is comprised of the break, implicit in the fictional character, with the presuppositions of the practice fields and the processes of reception. To have universal value, the configuration must surpass a description of isolated incidents, establishing itself in the sphere of the virtual. For it is there that the possible and the universal enter a relation of mutual reference, whereby the result is the creation of something new. Mimesis$_2$ thus names neither an imitation nor a representation of a reality; it leads instead, via the arrangement of individual elements, to the creation of a literary fiction that cannot be reduced to its presuppositions.

For plots and literary texts to be experienced as vital, mimetic processes are required on the part of the recipient of a work (Mimesis$_3$). Fictional arrangements can be understood only if the recipient has already acquired a practical knowledge of human action in the context of daily behavior. As the author needs to have experienced action in his or her daily life to be able to produce a plot, so does the reader need similar experiences to understand the plot. The plot can be opened up mimetically only on the basis of the reader's own life experiences. This mimetic processing of literary works is circular; it establishes a state of oscillation between the work and the recipient. Every confrontation with a literary work, understood in terms of this process, will contain moments of caprice, of the power of interpretation, and of redundancy.

The reading of a text is simultaneously the mimetic refiguration of the plot. What this looks like precisely is a question of the recipient's presuppositions;

reading leads, in any case, to the recipient's actualization and metamorphosis of the text.[15] Plot transpositions are inevitable. The refiguration that occurs in the imaginative world of the recipient in the course of mimetic processing is both similar to and distinct from the configuration created by the author. Every recipient creates in his or her imagination a partially new work. Not least among the determinations of a reader's modifications is the temporal distance separating the time of the action, the time of the telling of the action, and the time of its mimetic reception by the reader.

Part II

Mimesis as Imitatio, the Expression of Power, and Literate Subjectivity

For a lengthy period encompassing all of the Middle Ages and continuing well into the Renaissance, mimesis was understood as creation in reference to a model. God, as the supreme object of imitation, was the source of the creative. The creativity of imitation was understood less in the sense of producing a product than as an intellectual endeavor expressed in deeds, in particular, in the *imitatio Christi*. It proceeded according to models of mimetic action supposedly established in immutable form and for all time. During this period mimesis was characterized essentially by three qualities: it is reproduction in accordance with an idea; it constitutes a relation of succession in reference to a model; and it produces a similarity to the model and—a thought that emerges in the Renaissance—has the nature of the probable.

Medieval Christianity developed in part as an imitatio of the religion, language, and educational system of antiquity. Models and techniques taken over from classical culture and the Christianity of late antiquity were used to prompt mimetic processes, which, in turn, involved more than mere reproduction. New works came into being in literature, art, and music as a result of the mimesis.

Medieval mimesis must be understood in terms of three aspects. The first consists in a relation of representation, which is determined by the question of the kind of relation that exists between models and the results of mimesis. Since no declarative statements about God or Christ are possible, all notions and images of them arise within a relation of representation, to which all new representations must also be referred in turn. That is, representations always refer to prior representations. The second aspect of medieval mimesis consists in the observance and investigation of the *processes* that lead to specific artistic and literary representations. Finally, medieval writers show great interest in the *results* of these mimetic processes and the exploration of the innovative potential inherent in medieval imitatio.

The Renaissance *historicizes* mimesis, at the same time sharpening awareness of the close relationship between power and mimesis. The historical question does not arise first in the "Querelle des Anciens et des Modernes," the quarrel between the ancients and the moderns, but already exists in concerns that are maintained throughout the Renaissance. What is the significance for the present of Greek and Roman antiquity? Do their cultural accomplishments represent pinnacles toward which the proper relation is mimetic, the expectation, at best, being able to equal them? Or does one's own time mark the pinnacle of development? Representatives of both humanism and the "moderns" dispute these questions and offer their answers. The moderns refer to the experimental method, to new knowledge in the natural sciences, and to the achievements of the present, before which the knowledge of the "ancients" declines in value. These discussions lead to a historical relativization of cultural products and thereby to a relativization of the claims to validity raised by mimesis, which nevertheless remains the paradigm for the appropriation of cultural products.

The contemporary theory of poetics discusses the significance of traditional rules for literary production. Alongside criteria borrowed from Horace, similarity and probability become important considerations in the assessment of literary texts. These disputes about the style and value of literary works are in reality the expression of a battle under way in society concerning who holds the power over symbolic expression and who dictates the obligatory worldview. From this perspective it is easy to understand the bitter struggles over adherence to rules and the mimesis of traditional models. Expressed in the context of these battles is *literary subjectivism,* the beginnings of which reach back into the late Middle Ages. It eventually assumes a complementary function over against the social control exercised by the church. The possibility, in other words, of giving expression to a personal style appeared by way of a mimesis of the "ancients." By appealing to the authority of ancient authors and writing under their protection, Renaissance poets bypassed the strictures of ecclesiastical and secular authorities to develop their own personal expressive forms. Thus does the commandment of mimesis lead, on the one hand, to the specification of formal obligations in literary representation and, on the other, to the emergence of individual subjective expression.

With the spread of the book and the increase in the number of readers, texts attain an unprecedented importance. Of greater interest for this period is also the question of how commentaries and readers' guides influence the reading of texts. *Intertextuality,* the direct reference of texts to other texts, becomes an issue. What does it mean for literary production that texts are related mimetically to other texts, that they thereby give rise to new complex texts? What is the relation to textuality of the use of *fragments,* which is so evident in

Michel de Montaigne's work and so important for literary composition? Certainly the intentional use of fragments represents a modern compositional principle; it originates in the inadequacy of human knowledge and, in Montaigne, appears in connection with *self-referentiality,* in which the *I* arrives always and only back at itself. This self-referentiality comprises the single mimetic structure most central and fundamental to an understanding of the modern subject.

6

Mimesis as Imitatio

Throughout the thousand years that make up the "Middle Ages," mimesis, usually designated "imitatio" at the time, plays a major role. There is scarcely a sphere of medieval life in which its effects are not felt and which cannot be characterized as mimetic. Reference back to antiquity is frequently made at this time; things are taken up, modified, and introduced into a new context. When, for example, a Carolingian author takes over Cicero's definition of philosophy as "fundamental knowledge of divine and human things," the substance of the definition undergoes a retrospective change. The words remain the same, but in the context of Christian thought, a new meaning emerges. This process by which classical elements are taken up and incorporated into Christian thought, which is characteristic of the Middle Ages, is mimetic. A detailed examination would exceed the scope of our study, but we can offer brief clarification by way of a few examples.

One example of a complex mimetic process is the processional cross, referred to as the Lothar Cross and among the holdings of the Aachen cathedral, which was probably made for Emperor Otto III. The cross is composed of parts representing various historical periods, which makes a reinterpretation of its different elements the consequence of considering its overall meaning.[1] The reinterpretation derives from the combination of pagan Roman and Christian elements, making the cross a sign for the *renovatio imperii* sought by the Ottoites in the hope of merging the *populus christianus* and the *populus romanus*. To render this palpable as an image, the cameo at the center of the Ottoite cross, with the crucifixion of Christ on the reverse, depicts Caesar Augustus bearing the sign of Roman sovereignty. Thus a representation of an emperor from the time of Christ's birth is used to express the Ottoites' claim to power as the legitimate successor of the Roman emperor; at the same time, the representation takes place on a cross, that is, in a Christian context.

This amalgamation of signs from separate traditions is characteristic of the Middle Ages. It expresses the Holy Trinity—Father, Son, and Holy Ghost—and with it the triumph of Christian order over the world. The Roman eagle, appearing as a dove in the right hand of the emperor in the cross's central cameo, makes the new meaning obvious: it is the self-referentiality of the Christian order in the context of world domination. It entails transposing the Roman Empire into a Christian empire with its allusion to divine Jerusalem, to which the symbolism of the Ottoite crown explicitly refers.[2]

Such processes of simultaneous mimesis and innovation are also at work in medieval literature. In Spanish literature of the fourteenth century, Juan Ruiz, the archpriest of Hita, offers one example. In his *Libro de buen amor,* he created a work that clearly manifests mimetic reference to the *Confessions.* Ruiz develops a highly ambivalent relation to Augustine's great model, which established the first standard of autobiographical writing. On the one hand, the *Confessions* represents to Ruiz a model according to which the reader may experience an equally profound religious conversion. On the other, Ruiz distances himself from the Augustinian model by lending his own work an ironic touch, thus rendering it ambiguous. While in Augustine all events are subordinate to divine objectives, in Ruiz some of them seem opaque, unclear, and contrary to divine intentions. There thus arises an unresolvable tension between the lofty objectives of a pious life and the tendency of the overtaxed author, and the reader, to fail to achieve them. While Augustine proceeds pedagogically in his *Confessions,* Ruiz is skeptical about the degree of Augustine's success and even more so about achieving the necessary effects with his own work. He therefore abandons a Christian rhetoric that counts on the conversion of his reader, contenting himself with a representation of the inadequacy of the human situation. In distinction to Augustine's view, which regards a linear development of the individual from a longing after physical love to a longing after divine love as necessary and possible, Ruiz stresses the cyclical character of life, which the individual cannot escape and which leads to a repetition of the same sensual desires and moral failings. It is all the less possible to overcome desire, Ruiz argues in contrast to the Augustinian view, because memory is inadequate; it fails to prevent people from repeating mistakes. The work of Ruiz thus abandons the unequivocal voice of the Augustinian model; it remains ambiguous, leaving to the reader the matter of finding a way through the ambivalences in the text.[3]

No less marked is the mimetic relation between Boccaccio's *Decameron* and Dante's *Divine Comedy.* The works of Ruiz and Boccaccio are similar to the extent that Boccaccio endeavors to prove, throughout his discussion of the *Divine Comedy,* its failures of poetic truthfulness and moral utility. Boccaccio admires Dante's lofty intentions, on the one hand, while he is unable, on the other, to accept his idealistic goals. Instead Boccaccio refers to characteristic human egotism and self-indulgence, which, in another contrast, this one to the lofty language of the *Divine Comedy,* he represents in the vernacular. Boccaccio's numerous allusions to Dante's masterpiece are made ironically, an expression of Boccaccio's distance from and skepticism toward Dante's idealistic design. Even the title, *Decameron,* can be understood as an allusion to the six days of creation. There is no mistaking Boccaccio's mimetic reference to Dante's *Divine Comedy.* Robert Hollander, by analyzing the differences in the use of the word *quill (penna)* in the *Decameron* and the *Divine Comedy* (for a writing utensil and a paintbrush), identifies the differences between Dante's and Boccaccio's conception of art, which provides a clear indication of the "mimetic distance" that separates them.[4] The artist, for Dante, falls far short of the "mimetic capacities" of God; Boccaccio, explicitly distinguishing himself from Dante, emphasizes the surpassing abilities of the painter Giotto di Bondone. Giotto, not God, is, for Boccaccio, the quintessence of the mimetic genius.

The context in which these three medieval works were constituted indicates once again that mimesis is not adequately conceived as the reproduction of a model. A confrontation with literary models obviously gives rise to new works made up of an amalgamation of heterogenous elements. What becomes manifest in the process of mimetic literary development, given in the examples of Ruiz and Boccaccio, is the distinction between an idealistic and a more skeptical view of humanity, along with the anthropological difference the latter implies. Unable to escape the influence of Augustine and Dante, both later authors use irony and mockery to overturn the relations of representation found in their respective models, thereby carving out for themselves a space of creative freedom. Mimesis necessarily exceeds the meaning of something being represented again as it was once created. The mimetic process gives rise to the production of new works precisely because authors and artists do indeed make reference to other works in their representations, but the reference fails to offer a satisfying account of the specific character of the new work. In addition to mimesis, the social and individual conditions of an author's life belong among the active factors in the process of ongoing literary creation. Our examples from different periods in the Middle Ages show mimetic processes are involved in artistic and literary developments, which give rise to new works that cannot be reduced to their underlying models.[5]

Two further examples will help clarify the medieval understanding of mimesis, one drawn from the area of *aesthetic philosophy* and the other from *political theology.* Both terms are problematic in reference to medieval circumstances, in which art and politics do not exist separately as autonomous spheres. If we nevertheless insist on the terms, we do so in the awareness of the epistemological problems entailed in applying them to the medieval period.

Aesthetic philosophy and aesthetics do not appear as concepts in the Middle Ages, but there is an intense preoccupation with theories of the plastic arts and literature, as well as with artistic and literary production as such. There therefore develops a sensitivity for the beauty of artworks and natural objects, which finds expression in the twelfth century, for example, in the criticism by Bernhard von Clairvaux and Alexander Neckam of the "superfluity" (*superfluitates*) they find in works executed in the style of Cluny. Clairvaux refers to "inner beauty," which cannot be achieved by an elaborate style but which remains the primary goal of Christian art. People of the Middle Ages seem not to have made a principled distinction between the beauty of a sunrise, an artwork, and a person. The respective beauty of each had always to be a reflection of the beauty of God, and thus the three different forms share in common a mimetic relation to the beauty of God.

The creative power and beauty of God supply the artist's unattainable models. Artists remain inferior to God and nature insofar as they are God's creatures and part of nature. Artworks have a "borrowed substantiality"; as incomplete reproductions they remain secondary to things in nature. Their quality of bearing multiple meanings is overshadowed by the manifold meaningfulness of nature. There were several interpretations available for the statement "Art imitates nature."

> It could make nature appear to be an epiphenomenon of all-encompassing nature and thus call art as such into question; but it could also cause one to subordinate nature to art, on the justification that a thinking being is better able to imitate nature than sensuous objects can. It could be meant as a reminder of the limits of human ability: we imitate nature without being able to equal it.[6]

The activity of the artist never equals the creative activity of God; as art, it never escapes its need for what is given in God-created nature. Art is therefore limited by the "creaturality" and dependence on nature of the human artist, whose works are necessarily inferior to the eternal art and creative power of God. It is in this connection that contemporary aesthetic theory makes its references to ontology and metaphysics.

Following Plato, Plotinus assumes that art entails a three-step imitation of the idea.[7] Even if artists think that they are imitating nature, they are nevertheless working with an idea, since nature, for its part, imitates mind; and many of the arts endeavor to rise to the level of the rational forms, which are the source of nature. Thus the self-conception of the artist derives, not primarily from nature, but from his or her status as a thinking, creative individual, who introduces form into nature. The result, since the arts have access to beauty, is that they are capable of creating something out of themselves. To this extent, art can also correct and perfect nature.

For John Scotus Erigena, a ninth-century Irish monk, human being is not composed of "two substances, a general one in the divine ideas and a particular one in time and space";[8] rather, there are only two modes according to which the single substance of human being can be conceived. Since the nature of things is divine, so is the human mind "a living and productive mirror of the universe" and, as such, also divine. Individual human being, as microcosmos, and nature, as macrocosmos, are in a relation of correspondence. Since objects are more real in the mind of the artist than they are in themselves, the artwork can attain to a rank higher than that of natural things.

Everything falls into three areas in the Chartres school: the works of God, the works of nature, and the works of the artist imitating nature.[9] Nature in these terms is the simulacrum of the divine idea, and the productivity of the human mind is a precondition for the apprehension of the divine spirit. What human being produces, however, is as nothing compared to the creations of God, a point that applies with equal force to the artwork, which, like the artist, is nothing. There becomes evident here an unresolved tension between the potential of the human mind and what it actually realizes.

Plato, Plotinus, Erigena, and the Chartres school all assume that nature is of the spirit and that every thing presupposes its idea. For Nicholas of Cusa, human reason corresponds to the world soul; nature and art both imitate the idea. The idea of a thing is not sensuous; it is the unity of a multiplicity of determinations of which the idea is not itself the basis. Nature and art thus do not stand alongside each other in isolation. Reason emerges as the constitutive unity of nature and art.

It is possible to conclude as follows regarding relations among art, nature, and mimesis in the medieval period.

> Nature and the idea are not separated; the concept of nature is not the deterministic one of the nineteenth and twentieth centuries.
>
> Concepts, thinking, and art are not applied retroactively to nature; they are prior to nature. Nature is the copy; it is not possible to interpret mimesis naturalistically.
>
> There is no phenomenology of the artwork, nor is there a sense of the historicity of art.
>
> Divine art is eternal art and the standard of all human art. Nature, as nature, is something spiritual, just as human being is the creation of God. It makes sense to imitate nature because of the way nature and reason are interrelated. Human beings are able to imitate nature because they, in their sensuousness, are similar to it.
>
> Art, in imitating the essence of nature, does more than lend phenomenal form to a surface; imitation therefore means more than a simple replication of externality by artistic means; this "more" implies the in-

dividual freedom to create something new that has no model existing
in nature. Here individual human being is conceived in the image of God
as creator and artist.

In imitating the essence of nature, art must lend phenomenal form to more
than its mere surface. Imitation therefore means more than the simple replication of externality by means of art; in this "more" lies the freedom of the
individual to create something new that has no model in nature itself. In this
sense, individual human being is made in the image of God as creator and
artist.

The works of Thomas Aquinas make especially clear the spiritual character
of nature, its connection with art, and the experience of the divine. He defines
nature as the intellectual content of divine art. Human artists necessarily imitate
nature, because, through the senses, they acquire knowledge from things of
nature. Natural things can be imitated because they are ordered according to
a spiritual principle concerning their purpose, so that every *opus naturae* is an
opus intelligentiae.[10] For Aquinas, things are preconceived by God and therefore accessible to human knowledge. Human beings owe their capacity for
knowledge to God. Art and nature are similar to each other insofar as they
pursue their ends in a comparable way.

The experience of beauty is central to the relation between human being and
the world, because only human being is capable of experiencing beauty.
Beauty, like the good, the true, and being, has, for Aquinas, a *metaphysical*
value, a moment of universal objectivity that never changes. Beauty refers to
God and becomes one of his attributes. The beauty of this world is thus regarded
as having a mimetic relation to the beauty of God. The metaphysical view
underlying the concept of mimesis here stems from the Bible and Plato's
Timaeus, in which the temporal world is regarded as a mimesis of the eternal
world. The relation becomes one step clearer in the concept of *pankalia:* All
that God has created is beautiful and good. "Beautiful" and "good" exist here
in mutual reference; as attributes of the being of God, they are not to be
distinguished. That which can be perceived as beautiful, as the work of God,
stands in mimetic relation to God.[11]

If only humans can perceive beauty, the question arises of how their
perception must be constituted such that the world is pleasing to them. What
does it mean about the internal organization of a human being that perception
occasions the feeling of beauty? What correspondences must be said to exist
between the world and the individual? Is there a mimetically mediated structural similarity between the beauty of the world and its perception? Whatever
the answers to these questions, beauty must appear as a relation between a
human subject and an object offering itself for contemplation in accord with
specific criteria.[12] Among the latter are, primarily, proportion, wholeness, and
clarity, all three of which imply a reference to the representational form of the

contours of the body. The first criterion, proportion, refers to the claim that beauty consists in a harmonious relation of parts to one another.

Pythagorean thought, Plato's *Timaeus,* and the thought of the Chartres school all have a part in the development of these ideas, according to which various aspects of the criterion of proportion can be distinguished: (1) as referring to the suitability of matter for receiving a form; (2) as a relation between essence and existence; (3) as in a relationship among a multitude of fixed items; (4) in reference to logical relationships among thoughts, for example, to the harmony in a thought chain; (5) as the adequacy of a thing to itself; (6) as the mutual multiplicity of a dense network of relations; (7) as the relation between ontological and psychological factors; and (8) as the embeddedness of a relation in the vital reality of form.[13]

The second criterion, wholeness or integrity, is scarcely less important, though it overlaps in some respects with the first. It refers to a notion of balance and perfection inherent to the medieval understanding of the beautiful. The third criterion of beauty, clarity, encompasses multiple aspects, with four significant meanings of "clarity" to be distinguished in Aquinas's work: (1) light and physical color; (2) the light of reason that makes things known, *lumen manifestans;* (3) the shining forth of earthly renown; and (4) the celestial glory of the blessed.[14]

If the criteria of clarity, integrity, and proportion are at least partially satisfied, the result will be the experience of beauty, which is formally determined by them. Beauty is constantly manifest in the Son of God and in the human person. Things and their beauty also stand in mimetic relation to each other and to their common origin in God. We are not speaking here of a relation of correspondence; it is rather that things and their beauty are conceived as symbols or allegories of God. Worldly phenomena are referred to something and interpreted as the expression of that referent. The same applies to the metaphors and allegories of literature and painting. Literal meaning reproduces results; allegory refers to God; the moral is a manifestation of the appropriateness of an action undertaken.

According to Aquinas, metaphor belongs primarily to the province of literature. The allegories of the Holy Scripture, in contrast, convey "divine and spiritual realities under bodily guises"[15]—for the reason that all human knowledge originates in the senses, implying that spiritual and divine knowledge can be better understood in sensible form. Thus do the symbols, allegories, and analogies of the Holy Scripture stand in mimetic relation to the incontrovertible, universal, spiritual, and divine truths lying behind intelligible forms. The spiritual meaning, however, is characteristic, not of the poetry, but of the stories in the Bible, which "have no other end than to have meaning."[16] Aquinas thus attributes to the Holy Scripture a special value and a special mimetic relation to God, which makes it superior to poetry, art, and music. In religious images God is represented by a surplus of truth; nonsacred poetry and art make use of figurative expressions, which, however, are not possessed of the whole truth.

Aquinas defines art as right judgment concerning things that are made and as knowledge about how something can be made. The definition encompasses two elements: a rational one and a productive one. Art thus signifies the knowledge of rules by means of which works can be produced.[17] Smiths, painters, and poets are designated *artifex*. Their activity is a productive process guided by rules, which, insofar as it refers to preexisting knowledge, is mimetic. The mimetic character of artistic processes is composed of "invention and remaking"; art composes different elements in such a way that a work results. This process is similar to nature's process of creation. "Art in its works imitates nature."[18] What is meant here is not imitation that is faithful in its details, a copy of the *natura naturata*, but imitation of the *natura naturans*, the formative power of nature. In it is expressed the omnipotence of God. "All creatures are in the divine mind as a piece of furniture is in the mind of a cabinetmaker. Now, a piece of furniture is in the mind of a cabinetmaker by means of its idea and likeness."[19] This similarity is the result of a connection between an idea and something of which the idea is the model. The idea is thus a model in reference to which things are created formally. Artistic and artisanal production is therefore a making by means of mimesis of the model forms that themselves guide the production process. "Hence, properly speaking, there is no idea corresponding merely to matter or merely to form; but one idea corresponds to the entire composite—an idea that causes the whole, both its form and its matter."[20] The idea is given to us by God; it is knowledge he instills in us, which artists and artisans discover in themselves.

The problem of creativity remains unsolved in this understanding of the idea. The imagination, which in Aquinas's conception belongs with common sense, judgment, and memory as one of the four inward senses, is a faculty that can lead from the perception of similarity to the production of something other.[21] There is no doubt that what results is a production process and not a process of creation whereby, for example, new life comes into being. Only nature is capable of creation in this sense; only it can produce substances. The forms of art, in contrast, are always artificial and accidental. Artistic forms depend for their realization on the material used, the substance of which remains unchanged. In the building of a house, for example, the architectural design calls for materials already available in other contexts; for the design to be realized, the materials have to be removed from a prior use and integrated into the new context. Artistic forms are produced by people; they can only change the natural appearance of an object. When a block of stone becomes a statue, its original form disappears, but not its material. The latter merely acquires a new form (*figura*). While natural objects are substantial in material and form, products of the artist and artisan are substantial only in reference to their material; their form comes from without, from the human artist or artisan. Insofar as the artist strives to make the objects of art as perfect as possible, the objects themselves incline toward similarity with God, to which all human action and making refers mimetically.

Mimesis is also involved in the foundation of the political system, a point that is made clearly in Ernst Kantorowicz's *The King's Two Bodies*.[22] According to this study of the *political theology* of the Middle Ages, the king has two bodies, an individual human body and a supernatural divine body; the king is termed the "twice-born majesty." As a natural man, he is subject to everything human; as a supernatural king, he has a dignity deriving from his special relation to God. The two are incorporated into an indissoluble unity in a *gemina persona*. The political body is bigger and broader than the natural body; the space of the latter changes under the influence of the former. The political body transcends the imperfection of the natural body, rendering it beyond comparison. On the death of the king, the two bodies separate. The political body does not die; it is transposed to a new natural body, with the result that the immortal part of the king is passed on from one incarnation to another. There is less distinction between the political body of the king and the "mystical body" (*corpus mysticum*) of the Christian community, with Christ as the head. The king is understood in analogy to the God-man Christ. Thus was it possible in England to execute the natural body of Charles Stuart without destroying the political body of the king.

The anonymous Norman author whose work of circa 1100 contains the elaboration of the idea of the king's two bodies sees the kings of the Old Testament as forerunners to the kingly Christ. After Christ had been on earth and ascended, the role of kings changed. They are no longer forerunners but now imitators of Christ. "The Christian ruler becomes the *christomimētēs*— literally the 'actor' or 'impersonator' of Christ—who on the terrestrial stage presented the living image of the two-natured God, even with regard to the two unconfused natures. The divine prototype and his visible vicar were taken to display great similarity, as they were supposed to reflect each other."[23] Christ and the king are distinguished in this view in that Christ is an eternal king by nature, while the king possesses divinity only for a time. In the consecration of the king, it is only the grace of God—the attainment of divinity through divine grace—that elevates him and makes him a different person. The power of the king derives from the omnipotence of God and is ceded to the king for a limited period. "Hence, the king, too, is God and Christ, but by grace; and whatsoever he does, he does not simply as a man, but as one who has become God and Christ by grace."[24]

Also in regard to his power, the king appears as christomimētēs. When he fulfills the functions of office, he acts as the vicar of God and Christ; thus the medieval model of the Christ-centered kingship, which flourished from roughly 900 to 1100. The concept of christomimētēs expresses the mimetic character of the relation between Christ and the king. The king provides a representation of Christ, embodies him, and in his actions renders him available to people's experience. He is the "image of Christ," the "vicar of Christ," an understanding of the emperor that is clearly illustrated in the frontispiece of the Aachen Gospels. The ruler on earth is on his throne; his head reaches into heaven, we see, because it is being blessed by the hand of God; the ruler is surrounded by the four beasts of the Apocalypse; he is being venerated by two dignitaries at his feet.

The Christ-centered justification of kingship declined in significance from the twelfth century on, its place taken by ideas of kingship centered on law. In the fourth book of the *Policraticus* by John of Salisbury is found the idea of *rex imago aequitatis,* the metaphor of the king as the image of justice. By the beginning of the thirteenth century, "legal thought unmistakably prevailed over the spirit of the liturgy."[25] Abundant evidence to this effect can be found in the *Liber autustalis,* the extensive collection of Sicilian constitutions published by Frederick II in 1231. Here the emperor is called on to be at once the "father and son of justice."[26] What is the meaning of this paradoxical formulation? Clearly the emperor is being accorded a mediating role, which from now on determines the self-conception of the medieval emperor. A connection is established "between divine reason and human law."[27] Not infrequently the emperor is termed the "animate law."[28] As the father of justice, he embodies laws; he has precedence over their lifeless codifications. As the "animate law" given to the people by God, he represents divine justice; as christomimētēs, he enters into a mimetic relation to Christ, which means, likewise, that he stands in a mimetic relation to the laws. As the son of justice or the servant of the laws, he must correspond to them in his actions. There gradually occurs a "secularization of royal mediatorship through the new jurisprudence,"[29] which forces the ideals of the king and the priest into the background. In place of the grace of God, which was at the heart of the Christocentric monarch, now comes the idea of divine and animate justice embodied in the king. The ruler is no longer the christomimētēs. "A new pattern of *persona mixta* emerged from Law itself, with *Iustitia* as the model deity and the Prince as both her incarnation and her *Pontifex maximus.*"[30]

In England the development of a law-centered monarchy was further prompted by the works of Henry of Bracton, a contemporary of Frederick II, according to which the king stands both over and under the law.[31] It is this conception that ultimately replaces the idea of the emperor as the "father and son of justice." What is new here is the insistence with which the superordination of the law over the king is demanded. "The king has no other power, since he is the vicar of God and His minister on earth, except this alone which he derives from the Law."[32] The king is subordinate to no person, only to God and the law. God and the law make the king. Where no law rules, there is no king. God and the law overlap. The king behaves mimetically toward divine law and attempts to realize it in his realm through his actions.

There arises a division of labor between the king as a private person, who falls under the law, and the king as a public person, in whom divine law is embodied. A difference gradually develops between the feudal and the fiscal king. "Feudal" designates the king's personal relationships with his vassals; "fiscal" refers to matters "affecting everyone." Inalienability and exclusion from annual prescriptions come to apply not only to church possessions but also to the property of the crown, the fisc. Church possessions and the possessions of the fisc become more and more alike in terms of rights, until they become essentially equivalent. The question of what constitutes the fisc remains controversial; it is likely to have referred to "the *aerarium,* the treasury, not of the people or the Prince, but of the empire."[33] In the increasing parallelism between the rights of the fisc and the rights of the church, the fisc becomes analogous to the *res sacrae* of the church, which was held in the name of Christ, until "something definitely secular and seemingly 'unholy' in the Christian and every other sense, namely the fisc, was turned into a thing 'quasi holy.' The fisc finally became a goal in itself. It was taken as a hallmark of sovereignty, and, by a total reversal of the original order, it could be said that 'the fisc represents State and Prince.'"[34] This development gradually leads to the hallowing of the state, including its administrative institutions, goals, and needs. The new state comes to be "equated with the Church also in its corporational aspects as a secular *corpus mysticum.*"[35]

Evidence of the process is found in the mutual borrowings of political insignia by the pope and the emperor. A golden crown adorns the pope's tiara; the emperor wears a miter under his crown. The exchange between church and state goes on. The hierarchically organized apparatus of the church "tended to become the perfect prototype of an absolute and rational monarchy on a mystical basis, while at the same time the State showed an increasing tendency to become a quasi-Church or a mystical corporation on a rational basis."[36] The designation "corpus mysticum" serves "to hallow the secular polities as well as their administrative institutions."[37] If corpus mysticum initially retains the meaning of the host, the body of the church with Christ as the head and the ecclesiastical officials as its limbs, then this meaning gradually shifts to the *corpus politicum* and the *corpus juridicum* of the church. The mystical character of the church, founded on its similarity with the body of Christ, declines in importance, until finally all that the term signifies is the church as a political organization in the secular world. Analogously, the state will be designated a little later *corpus respublicae mysticum.* Here the "mystical body of the commonweal" overlaps with the "political body of the state." "And just as men are joined together spiritually in the spiritual body, the head of which is Christ . . . , so are men joined together morally and politically in the *respublica,* which is a body the head of which is the Prince."[38] Occasionally the king is designated "the mystical spouse of the *respublica.*"[39] The state becomes a corpus mysticum, which maintains continuity since it, like the church, is immortal and lasts "eternally." The transposition of the appropriate ideas from the sphere of the church onto the state renders it sacred. What was initially guaranteed by the continuity in relation to Christ and then by law is now guaranteed by the corpus mysticum of the state. Notions of the state as *patria* reinforce this development, in which the earthly fatherland comes to be juxtaposed to the church. There thus arises gradually "the new polity-centered rulership . . . vested in the *universitas* 'which never dies,' in the perpetuity of an immortal people, polity, or *patria,* from which the individual king might easily be separated, but not the Dynasty, the Crown, and the Royal Dignity."[40]

The development of medieval kingship can be understood in these terms as a complex mimetic process, with distinctions to be drawn between Christocentric, law-centered, and polity-centered rule. Transitions from one phase to another are continuously under way, with models and patterns of thought changing in the process. Now it is the double body of Christ that provides the model for the king's two bodies; now it is divine law and divine justice, both of which are incorporated in the king and can be realized only through his action. Finally, it is the law that demands the subordination of the king, or seeks a new relation between church and state that promotes the development of the law as the king's new point of reference. Involved as well in each of these changes is the mimetic relation of the king, the church, and the state to God, which, by way of revisions of prior interpretations, is newly interpreted and defined.

7

Poetics and Power
in the Renaissance

Central to the elaboration of the self-conception of many historical periods has been the question of their relation to antiquity, that is, to the origins of European culture. An answer requires that a given period specify, in terms of its own concerns, the significance of the classical era. Just as individuals are "begun" before they are able, through memory and behavior, to understand the question of origins and thus to lend autonomous form to their lives, so are historical epochs subject to the influence of what came before. But just how the influence of prior times operates exceeds available knowledge, whether in reference to particular individuals or to historical periods. Neither individuals nor cultures have access to their beginnings. All that can be said for certain is that all individuals and all epochs are shaped by mimetic processes, which take up what already exists and transform it. In the continuous process of cultural appropriation, some cultural legacies offer models and orientation, others prompt self-delimitation, spur new thinking, and inspire cultural accomplishments. Constantly under way is a confrontation with tradition, the validity of which is determined anew for every time and every person. Every historical period is in this sense a "double"; conditions prior to its sense of its own beginning tend to be forgotten in favor of emphasis on uniqueness and originality. In the moment of repression contained in this maneuver of self-identification, the mimetic character of cultural creation is lost sight of, overshadowed by a shorthand understanding of productivity and originality.

A prime example of such an encounter with classical antiquity is the "quarrel of the ancients and the moderns" in the last decades of the seventeenth century and first decades of the eighteenth century in France.[1] The focus of the discussion was the importance of antiquity to French classicism. Did it serve as a model? If so, in what respects? Or was it more advisable, at least in certain areas, to get free of the past and thus have a chance to surpass it?

These were already important historical questions in their early form.[2] Cassiodorus, for example, juxtaposed in the sixth century the champions of antiquity (*antiqui*) to the moderns (*moderni*). The task of the moderns, he argued, was necessarily the renewal of inherited culture in the spirit of the Christian worldview.[3] The Carolingian Empire makes the argument, under the rubric *translatio studii,* that the cultural productivity of the Greeks passed via the Romans to the Franks.[4] Writers in the twelfth century announced that this initial phase had been accomplished; Adelard of Bath calls for the moderns to complete the work of the ancients.[5] John of Salisbury emphasizes the significant accomplishments of his own time.[6] Walter Map voices his opposition to the overevaluation of the ancients, in his judgment a major affliction of his time.[7] Articulated in these statements is a powerful tension between a traditional consciousness, which recognizes the authority of antiquity, and a new self-consciousness based on autonomous creative energy. Mimesis of antiquity appears in the twelfth century to remain the precondition of the knowledge and intellectual creativity requisite to advances beyond the achievements of the classical era.

Grammar and rhetoric, which include the study of classical literature, suffer a temporary decline in the thirteenth century. Classical authors are read less as scholars come to devote their attentions to dialectics. Also, in the universities arising at the time, literary studies, and with them the classical authors, slip into the background, especially once medicine and law begin to compete for attention. The University of Paris did away with the reading of classical authors in its entirety in 1215, so that the talk of a "secolo senza Roma" seems almost justified.[8] Benjamin Nelson sees in the first signs of the modern revolution in science and philosophy that appeared at this time a gradual emancipation from the authority of antiquity.[9] Despite such developments, however, there remained many defenders of the ancient heritage, calling study of the classical writers indispensable on account of their high cultural value.[10]

Extending through the Renaissance is a dispute between the champions of humanism, who argue the necessity of a "rebirth" of antiquity, and opponents of such veneration of philosophy, the natural sciences, and art, who emphasize with marked self-awareness the cultural potential of their own period. In the context of the *studia humanitatis,* developed out of the ancient trivium, the early humanists taught poetics, in addition to literary studies, history, Greek, and moral philosophy. In doing so, they considerably broadened literary studies based on the classical authors. One of the important aims of such studies was learning how to write poetry, which is to say, Latin verse.[11] Although a wide-ranging literature in Italian began to develop in the sixteenth century, its choice of themes, structure, and organization were all oriented on classical models, more precisely, Latin writings from the fifteenth century. Native-language literary developments also led to the discovery of new themes, principles of organization, and literary forms, but they took place in the context of a mimetic relation to the older Latin models.[12]

With the rediscovery of Platonism and especially the dissemination of knowledge of Aristotelian poetics, numerous works appeared over the second third of the sixteenth century which attempted to develop a poetics for contemporary literary production on the basis of Aristotle's text. There were analogous efforts in the areas of the theory of painting, sculpture, and music.[13] Concentrated largely on the preservation of the classical texts and their adaptation to the new conditions of the Renaissance, the poetic and aesthetic discussion proceeded in reference to Plato, Aristotle, and Horace as models. Evidence of changes in the estimation of antiquity and its significance for contemporary cultural production are clearly found in the numerous sixteenth-century writings on poetics and aesthetics. Although this material has yet to be thoroughly investigated, most extant poetics texts do aim primarily at the reception and adaptation of classical thought.[14]

The counterpart to classical retrieval, and the essential representative of the moderns, is a group of natural scientists and individual artists represented by Leonardo da Vinci, who proudly marks his distance from humanism, a "uomo sanza lettere," who doubts the value of the type of knowledge that can be wrested from tradition. For Leonardo, the humanists are book scholars, not inventors; they study and cite only other people's works.[15] He considers them unproductive imitators, while scientific researchers and inventors, from their position in between nature and humanity, strive for new knowledge. Their work is, in principle, endless, the human life span scarcely long enough to permit a fundamental contribution to the knowledge process. The natural sciences, especially astronomy, operate in longer temporal units. A statement such as the following appears justified against such a backdrop: "Truth can only be the daughter of time."[16]

A central question in the poetics of the Renaissance is that of the proper relation to the seven liberal arts and thus to the canon of knowledge. Authors like Sperone Speroni became interested in the distinction between poetics and rhetoric; in his *Dialogo dalla rhetorica* of 1542, Speroni assigns to poetry the task of pleasing, while he demands of rhetoric that it both please and persuade, thus holding the latter to higher expectations. The elevation of rhetoric above poetry, in which Horace was a major influence, remained in force for a long time in the Renaissance. Poetry finally freed itself of the determining influence of the rhetorical tradition only via the central position that was carved out for the imitation of nature in seventeenth- and eighteenth-century France and Germany.[17]

The relation between poetry and the writing of history is likewise an important topic in the poetics of the time. Julius Caesar Scaliger, in his *Poetices libris-septem* of 1561, draws no unambiguous distinction between poetry and the writing of history, history and poetry being what results from his division of the expressive form *delectatio*. History and poetry are characterized by the central role played in both by the mimetic principle, for both, albeit with a difference, imitate nature. History writing imitates what really happened; it is pledged to the truth. Poetry adds fictions to the truth; it represents what it is possible to represent, hoping to make an impression by doing so. In both cases, the goal of mimesis is to convey something pleasurably.[18] While in Aristotle the elaboration of a mimetic fiction is the goal of poetry, mimesis here subordinates itself to a goal. Mimesis in Scaliger, relying on Horace and the rhetorical tradition, becomes an instrument of *teaching;* but a precise formulation of the concept of mimesis is not offered. Sometimes Scaliger even distances himself from mimesis as the principle underlying poetry; instead he speaks of a different type of nature, one that comes into being when the poet transforms reality by adding something to it, thus making of himself a second God. Scaliger issues a stern call for poetry to exercise a morally valuable effect, though he stops short of dealing in more detail with the catharsis theorem. Like the rhetorical tradition, he differentiates the effect of poetry, in terms of teaching, moving, and pleasing (*docere, movere, delectare*). Looking from this perspective toward Horace, Scaliger prefers Roman to Greek antiquity. It is clear to him that the great authors of antiquity were themselves following timeless poetic rules, so that they are not to be surpassed in principle.

In most treatments of poetics in the early Renaissance, the theory of poetry is assigned to the category to which logic, grammar, and rhetoric also belong; dialectics, sophistry, and history are sometimes classified in this way as well. There could be a number of reasons for this:

1. All members of this group belong to the "discursive" disciplines.

2. Poetics belongs neither to art nor to science; it, like logic, grammar, and rhetoric, is better regarded as an intellectual ability.

3. The object of poetics is not truth but variations on the probable or the similar, and in this it is the same as sophistry or rhetoric.

4. The group of disciplines as a whole tends toward the instrumental; none of them produce their own knowledge; they are more about analyzing interrelationships in terms implied by the needs of representation and persuasion.[19]

In all of these variations on poetics, poetry is subordinated to moral imperatives; incumbent upon it is the task of ethical education.

Over the course of the sixteenth century, poetological knowledge undergoes a process of differentiation. Authors such as Dionigi Atanagi, in his *Ragionamento de la eccellentia et perfettione de la historia* of 1559, elaborate the precise indicators of the difference between history and poetry. In *La deca disputata* of 1586, Francesco Patrizi criticizes the Aristotelian concept of mimesis, charging above all that it is lacking in precision, although he is not able himself to offer a more precise account. In many Renaissance poetics, representatives of both the ancients and the moderns focus the dispute primarily on one's understanding of nature and the rules and criteria of art. We find in this literature strong reservations, inspired by Plato, against poetry; doubts are voiced, from one vantage, by the humanists, who remain in a state of complete surrender to the early Plato, and, from another, by adherents of the Counter-Reformation. Still other critiques emphasize the pagan character of classical literature.

If it was going to remain possible to find orientation in the literature of antiquity, arguments against such negative assessments had to be found. One such argument lies in an emphasis on the ethical obligations of literature in reference to its moral and pedagogical effect. Other points are raised by Panicarola, Viperano, and Posserion, who represent poetry from the angle of their Christian commitment. The *utile* of poetry emphasized by Horace becomes a popular criterion of poetic worth, the argument fortified by reference to Plato's ideas about the utility of poetry. Superordinate to this specification of the task of literature is the Aristotelian theory of catharsis, according to which poetry, with its purifying effects, contributes to the improvement of the individual. In the cinquecento the objective of poetry is widely regarded as its capacity to further moral education. From its appropriation of poetic figures and representations, poetry acquires a certain mimetic potential, the results of which are regarded as educational. Writers, relying on the authority of Aristotle, argue that mimesis is at the heart of poetry.[20] Mimesis is understood as imitation and/or production of an image and/or representation. "Similarity" and "probability" become important concepts in the description of the tasks of poetry; the same is true of "action" and "fiction." Poetry, without exhausting itself in this task, is supposed to create similarities to life.

The norms of *decorum* (embellishment) also become important determinants of the character of poetic works, rising to the status, under the influence of Horace, of an essential formal principle. Aristotle's argument for "necessity" and "probability" and Plato's insistence on "truth" all overlap in a consideration of decorum.[21] Texts considering issues of poetics in this context continue the discussion of the interrelationships between art and nature, as well as the problem of similarity to nature, which later becomes so important. Most of these studies, Castelvetro's "Poetica d'Aristotele vulgarizzata e sposta," for example, lay more stress on the significance of nature than on the potential for formal freedom inherent in the poetic imitation of nature. Only a few authors broaden the parameters of the poetic imagination beyond what is indicated in contemporary understandings of Plato and Aristotle. The possibilities raised in the tenth book of the *Republic* regarding the establishment of artistic autonomy by releasing art from expectations of truth and utility do not correspond to the ideas of the time and therefore receive no further consideration.

Style, again signaling the importance of the rhetorical tradition in the Renaissance, becomes an important formal criterion.[22] For every poetic form there are a series of established styles, one of which had to be chosen. While Plato and Aristotle offer little assistance here, Renaissance authors do find support in Horace. A work is regarded as successful when the criteria *inventio, dispositio,* and *elocutio* are fulfilled. Inventio refers to the similarity to nature, to truthfulness, and the interests of decorum; dispositio concerns structural appropriateness; and elocutio concerns proper style, that is, right word choices and correct figures. The overarching criterion of ''unity'' gets reduced to the *simplex et unum* of Horace and thus to the appropriateness of all elements in reference to each other. Naturally there were also authors in sixteenth-century Italy, such as Bartolomeo Maranta and Francesco Buonamici, who resisted the incursion of rhetoric into poetry.

Rhetoric gains in importance as the doctrine of speaking and writing with the aim to persuade. Central here are the mediation and reflection of techniques of persuasion and the analysis of rule-governed systematicity. Rhetoric strives for a linguistic ordering and shaping of things, such that things are put to their proper use in every respect and made available for the general good. Rhetoric eventually resolves into a mimetic verbal self-production, as becomes evident in the mutual relations among object, person, and situation. Words have a mimetic power; they point the way so that the actor will follow them. Imitative confirmation and prior imagination coincide in mimesis. This understanding of rhetoric is quickly restricted, to be sure, to literature and literary speech. In Renaissance poetics, the ability to specify the possible persuasive devices in every case becomes the doctrine of literary speaking and writing, the goal of which is the identification and representation of ideas that are adequate to their objects.

Since many Renaissance scholars also wanted to write poetry themselves, they endeavored to acquire the requisite knowledge for it. Prescriptions, recommendations, and rules seemed the appropriate means to that end, and Renaissance poets, such as Giraldo Cintio, Speroni, Tasso, and Guarini, used classical texts to refine their elaborations of all three. Their goal was to further development of the *artes poetica,* for which they had a model in the *ars poetica* of Horace, in which the latter left precise instructions as to the proper activities and tasks of the poet. When it came to genres that did not exist in antiquity or were not examined theoretically in extant classical texts, Renaissance writers faced new tasks. Here the conflict in poetics between the ''ancients'' and the ''moderns'' flares with particular vehemence. Where there were no classical models, it was easier to get new ideas on the theory of poetry established, whereby it remained controversial whether and to what extent an author should follow classical models. The ancients regarded classical norms as valid for new literary forms as well, while the moderns took advantage of new forms to invalidate, if only partially, the norms—which, however, appeared heretical to the champions of antiquity. Both camps resorted repeatedly to the authority of Aristotle, turning his arguments to their utterly divergent aims.

Regulations abounded on both sides of the dispute. Many principles were converted into rules; poetry was standardized on the basis, above all, of Aristotle. The goal of both the ancients and the moderns was to weave the network of rules for poetry as finely and comprehensively as possible. The desire to discover the essence of poetry, its principles and criteria, and to defend it against reproach led to a considerable elaboration and differentiation of poetics. The outcome was a series of confrontations over the goals, contents, and procedures of poetry, which is also to say, over specific works. These disputes began with a conflict about Dante and were continued in reference to Speroni, Ariosto, Tasso, and Guarini.[23]

The discussions combined theoretical and practical critiques of poetry, centering on the question of literary genres. Pietro Bembo initiated the dispute in 1525, before the spread of Aristotelian thought, but the arguing did not cease following Castelvetro's reception of Aristotle in 1570. Was the *Divine Comedy* an epic or a tragedy, a satire or a theological poem? The question of what defined tragedy began with a focus on Speroni's *Canace* and then was posed more fundamentally in reference to Guarini's *Pastor Fido.* An important part of the controversy concerned the goals of individual works and their audience, as well as the didactic and moral aims of literature. Closely connected was the question of how literary works should be structured and which of the classical authors could be regarded as models. For Dante, Ariosto, and Tasso, it was Homer and Virgil; for the dramatists, it was primarily Sophocles, with the identification of a reference to classical models making up a generally accepted procedure for evaluating contemporary works.

The conflict thus centered on an assessment of both classical models and contemporary literary products. Varchi's appraisal of Dante as superior to Homer, which began the discussion of Dante, also led to a new evaluation of Homer and Virgil. Dante's opponents emphasized the quality of transhistorical inspiration in Homer and Virgil, which had already persisted over many generations. Since the chief aim of the moderns was to relativize the value of the classical authors, they required criteria that would enable them to do so, and these criteria could not be extrapolated from classical theories of poetics. The result was the gradual discovery of further criteria of comparison, differentiation, and relativization. Among these new discoveries are the differences between historical epochs; the needs of the respective audiences; the possibilities and limitations of literature inherent in different languages; the forms of polity and society; religion; and the overall situation as regards the development of civilization.

The quarrel between the ancients and the moderns made constant use of *metaphors,* and these, in turn, offer a graphic depiction of the tension that accompanied the split: the image of a giant sitting on the shoulders of a dwarf;

the image of nature as an old woman worn down by birthing many children; and finally, the image of truth as a daughter of time, or, reversing and modifying that image, time as the father of truth. The metaphor of the dwarf of the present sitting on the shoulders of the giant of antiquity already appears in the Middle Ages, in Peter von Blois, for example, with the addendum that the dwarf can see somewhat farther than the giant.[24] Antiquity is the precondition of the present; absent its towering works and their mimetic appropriation, there is no way for the present to come into being. Once the present accepts the support of antiquity, however, development can proceed. Alexander Neckam insists to his contemporaries that they remain conscious of what they owe to antiquity, that they not act as if they had created everything themselves.[25] From this time on, the comparison of contemporary times with a dwarf functioned primarily to refer to the autonomy of the present and the possibility of progress.

In a certain sense the dwarf metaphor occupies an intermediary position between the other two, but it nevertheless permits of varying points of accentuation. Sometimes it is used to express the possibility of surpassing the ancients, which, in the view of Ambroise Paré, for example, existed for inventors and students of nature in the form of an ethical obligation.[26] Luis Vives, friend of Erasmus and the most important representative of Spanish humanism, self-consciously rejects the dwarf metaphor, because he sees in it an overestimation of the past and a disparagement of the moderns.[27] Frequently in the conflict between the ancients and the moderns the image serves to define the relation between "having been begun" and "beginning oneself." It appears in the seventeenth century in this form in Honoré d'Urfé, Pierre Pigray, Blaise Pascal, and Sir Isaac Newton,[28] enjoying favor for a particularly long time because it justified equally the ancients and the moderns, while permitting them to be variously weighted.[29] The metaphor's optimistic rendering of the course of civilization inspires skepticism only in Montaigne, who regards the chances of civilized development and human progress as slim to the point of vanishing. His pessimism deflates the vividly pleasing sense and the persuasive power of the metaphor, which betrays a belief in a progressive historical dynamic, with which it has once again become difficult to identify in our own period.[30]

The dwarf metaphor allows both ancients and moderns to characterize their respective situations; the position of the ancients is expressed more specifically in the metaphor of the woman weakened by many births. This image, probably traceable to Lucretius, is unambiguous.[31] Nature in antiquity achieved a pinnacle that will never again be equaled; the fruits of classical culture were uniquely perfect. The definitiveness of the metaphor and the determinism it implies have repeatedly provoked vigorous reaction. Alberti, for example, in a letter to Brunelleschi, doubts its validity. He points to great contemporary artists, Brunelleschi himself, Donatello, Ghiberti, Luca Della Robbia, and Masaccio, who have produced works of incomparable quality. Nature remains very capable of producing outstanding individuals and works.

Pico della Mirandola argues similarly in his dispute with Bembo.[32] Vives modifies the image, contending that nature has gained in strength over the course of the centuries. For the knowledge of the ancients has been increased by the moderns, so that it is more comprehensive than before.[33]

Metaphors that make time the father of progress or knowledge the daughter of time express the radical superiority of the present over the past. The self-assurance of the moderns becomes evident here. The progress of knowledge is a function of the passage of time. The longer time goes on, the better and more comprehensive knowledge becomes. Thus Galileo no longer recognizes the authority of antiquity; it has been supplanted by the later developments of science. Confidence in the methods of the natural sciences and in the progress of knowledge produced by the methods over time becomes unquestionable. Time is the father of truth; our intellect is its mother.[34] Beginning with this same statement, Giordano Bruno goes so far as to conclude that, since they build on the beginnings of culture, the moderns are in truth the ancients.[35] In this sense, the ancients are able to draw on the experiences of earlier generations, using them to advance their own progress.

We find this rhetorical figure frequently in the ''querelle des anciens et des modernes'' in cases of thinkers invoking the support of the natural sciences and the scientific method of René Descartes. Truth is also the daughter of time in Francis Bacon and Nicolas de Malebranche,[36] implying that the knowledge of truth, its authority and a consensus over what truth is, cannot have been present at the beginning of European history. Because they are lacking in time, the ancients cannot be capable of knowledge; thus must their authority be diminished. Since the stores of knowledge are preserved over great historical spans, Descartes's universal scientific method results in the saving of time in the knowledge process. Because of the expansion of the knowable, however, the time required for knowledge to be acquired grows. An individual life span has ceased being long enough to allow one to arrive at truth; progress must be carried on from generation to generation. The Copernican revolution and the discovery of the cosmic dimension of time relativizes the human capacity for knowing the truth.[37] The moderns, making common cause with the rising sciences, lend vigorous expression to the progressive optimism implied in the statement that knowledge is the daughter of time.

The actual ideas of antiquity are not so much at the heart of the quarrel between the ancients and the moderns as is generally assumed. What we find here is more a reclaimed antiquity, one already subjected to modern commentary, and not a philological reconstruction of authentic positions. The issue is the proper interpretation to be placed on classical texts; the obligation of the moderns toward the ancients, the commandment of imitatio, is thus not to be taken literally but implies, perhaps primarily, a reference to classical-style models. The obligatory nature of the reference defines and strictly organizes expressive form, which, rather than being free, is the target of social pressure.

We are on safer ground if we presume the motivation behind the prowess to exist outside rather than inside literature, in a completely different field, in fact, namely, the field of conflict over the social power to regulate symbolic expression and enforce a worldview. The intensity of the struggle we are considering here further recommends a search for evidence of such competition for symbolic power among social forces. From this perspective the otherwise incomprehensible rule-bound literary dogmatism of the period gains a certain plausibility.

The immediate question now is how to bring this thesis regarding the social standardization of symbolic expression and the strictly obligatory nature of traditional, foreign models into line with the circumstance that the Renaissance offers us the first marked expression of modern individualism. The question calls for consideration of a number of factors. At the beginning of the modern period, the individual is still constituted differently than will be the case as the modern period continues, given that traditions left from the Middle Ages remain powerful forces in the rise of the Renaissance individual. The attribution of subjectivity to the individual is just beginning: autobiographies appear; there is a great interest in letter writing; portrait art and sculpture become personalized; there are changes in people's ideas of intention, sin, and atonement. But these developments do not imply a subjectivity comparable to our own modern one. The way to a wholly free choice of expression and representation has not yet been cleared, not even prepared. The creation of personalized worlds remains beyond literary capabilities, whether from the perspective of the degree of freedom allowed authors or the expressive and representational devices that were available at the time. Imitatio of the ancients, in this situation, actually contributes to the rise of the first forms of literary subjectivity. These suppositions are confirmed in a historical interpretation laid out by Luiz Costa Lima, when he analyzes systematically the context in which imitatio represents not only an important but a necessary contribution to the constitution of the individual.

Costa Lima begins by identifying an early version of medieval subjectivism, which, in the view of Hans Ulrich Gumbrecht, originated in a condition of crisis. Christian thought had become immobile and rigid in the face of novel experiences that stood in need of interpretation, in particular, those having to do with the perception of time.[38] When the traditional cosmic order, given in religion and systematized by theology, can no longer justify adequate answers, the individual gains a certain latitude for discovering a new orientation:"Subjectivity takes on a supplementary function, so to speak."[39] The thesis gains support from the fact that forms of individual subjective expression do in fact begin to appear from about the twelfth century on. The *I* that is speaking in these early texts is naturally not yet a subject in a Rousseauian sense. According to investigations carried out by Paul Zumthor, the majority of poetry written in the first-person singular remains objective expression; the *I* in the texts does not designate a potentially individual and certainly not an empirical person.[40] In Zumthor's view, the situation begins slowly to change in the fifteenth century. The *I* begins to refer to an external subject and can be identified with the person of the author. The appearance of an empirical first person can be identified in Castilian prose in the fourteenth century.[41] Jacqueline Cerquiglini arrives at a similar judgment in her study of the work of Guillaume de Machants (ca. 1300–1377), in which the truth is supposed to be guaranteed by appeal to lived experience.[42]

Subjectivity, undergoing slow formulation in terms of its own judgment and individualized attributions of meaning, comes into collision with traditional theological knowledge. But how could a poetic fiction be legitimated over against ecclesiastical authority? How could even its existence not call for the physical punishment of the author? The subjective *I* in this early stage of incipient formulation cannot stand its ground against authorities. In this view, the classical theory of the poetic self turns against the fictional and contains it, securing through this reduction of subjectivity a minimal degree of latitude, which is vital to its development. To defend poetry, humanists had to play along to some extent in the game of their clerical opponents. They had the option of construing poetry as theology, or of interpreting it as a didactic device. Followers of Cicero combined "the study of the ancients with the development of a personal style," in which individual knowledge could be expressed, and "leant autonomy to the search for a poetic language." The Augustinians subordinated this knowledge "to the utility of the faith." But humanists and the adherents of Cicero ran the danger "of being surprised in their defense of alternatives by the charge of heresy, potentially ending up at the stake."[43]

Under this enormous social pressure, it became purposive to reconcile the principle of imitatio of classical writers, which had occupied a central position in humanism from the start, "with the expression of individuality." The principle of imitatio, undisputed in any case in terms of artistic creation, now offered an opportunity to circumvent the primary thrust of social control by encouraging the development and publication of individual expression. There is more to this maneuver than the cunning of reason or mere strategic behavior. For "without the principle of a model, on which the standing of imitatio was based, the *I* became a wild, *uncontrollable* entity with no respect for hierarchies."[44] We cannot say that subjectivity here was on the verge of utterly unconstrained expression, yet the imitatio enshrined in the Christian veneration of antiquity appears to have been reconciled, indeed combined, with subjectivity. The voluntary control of fiction among the humanists, the "veto," is therefore more than an instrument opposed to subjectivity; it also opens up the possibility of legitimation, "which may be achieved in reference to a model that is acceptable to scholars and lay persons, humanists and the representatives of ecclesiastical thought."[45] Poetic freedom "never oversteps the specific boundary of a special permission, which was always subject to the censor's zeal.''[46]

Once one further necessary condition is fulfilled it becomes possible for such subjectivity to come to expression: the texts must possess the character of the *elegantia sermonis,* which, in turn, is legitimated by *eloquentia* as ''the instrument of *sapientia,* knowledge and wisdom, science and virtue, responsibility and the exercise of responsibilities.''[47]

> The obligatory consummation of the *elegantia sermonis* implied (a) disdain of the status of perfection, (b) the affective possibility of reconciling service to the faith with reverence toward the classical models, (c) the necessity of combining individual expression with 'objective' parameters, that is, with excerpts from the classics. These three results occur in fact in combination with one another; they originate in the same pressure.[48]

Mimesis as imitatio plays a conciliatory role in relation to the responsible ecclesiastical authorities. Its price is the subordination of poetry to legitimate models and its demotion to an ''inferior position'' far beneath theological truth. But the reference to an empirical *I* nonetheless shifts the Aristotelian reference system; for now lived reality unmistakably encompasses the theory of aesthetic products, in particular, those of the theater. In Aristotle's definition, mimesis introduces the possible in the sense of the probable; in the Renaissance, mimesis is used to mediate the factual. In the theory of the theater the argument for the representation of the probable becomes an argument for the unity of time. As such, it stipulates what is to be expected given the routines and settled assumptions of lived reality. Measuring the time represented in a theatrical performance according to the time of the representation becomes customary, with the result that a practice of daily life is raised, above the play, to the status of a standard; the result is an ''explicit subordination of poetry under the principle of reality.''[49] Probability begins to dominate ''inventio''; yet authors do not experience the subordination as suppression. For their goal remains as before the verification of the universal and not—as in romanticism and later literary tendencies—the expression of personal experience. In the Renaissance, truthfulness and sincerity are not yet the themes of poetry.

Contrary to widespread interpretations, imitatio, conceived as a category of symbolic power, has little to do with a call for similarity to a model. Literature is not written in terms of the regularities of a classical model, as if the latter were a terrain through which Renaissance poets could move. What is being required of those who exercise power over symbols is a *formal commitment.* The demand is made in the name of antiquity and truth, in the interest, not of the exercise of power to the advantage of individuals, but of supporting the social order and the universality of knowledge-bearing institutions. All but constitutive of this complex of control over the imagination, over the aims of imitation, over the norms of linguistic creation, and over the permissibility of subjective expression is a systematic misunderstanding, or nonunderstanding, of the aspect of power inherent in the demand for imitatio. No one profits personally from power; but the restrictions and controls to which poetry is subjected, as paradoxical as it sounds, carve out room for individual subjective expression.

The potential for subjective expression continues to increase in the seventeenth century. In the drama particularly the position advanced by the ancients and the obligation to adhere to classical models takes on a meaning other than the one it had in the Renaissance. The power aspect of social pressure exercised over representation becomes yet more visible; it is no longer possible to mistake the aim of the pressure, and the means by which it is enforced have become personal. The power claims contained in the symbolic interpretation of romantic poetics, alongside its veneration of individual expression, remain largely unappreciated.

8

Intertextuality, Fragmentation, Desire

Erasmus, Montaigne, Shakespeare

We began our discussion of the role of mimesis in the constitution of a relation between a historical epoch and classical antiquity on the level of philosophical and literary definitions. Our focus on both levels was the meaning of a particular relation to antiquity and the metaphors and discursive strategies used to specify the relation. Questions of how individual authors relate to antiquity, or, for that matter, to contemporary models, and the sorts of demands texts place on the mimetic abilities of their readers will prove equally fruitful for an understanding of mimesis. Mimetic processes mediate between authors and the texts that serve them as models, and they operate as well between literary texts and readers; in the absence of such processes, literature would have neither come into existence nor been subject to dissemination. Texts thus stand in a representational relation to other texts and to that which exists outside literature in the form of what constitutes the social. Texts refer to this extraliterary sphere, and they open it up to readers when they read.

The "rebirth of antiquity," for example, is a central concern of the Renaissance; the way the Renaissance goes about pursuing rebirth, however, presupposes the creation of something new that cannot be accounted for in terms of representation. The Renaissance, however fascinated it may have been with a number of the central ideas of the classical period, at the same time develops forces that press beyond the model, which is what makes the creation of new works possible; Renaissance originality derives from the circumstance that the mimetic processes operating in reference to antiquity end up producing cultural innovation. Artists and writers frequently misconstrue antiquity in this process, as well as their relation to it and their own activities. Yet it seems that precisely such a misconstruction is what allows new works to arise. Mimetic confrontation with classical authors and works becomes in the Renaissance a precondition of its own cultural creativity. Mimesis is a complex, multifaceted process of re-presentation and re-creation, in the course of which new works come into being via the misconstruction and transformation of a model. Involved in this process as determinative elements are the preexisting social, cultural, and life conditions of authors or artists and their respective interpretations of the world and themselves. To restrict mimesis to the mere reproduction of existing models thus falls far short of a satisfactory conception. We shall get farther in our efforts by attempting to conceive this process of re-presentation as a process of *creative transposition.*

When mimesis is understood in a restricted sense as the imitation of a certain "reality," of an established knowledge, a recognized canon of rules, or the like, the dynamic that it unleashes in the writer, artist, or reader attracts little attention: the subjective, unique aspects of mimetic processes are left out of consideration. We maintain that the creative element in the mimetic process is an essentially greater force than generally assumed, and the accomplishments of literature and art that base themselves on the mimesis of antiquity and/or nature justify the assertion. The mimesis of classical models eventuates in works, the "reference pattern" of which can scarcely be identified.

If we consider not only the author or the artist but also the reader or observer of works, the concept of mimesis expands once again. Inherent in the reader's or observer's performance of the reception of a work is an additional mimetic process, which once again, internally to the recipients, changes the text or image, reshaping it in terms of personal life experience. The dissemination of literary or visual products can thus be described as a mimetic process as well. Every new reader or observer once again brings a text or an image "to life," thereby changing it in accordance with his or her personal predilections. These mimetic processes operate both diachronically and synchronically. As diachrons, they refer to works of past periods, which they fill with new life, which is to say, use as models for creative processes. Synchronous processes designate mimetic encounters among contemporaries or between authors and readers. Synchronous and diachronous mimetic processes take on significance in a history of the effects exercised by artworks. Both work to determine the degree to which a literary or artistic work is effective and to guarantee the ambiguity and heterogeneity involved in their reception.

The significance of mimesis for individual authors and works is independent of whether they find their models in antiquity, the immediate past, or the present. We want now to illustrate, by referring to a variety of works, the ways in which both diachronic and synchronic mimetic processes produce their effects. In all of these processes the relation between presence and absence is subject to multiple determinations. Literary and artistic products that refer mimetically to other works establish reference to them with the others actually being present. Though they are not represented as a whole, something of them is represented. The new work merely cites a few aspects of the model; it changes and supplements the model, bringing into existence something that did not previously exist, for the production of which the prior model has meaning, even though the new work cannot be reduced to it. Insofar as mimetic reference occasions something previously unknown, it does not merely reproduce the absent model. It is better to say that the absence of the prior model makes possible the presence of the new work. In an intertextual or interpictorial dialogue with the reference text or image, a new work emerges by way of the production and new combination of elements, forms, signs, and meanings.

Over time readers, observers, and spectators come to play an increasingly important role in Renaissance literature. This is more true of examples of works in which the immediately palpable aspect of mimesis plays a lesser role and its individual subjective aspects take on greater significance. This development gets under way with the writings of Erasmus and gains intensity in Montaigne and Shakespeare, where intentional ambiguity expands the reader's or spectator's mimetic latitude. This expansion, to be sure, is soon reversed, in the name of clarity, straightforward meaning, and transparency, by neoclassicism.

Erasmus

Erasmus's *Adagia* belongs among the sixteenth-century works that, while themselves mimetic, place high demands on the mimetic abilities of the reader. The work contains 800 entries in its initial version, then, by 1508, 3,200, and in later editions, more than 4,000. There is scarcely any structure to be identified in the organization of the entries, a circumstance that has made the work a difficult one for readers of every period. Moreover, supplementary material was always being grafted onto it already in Erasmus's lifetime. Each entry begins with a proverbial saying, a figure of speech, or a puzzling image from antiquity, which is followed by a philological commentary identifying the classical passage and/or author. Alongside the meanings assumed to have been applicable in the classical context, Erasmus lists the further meanings developed out of the original one up to his own period. In a few cases the commentaries turn into lengthy discussions concerning what Erasmus regards as important questions and problems. A work composed of two different elements thus emerges: an original classical quotation and a commentary. The latter stands in a mimetic relation to the former.

In his analysis of the dictum *Speûde bradéos, Festina lente* (Make haste slowly), Thomas M. Green refers to the particular character of the statement, for which Erasmus gives three interpretations.[1] It could be understood (1) as meaning that it is better to wait before tackling something; (2) as a summons to rein in impulsive passions by reason; or (3) as an admonition to avoid overhasty actions. Erasmus's lengthy interpretation—which expands on the statement and treats it by way of associations, memories, and anecdotes—alongside the miniaturelike concision of the original, creates an appealing literary tension. Erasmus was obviously quite taken by the gemlike character of the proverb "Make haste slowly." His view is that such sayings represent comprehensive bits of wisdom in concentrated form. They should sparkle like jewels, revealing an enigmatic character embedded in paradoxical formulation. As gold and precious stones lie buried and must be unearthed, so must the point of a commentary be to expose the numerous meanings of an adage or maxim. Every interpretation of a saying is simultaneously a reduction of its hieroglyphic character; every "translation" into an interpretation falls short of the enigmatic complexity of the original. By way of repeated mimetic approximation, however, the further dimensions of substantive content are opened up.

Developments in the printing arts prompted a broad dissemination of literary works, drawing a previously inconceivable number of readers into the interpretation process. The number of possible interpretations was increasing, if only through the expansion of reception. This process by which knowledge is expanded is one of the humanists' pressing concerns, though the value of such knowledge, in Erasmus's eyes, is limited by the uncontrollability of literary dispersion and its subversive effect on the church and family. Erasmus saw clearly the moral and religious ambivalence entailed in an intensification of the mimetic processes of appropriation. An appropriate commentary is needed to guide reception in the desired direction, so that the meanings contained in a saying can be deciphered and rendered unambiguous. Erasmus sees, as important functions within the process, both the preliminary structuring of meaning given in the text and the interpretation of preexisting material.

Erasmus adhered to the methods of biblical exegesis, according to which the value and meaning of a text exist largely independently of the reader. The result of the commentary, in contrast, should be to occasion a mimetic appropriation of the text. Erasmus thus grants commentary a great deal of room to work out the substantive meaning of the saying. The paradoxical character of the dictum we have chosen for analysis here, "Make haste slowly," represents a particular challenge to commentary—which expands, becomes autonomous of the saying, and finally represses it, the original point of departure, altogether. The individual parts of the commentary exist in mimetic relation with each other, in the sense of both attractive and repulsive aspects. A movement gets under way which is independent of the original, which is determined by the subjectivity of the author, by the latter's way of writing, by the views expressed. The contradictory quality of the dictum continues in the contradictory commentary, which becomes a work in its own right and an occasion for the unfolding of the commentator's brilliance. The commentary becomes the actual work that absorbs the reader's attention, because of its range and the structure of the entry; the dictum has the function merely of having gotten the commentary process moving. The commentary lets its point of departure slip into the background and becomes increasingly self-referential.

Despite the increasing autonomy of the commentary, it never abandons the dictum completely. In its initial proximity to the text, Erasmus localizes the saying philologically; he elaborates a time axis specific to the commentary, as well as an interpretation of the variations of meaning applied to the dictum. In our present example, variations run from ancient Egyptian theology through Aristophanes, Augustus, Titus, and Aldus up to the present of Erasmus. The result is a genealogy of meanings that resists complete dissociation between the commentary and the dictum. The humanistic and mimetic treatment of a text, its localization, and the commentary offered in reference to it maintain a balance between the irremovable point of departure given in the saying itself and its appropriation and supplementation resulting from the mimetic processes of interpretation on the part of the commentary and the reader. Interpretations advanced in earlier historical periods join contemporary conceptions to become part of the manifold process by which such a proverbial saying is appropriated. Historical and contemporary dimensions overlap. What this way of seeing forfeits is the transhistorical meaning of the text. Instead it has the text constituting itself fully only in the process by which its meaning is realized. This view does not rule out the text having a certain historical-semiotic character, which is constitutive of the history of the appropriation of the text and determines the plurality of possible interpretations.

In distinction to a view of the text, shared by Cicero and Scholasticism, according to which readers need to immerse themselves as much as possible in it in order to appropriate its enduring substance, there develops in the Renaissance a counterposition with lingering ties back to the work of Erasmus. The reader and the reader's subjectivity take on a previously unknown significance. Conceptions of the text as developed by the church fathers, according to which reading centers on the text's authentic intentions and follows established rules to identify them, slip into the background. Instead, by way of techniques of allegory and allegorical transformation, the reader is given a broader interpretive latitude, bounded only by the text's fundamental moral and theological goals. Humanism, with its innovative methods of philological and contextual commentary, carves out a central place for the reader. The situation is similar in the case of Protestantism, where via the reader's claim to his or her own reading of the sources of faith found in the Bible, the reader gains in significance. According to Erasmus, by reading substantial texts the reader attains to a mimesis of the divine logos. Through readings of the Holy Scripture, the believer is supposed to come into a direct relation with the fundamental ideas of Christianity and thus appropriate them mimetically. Erasmus's *convivium religiosum,* in which the intrinsic value and the meaning of independent mimetic reading comes to expression, as it does in the commentary on "Make haste slowly," provides another example of this intention.

Montaigne

The Renaissance figures Rabelais, Montaigne, and Cervantes place even higher demands on mimetic reading, involving the reader still further in the constitution of their texts. Montaigne's *Essays* quite specifically call on the reader's mimetic capabilities, without which the writings remain mute. The text presupposes an independent reader, who, in reading, participates in the making of the text. Montaigne no longer cites the authority of antiquity or Christian tradition; instead he selects complex statements by famous authors and then offers a commentary and a gloss, in an effort to move beyond them in his reflections. Montaigne takes up thoughts and insights without identifying their origin or context. He even attempts to conceal the origin of his own thoughts by omitting possible clues or leading readers astray, consciously putting them off on the wrong track.[2]

In relation to such a text, which supplies quotations and then comments on them, the activity of the reader consists in following the train of thought; those texts, however, in which Montaigne has inserted hidden quotations demand greater efforts of reading and deciphering. A new freedom for the author and reader accompany what Marc Fumaroli terms the disappearance of "quotational rhetoric." The critical reader is called on to discover the mimetic references to prior texts woven into the text by the author, to follow the traces of the transformation process undertaken by the author, and to find literary appeal in this activity. Montaigne pushes the mimetic interaction with texts, images, and materials still farther. He quotes falsely and disguises his quotations, so that they appear in a form and meaning that differs from their original instance. He completely changes the context of quoted matter and, finally, makes these operations transparent so that readers may follow them.[3] In doing so, he once more breaks the continuity of his activity, which lies in the concealment of his literary references.

The *Essays* develop their own idea of the reader. On the one hand, Montaigne says that they are difficult to read and appropriate only for his friends and family members, which is to say, for sympathetic readers. On the other, he plays with his readers: he puts himself in their place, addresses them, makes fun of them, and effaces the difference separating him from them. The text becomes, for Montaigne, a means to understand himself. He appears again to comment, order, and confuse, demanding that his readers follow his path mimetically. In either case the writing subject remains undefined and hard to grasp; it ceaselessly changes its position, its intentions, and its methods. Sometimes it is even addressed in the second person ("And then, for whom do you write?''). Although the subject of the author is present in various forms in the *Essays,* it remains, despite these objectifications, hidden. It oscillates between appearing and disappearing. Mimesis takes place in this ''between,'' marking boundaries only to efface them again.

As the subject of the author is constituted through writing, so is the subject of the reader constituted through reading. Operating in these processes is either a writing or a reading relation to the text and, in the appropriation of the text, a writing or reading relation to life. In both cases attention is directed to details—the use of a word in a specific context or the carefully prepared associative field of a concept. To enjoy reading fully, as a recently developed leisure activity, the reader is expected to appreciate the microstructure of the text as well as its refinements and imponderables. The demand is the more taxing as Montaigne's texts are composed of fragments with varying substantive content, various meanings, and written in heterogenous styles. There is a tension between the frequently contradictory fragments, which only lends to their fascination. The fragmentary quality of the text opens up the possibility of manifold interpretations; it demands that the reader, who must learn to deal with the opposition between unreconciled contradictions, participate imaginatively in the further development of the text. It demands a mimetic appropriation that does not sublate the contradictions. For the contradictions are not subject to sublation, either in the text or in life.

''Every movement reveals us.''[4] Such revelations also occur in statements and mental gestures, and they communicate something of the author, his thought, and his life. They communicate all the more as they are the fruit of a turn inward. Montaigne's gaze is directed, not outwardly, but inwardly. ''I take stock of myself, I taste myself. . . . Others . . . always go forward. . . . [A]s for me, I roll about in myself.''[5] ''The self is distributed'' as Jean Starobinski formulates it, ''over all these various levels of syntax: it enters the scene as an agent, an implement, and a point of application.''[6] The external aspect of the Other also falls under the author's gaze only in its meaning for the *I.* The subject is indeed an ''empty page,'' but it is always being touched by others, without that contact working to fix the subject's *I.* In Auerbach's description, ''I am a creature which constantly changes; ergo, the description too must conform to this. Here Montaigne is at the center of the realm which is peculiarly his own: the play and counterplay between *I* and *I,* between Montaigne the author and Montaigne the theme.''[7] Auerbach describes here a mimetic process between author and theme in the course of which each becomes the reference point of the other; the language oscillates between author and theme without allowing itself to be fixed. Theme and externalities interest Montaigne only in their reflections in the interior of the *I.* ''As for me, I roll about in myself''—this is the expression of Montaigne's version of self-referentiality, which would become so characteristic of the modern subject. There is no progress in this movement; there where the *I* finds the reflections of the Other in itself, it arrives at itself. It is constantly being thrown back on itself, without ever achieving unity. For its movements are polycentric. "We are all patchwork, and so shapeless and diverse in composition that each bit, each moment, plays its own game."[8] Rolling about in the self, while reflecting on the self in movement, is, for Montaigne, the most intense form of life; in it the *I* is "agent, implement, site, and purpose" simultaneously.[9] Self-observation amounts to a life task; the *I* allows itself to be swept along, to glide over life. The center of all this is the present and the self-certainty of the "I feel," from which there is no access to universal knowledge. The individual remains captive to contradictory opinions and radical plurality. Montaigne's uncertainty is deliberate; it is the consequence of his skepticism, against which nothing is proof. The *Essays* can be understood as a form of self-experimentation, the provisionality of which Montaigne repeatedly emphasizes—modestly, sincerely, and ironically. This intentional inaccessibility finds its expression in the "artless, personal, natural, and immediate character of his language,"[10] which is responsible for the polyphony of the text and through which the polyphony draws the reader into the conversation—which, lacking mimetic capabilities, the reader could not follow at all. In his *Essays,* Montaigne provides examples of a reflexive relationship with the self, of the search for self-orientation in the absence of secure points of reference.

Montaigne's *Essays* mark a radical turn away from the prescriptions and rules of rhetoric. Rhetorical conventions codify the production process, which leaves them ill-suited to the production of literary texts. They rid the problems under consideration of complexity, with the result that texts are produced which are technically sound but which remain abstract and sterile in their devotion to clarity and precision. Montaigne poses, as an alternative to surrendering to the conventions of rhetoric and science, reading in the *book of nature*— humanity's greatest textbook, according to an essay on childhood education. Yet man, more than nature, is the mystery and mentor of man. The point of departure for all knowledge becomes the physical existence of the individual in the world. The general conditions of human being inherent in this physicality are present and palpable in every individual; that is why thinking must avoid abstraction. Montaigne's constant theme is the individual and his or her bodily conditions. The natural capabilities of the individual are a mix of biological givens and the form they assume in society; capabilities come into being in the practice of life, which is ridden with contingency. Knowledge remains permanently fragmentary and inadequate. It is bound to the body and its relationship to the world.

We must take account of this situation in our thinking and speaking. In Montaigne's view, only a combination between philosophical and poetic speech, on the one hand, and daily speech, on the other, can render an account, and that is the goal of the *Essays.* The resulting texts contain elements of philosophical and anthropological reflection, as well as poetic beauty and references to daily life; they combine the critique of abstract knowledge with fundamental reflection and literary quality. They occasion the mimetic assimilation of nature and art to each other, whereby the determinate moment always remains conscious of the inadequacy of any attempt to gain human knowledge, and, along with this, Montaigne's trenchant critique of rationality. Montaigne ridicules those who think it is possible to have knowledge of human being. Contingency, in his view, intervenes in all knowledge; all self-knowledge is rudimentary; each individual is always "the Other of the Other." Any attempt to reach the truth must recognize, as its own precondition, the inadequacy in principle of the conditio humana. Cognition has no unmediated access to things. Between the individual and objects stand language, perception, and imagination.

Knowledge is autoreferential, autopoietic, and mimetic. It establishes reference between itself and other knowledge via language, perception, and imagination, and it constitutes itself out of this relation of reference; among the necessary conditions of reference are fragmentariness and temporality, which are related to human imperfection, forgetfulness, and contingency. Fragmentariness is bound to the excerptlike character of perception and an awareness of the temporality of perception. Montaigne goes so far as to find in these qualities a precondition of his creative power. He ascribes to forgetting, for example, a surprising degree of importance in his work. It is not only that he "forgets" which quotations and thoughts he has worked into his texts; in forgetting, Montaigne also finds the possibility of being in the present, living, and writing. If not for forgetting, people would be paralyzed, incapable of referring to the past and to things outside of themselves, which we in our forgetful state do even while we are producing something new. Seen in this way, forgetting becomes a condition of mimesis. The same is true of fragmentation. If it were not a precondition of human knowledge that it be fragmented, it would be impossible to make mimetic reference from one fragment to another. Likewise the temporality of knowledge. On the one hand, it is the precondition of a mimetic reference to things; on the other, the temporal difference is what the act of mimesis overcomes. A form of "contemporaneity" is produced beyond vast temporal differences. The fragmentary and temporal character of knowledge points to its incompleteness and imperfection in principle, which is what calls the mimetic faculty into action. Every literary fragment is *polysemous;* it cannot be fully opened up in any single interpretation but demands repeated approximations, in the course of each of which new knowledge comes into being. It is irrelevant here how great the temporal difference might be between the origination of a work and its mimetic disclosure. Requisite to the processing of knowledge and knowing are also mimetic abilities; in each act of knowing the assimilation of contradictory knowledge brings something new into being, which itself then enters into other knowledge processes that likewise remain incomplete.

Like forgetting, the contingent nature of life is also centrally involved in all human knowledge and in the production of texts. Montaigne is skeptical about all forms of systematic knowledge as produced by science and philosophy. Mimesis is also an important element in contingency. Montaigne describes it as follows in reference to the process of writing: A project is begun; a second step follows the first without the author being aware of precisely why this second step follows the first. Nor does the author know in general why specific dreams and ideas turn up at one rather than another place in the writing process. Montaigne's conclusion: to release himself to the process, following his inner impulses and feelings. The images, thoughts, and statements immediately supplied by the imagination then become the reference point for the further production of the text, without Montaigne being conscious of what happens and why. He merely registers that something new has been transported into the stream of consciousness and that the new element refers to a prior given. Mimetic processes occur in the space between what is given as factual or imaginary and what follows it. They combine to produce fragments, which is to say that they do not produce coherent rule-guided systematic knowledge. The production of fragments is of aesthetic appeal to Montaigne. Forgetting, contingency, and mimesis are all involved in it.

The *Essays,* despite their pronounced intertextuality, are ultimately self-referential texts. Montaigne's use of existing texts does not lead, as it does in Erasmus, to an accumulation of fixed points of reference. Readers are instead subjected to the simultaneous presence of several points of reference, which underlies the production of self-referentiality and places heavy demands on their own mimetic abilities, which, in turn, come to light in the assimilation of readers to the text. The *Essays* convey to readers the experience of their own relativity, the relativity of the *I,* of knowledge, of truth, and the dependency of all of these on language; self-knowledge is possible only in the medium of language, everyday language in particular. Montaigne regards the lack of precision of everyday language, its diffuseness and inexactness, not as weaknesses, but as responsible for richness and plenitude. In comparison, the language of science and philosophy reduces the complexity of approximation. Readers, by means of their mimetic abilities, assimilate themselves to Montaigne's text; the polysemy of the text causes the process of assimilation to lag behind the potential of assimilation. The text's permanent ambiguity makes of reading a task that is impossible to complete. Readers are drawn into the formative process of the text; they are required to engage themselves in the reduction of the imprecision inherent in the literary text. Aesthetically valuable texts contain empty spaces, calling on readers to direct their gaze at them. Each approximation brings only one facet into the field of view. Approximations begin to attach themselves to the text, increasing the complexity of its processing. Readers all open up different facets of the text to themselves, broadening their prior store of experiences and knowledge. The literary text in combination with the reader's reading give rise to a new *intertextuality*, which endures as a model for many authors into our own times.

Shakespeare

If Montaigne's *Essays* tax the reader's mimetic abilities, Shakespeare's theater intensifies the challenge. For one thing, there is the "mimetic desire," in René Girard's term, that characterizes a certain kind of conflict formation that appears repeatedly in the plays. For another, Shakespearean theater creates new mimetic representational forms.

The production of Shakespearean plays calls for the actor to refer to a text, lending individual expression to its narrative elements and its references to prior social conditions. Making use of the expressive potential of his body, which is to say, nondiscursive expression, the actor can distance himself from specific messages in the text and adopt his own, even subversive, accentuations. The text becomes "vital" by way of the actor's shaping of it; the actor translates it from a state of imaginary nonspecifity into a concrete form. He renders the text unambiguous, inviting the spectator to go along with his concretization mimetically.[11] The final element is the spectator's imagination: he or she mimetically appropriates the play, in reference to both its discursive verbal aspects and its nondiscursive physical aspects.

In any encounter with Shakespeare's work, mimesis guides not only the appropriation of verbal and visual signs but also the processing of character constellations and social realities. Mimesis has a hand in the process of theatrical representation, but it moves beyond that to apply to social conditions. It is not only a result of these conditions but it also plays an active part in their formation. From the angle of mimesis, theatrical representation is "understood as function *and* copy, as an event and a configuration of signs . . . ; communication and world appropriation enter a condition of intense reciprocity."[12] Hamlet's madness represents an event and a mirror image simultaneously. The madness is at once event, representation of the event, and the spectator's encounter with the event. The image of madness and the horror it inspires come together in a unity that is experienced in the mimesis of Hamlet's madness. It leads to his radical transgression of boundaries and the end of all discursivity, and it removes him definitively from the sway of courtly norms and relations of self-representation.[13]

Before Hamlet is torn from the world of the court by madness, he appears as its representative. Though not completely. He calls for moderation, flexibility, and restraint, but he is already acting in a manner opposed to his own admonition. He detests pantomimes, but he organizes one himself. The result is a play-within-the-play, in which, likewise, the simple relation of self-representation is destroyed. The gap between acting and thinking, high expectations and base practice, language and movement, sign and signified, grows too wide to be bridged. Whatever remained unambiguous in mimesis now collapses. Mimesis encompasses such heterogenous elements that it is no longer subordinated to an all-encompassing definition of goals; it remains multidimensional and contradictory. Verbal and gestural signs convey heterogenous messages. The gestural signs subvert the verbal ones; and the verbal signs, the messages of the dramatic action. Wordplay overlies and transforms gestural play. Attempts to produce identical messages, to specify roles, to establish any kind of regularity founder. Hamlet reflects courtly customs and the struggle over power and love and at the same time destroys the reflections. His character is much more complex than is required by the plot. ''More— mimesis plays a powerful role in all of this, but, then again, is so arbitrary in its power that it circumvents the social self-representation of Hamlet as prince and heir to the throne. His privileged status is undermined by the emphatic, popular, and subversive character of mimesis, which throws the entire classical theory of self-representation into crisis.''[14]

This crisis of representation is felt even on the level of the ''dramatic illusion,'' for the production of which Hamlet's character itself contributes more than does the process of creating or performing the character. As soon as attention turns to the performance process, actual theatrical endeavors (author, director, the role of the chorus, actors quoting texts, etc.) become conscious. At this point the process of performance, with all its mimetic seductions, moves to center stage. We begin to understand the tensions between the representational and nonrepresentational functions of Hamlet's language;[15] the relations between the role being performed and the actor performing it become evident.

A good example of the way in which Shakespeare produces manifold meanings is the performance of Hamlet's impertinence. Mimesis of impertinence relieves Hamlet of the norms of self-representation; it makes space for contradiction, for the ''arbitrariness'' of subversive mimesis. Hamlet's impertinence creates resistance to the function of self-representation, which comes to expression in the resulting comedy, in grins, in laughter (or, as the case may be, in ridicule).[16] Illusion and the perception of the play's social situation overlap. Spectators draw on their own experience to enter the world of the drama and expand it. ''Hamlet's use of mimesis remains extremely complex insofar as he is aware of its power to enchant and disenchant. The theatrical illusion is violated, but not actually broken. Self-representation is called into question (but not destroyed) by the circumstance that Hamlet combines his role at court with an awareness of the actual conditions necessary for the successful performance of theatrical work.''[17]

The subversive universe of mimesis manifests itself in madness, in impertinence, in what is foolish and utopian. Yet mimesis is not restricted to this area; this mimesis complements a mimesis of nature and humanity. This is what Goethe became aware of when, in 1771, he called out in Strassburg: ''Nature!

Nature! Nothing so natural as Shakespeare's people.''[18] If it can occasion an experience such as this, the character of Hamlet has assumed a degree of universality that far exceeds the bounds of a specific theatrical or social role. Hamlet's character concretizes general human traits in concentrated form; it represents a ''concrete universal.'' The representation of the socially stratified world overlaps with elements of universal socialization. We see that ''the arbitrariness of mimesis is so great in Shakespearean theater that it can, on the one hand, undermine the representation of the ruling interests, while being able, on the other and at the same time, to advance a new, concrete universal in the social image of true-to-life individual characters.''[19] Both the social character of mimetic processes and their oppositional force become obvious. Mimesis, as appropriation, refers to processes of expropriation, deprivation, and secrecy, to all of which it is related. Mimesis works toward the appropriation of the world in theater; its effect is to activate the spectators. It makes them capable of speech and judgment and prompts them to action of their own; and they discharge emotions in their mimetic involvement in the play. They come face-to-face with constellations of power; they are delivered up to contradictions and called upon to react. One specific power constellation in concentrated form is Hamlet; he embodies ''within himself the conflict between the represented mimesis of power and the representational power of mimesis.''[20] The same applies to his language and gestures. They are products of theatrical mimesis and are meant to be appropriated by the spectator. They are, however, also producers of mimesis and as such refer to the appropriation process. ''The represented appropriation of power through violence (that is, the murderous usurpation by Claudius) coincides with the self-representing appropriation of power through mimesis, through what is accomplished theatrically in discourse, thought, and movement derived from a collective convolute of writing, speaking, and acting in the world.''[21]

Not only in the relation of his plays to Elizabethan society, to the established relations of self-representation and power, and to the audience but also in their inner structure, in the character constellations, Shakespeare instills in mimesis an unprecedented intricacy. Mimesis is not only a force that refers people to one another and renders them similar to each other, but one that divides and destroys them; merging and diverging, that is to say, appear in equal measure in mimetic desire. Any two people sharing a desire in common are closely bound to each other; if they are no longer able to share the desire, they become enemies. The young Shakespeare, in his poem the *Rape of Lucrece,* has already accorded mimetic desire a central place; it is operative as well in the following plays: *Two Gentlemen of Verona, Much Ado About Nothing, Julius Caesar, The Merchant of Venice, Troilus and Cressida, Hamlet, King Lear,* and *A Winter's Tale.* These plays lend manifold conceptual expression to mimetic desire: love, jealousy, envy. Shakespeare represents entanglements in mimetic desire in plays with both comic and tragic outcomes. In the former case, the mimetic conflict is playfully resolved; in the latter, it is unresolvable. The destruction of the social order in a "mimetic crisis," the sacrifice of a "scapegoat,"[22] is the result.

The mimetic paradox is obvious already in the early play, *Two Gentlemen of Verona*. Proteus falls in love with Silvia, who is in love with his friend Valentin, who, in turn, has gone off alone to Milan. When Valentin follows Proteus to Milan, Proteus's love arouses passionate desire in Valentin, who forgets Julia, the woman with whom he thought himself in love in Verona. Proteus so loses control of himself that he nearly rapes Silvia and is stopped only by the timely arrival of his friend. Because he is inwardly disposed to follow Valentin, whether to Milan or in loving Silvia, Proteus falls victim to excessive desire. As friends they have been able to share everything until now, but it is not possible to share Silvia. The result is rivalry and hatred. Mimesis displays here its ambivalent character; its destructive side becomes obvious. Valentin is the model of imitation for Proteus, the mediator through whom desire develops mimetically, but Valentin himself seems immune to such desire. As regards Julia, it may even be that Valentin's reserve is part of what causes Proteus to lose his love for her. Then the latter's enthusiasm toward Silvia, expressed in his hyperbolic rhetoric, awakens and intensifies Valentin's desire. The structure of the mimetic desire is thus paradoxical insofar as it contains contradictory imperatives: "imitate me" and "do not imitate me." Mimetic desire is a "double bind" and as such, laced with violence. The only possible outcomes are either tragic or require one of the rival doubles to relinquish the woman. Valentin is prepared to do so; he appears willing to sacrifice his desire for his friendship with Proteus. But appearance deceives. "Valentin and Proteus can be friends only by desiring alike and, if they do, they are enemies. Neither one can sacrifice friendship to love or love to friendship without sacrificing what he wants to retain and retaining what he wants to sacrifice."[23] The identity between mimetic friendship and mimetic hate is indissoluble. *Two Gentlemen of Verona* avoids a violent ending, but in the *Rape of Lucrece* a similar mimetic conflict ends in tragedy. Collatin effusively praises his wife, Lucrece, which awakens desire in Tarquin such that he cannot resist it. The ultimate result is the disgrace and suicide of Lucrece.

It is possible to identify a similar structure in *A Midsummer Night's Dream, Much Ado About Nothing,* and *As You Like It.* They all pose a paradox: love and love not—because I do. It seems impossible to avoid mimetic desire, to escape love and rivalry; or, in Pascal's unsurpassed formulation, "Qui fait l'ange fait la bête." If we accept this interpretation, desire in Shakespeare is never a subject-object relation and never solipsistic; rather, it requires, if it is to burn, the Other as a mimetic rival. Desire seems eternal and imperishable as long as it is not satisfied. The only thing that has power against mimesis is more mimesis, and thus does Shakespeare create over and over in his plays a cycle of mimetic desire. For this cycle to operate, it is critical that the characters involved not understand the structure of mimetic desire; if one once sees through it, its power is lost.

Mimetic desire can also be directed onto the self. If I am the object of my model, I will desire myself and endeavor to prevent my model, which is also my imitator, from possessing the object, which is myself, which we both desire.

Part III

Mimesis as Enactment of the State

Systems of literary codification in the Renaissance were continuations or further developments of classical poetic and rhetorical patterns (of decorum in particular), which were subject to strict normative control. The seventeenth century builds on this position, which remains, if with significant changes, the basis for the production of aesthetic objects. The most important change lies in the shift of aesthetics to a different social location, which allows it to fulfill a new function inside power structures. Mimesis operated in the Renaissance to sustain the social order as well as augment universal knowledge, this at a time when the opportunities for subjective expression were being broadened. Poets, musicians, historiographers, architects, and painters under Louis XIV put themselves at the service of the institutions of power. The development of subjectivity in artistic mimesis became part of the project of the absolutist state.

There is nothing a ruler requires more urgently, alongside military strength and financial resources, than power over the symbolic expression through which political power is ultimately enacted. If there is no enactment of the state, there is no representation of the center of power, no omnipresence, no permanent heroism on the part of the king, whose deeds, even as they are undertaken, are being transformed by the historiographers into history. The greatness, perfection, absolutism, and legitimacy that the king seeks cannot be achieved without representation. Mimesis has a constructive function in French absolutism; it produces the world of political aesthetics. Theater and architecture are the most important arts of the era.

The querelle des anciens et des modernes, the great controversy over the relation of the present to the past, shows how strong the desire is for personal subordination to the normative standards of the classical heritage, for support from the nonpolitical authorities of the past, and for authorization of one's own share in power. This endeavor on the part of the "ancients" is opposed by the position of the "moderns," who are no longer prepared to conceive the present as a variant form of the classical past. They understand the age of Louis XIV in historical and political terms; they juxtapose it to antiquity as a world in its own right. The self-evidence and uniform functioning of mimesis is now definitively a thing of the past. Unlike the querelles of the previous century, the conflict in seventeenth-century France establishes a competitive relation between the contemporary and the classical periods. As an inherent part of the defense of the modern position, contemporary aesthetic practice becomes increasingly self-conscious and secure.

The seventeenth century gives rise to a new understanding of symbolic systems; it discovers both the conventional nature of symbolic rules and the function of definitions. Systems of signs, as thinkers of the time come to recognize, can be made to operate in accord with a will capable of mastering them, a will that is powerful enough to raise its own symbolic order to a position of dominance. The codification system that is formulated in this way raises a claim to universal validity. All symbolic areas are involved in its elaboration, which binds them together into a single comprehensive fiction.

The overwhelming pressure of the fictions of the king, power, and the state is met by an astonishingly effective and consequential counterpressure. A profound skepticism regarding the representational function of language and painting is introduced from the Jansenist perspective (especially by Racine, La Rochefoucauld, Pascal, and Madame de Lafayette). Other critics also call the mimetic representation of reality into question: Descartes, by putting the scientific method in the place of representations; the representatives of Dutch painting, by rendering exactly what the eye sees.

Particular emphasis must be reserved for an offshoot of antimimetic skepticism, the modern novel, which arises as a new literary genre in the sixteenth and seventeenth centuries and takes up an ambivalent attitude toward the representational function of language. It is ambivalent insofar as the novel formulates fictional worlds, the existence of which it calls playfully into question. Several variants of skepticism flow together in the novels of Madame de Lafayette. The *Princess of Cleves* shows how the heroine of the novel—a representative of aristocratic society, which feeds off the simulation of political power—becomes fascinated by images, by images of a man whom she begins to love without ever being able to break through the mimetic representation to make contact with the original. The political exploitation of mimesis in the court of Louis XIV inspires resistance on the part of artists, who are specialists in the making of symbolic worlds. A question deserving of further research is whether other political regimes that make use of the simulational qualities of mimesis with equal determination also meet with resistance on the part of the producers of symbols.

9

The Conflict
Over History

The Querelle des
Anciens et des Modernes

On the History of the Conflict

The querelle des anciens et des modernes reached its peak in the last third
of the seventeenth century in France. It is made up of several interlocking
processes, which suggests at first glance that Jean d'Alembert's judgment—that
the conflict was precisely as useless as so many others and had taught humanity
nothing—might be shortsighted. The quarrel can be traced back to the time of
the Hundred Years War, where it also betrays a strong national element. Part
of the development of the nation during the reign of François I, who aimed at
the cultivation of a specifically French culture, was a confrontation with Greek
and Roman antiquity and the Italian Renaissance. The result was a high
valuation of the national poetry written at the time in France, accompanied by
a slight distancing effect in relation to antiquity and Italy. Part of the process
as well was the development of the French language and literature, which
eventually led to the founding of the various French academies.

Joachim Du Bellay, in his *La défence et illustration de la langue française,*
spelled out what he regarded as the preconditions of a modern national culture
for France,[1] and it is possible to understand seventeenth-century classicism as
the realization of Du Bellay's ideas. His central concerns are the specific value
of the French language, the equality of French culture with antiquity and the
Italian Renaissance, and the idea of cultural progress, of which the moderns
provide us an emphatic representation. His aim is liberation from the authority
of antiquity and the domination of Latin, but he wants to achieve these goals
without disputing in principle the accomplishments of classical and Latin
culture. Another contribution to the developmental process by which a national

culture comes into being was the founding of the French academies; they also became the sites where controversies over the relation of the past to the present were carried out with particular vigor. Du Bellay calls Greek and Roman historiography into doubt as regards the historical emergence of the French state; he speaks of "mendacious Greece" and "Roman charlatans."[2] Such claims are part of a broader discovery of the significance of French-Gallic history and historiography in the rise and development of French civilization. Meanwhile, Christian values are also working to relativize the classical tradition. A link is forged to the Italian Renaissance, a link with a specifically French accent. Here as elsewhere the moderns stress the permanence of the forces of nature, the idea of progress, the idea of the superiority of the moderns over the ancients. The seventeenth-century controversy over the relation of the past to the present is determined by these issues.

The literary academy in Paris holds firm, at first, to the precepts of Aristotle and his successors. As in Italian poetics of the time, the dominant voice in France remains fixated on the *rules* by which literary texts are produced, as mediated through the *ars poetica* of Horace. Such dogmatism coincides with a nearly religious veneration of Aristotle and the conviction that it is the application of rules that brings literature into existence. Mimesis is understood here as the ability to follow rules. The results of such a system of reproduction are predictable: the great literature of the time (Rabelais and Montaigne, for example) does not hold to the rules and is written outside the academies. The academic literature makes clear how unjustified it is to reduce mimesis to adherence to rules. Literary mimesis is a much more complex process than following rules and imitating models; the relation between texts and rules is not determined by the priority of rules over texts. It occurs, in fact, much more frequently that great texts anticipate the formulation of the rules to which they adhere. Rules and texts condition each other reciprocally; the application of precepts and recipes alone does not lead to "good literature."[3] This is the experience of the academies, where antiquity is largely reduced to a canon of texts, knowledge, and rules.

Academicism also develops in the plastic arts, culminating in the work of Fréarts de Chambray, who published his *Parallèle de l'architecture antique et de la moderne* in 1650 and *L'Idée de la perfection de la peinture* in 1662. Here as well the goal is to produce a copy of antiquity. Painters and architects are to follow specific rules in order that their works satisfy the criteria set down by the academies in the first half of the seventeenth century. Chambray formulates the ideas of the moderns concerning the development of taste and the change in the idea of the beautiful over the course of history, only to reject them in favor of a representation of antiquity as the unique pinnacle of perfection.

At the same time polemicists take aim at academicism, criticizing its underestimation, in the context of an overestimation of strict rules, of the formative power of the writer and artist. The conflict for and against mythology, for and against the French language, for and against Corneille's *The Cid* are examples. What initially sparks the dispute is the question of whether and to what extent correspondence with the poetological ideas of Aristotle is to be considered in an evaluation of the quality of a play and, indeed, whether such correspondence is necessary at all. Prior to this time rules enjoyed such general recognition that a correspondence between them and a literary work was regarded as the decisive criterion in its assessment. Thus, having compared the *Cid* to classical plays and rules, Mme. de Scudéry comes to the conclusion that it is an inadequate play. It is, in her view, neither tragedy nor comedy but a mixed form satisfying neither the demands required of a "plot," nor the unity of time, nor the concerns of moral practice and action. She regards the violations of valid rules as so grave and inexcusable that the *Cid* can have only minor artistic quality. Defenders of the play argue that a spectator needs to be aware neither of Aristotelian nor any other rules to know whether a play is good or bad; for these rules are external to the concrete literary work and thus inappropriate to its judgment. The point, in their view, must rather be to identify the criteria inherent to the work. And the decisive issue is whether the spectator or the reader likes it.

The primary criterion of literary quality gradually shifts from a concern with whether rules are being followed or broken to a *judgment of taste.* Adherents of the new standard refer to the literary force of Corneille, who with the *Cid* had produced a new play for which there was no classical model and which therefore represented a genuine innovation; they demanded that its legitimacy be recognized. The play was written for an audience of the present, not antiquity, and one may expect of living spectators a degree of spontaneity and lack of restraint. Corneille's accomplishment, according to his defenders, lay precisely in the adaptation of classical dramatic ideas to the present and its different tastes. Moreover, Corneille succeeded in replacing classical values with Christian morality and thus broadened the range of dramatic possibilities available to the age. In the view of the "moderns," the significance of the *Cid* consisted precisely in its violation of the dogmatic standards of the academy as laid down by Jean Chapelain; it subjected classical dramatic doctrine to development and created works of universal value.

The success of the *Cid* unsettles a number of established beliefs: the infallibility of Aristotle; the necessity of adhering to rules; and the absolute perfection of the classical model. The authority of Christian values, Christian morality, and Christian poetry displaces classical antiquity, leading to the development of alternative ideas of human perfection. Modern natural science and Cartesian philosophy also work to undermine the classical model, whose accomplishments in these areas of knowledge appear little worthy of imitation. Champions of new doctrines are able to refer to the innovative character of their insights and discoveries. They emphasize the significance of the experimental method and the production of universal knowledge; they claim the status of necessity for their approach and point out that there exists no prior model for their procedures.

Before all this was accomplished, however, and alongside the argument over the significance of the French language, came a dispute in art between the representatives of the ancients and the moderns. In 1635, Richelieu founded the Académie française for the promotion of the French language, poetry, and literature; in 1648, Mazarin founded the Académie royale de peinture et de sculpture. Additional academies followed. They came to be of increasing importance in the separation of art from the sciences and for the differentiation and development of individual areas of specialization, formulating, with antiquity the standard of the present, official tenets for each. The representatives of such tenets in the plastic arts were the "ancients," Raphael, Poussin, and Le Brun. The controversy came completely into the open in the "querelle du dessin et de la couleur" of 1668. On one side were arrayed the advocates of tradition, emphasizing the priority of drawing and sketching. They took up the argumentation of the Italian Renaissance over the meaning of *desegno* and the similarity to God of artists capable of desegno. As God sketched the world, so do artists sketch the world of images.

The representatives of "color," including, among others, Roger de Piles,[4] rejected Poussin and Le Brun. They found their model in the work of Rubens. De Piles criticized slavish imitation, the copying of works of the Renaissance and antiquity. As important as the sketch and the rules of perspective might be, he argued, they must not be allowed to place constraints on the artist's formative power. Rubens, for example, was able to create works for the "modern taste" precisely because he disregarded the rules of "ancient" works; his genius is most evident in the color composition of his paintings. It must not be measured against the great simplicity and refined expression of the works of the "ancients" and thereby mistaken. Instead the artist must do justice to Rubenesque expressivity, which is pleasing to today's tastes and which opens up new aesthetic possibilities in the area of color composition. Rubens's painting, the argument continued, is expressive and nuanced; it is more vital, more individual, more manifold in its selection of themes, and a better imitator of nature than some of the works of the ancients. Moreover, it embarks on paths that lead beyond classical norms. A genius like Rubens has the right to such latitude; he knows better what modern painting demands than any number of "preservers of rules." What could show better than Rubens's own works that the rules of the ancients are not universally obligatory? This discussion soon achieved a broad currency, with sympathies going increasingly to the representatives of the new color composition, to the independent painters, to the innovators.[5]

In the academy session of 27 January 1687, the querelle des anciens et des modernes broke out with unprecedented vehemence. The topic of discussion was Charles Perrault's "Poème sur le siècle de Louis le Grand,"[6] which so incensed Nicolas Boileau Despréaux that he said its being read in its entirety was a disgrace to the academy. Tensions evident already in previous decades now came to a head, with issues raised in the conflict over the role of antiquity in the present now focusing on the self-conception of the "great century" of

French classicism—which is defined essentially in terms of mimesis of antiquity. Both the ancients and the moderns now assume a mimetic stance toward the past. The former are oriented on a strict understanding of Aristotelian thought and their claim that they practice a direct imitation of antiquity; the latter postulate the equality, even superiority, of the cultural accomplishments of the contemporary age. A historicization of culture, in particular, of the beautiful and the rules of literary creation, is the result; it in turn fosters a broadening of the latitude ceded to literary activity. As important as the ancients might be, the tasks of literature, art, and science lie in the present; the fruits of literary, artistic, and scientific creativity must satisfy current requirements.

Our reference to the mimetic elements present in the position of the moderns implies a specific concept of mimesis, one that also entails the modification of the preexisting model by the author, artist, or reader. According to this conception, the change in relation to the model appears even as the decisive quality of any mimesis that is not mere reproduction. Mimesis in this sense is a productive process in which, if it does not degenerate into mere imitation, something new and previously unknown comes into being. Something unknown is represented in the process of mimesis, something expressed that has never been communicated in this way. By establishing reference to the unknown, to what is now to be represented for the first time, mimesis moves beyond the imitation of the preexisting to become an anticipatory imitation of what does not yet exist.

The two sides in the dispute thus advance a similar series of arguments. And it is precisely representatives of the ancients who create the great works of the age—Racine, La Bruyère, and La Fontaine. Authors who proclaim the necessity of a mimesis of classical works, in other words, produce works of their own which rank among the greatest and ''newest'' of the time. Their insistence on maintaining the standards of the ancients, in the context of the creation of works of equal stature, leads them to bring something new into existence, which cannot be fully explained as adherence to tradition. Perhaps tradition contains something of the Other of the new, which is necessary to assist the new into being. Should that be the case, then antiquity is the background that, by drawing attention to itself, contributes to the creation of the new. Perhaps circumstances here are similar to other situations in which action is undertaken: there remains a difference, which cannot finally be fully elucidated, between what people intend and believe themselves to be doing and what they do and, in turn, what turns out to be the result of their action. It appears that in the process of literary and artistic production, this difference cannot be transcended.

Racine and Molière

What are the effects of the querelle on individual authors of the time? Is it possible to identify in their works adherence to one or the other side, and to document the role of mimesis in their creative process? If so, an analysis of their works would secure new insights into mimesis, beyond the literary theoretical and philosophical reflections on the surface of the querelle itself. We want now to pursue this question in reference to the works of Racine and Molière.

What must be established at the outset is that Racine's tragedies operated in accordance with mimesis of the classical model, which included, however, the interweaving of traditional and contemporary elements such that new tragedies of a sort never seen before came into being. In comparison to social comedies, tragedies are required to separate more emphatically the tragic from the daily conditions of human life. Racine excludes the daily and the creatural more radically than his Greek models, such that he brings to representation "a type of tragic personage unknown to antiquity."[7] He develops a "higher style" that is neither the classical tragedy nor any other form of dramatic literature in the period since. It is possible to interpret this style as the expression of a closed society, the structures of domination and violence of which are secured by the power of the absolutist king and the norms of the Christian faith.[8] In Racine's tragedies, the "tragic personage . . . is pervaded in its very substance by its consciousness of princely rank,"[9] by his social situation; the social activity of ruling appears only in generalized allusions. "Being a prince is much rather a posture, an 'attitude,' than a practical function."[10] Such a construction represents human activities and entanglements on an "exalted level," though, at the same time, that which is represented retains its exemplary and human character.

Racine anchors the political in the personal aspects of his characters; like Molière, Racine understands the political as a question of the moral behavior of individuals. This restriction of the political to personal behavior neglects factors, such as economic circumstances or adverse conditions, that often are the cause of morally irreproachable behavior foundering in the real world of political action. For Racine, the well-being of the state depends on the morality of its rulers. If they succeed in restraining their passions, the well-being of the state is assured; if they are overcome by their passions, it is threatened. This moralism does not derive from Greek and Roman antiquity; it is of a Christian origin and has its sources, for Racine, in the powerful influence of Jansenism. The royal omnipotence of his characters implies a reference to God, even as it lends symbolic expression to a specific understanding of absolutist rule. All that is base, frail, and creatural is excluded. The elevated style is the tragic expressive form of rulers who surrender solely to their passions, which means that the tragedies set up experimental conditions for representations of the way people get entangled in their passions. Whatever happens, the characters remain physically intact; the plays eschew all sign of physical decay. Even death is something to be treated in an "elevated style." Bodily decency and *contenance* are obligatory.

While love in antiquity appeared only in its connection with other instruments of fate, in French classicism, particularly in the work of Racine, it becomes one of the defining themes. Racine, though he neglects the physical and sexual side of love, sees in it one of the psychological forces by which people are exalted and destroyed. Dramatic rules of unity mean that the action must be concentrated in one location on one day. The result is an effect Auerbach describes as follows:

> On the whole it is possible to say that the unity of time and place lifts the action out of time and place. The reader or listener has the impression of an absolute, mythical, and geographically unidentifiable locality . . . in which tragic personages, raised high above all everyday occurrences and speaking in sublime stylization, abandon themselves to their passionate emotions.[11]

The tragedies of French classicism definitively separate the tragic from the quotidian and from social reality. The underlying understanding of tragically entangled people and the elevated stylistic expression of that predicament are the result of a mimetic process, one that could only have occurred in the historically unique situation of French absolutism.

Racine's contemporaries appreciated in the tragedies of antiquity the realization of classical simplicity and expressive elegance. They believed that the rules of unity were the mechanism by which the same effects could be realized again. The plot counted as "probable" if the narrative structure was concentrated into one place and time, so that the events of a play all take place within the few hours of a performance, not in many places and at very different times. The plays appeared "natural" to contemporaries because plot was stripped of anything base or extrinsic to it. For "to call something natural was almost tantamount to calling it reasonable and seemly."[12] Nature is not being understood here as the contrary of civilization; rather, a person was "natural" whose behavior was harmonious and reasonable. Naturalness was taken to be a product of culture, the result of education. The natural was the eternally human with its great passions, and it was literature's responsibility to express them. The tragedies Racine wrote for the court and the *haute bourgeoisie* were meant to give expression to the eternally human; by elevating his characters to extreme heights, where the inner and outer aspects of their dignity were supposed to harmonize, Racine composed tragedies that exceeded the limitations of a particular time.

No less significant an event of the period are the comedies of Molière. He fashions in them a bourgeois space that distinguishes itself from the *more geometrico* of classical tragedies. His comedies amount to an aesthetic contemplation of the bourgeois self, a frequently caricaturing mimesis of bourgeois conditions under the warrant of expressive directness, authenticity, and the psychology of probability—all of which somewhat baffled some of Molière's contemporaries. Thus the criticism of Molière, in more respects than one, by La Bruyère and Boileau, both representatives of the ancients. La Bruyère considers Tartuffe in terms of the type of the hypocrite and discovers in the process that Molière's character fails to correspond to the pure type.[13] But La Bruyère mistakes Molière's intention.[14] He achieves his comic effect by placing Tartuffe in the role of a hypocrite in opposition to the natural character of the hypocrite. It is precisely what La Bruyère criticizes, the inappropriate combination of character traits, that creates the comedy. Molière individualizes more and typifies less than was common among the moralists of his century. We find the same device in *The Misanthrope,* which works not simply with the representative type of the ''hypochondriac'' but with a much more complex character. Molière aims at a comic effect by ''mixing'' contradictory traits, subverting unambiguous characterization and creating individuality. Molière reveals his genius in his violation of certain dramatic rules otherwise regarded as valid. Within the frame of reference of the seventeenth century, it is the violation of rules that gives rise to great comedies. No less instructive is Boileau's critique of Molière elaborated in his *L'Art poétique.*[15] He begins by distinguishing three styles: elevated, as reserved for tragedies; intermediate, suited to social comedies; and low popular. Then Boileau demands that social comedies like Molière's conform to an intermediate style. He supposes it suited for the ''court'' and the ''city,'' that is, for the elevated public of the higher aristocracy and the haute bourgeoisie, the leading social stratum of Louis XIV's France. This he contrasts to the use of the language of the common people, which he regards as impermissible. The common people and their language are not fit for representation in social comedies—an imperative Boileau charges Molière with having repeatedly violated. There is no doubt that Molière was always looking for opportunities to produce comedy by means of exaggeration and burlesque techniques. In the *School for Wives,* he invents a *marquise ridicule* in an analogy to the stock character of the comic servant. While Molière thus does ridicule persons from all social strata, the people appear in his works *only* in the form of ridiculous characters. Molière's critique focuses less on the social conditions of the various strata than it judges human behavior as such from the perspective of a moral universal. What this social ideal of the *honnête homme* dictates is the most general education and attitude possible. Those who desire social acceptance must refrain from revealing details of their economic lives or professional specialization, should they have one; the alternative is to be regarded pedantic, extravagant, and ridiculous. The only abilities that may be displayed are ones that can also be regarded as elegant hobbies and that contribute to light and pleasant entertainment in society.[16] When bourgeois characters, instead of conforming to this ideal, attempt to imitate an aristocrat or a *gentilhomme,* they necessarily fail, which has a comic effect and elicits laughter.[17]

On the one hand, Molière violates the imperatives of the pure intermediate style; he breaks rules that the representatives of the ancients regard as obligatory. On the other, he sticks to the conventions of his time by failing to treat the common people and their problems. He outfits his characters with a high degree of timelessness and universality and pronounces moral judgments that do not raise the issue of the social conditions of morality.

This combination of following norms and violating rules is what characterizes the mimetic process that eventuates in the creation of Molière's comedies. In his plays mimesis operates in reference to the society's moral standards; this is what he represents in his characters. The codification of social behavior, of the characters' behavior toward one another, is subject to disruption. The expressive possibilities that had previously been developed by way of dramatic gesture in the comedy and the farce allow Molière to surpass social conventions.

Structural Results

While, at the beginning of the querelle, the champions on either side stood irreconcilably opposed to each other, an intervention by Antoine Arnauld ultimately made it possible to put aside the conflict. Remaining nonetheless were several conflict formations, and we turn now to an investigation of their contribution to the theory of mimesis.

One conflict formation arose in reference to the issue of *perfection,* which was taken to be the goal of all individual and collective development. Representatives of the ancients believed that the highest degree of perfection had been attained in the classical period; mimesis of antiquity was, for them, the way to achieve, or at least approximate, the former level of perfection. To radical adherents of this position, antiquity was unique and impossible to equal. The period subsequent to the classical age represented a decline in cultural development, suggesting that mimesis of antiquity was the only way to reverse the downward trend.

Some of the ancients then advanced the thesis of *bipolarity* in the development of culture and civilization. They saw a high point in the age of Augustine and a second one in the time of Louis XIV. Separating the two are periods of meager cultural productivity. It is therefore the task of the epoch of Louis XIV to advance its own cultural development by way of mimesis of antiquity. The norms, rules, customs, and laws of the contemporary period are an integrated part of any such process and bring, through mimesis, something new into being. La Fontaine, for one, represents the relation implicit here between antiquity and classicism when he designates mimesis of antiquity as the task of literature and art, emphasizing at the same time that he is not calling for slavish imitation.

The result of these arguments is a relativization of the character of antiquity as a model. Perfection is no longer tied exclusively to a particular period; it becomes historically relative and thus also a possibility in principle for the future. A further relativization of the ancients' position is the consequence of reference to the perfection of Christ and the call for an imitatio Christi, for it questions the priority of antiquity, now in the name of the Christian religion. Final perfection lies solely in God, the creator of humanity. An emphatic representative of this position is Jean Desmarets de Saint-Sorlin. He encourages a novel treatment of Christian material, the development of a "poetics of Christianity," which, given the decline in the importance of classical material, presupposes a high degree of ingenuity. Desmarets's position also works to destabilize classical norms of similarity and the imitation of nature; they are displaced by a claim to a mimesis of the true (*vrai semblance*) and a mimesis of Christ, as well as of God. Perfection lies at the end of these two mimetic paths. Given the absolute perfection of God, the perfection of antiquity is also merely relative. Such arguments as these, deriving from the Christian tradition, offer thinkers the opportunity to deny idealizing exaggerations of classical greatness.

The moderns turn more directly against the norm of classical imitation, judging it to have become thoroughly mythical. They do not deny antiquity its accomplishments. Yet, by referring to the progress humanity has achieved in the meantime, they plead for its character as a model to be relativized. These thinkers are now conceiving human history as the history of progress. Progress has been especially vigorous, in their eyes, in areas where "discoveries" have been made. One example is painting, in particular, as regards perspective and the composition of light and shadow. Such advances imply the superiority of the moderns over the ancients. But where incomparable progress has been achieved is in the natural sciences and quantifying knowledge, examples of which are evoked in arguments favoring the eventual perfectibility of human knowledge over the course of history. The perfection of the ancients in art and literature is scarcely disputed, but the moderns achieve perfection in the area of reason, which comes about as a function of the passage of time. Thinkers frequently identify antiquity with youth, a time of effusive imaginative power, and the epoch of Louis XIV with maturity, a time of reason. Their arguments also work to emphasize the specific character of the present over against that of antiquity.

Reason (*raisonnement*), free judgment (*libre examen*), and good taste (*bon goût*) come gradually to displace the rules, norms, and models of antiquity. Theorists identify a distinction in art between the "relatively beautiful" (*beau relatif*) and the "absolutely beautiful," arguing that the difference appears as a function of taste, whereas in previous times the decisive aesthetic criterion would have concerned adherence to rules. People begin to understand art now as being incomparable, as corresponding to different criteria in different periods and cultures. The unavoidable conclusion is the historical relativity of aesthetic norms. Ideas such as these had already made their appearance in the Renaissance, but now they take on greater clarity. A distinction is drawn between the arts, which are based in imagination, and the sciences, which derive from reason. In the arts, closure is impossible in principle, the development toward perfection unceasing. Progress in the sciences, in contrast, appears to be capable, over time, of actually achieving perfection. Thus the sciences are the primary guarantor of historical progress; they make possible a form of linear progress founded on the accumulation of knowledge. It seems possible, on the basis of the Cartesian method and Baconian experimentation, to create a universal knowledge that is independent of geography and remains valid over succeeding generations.

The accumulation of this knowledge becomes the defining characteristic of universal human being (*homme universel*), with the arts and sciences the instruments by which it is to be perfected. Persisting in this model of human development is the humanist idea of perfectibility, the realization of which appears a mere question of time and history. The idea that both science and art are based in part on paradigm shifts and are therefore not perfectible is a product of our own period. Nevertheless, the idea did make an initial appearance at the time, in La Fontenelle's insistence that humanity's overall moral striving must be conceived in finite terms as operating under the laws of illusion.

The credo of the ancients—the infallibility of Aristotle, the necessity of rules, and the absolute perfection of classical models—has thus suffered a marked destabilization by this time. Its place is taken up by a belief in progress. Instead of turning to the past, thinkers start to place their hopes in the future: humanity strides on, led by God (Fénelon). Meanwhile, the forces of nature and the human spirit continue to develop; the number of ideas and works increases. The moderns oppose classical rules and models by insisting on applying their free judgment to works of art. They develop the conviction already articulated in the Renaissance that aesthetic judgment is possible only in terms of criteria derived from the works to which they are then applied. Aesthetic judgment becomes a circular movement, which will later be interpreted as a hermeneutic circle[18] or, in a variation on the same idea, a hermeneutic spiral.[19]

The authority of reason and evidence as postulated by Descartes, not the authority of antiquity, is the only principle capable of founding the maturity of humanity. The seventeenth century calls a halt at its threshold to the parallel between phylogeny and ontogeny; maturity has been achieved and the focus remains on the present. Fontenelle, for example, does not raise the question of whether, according to the model, maturity is not necessarily followed by a period of decline. Perrault suggests that not only in the natural sciences but also in geometry, perspective, color composition, architecture, and sculpture the present can claim superiority over antiquity.[20] The present's concept of beauty and taste is specific to itself; from that perspective the absolutist claims of the classical period are necessarily relativized. The modern secular literature of the *salon* comes into being. Its audience is made up of individuals from both the "court" and the haute bourgeoisie—of persons, in short, who no longer have the broad linguistic knowledge and classical education of the humanists and who are thus less familiar with antiquity. New ideals and issues, originating in both "court" and "city" and shaping the taste of the time, become important with the gradual decline of education in classical antiquity. The *grand goût classique* is no longer called for; the honnête homme is now the embodiment of the *esprit critique* and libre examen. This person is not a *savant* but an *homme galant,* whose ideas are determined by the norms of the king.

Also incompatible with an undisturbed veneration of antiquity is the self-conception of Louis XIV. His role implies a strong self-consciousness of the contemporary epoch, which can only be maintained given a strict distinction between itself and antiquity. Of burning concern is no longer the authority of tradition but the ability of the present to give birth to universal human being. The golden age lies not in the past but in the present and the future. The two forces that are supposedly capable of securing this development toward human perfection are the natural sciences, with their capacity for accumulating universal knowledge, and the universal power of the king. It therefore comes about that universalist images of the world and the individual are characteristic of French classicism, but such images are already being relativized and historicized. Fontenelle, for example, is not yet aware of the category of historical time; the idea of the uniqueness and specificity of a historical epoch is alien to him. At the same time, however, he no longer subsumes human history under a unified principle. The idea of eventual perfection in the natural sciences remains restricted to the influence of time's passage, and Fontenelle accepts the inevitability of uncertainty and error in individual and social action in all historical periods.

According to the narrow concept of mimesis that has long been standard, the situation is simple: representatives of the "ancients" have assumed a mimetic relation toward antiquity. Convinced of the superiority of antiquity, they imitate its themes and rules. The representatives of the "moderns" seem at first glance not to be acting mimetically; they emphasize the autonomy of their own epoch, the inventions that have only now become possible, and their trust in the progress of humanity. If, however, we presuppose an expanded concept of mimesis, the unambiguous character of the difference vanishes. In terms of a less restricted concept, the autonomous and creative aspect of French classicism, within a mimesis of antiquity, comes to light, and, in the case of the moderns, who emphasize separation from tradition, the mimetic aspect of innovation becomes evident. Present in both cases are conceptual images in reference to which creative work takes place. The ancients take these images from the universe of ideas formed by French classicism of antiquity. The moderns develop their ideational world around the homme universel, which likewise forms the basis of their creative activity, though in their case, to be sure, the point of reference lies in the present, or even in the future, which is only now to be brought into being in accord with the homme universel.

Ricoeur, using Augustine as an example, has shown how the narrative perspective erodes the significance of past, present, and future to the extent that the process of narration reduces all tenses to the present. Historiography is likewise subject to detemporalization because of the way differences between tenses break down in the present of the narration. A present of the past and the future is implied in the present of the narrative in fictional and historical narration. The same, modified appropriately, is also true of conceptual images in reference to which something new is produced. The images are available in the present of the conceptual world of the author and artist, independently of whether they stem from antiquity or the future. They differ only slightly from each other as conceptual images, and it is these images to which the mimetic process refers.

If we understand "imitation" as only one of the significatory variants of mimesis, regarding "to represent" or "to bring to representation" as a better translation of the concept, the differences between the ancients and the moderns diminish once again. If, in other words, mimesis designates not a passive process of reproduction but the process of creation, representation, or enactment, it denotes an active process. It involves, in the Aristotelian sense, the "production of a plot," the "arrangement of the facts," and the "representation of a course of action." This process entails the construction of an order in which the individual elements all have their place. The elements are structured in temporal terms as the order is worked out. The issue of whether this structuring is undertaken from the perspective of antiquity or an anticipated future is of secondary significance. For ultimately the temporal structure of the literary work results from the specific enactment of its elements. This enactment also determines, relatively independently of content, of the how and why of the organization, the degree of universality of the literary or artistic work. Critical to the mimetic process is the break with a given reality, the emergence of an "as-if," which opens the imaginary space of artistic production. Mimesis of antiquity can thus be conceived as a vehicle for moving into the world of the as-if. The reference back to antiquity becomes a means by which an advance into a new fictional world is assisted. Something quite similar applies to the moderns and their images of universal human being, of the progress of knowledge and the sciences and humanity as a whole. Both cases imply reference to constructed worlds that make it possible, by way of a process of metaphorical transposition, to forge something new.

10

Mimesis as the Self-Representation of Political Power

Artistic mimesis under French absolutism operates in the service of political power and helps to constitute this power.[1] It is returned to its old role of creating and controlling systems of classifications, with the goal of creating an absolute position for the king. This is not a marginal, but an essential, part of the process that can be defined as the emergence of the king's symbolic power. Our question now is the function that mimesis acquires within the power structure of absolutist rule in seventeenth-century France. Here mimesis is not the self-authorization of the individual speaking as an *I* in the name of a higher power, protesting and attempting to correct the course of worldly things. Mimesis does authorize individual persons even here, namely, historians, dramatists, painters, and architects of palaces and gardens, but it does not authorize an individual attitude. Rather, it legitimizes cooperation in the construction and fashioning of political power in a critical area, that of signs and the imagination.[2]

The Portrait of the King

Mimesis becomes the political art of disposing over symbolic power, which aids in the constitution of the authority of the king. The great stories about the king, reports of the deeds through which he is written into history, the pictorial representation and textual description of the body of the king as expression and constituent element of his power[3]—all of this is mimetically produced, invented, fashioned, and disseminated; and it is all produced in such a way that mimesis of the king evokes calculated effects in readers and observers. In the process, a comprehensive imagination is created which is indispensable for absolutist rule. In the absolutist state, the producers of mimetic worlds are overseers of symbolic power; their essential concern is to produce the ''portrait of the king.''[4] They have not broken with the rhetorical tradition, as what they do amounts to a very advanced political rhetoric. But one critical element is new: symbolic producers construct an image of the king, a proprietary image of a product, and enter it among the collection of symbols circulating between the king and his subordinates and back to the king; it is a product the consumption of which is controlled, just as the image itself is subjected to control.

The officially commissioned producers of mimesis are those who transform the deeds of the king into *plots*.[5] The historian, the dramatist, the portraitist know how to read the world of events correctly, to capture this world in the appropriate symbols, and to construct a narrative context in which to place the events: dramatists focus on the king in their plays; chroniclers, on the official story of deeds and events; painters, on the pictorial representation of the king's expression, bearing, decor, symbolic objects and environs, and taste. Louis Marin uses the example of the historian to demonstrate the power of mimesis: chroniclers produce out of past events a succession of significant state actions. To do this, they imagine ideal readers to whom they present the king as a reality, readers who understand the events being interpreted in the right way so that they recognize in what they read a picture of the king. The king, too, must insert himself in this circulation; he must present an image of himself, must produce in the world of events an iconic imprint, such that the latter corresponds to the anticipatory impression given form by history writers in their chronicles.

The historians' mimesis becomes an all-encompassing fictionalization of everything significantly involved in the formation of the image. The portrait of the king, in this process, becomes more real than the world of events. Cast in the forms of the chroniclers' stories, the portrait takes on the certainty of an ideal construction. The portrait stands for the king, who is otherwise subject to contingent life circumstances. It is less variable than the physical king, since it remains effective even when it is empty; perhaps it is most powerful in that case. As a normative model, it imposes burdens on the king down to the details of his daily life.[6] Marin's analysis subtly demonstrates how a metadiscourse was constructed in Versailles and how it was ultimately those who had mastered mimesis who controlled it.

Absolutist power is essentially representation, and representation in the baroque period must be considered in its relationship to power. The portrait of a prince is more than an illustration of a physical entity. It is what one imagines a royal body to be, in the threefold sense attributed to it: the king's physical body is historical, his political body is juridical, and his signifying body is sacramental. This is the thesis Marin attempts to confirm in his investigation. He begins with a text regarding Paul Pellisson Fontanier's plan for a chronicle of ''the last war,'' submitted by the minister to Jean-Baptiste Colbert in 1670. Reduced to a few points, Pellisson's project is based on the following train of thought.

The king is an ideal actor, for, in the history of his time, he is the only actor on earth. What the king produces becomes history. He is the producer of historical time, a singular time created by a singular individual to which the times of all other individuals are linked. The historical time of the king is not that of an empirical individual but that of the portrait of the king; it is not lived time but represented time. Historians who report on historical time likewise produce it in their texts; they keep their own persons with their own time out of the historical text. Their texts rewrite everything that could appear in the first person, all the *I* sentences, into sentences with a third-person subject. Political power represents, as it were, itself; it seems to tell its own history through the instrument of the anonymous voice and text of the narrator, who sees only that which power offers him to see.[7]

The plots produced by the chronicler take place in an ideal space, in that of world history. Historical narrative is supposed to make readers into spectators of a theatrical event, to move them into a position that allows them to cast a glance from a distance at the theater of world history. Louis XIV pulls the strings of historical actors before their eyes, causing deeds to be accomplished which become history. In fact, however, the entire theater, with its scenery and participating characters, is a product of the narrator, the "great simulator" of the images. Readers are captivated by the pleasure they take in the historical narrative. They are supposed to believe what the text represents: they are supposed to see the king as if they were by his side or even in his place. The theatrical text must stimulate the readers' imaginations, but also the king's, who himself must inhabit the position designated for him in the narrative. The theater of history is characterized by the extraordinary, which only the king is capable of producing: "All the king's actions are miracles."[8] The extraordinary event has the quality of an exemplar; as a model event, it is written into the history of the king.

Nothing exceeds the reach of simulation and calculation in Pellisson's project. Its goal is the production of political omnipotence. For royal omnipotence to come into existence, the king obviously has to share it with the chroniclers; Pellisson is named the official chronicler of the king. There arises a split—or a division of labor—between the action in which political omnipotence is manifest and a narration of this action, which is supposed to produce its omnipotent effects: the action of the king and the presentation of the narrator. Historians need the king for their narrative, but the king also needs the historians; for political power can achieve perfection, can identify its absolute, only if its force is joined with, as its object, the force of the narrative. Thus arises the chiasma between political power and discursive power; the king becomes a portrait of the king.

Precisely because the effects of history writing are simulated and calculated in advance, the historical narrative must dissimulate all fictional qualities[9] that could betray the king's manipulations. Only in this way is it possible to achieve the political goal, which is the subordination of the reader to the sovereign subject and his absolute power. We have here a question of the tactics of narrative presentation. Pellisson determines to obliterate from the text all trace of his person; the living vitality of the narrative is supposed to convey to readers the impression that the words are coming from their own mouths.[10] The chronicler assumes a privileged position directly next to the king, who is in the course of accomplishing the acts from which chroniclers derive the beauty of their representations, preserving them for posterity. To this end, they develop a performative mode of writing, which is supposed to transform readers into an admiring audience. The account of a war, for example, in its own way and on the field of narration, must consider strategies and tactics. It allows the events in time and space to appear as a permanent and universal attribute of the king's substance, which is inscribed into history, past, present, and future, by repetition.

The goal of such a historical record is not what we customarily regard as the representation of events, developments, or times. Rather, it lifts precisely what is timeless out of the historical flow: the final reference of historical narration and its justification lies in the picture of history it produces.[11] The historical picture represents the substance of the king in its perfection.[12] Pellisson's final goal consists in making manifest the substance of the king so that it, by being manifest, works its effects on the readers.

In such a representation, all differentiations between event, speech, image, and text must be transcended: what is written down must convey the vitality normally reserved for listening to a speech; the text must work imagistically; the picture must capture the substance of history; the written text must make it possible for the substance to become manifest, and readers must be put in the position of seeing the incarnation of absolute power in the portrait of the king. Legibility creates visibility and the visible becomes legible; at the center of the theory of representation under French absolutism lies the transcendence of the duality between the visible and the legible. It therefore favors manifestations that produce legible pictures, which, in turn, represent substance visibly and transform the empirical into the ideal without forfeiting empirical qualities. From this perspective phenomena other than the portrait of the king—war, festivals, gardens—take their place alongside the portrait as the prominent elements of a fictional envelopment of real events, which are all entered into presentational circulation.

The fête, in particular, represents a great metamorphosis of the exterior space outside the palace; the space is manipulated, represented, remodeled, and made the object of play. It is consumed and destroyed, experienced sumptuously without regard to purpose: a spectacle of air, water, and fire in a wholly mastered nature, a metamorphosis of the real.[13] "War is the fête continued by other means, as diversion is politics pursued on another register."[14]

In one respect the portrait of the king is itself the person that it represents. The image does nothing other than represent the pictorial characteristics the king already possesses before an image of him is made. There is no difference between the king's royal aspect and the object of portraiture. When the king looks at a portrait of himself, two kings find themselves face-to-face; the king himself is simultaneously a portrait. Such an all-encompassing idea of representation risks endowing images with magical power. Such a strategy of symbolization necessarily appears suspect to a theory of signs, like that of the Jansenists of Port-Royal, which refers similarities and meanings essentially back to conventions.[15] To the great representational tasks of the state, however, the absolutist conception of the pictorial renders an extraordinarily valuable service, such that political absolutism is presumably altogether impossible without it. Yet beneath the level of the actions undertaken by crown and state, especially in the personal sphere, the pictorial becomes problematic. It is perhaps not without significance that the person who referred more penetratingly than anyone else to the difficulties inherent in this conception of representation was a woman, the novelist Madame de Lafayette.

On the Dramatic Practice of French Classicism

The essential features of the theory of representation that the political system of French absolutism helped to constitute also determine the oddly strict, signlike, and elevated form of French classical tragedy. The tragic drama belongs among the essential symbolic representations of absolutist rule. Racine was, like Corneille, a court writer and, moreover, the successor to Pellisson as royal chronicler. The same theory of signs underlies the composition of tragedies as the one used in the production of the portrait of the king, though to regard the drama as a subdivision of state rhetoric would be to mistake the particularity of the dramatic arts. There is indeed a correspondence between the essential principles of political and artistic mimesis, but the drama and the novel maintain a certain latitude for themselves over against the political goals of the king.

Like the state, art must be subjected to order. There exists as well a strict system among the various areas of life. "The vision of neo-classical drama is that forged by Richelieu and imposed by Mazarin: there had to be order in life as in art."[16] There is always a political substratum to the tragic literature of French classicism, even when it is concerned with personal passions. Order is expressed on every level of tragedy, most obviously on that of style. Classical French tragedy, writes Auerbach, is without exception written in the elevated style; "the separation of the tragic from the occurrences of everyday and human-creatural life was carried out in such a radical way as never before."[17] Dramatists banish from the stage both the quotidian and the creatural aspect of tragic characters, with the result that they are elevated in the extreme. Characters achieve a great loftiness in their actions, which is manifest in personal terms, in particular, in passions, but which never appears private or intimate; still less is it the subjective expression of the author.[18] The characters speak a rhetorical language, with Corneille drawing on elements of political rhetoric while Racine develops a highly formal language of interiority, a rhetoric of the emotions.

In classical French tragedy, the personal always functions as an exemplar, never as private passion; the personal provides the occasion for a picture of passion and in this way gains the quality of political expression. The dramatic action of a tragedy, while indeed the depiction of individual characters, is meant to be perceived by the audience as an embodiment of substances. Only those closest to the prince are allowed to appear with him on the stage. Thus the tragedy achieves "the strictest seclusion of the tragic personages and the tragic action from everything below them";[19] the effect of the play is intensified and the thesis demonstrated that only the king and his immediate associates make history. From the conception of the portrait of the king arises a further imperative, that the tragic characters remain physically intact. To be sheltered from physical impairment belongs to the characteristics of the absolutist king, in particular, to his capacity to express majesty and supreme rank of birth by means of his body; these are manifest in beauty, the pose of a conqueror, elegance, and a superior attitude.

That dramatic movement is restricted to a unified plot, a single place, and a brief span of time is related to considerations of economy in the employment of dramatic signs but is certainly not reducible to this point of view.[20] Tragedy is never concerned with the times and places of events but, as in the writing of history, with the production of an ideal plot in an ideal time at ideal places. These two forms have so little to do with empirical ideas or experiences of time and place that we may speak of time- and placelessness in reference to them.[21] The passing of the tragic plot cannot be measured in time; whatever standards we might use—hours, phases in a lifetime, experiential values—either do not apply or would lead to results we cannot interpret. Our object here is more precisely identified as a construction of signs containing nothing temporal or spatial within it. Temporal and spatial concepts appear only in a figurative sense. A work of literature produced in this way does not allow the audience to establish a relationship to the practice of life, which means that the life experience of the audience is excluded from consideration. The work thus resists interpretation of its temporal and spatial structures in terms of the concepts of human experience; what time and space can otherwise mean remains an open question. Put the other way around: only through reference to concrete practice, which is precisely what dramatists leave out of French classical tragedy, can the literary work take on temporal and spatial dimensions.

The space of baroque theater is construed according to a central perspective;[22] it thus absorbs advances developed since the Renaissance in visual perspective. This specific spatial form is what the absolutist theatrical spectacle requires. Space is arranged to be optimal for the spectator: it is closed in the back, with all lines coming together in a single vanishing point;[23] and it is closed in the front in the sense that all lines of sight come together in the eye of the spectator located at this optimal point. There are in reality, then, two spaces, the one for the stage and the one for the audience, which are so arranged in reference to each other that together they completely close themselves off from the space external to the theater. In this construction of two communicating funnels, everything that happens on stage becomes ideally visible from the point at which all visual lines meet.[24] The person observing from this point has an overview of everything, which he or she can also know and control. On the one hand, the space of the theater fulfills the requirements of theatrical representation; on the other, it represents the power of the absolutist king.[25]

While the space of the classical French theater is influenced in at least a few of its characteristics by the *physique nouvelle* of Descartes, the time of the performance is far removed from the linearity, homogeneity, and constancy of physical time. The theatrical performance is a ritual.[26] Everything in the theater transpires as ritual, from the entrance of the king and audience and the raising of the curtain to the performance of the play and everyone's exit from the theater. The individual steps in the process make up a succession, whereby the first must be accomplished to make it possible to move to the next. As early as Aristotle, tragedy opens up no genuine temporal dimension; it moves a series of obligatory stations to its end point. The only thing that is temporal about this is the sequence of steps—first . . . then—while other principles organize the drama itself: the reversal of fortune into misfortune; recognition; deep sorrow; purification. If temporal considerations play any role at all, it is only in reference to the question of how the temporal dimension can be organized as economically as possible.[27]

The succession of events in tragedy must also satisfy the requirement of knowability: everything must be said, everything essential brought to its conclusion. Like dramatic space, the dramatic time of what happens also works to objectify; the individual experience of time, whether that of the author or the spectator, must not be part of the performance. Time and space produce an objective order of things and events; they show them as they have to be. What is represented are the essences of the characters and the nature of things; the claim to truth involved is that of an intellectual likeness. This kind of tragedy has no place for subjective expression, which would interfere with the transmission of a true view of the world by means of spectacle. Political power represents itself theatrically with a claim to objectivity and truth.

The discovery of the true order presupposes a unified plot, since only a tautly executed, coherent chain of events illuminated from all sides is capable of revealing characterological essences and the nature of things. The plot, as Racine writes in the foreword to *Britannicus*, must be complete: "As for me, it was always my understanding that, as the tragedy was the mimesis (*imitation*) of a complete action in which several persons cooperate, that action is not finished until we know the situation in which it leaves these persons."[28]

Our investigation demonstrates that the three unities in classical French theater are bound to absolutist strategies of power. Without the demand for visibility, knowability, and controllability, however, the doctrine of the unities would remain empty words.[29] A singular constellation comes into existence in French absolutism which is capable of adopting anew—perhaps is even obliged to adopt—the structural organization of Greek theater. The enactment of the French monarch's power is the decisive (political) reason for French authors' resort back to Greek drama. The strict conception of dramatic mimesis manifests its meaning as a political rhetoric of power that is impossible under other conditions.

French classical dramatists have a second reason for appealing to Greek tragedy in the ritual character it lends to their plays. At issue here, in Jean-Marie Apostolidès's interpretation, is a disguised continuation of the ritual battle through which the king legitimates his claim to power. The tragic plot represents a symbolic sacrifice in the archaic sense that such battles establish new orders or fortify an existing one; the tragedy enacts the *myth fondateur,* the founding myth of kingly rule.[30] The ritual character of tragedy calls for a specific mode of representation: political rhetoric, declamation, complete exclusion of the quotidian, verse form, festive decor, antique costuming, and lordly gestures.

It is surely too one-sided to restrict classical French tragedy—as Apostolidès does, citing the sixteenth-century author Pierre de Laudun d'Aigaliers—to the moment of the king's sacrifice, regarding the latter as the "natural complement of the battle," the duel, the *ordalie,* eventuating in divine judgment.[31] Nevertheless, we may take over two points contained in this position in expanded form: that tragedy is the spectacle of the king and that it has the function of commemorating in ritual the end of violence directed against the state.[32] The king on stage is an image of the king, but not one of the empirical historical king. This image is, on the one hand, involved in the production of the political portrait of the king and, on the other, simultaneously the object of a theatrical play. Thus the author of the play, like the real king, has a certain latitude over against the mediating theatrical image. This situation makes it possible to represent the king on stage in a way that the real king could never be shown: he is made to appear as an essence that determines the course of history. The marks of sovereignty are displayed on the represented body of the king, which allows the authority he acquires by birth, and thus his legitimacy, to become visible. At first, dramatic spectacle allowed the role of the priest to be recognized behind the role of the king, but this practice gradually declined, making room for the aesthetic dimension of the tragedy to appear.

Poetic mimesis does not maintain its position at the center of political power for long. It is destabilized by a number of concurrent developments: by advances made in dramatic theory, which, through comedy, open access for the bourgeoisie to theatrical representation and raises the quotidian, vernacular language, and *bon sens* to a central position; by the attitude of a "negative anthropology" and a critique of representation, which, under the influence of the Jansenism of Port-Royal, found important advocates even at court; by a new orientation toward the verbal making of worlds, which comes to particular expression in the genre of the novel; by the rise of the new scientific spirit, the goal of which—to apprehend the truth of the world—banishes mimesis from epistemology and the processes of knowledge. We consider all of these tendencies typical of the reformulation of mimesis that takes place at the end of the seventeenth century. Before discussing them in detail, however, we must mention a significant change in political conditions that had a decisive effect on the work of Corneille: the construction of the absolutist state, in which the heroic comes to play merely the role of a traditional value.[33]

Corneille's theater represents the supreme values of the old feudal society: fame, pride, gallantry, love, stoicism, aestheticism, generosity, the readiness to sacrifice. The traditional understanding of aristocratic society is called into question in the absolutist court, and the development of Corneille's oeuvre reflects this severe crisis in relations between the aristocracy and the absolutist state. In his early comedies, Corneille enacts the genesis of heroism as one and the same with the birth of the state. As nature and history are overcome, the values of the nobility of the time of Louis XIII triumph. The success of Corneille's first tragedies comes about in the meeting between a cultivated and educated public and a modern political sensibility.[34]

In the intervening phase, the confrontation between the hero and the state has changed: glory no longer has the creative significance it once had; it remains merely the continuation of an established plot. If, however, the tragic hero no longer exerts a historical effect, he is accorded the role of resisting power; the hero becomes a victim.[35] "Political heroism is transformed into heroic politics. . . . The state thus becomes the continuation of the hero."[36] In the final phase of Corneille's theater, the omnipresent and omnipotent state no longer tolerates the presence of the hero;[37] he takes leave of the stage, which from now on is monopolized by the state. What had earlier been a heroic story now becomes political; the state deteriorates into tyranny and annihilates the hero (in *Suréna*). In Corneille's last play, "heroes without power fall under the blows of power without heroes."[38] While the heroic individual succumbs and is forced to endure the state, the latter construes itself as the historical form of fate by styling its *libido dominandi* as tragic greatness.[39] Politics becomes tragic, becomes the passion for domination, which destroys order; the origin of a state that creates this passion is hubris.

The fatal vision of the absolutist state expressed in Corneille's late (and unsuccessful) tragedies is less trenchant than the radical skepticism of Port-Royal: it causes the old values of individual glory and vying for honor, which were bound up with the morality of the nobility, to be called into question. The old rhetoric, which since the Renaissance had served to represent the aristocratic notion of the individual and a noble existence, is devalued. Port-Royal maintains that the individual is subject constantly to illusions about the self, is led on by *amour-propre,* seduced into a false self-consciousness that always ascribes to the self better motives than it in fact possesses.[40] Jansenist rhetoric is oriented wholly toward the inner self, of which, aiming to extinguish the *I* and all its values, it makes a public matter. It becomes an entirely negative rhetoric, is no longer able to find any occasion for a positive representation of the individual. If it cannot thrive on the verve of its indictment, its doubt, its condemnation, then it denounces rhetoric as such and prefers to withdraw from the world—as in the denouement of Madame de Lafayette's *Princess of Cleves.*

Racine imports this negative rhetoric into tragedy, endowing it there with a fatal violence.[41] He represents human passions as brutal and usurpatious, as achieving a kind of matchless intensity. Love is driven to the extreme, where it loses its human appearance.[42] This is the one side, the negative and psychological; the other side is the sublimity, rigor, linguistic elegance, and atmosphere of brilliance and power that is preserved in the tragic form.[43] The poetic laws of the genre enter into a peculiar combination with the moral disposition of the poet and the political situation of French absolutism. "The king, close to divinity, is in the Christian and Jansenist view close to sacrilege. This explains the incessant threat of divine punishment which hangs over him."[44]

A comparable involvement of poetic mimesis in the constitution of power—with the simultaneous distancing[45]—will not be achieved later. In French court society, the degree of social pressure exerted over the literary production of symbols was extremely high, higher than in later periods. At the same time, however, literary figures had the opportunity to exercise a counterpressure, which becomes available to them in their involvement in constituting the portrait of the king.[46] Writers take on a role in the game of power, the importance of which is increased by their political, spiritual, and rhetorical attitude and which leads to the development of an extraordinarily elaborate codification system that favors a strict conception of the theater. There thus emerges a unique, unrepeatable historical constellation, and the concept of mimesis necessarily changes fundamentally.

Drama that is formally strict in this way can be plausible only if dramatic requirements coincide with a particular worldview, with political pressure, and with an especially pronounced system of codification. Mimesis, the validity of which had been particularly tied to tradition, acquires a new role in the future; it appears in other social locations, initially entangled in a rearguard action with the traditionalists, but then ever more clearly involved in the production of wholly other worlds. It may seem on a superficial viewing as if the validity of mimesis extends without break into the Enlightenment, indeed, as if its true significance is only discovered in that later period. In fact, however, all the elements involved in mimetic processes in the eighteenth century have changed fundamentally in comparison with the seventeenth century. Not the least of these changes is a shift in the relation of genres to one another: following the heyday of French classicism tragedy is forced to share its role as the leading literary genre with the novel, with a bourgeois medium that has emancipated itself from rhetoric and will henceforth distance itself from traditional mimesis.

The Representation of Daily Life in Comedy

The significance of theatrical representation for social reality lies in the circumstance that the performance of a play affirms the world depicted concretely on the stage. It becomes the more significant when tendencies appear in seventeenth-century French drama which seek to make the daily reality of the bourgeois world representable in the theater. This happens very early, with the beginning of the classical comedy in France from 1625 to 1629; it is "constructed *against* the essential norms of neo-Aristotelian doctrine."[47] Comedy opens the stage to bourgeois daily life; bourgeois characters appear "no longer as comic types, but as *honnêtes gens* who act and speak in accord with the rules of *bienséances*. That is, the emancipated bourgeois appears for the very first time in the history of modern French literature in the literature of high culture. Thus at the same time the real world of the bourgeoisie becomes the object of dramatic reflection."[48]

Everything in drama changes; "that is, the personal and with that the conflict, the emotions, the language, the style, or level of style—alexandrines are suddenly possible—and thus the heroic diction, etc. And the place changes."[49] The idea that the literature of French absolutism follows a unified plan and is composed according to a fixed canon of rules (*doctrine classique*) is nothing but a myth. The doctrine of the three unities takes on a completely different meaning in the comedies, particularly those of Corneille and Molière, than in contemporary tragedy. With Corneille begins the turn to the empirical social space of the bourgeoisie, which is identified with ever greater precision and represented ever more concretely.[50]

Corneille takes a further step in his considerations on a bourgeois drama: when he puts the honnêtes gens into action on the stage, the relation between the public and the dramatic characters changes fundamentally. The function of the drama, to stimulate fear and compassion, can now be constituted in a new way: both fear and compassion arise out of a relation of equality in principle between persons on the stage and in the audience. Corneille writes in the foreword to *Don Sanche d'Aragon,*

> If, then, it is true that a representation of this latter sentiment [compassion and dread] stimulates the same in us only if the people we see suffering are like ourselves, so that their misery causes us to fear the same condition for ourselves, then is it not also true that it could be all the more powerfully stimulated in us

by the sight of misfortune befalling persons who share our circumstances, who are utterly similar to us, than by the kind of images offered us by those who have the greatest of monarchs topple from their thrones, persons, that is, with whom we have no rapport whatever, aside from the fact that we too are susceptible to those same passions that drove them over the precipice, which is not something that we encounter everyday?[51]

If readers find this argument reasonable, Corneille continues, then they will have no objection to the idea that "one could create a tragedy with middling characters, as long as their misfortune is not beneath the dignity" of the form.

Corneille is elaborating here a relation of similarity between everyday individuals and dramatic characters. The similarity refers to the possible fate of both. His argument is constructed on the basis of equality between the audience and the characters postulated in a twofold sense: the equality of their social positions and the equivalence of their reactions to misfortune. This presumed double equality is of fundamental significance for the later development of mimesis. It finally results in a potential exchangeability between theatrical representation and bourgeois action. The equality maintained here makes it possible to reverse the direction of the respective arguments: the drama functions—from the standpoint of emotions—like society; to this extent, social life becomes an object for the theater. But the reverse of the argument is also valid: society functions like a drama; to this extent, the theater becomes a model of society.

The institution of the theater supplies a model for mimetic social processes. This is its new role; the drama is complete only when it has registered, shaped, and intensified the mimetic processes active in society and sublimated them into art. It devolves upon theater, as the first social institution so charged, to educate and refine bourgeois social mimesis and transform it into art. The stage, to this extent, has played an essential role since the first realistic comedies, especially Corneille's, as the institution that catalyzes and provides models of the mimetic process responsible for shaping society. With the bourgeois drama, social mimesis acquires public and aesthetic representation.

In Boileau's *L'Art poétique,* the exchange between social reality and the world of the stage is organized around the concept of bienséance. The writer is to respect bienséance, just as his characters are required to do.[52] Their behavior in the play must correspond to that of persons of the same position in the real social world, "so that the audience can regard their behavior as possible and probable."[53] The psychologization of dramatic technique ultimately amounts to a socialization of mimesis and an aestheticization of the world of experience.

What does it mean that the theatrical and empirical worlds begin to approximate each other in this way? In the first instance, it means that theater loses its autonomy; it becomes a secondary medium tied to social practice. As we have seen, however, this relationship is reversible: social practice can be subsumed under the paradigm of imitative mimesis. For it is now possible to position bienséance prior to social reality in the form of a model, whereby the theater—that which pertains to the theatrical and dramatic as a whole—becomes integrated into social practice. The result is a process of reciprocal reflection; given the proper social compulsion, a kind of modeling can take place. Specific agglomerations of characteristics in one of the two worlds are evoked in reference to existing agglomerations of characteristics in the other. If, therefore, society demands bienséance from the theater, it is obliged to behave accordingly itself. Such social pressure is always exercised only by specific class factions in society; they come into confrontation with rival social groups via a detour through the theater.

Corneille's thoughts on a bourgeois tragedy, which is where we began the current discussion, never get beyond the stage of argument; he is never to write one, and the bourgeoisie gains access to the theater, not in tragedy, but in comedy. Corneille's argument, quoted above, appears finally to amount to something else, to a remarkable, we could almost say muddled, "reversed conclusion." He extends it as follows: if a tragedy can be written with middling characters, then "allow me to conclude, *a simili,* that we could also write a comedy dealing with illustrious persons." What Corneille is no doubt aiming at, in reference to dramatis personae, is a lowering of tragedy and an elevation of comedy.

Twelve years later "the first comic (that is, bourgeois) tragedy is performed: *The School for Wives,* by Molière."[54] Unlike Corneille's plays, this play, according to Michael Nerlich, is part of the larger context of contemporary French political struggles. Considered in this context, it becomes fairly obvious that Molière's theater takes the side of the activist bourgeoisie, which supports the absolutist king in his struggle against the feudal nobility, a progressive commitment at the time. The playwright spares the utilitarian and progressive bourgeois his ridicule.[55] Molière's critique aims initially at opponents of the policy the king had been conducting with Colbert since 1661, "and only once Molière has lost his revolutionary optimism, once he has become the incorruptible voice of admonition, does this relationship [to the king] cool considerably."[56] Though Molière also fails to develop the bourgeois tragedy, which is a task reserved for the next century, he opens up the bourgeois space in his comedies, a space that is completely different from the unified space, the more geometrico, of classical tragedy. Molière's theatrical space is no longer an idealized but rather a typified space, a kind of model of the "intellectual and material space of French society of the time, which is to say, an essential part of this space."[57] Within this space there is no more important location than the bourgeois household, inside of which the operations of society, social forces, the potential of society, and the conditions of its health are manifest. The spatial center of the French state is the king's *appartement* in Versailles. A festival is held in honor of its opening as the seat of king and court, which includes the premiere performance of *Tartuffe:* "On May 12, 1664, at the heart of the most powerful monarchy in the world, at the geographical, physical, and intellectual center of the absolutist rule of Louis XIV, in an apologetic moment in the *appartement même du Roi,* Molière's play erects the bourgeois house."[58]

This important event is the first sign of what will eventually happen with the three unities of the theater: the unity of space will become the sphere of bourgeois daily life; the unity of plot will be judged from the vantage of the rational conduct of life; the unity of time will be set in relationship to the empirical time of the audience, society, and author. That these changes necessarily affect dramatic heroes was fully apparent to Molière. In the *Critique of the School for Wives,* he writes,

> When you portray heroes you can do just what you please. These are fanciful portraits; no one looks for lifelike resemblances in them. . . . But when you are painting men, you must paint from nature. Everyone insists that the likenesses resemble reality; and you haven't accomplished anything, unless you make your audience recognize the men of our own time.[59]

11

Against Mimesis as
Self-Representation

In the age of French classicism, the idea of social self-representation in-cluded using the devices of rhetoric and enactment to intensify the effects of the signs of power, to the end of forging a strong connection between the signified thing and the signifier. No other means could make it possible for the empirical person of the king to be represented indubitably and permanently by the portrait of the king. In the novels of Madame de Lafayette we encounter the resistance of signs; she shows a preference for situations in which repre-sentations fail to function, thus signaling opposition to the representation of absolutism promoted tirelessly by the king.

There was room in the classical theory of signs for stunning developments in respect to conventional signs, calculations and tableaus, grammar and logic, and the formal sciences. But problems arose in reference to "natural signs," whereby political representation is a matter almost exclusively of natural signs. "From the seventeenth century, the values allotted to nature and convention in this field are inverted: if natural, a sign is no more than an element selected from the world of things and constituted as a sign by our knowledge. It is therefore strictly limited, rigid, inconvenient, and impossible for the mind to master."[1] In Lafayette's novels the "representivity" of the natural sign be-comes the occasion, prompted by the classical theory of signification, for a critical examination of mimetic processes.

The Critique of Self-Representation
in Madame de Lafayette

Lafayette's novels[2] develop toward social self-representation a critical at-titude of unprecedented clarity and radicalism. The story she tells in the *Princess of Cleves* begins with a depiction of courtly splendor. In the world of functioning self-representation, the narrator, almost unintentionally, sets in motion a plot that destroys its own world even as it develops it. At the end this narration of resistance arrives at its goal: a withdrawal from the public world into an otherworldly piety. Lafayette offers the reader the vision of an amorous train of events, in order then to destroy it. What remains is an attitude of shock regarding the effect of mimesis in social reality, an attitude of disgust.

Lafayette marks an end point in courtly representation in literature. The representational multiplies itself, presses out beyond the boundaries that had been set for it, and produces images, which, in turn, become autonomous and draw people under their spell. All the major characters in Lafayette's novels are fascinated by images. They see in them reflections of reality. The images are representations of people, and for the possessors of them, possession signifies love; Zaide's love for Consalve arises out of her inspection of his portrait;[3] the Princess of Cleves and the Duke of Nemours assure themselves of their passion by regarding pictures of those whom they love in the privacy of their solitude.

Yet the plots of *Zaide* and the *Princess of Cleves* cause the referential relationship between pictorial representation and the represented persons to come unhinged. The novels come surreptitiously to center on the pictures because reality offers up their objects of reference either not at all or only with extreme difficulty. Over the course of events in the novels, the reflectionlike images acquire a remarkable superiority over their models, a predominance that ultimately undermines the represented persons: the images begin to act; the originals accept the role of imitating their own pictorial representations. Pictorial mimesis becomes the point of vulnerability in the subject.

What Lafayette's novels demonstrate, at a time in the seventeenth century when social representation had achieved its classical form, is the crisis of representation. She depicts the representation of the self, which is supposed to be the special service of the novel as a genre, as problematic. Wrapped up in the events of the novel is a critical discussion of the presuppositions of worldmaking by means of images and narratives.[4] Lafayette's novels demonstrate how mimesis can establish a relationship between people and lead to the making of a world shared in common.

The *Princess of Cleves* is unusually rich in scenes constructed according to the mirror principle: an intercepted glance; an observed facial expression; a statement answered by a blush, whereby the observer recognizes himself or herself in the physical reaction of the other. A painter, for whom the princess is presently sitting for another painting, is charged with altering a small portrait of her that belongs to her husband. During the sitting, with the pure dauphine and her retinue in attendance, the portrait lies unnoticed on the table. The Duke of Nemours is in love with the princess, though she does not know it; he seizes the moment to steal the portrait. Through a split in the curtains the Princess of

Cleves watches him deftly pick up the portrait; she immediately guesses the true situation. When the Duke of Nemours turns, he meets the princess's eyes, still fixed on him, and is immediately certain that she has spotted the theft. After quick consideration the princess decides to preserve silence to avoid making an affair of the deed—a decision that the duke interprets as reluctant love on her part.

To avoid the temptations of her love, the princess withdraws to her country estate. The duke secretly follows and observes through the window in the dark how she, with a candle in her hand, approaches a painting of the siege of Metz, which includes, among the others pictured, his own portrait. He sees how she dreamily examines the portrait. The prince stands rooted by his passion; as he finally moves to approach her through the opened French doors, she turns her head, recognizes him, and flees. The Duke of Nemours has become a witness to his own possession as an object of representation, similar to the princess previously. As observer he is, as John D. Lyons points out, "both within and without, both included as a painted object and excluded from the spectacle of the object's possession."[5]

According to Lyons, Lafayette's novels deal with the inability of pictorial signs to unveil truth. In Jansenist logic, in contrast, truth requires no sign at all; it unveils itself.[6] Pictorial representation is almost the polar opposite of the rational conception of Port-Royal. The cause of error is the indefiniteness of the image; but it also constitutes, as we can establish by moving beyond Lyons, the power of images over us. This power does not constitute genuine possession: the Duke of Nemours possesses the princess not truly, but only as an image, the same way that he is possessed as an image; he sees her absorbed in an examination of his picture but "cannot introduce himself into this scene."[7] Images take the place of reality; Pascal's warning against the *vie imaginaire* that we live in the eyes of others is reformulated by Lafayette as a literary text. Our self-presentations, and that of others, fool us; they do not lead to understanding. The latter, in Lafayette's philosophical conviction, can "only come from within, from an interiority that is made inaccessible by its dim reflection in the outside world."[8]

With Lafayette, the mimesis of action, thinking, and desiring is pushed to a high point and its fundamental weaknesses revealed. The similarity of pictorial imitation, the emphatic understanding of the Other, the observation and interpretation of physical reactions all founder on the ambiguity of representational symbols. Yet, instead of attenuating imitation, these weaknesses lead Lafayette's protagonists to ever more passionate mimetic reactions.[9] Lafayette herself is concerned with the problems of interpreting signs; in this we may agree with Lyons. But she directs her considerations at a fundamental philosophical problem. Relationships among characters in her novels are shaped by mirror images that constitute a world of their own. In comparison to the world of images, reality becomes a reflection of a reflection; mimesis intrudes into the hierarchy of court society and refashions relationships among the persons involved.

Once these relationships become dominated by mimesis, the social order deteriorates, with everyone searching for the Other within a general state of untruth. The reality of court society is stripped of its truth, and those things that have previously been valued—name, nobility, aristocracy and family, character—are destroyed by the mimetic mirroring that goes on all around. In preabsolutist society all of these things had been endowed with the permanence of substances, but now they cannot withstand mimesis. Lafayette's novel has the depth that it does because the emotions she uncovers never achieve their real goals. Action becomes organized in mimetic chains; it produces interior worlds that can never attain to the status of the real world. The only things that are real are the external signs, which express the movements of interiority.

The political and the private form complementary spheres in the *Princess of Cleves:* the private exists for the characters only when they remove themselves from the political space. The protagonists, over the course of the novel, play an ever-smaller role in the network of political relationships; strictly speaking, they are political failures. In her mother's wishes the Princess of Cleves was destined for a marriage alliance of the highest rank. But once the marriage project gets drawn into the vortex of politics, it has to be abandoned. M. de Cleves is just barely able to save the princess's career at court, but he enjoys no political distinction of his own. His interest in her is entirely private, his desire to marry her innocent of all political calculation. The Duke of Nemours, at the beginning of the novel, has in mind courting the English queen Elizabeth, and he has solid expectations of success. But his passion for the Princess of Cleves causes him to neglect his grand political project, which ends up serving only as the object of his boasts, thus raising his value in the eyes of his beloved. In contrast to Diane de Poitiers, the king's mistress, who treats love and desire strictly in terms of political calculation, converts the private into public power, and has a critical share in the shaping of French politics, Nemours takes leave of the complex of politics and sinks into the tangle of passions. Passions are in turn reduced to *plaisir,*[10] which is characterized by the renunciation of influence and power and strictly confined to the personal.

Contrary to the theory put forth by Norbert Elias, in which the psychological is interpreted as the result of a process of interiorization prompted by external compulsion, the psychological sphere opens up here as the equivalent of the development of a secondary network of relationships that operate beneath that of the political hierarchy. The constitution of the individual psyche runs counter to the claims of the hierarchical system; it demands autonomy for the body and soul, for individual emotions and the unfolding of the capacity to love. This withdrawal from hierarchy, the call for the possession of one's own body, the turn toward the private, and the striving for equality are all characteristics of individualism. The structural center of the novel becomes the conflict between mimetic action geared toward equality and the antimimetic hierarchy, which has scarcely begun to work out the split between exterior and interior observation.

Only the main characters in the novel are active in the creation of the signifying system of emotional expression, which is critically mediated over the observation of the psychological life of other characters. Nothing that is supposed to be secret escapes the curious eyes of the Other; there develops accordingly the counterstrategy of concealment. But the gaze of precisely that person who should not see penetrates into the personal sphere as well: the intimate fact is shared with the observer, which is precisely the mechanism by which it becomes identifiable and stable. This process deploys the reservoir of shared symbols in such a refined, reflected, and psychologized way that it operates largely outside the notice of those in the immediate environment, who must be prevented from understanding it. It regulates relationships arising out of the chaos of passions, taking on a reciprocal and therefore persistent structure. The rules no longer share anything in common with the customary relationships of the court hierarchy; they do, however, possess a freshness, as well as the ambivalent attraction of a fully regulated intimate world.

The three main characters in the novel violate the essential prohibition on reciprocal action, thus undermining the regulation of court life. The world they share among themselves has split off from the political world of the court. Their world is organized mimetically and includes spaces of individual latitude that are inconceivable inside the hierarchy. Mimesis and individualism, in this apparently paradoxical fashion, become bound to each other.

The world brought into being by the mutual action of the main characters endures in remarkable fashion through the mechanism of mirror images. The beloved Other, in the novel's central scenes, becomes a portrait: the reflecting surface of the images opens up; the observed person approaches the likeness of the observer. Unification takes place in the mirror.

Amorous fantasies seem an adequate source of the desire for unification, but, in fact, it is equally consonant with a contemporary preoccupation with the problems of pictorial representation. The desire portrayed in the novel coincides with the interpretation Michel Foucault has offered of the painting *Las Meninas* by Velázquez, in particular, with his considerations on the mirror that is centrally located in the composition. "The function of that reflection is to draw into the interior of the picture what is intimately foreign to it: the gaze which has organized it and the gaze for which it is displayed."[11]

If the medium of mimesis is the mirror, its object is the body. The body-soul dichotomy established by the constitution of a mutually produced intimate world endows the physical with a free space of individuality that it did not previously possess. When the protagonists meet, it is always the body that reacts—with reactions ranging from blushing to dying. The body becomes a disturbing factor in court society because it introduces the principle of (relative) equality: it becomes a carrier of signs and thereby loses its particular substance; all that remains important in it now are the signs. At the same time, however, the signs individualize the body insofar as they make it possible to express particular emotions. The principled comparability of persons had opened the way for the ascription and the production of passions; now the shared intimate world brings forth analogous passionate reactions. Equality, mimesis, the making of worlds, and the individual psyche form the kernel of the new, which will soon dissolve the hierarchical world.

The central characteristic of all the important signs in the novel is the way they address the observer and either stimulate or intensify in him or her an emotional relationship to the observed Other. They open a path by which the observer can enter into the world of the Other. The address is always issued by representations of the enamored person, never, however, from the person as such. When M. de Nemours steals the portrait of Mme. de Cleves, he behaves like a thief, regarding her as an object. But is she, for him, also something more than the copy of a portrait? Lafayette's *Zaide* has already taught us to see that when the relationship to the Other is mediated over images, image and person become interchangeable.

It is not merely that the image that addresses the observer shows the Other as an object; the observer is also nothing but an object for the real viewer—who is simultaneously present as a represented object in the portrait. In the eyes of the observer the observational scene itself becomes an image, which, in turn, issues its own address. The address operates reciprocally, because both lovers regard their respective Others in a mirror. M. de Nemours knows that he is loved as an image, and Mme. de Cleves is aware that she manifests her love to an image. Their love takes place in a mirror; their relationship is one between images. The two mirrors stand opposite each other and reflect the Other. What is remarkable is not that the real Nemours would like to find his way into the image but that he, who is present in this scene, becomes doubled, whereby the central role is played by his (represented) doppelgänger. The doubling is no longer subject to transcendence. As a real observer, he belongs to a world that is different from the shared world: his attempt to put himself in the position of the portrait necessarily fails; for in order to transform the imaginary world into a real one, he has to release Mme. de Cleves from her existence as an object.

Only images have an addressive character in the *Princess of Cleves*. Transformed into imitations by way of their mediated addresses to each other, the protagonists act against convention, liberate themselves from rules, break open the hierarchy of courtly customs, and set emotions in movement. But they do this, indeed, not as real persons. The individuality constituted through the production of an emotional world remains confined to images. No one appears in the novel to explain everything and reinsert the individual as the original. On the contrary, the end of the novel is reserved for Mme. de Cleves, who delivers the sharpest indictment against mimesis since Plato.

After having repeatedly attempted to escape the address through images, at the end of the novel and following the death of her husband, Mme. de Cleves sees through the fundamentally mimetic construction of the world of mirrors. Nemours's love, she presumes, might have been so passionate only because it was never fulfilled; the same had presumably been the case with her husband's passion. She sees herself as the object of two passionate loves, which, via mimesis, reciprocally intensified each other, without her, in her capacity as a real person, ever having been the object of the love. All of the main characters, herself included, betray the same weakness: they secretly desire the feelings of the Other and flatter themselves with the Other's love. That the Princess of Cleves is acute in her judgment here is attested by the fate of her lover: once he learns that she is definitively lost to him, he begins the gradual process of forgetting her.

Mimesis, as the Princess of Cleves recognizes at the end of the novel, belongs to a different order of being than reality. With this recognition she closes off the past, without either denying or recanting it; she acknowledges love and her relationship to Nemours but refuses it a future. She will put an end to mimesis, take definitive leave of the privately produced world. By renouncing mimesis, the Princess of Cleves gains truth about herself and her relationships to the others. At the end of the novel she withdraws into the mirrorless spaces of her cloistered solitude, relinquishes her individuality and her body; she leaves behind "des exemples de vertu inimitable."[12] "Inimitable"—this quality of Mme. de Cleves's behavior following her withdrawal from the world is in a twofold sense the novel's last word.

The introduction of perspective in Renaissance painting prompted a new organization of seeing. In literature it prepares the way for the unfolding of subjectivity. Both developments mark points along the path of an increasingly artistic imitation of life. The mimesis of desire draws attention to a change in the way people relate to each other, to the production of subjective worlds, and to the blurring of distinctions between the separate spheres of social reality and individual constructions. European civilization, ever since the rise of modern subjectivity, has been searching for the genuine reality of the human original. The novels that come into being as part of this tradition order relationships to the Other as a striving for possession; they deal primarily in representations, in objects. While individuals are entered into the order of things as reflections, lovers behave toward the reflected images as if they were individuals.

Negative Anthropology

Our consideration of Corneille, Molière, Racine, and Lafayette warrants the presumption that the literature of French absolutism opened the door to later developments, all the way up to the bourgeois tragedy and social mimesis. In opposition to interpretations that force the manifold literary production of the age into the narrow concept of the doctrine classique, we have emphasized the breaks with tradition that emerge from the complex of politically determined ways of seeing, new understandings of mimesis, and the ongoing development of literary genres. We see this process as reaching its most advanced point in Madame de Lafayette. Karlheinz Stierle, in his essay "Die Modernität der französischen Klassik," offers an interpretation of the literary works of Pascal, La Rochefoucauld, Racine, and Lafayette that reinforces and extends the reading we have given here.

Stierle also rejects the image of the *siècle classique,* which he sees as "masking" the meaning of the period.[13] He sees something fundamentally new arising in French classicism: a "negative anthropology" and a "functional style." With extreme consistency, all four authors he examines push the question of human nature toward an unresolvable problematic from which there is no escape. The question can only be raised as the product of the utmost concentration and ever again reflected anew; it cannot ultimately be answered.

In Pascal's *Pensées,* the *I* is experienced as decentered; it still indeed recalls its original determination, but it is at variance with itself, it is internally bifurcated, resulting in a *moi haissable.*[14] Pascal searches for orientation in the model of Montaigne's researches into the *I* but finds himself unable to achieve any "trust in one's own 'âme bien nèe.'" In a fashion that resembles Descartes's thinking, Pascal pursues a strategy of radicalization that aims at a point of final, indubitable certainty; but he is capable of neither supplying a positive definition of it nor, therefore, naming or describing it. His anthropology remains empty, "negative"; it is not knowledge "but rather an open movement of reflection."[15]

Stierle also identifies in the reflections and maxims of La Rochefoucauld a rejection of Descartes's positive anthropology and, indeed, of his theory of emotions. "The love of the subject for itself fails to sate itself in self-referentiality, creating instead an emptiness, a longing for the self, that can only be fulfilled in that the self presses beyond itself to become conscious of itself."[16] Here, too, the self is conceived as the empty midpoint of the world. While the established order retains its validity, it rends human interiority, leaving behind a bifurcated ego obsessed with amour-propre and lacking its own center. La Rochefoucauld finds in his own depths nothing but "a dynamic ceaselessly exhausting and renewing itself, as if the only need of the self were to remain conscious of itself in its own activity."[17]

Racine's negative anthropology is evident above all in the *I*'s reference to others and to itself: the main characters in his dramatic works find themselves cast "under the spell of a *moi caché.*"[18] The tragic *I* is thrown back on itself by the boundless desire it projects toward others; the *I* suffers an internal split, "positions itself as a lack at the empty center of its world."[19] As soon as the experience of the lack, of the loss of the self, begins to contemplate action, "the question of the *I,* the question of identity, arises: who am I, what have I done, where am I, what have I said? The question is the expression of the destabilized identity becoming aware of itself; it finds no answer, but leads only into the impenetrability of its own fate."[20]

We have already pointed out that the *Princess of Cleves* is pervaded by a negative anthropology. Stierle finds in the novel a "plurality of the *I,* the dynamic of which La Rochefoucauld had been the first to represent," an ambiguity brought about by the operation of the *I:* "the *I* reveals and conceals itself, reveals itself in concealing and in this revelation is already concealing itself anew."[21]

An anthropology such as this, one that breaks radically with all previous ideas of human being and for which human nature has become an unanswerable question, which it nevertheless poses continuously, seeking new avenues of approach, an anthropology that is precisely incapable of enduring in silence, although it cedes ample space to silence, can no longer find expression in rhetorical language. A new conception of language, which permits it to be articulated, becomes necessary. If the search is under way for a new problematic, if questions are asked that no longer have answers, what remains accessible to representation? The answer: the movement of thought itself. For that there are no style models, so that a radical break with the rhetorical tradition becomes inevitable. Thinking searches, as it were, for a language for itself; it wrings out of language the order of its movement. It does not flow into preexisting molds but searches for the means of expression that devolve upon it even as the search progresses. Neither the artificially formed signs of specialized languages nor those of systematic philosophical discourse are suited to the task thinking now sets for itself; instead it searches for the language won of experience, the language that derives directly from human practice and the needs of mutual communication, from "the normal conversations of life."[22] This sought-after language is the vernacular.

This recourse to daily linguistic practice, to oral and dialogical situations, the recognition of the vernacular with its wide versatility and proximity to lived reality—and all of this not as the isolated personal act of the author, but as an anthropologically justified prior commitment to another way of thinking—represents a momentous turn in the history of mimesis. Negative anthropology will henceforth express itself in the vernacular and chart the movements of thought as precisely and authentically as possible, guided by neither technical nor systematic concerns, but by an *esprit de finesse* (Pascal). The vernacular will henceforth be conceived as the medium in which thinking *manifests itself.*[23] While classical authors develop their negative anthropology on the basis of the idea of an order given from above, in later centuries the movement will proceed from the other direction, from an "order from below."

One critical qualification must be mentioned here: the vernacular is not employed in conformity with everyday usage, but rather in the particular way called for by "finesse," that is, in aesthetic writing. According to Starobinski, the perfection of the literary form achieved in La Rochefoucauld's "maximes et réflections" can be "understood as aesthetic compensation for the negative anthropology."[24] Such a sublation of the negation in the "sphere of the aesthetic and literary" is also found in the other theorists of the negative anthropology. Whether it is best regarded as "aesthetic compensation" or "rescue from the sphere of negation" (Starobinski), or whether it comes of the conscious effort to develop an instrument capable of penetrating the most distant corners of intimate experience, cannot be decided here. What is certain, however, is that writers from now on refine and make more precise the vernacular, such that the historical evolution of the psyche falls under the influence of these same accomplishments.

The use of the vernacular with finesse in aesthetic writing anticipates a development that exists here in incipient form. It is still too early to speak of aesthetic autonomy, but a certain liberation of the aesthetic dimension of literary works can be observed at least in La Rochefoucauld and Racine: the negative anthropology combines with what are already almost individualistic linguistic forms that themselves combine knowledge with pleasure. "Le plaisir poétique" evokes neither decorative nor culinary models and is no longer satisfied to be measured against publicly accepted standards of beauty and value. The poetic work on the vernacular that now gets under way prompts aesthetic decisions in its own right, which prepares the ground for the future emergence of a plurality of single aesthetics.

Along with the canon of norms, the privileging of specific linguistic forms in relation to other modes of expression now slips into the background. Tzvetan Todorov regards this destabilization of the privileging of specific forms as one of the essential reasons for the disappearance of rhetoric.[25] The process by which rhetoric is done away with will persist for another hundred years. But already in the seventeenth century, in the midst of the great age of rhetoric, literature begins to respond to the influence and transmutational forces of the *spoken* language, thereby developing a personal aesthetic expression for thought. What becomes evident here is the approaching end of the tradition that began with Augustine, in which "*the* truth is believed to be known," in which "there is no question of allowing each individual to appreciate his own truth and to love objects (in this case linguistic ones) simply for the sake of their harmony and beauty," and which regards poetic pleasure as useless and ultimately "unacceptable" to the social order.[26]

A century later it is the idea of the necessity of regulating discourse that is unacceptable. The view emerges, under the influence of romanticism, that "everyone, by drawing upon personal inspiration, without techniques or rules, can produce admirable works of art."[27] The split between thinking and expression is definitively transcended. In the historical moment that rhetoric ends, modern aesthetics begins.[28]

Two Attempts to Transcend Mimesis

The protest against mimesis in the seventeenth century is a protest against the mimetic medium, against language, writing, the mirror, enactment, narration. We turn now to Descartes's philosophy, an example of one way in which mimesis was supposed to have been rendered superfluous: by means of establishing a new foundation for thought, expressed in axioms and formalized language. There was also an effort to neutralize the medium in art, to postulate painting as pure replication. Dutch art of the seventeenth century, as Svetlana Alpers has shown,[29] turns away from the narrative mode of the Renaissance, toward a total transparency of the image as pure description. Dutch art, no less than Descartes, is mistaken in its assessment of its own presuppositions. Both tendencies, scientific philosophy and descriptive painting, are the originating points of antimimetic currents that continue into the present; they oppose to worldmaking undertaken by means of media a technicalization and mechanization of description, or, as the case may be, construction, divining their respective methods in the process.

Descartes

No one has formulated the analytic breakdown between science, art, and quotidian knowledge more starkly than Descartes. In a dramatic turn, he opposes his philosophy of consciousness to the mimetic thinking of the sixteenth century. Yet Descartes's attempt to overcome the mimetic thought of tradition itself makes use of mimetic processes. He makes a new world, a new world of the philosopher, the setting in which the latter conceives and elaborates rationalistic thought.

Descartes breaks with the theory of similitude, renounces reflection on the limits of language, and eschews skepticism in regard to the intermediary character of self-image—all of which are marks of Montaigne's work in particular. Descartes is concerned to abolish doubt, skepticism, and illusion and finally even to do away with the empirically given. The notion, he says, that human knowledge is fundamentally insecure comes into being in the intermediary space between the subject and the world; the medium of language is supposed to mediate between the two, but it fails to do so in a reliable manner. Somewhat starkly formulated, Descartes's philosophy aims at a ''neutralization'' of representation, opposing all aspects of language that grant it any latitude or even allow it to have its own particular coloration. Descartes would have language completely purified, made utterly transparent so that it can depict the order of the world with unsurpassable clarity.

Descartes represents the first great attempt of modern philosophy to purify language. Whatever exists outside the subject can in principle be a source of error and illusion; Cartesian reflection charts the course from complex forms saturated with daily processes all the way to the ultimate point, the Archimedean point of the completely emptied *I,* from which all traces of quotidian life experience have been purged. From this point of departure, the world comes into being anew through the mediation of artificial rules, a formal language, and a method derived from the ultimate certainty of the *I.* The world becomes a construct, a recognizable object manufactured according to strict prescriptions, the construction of which is also verifiable. Descartes explains thoroughly each methodological step, each one of which is unambiguous and derived axiomatically. He offers us the dream of reason.

But Descartes fools himself as to the prospect of perfect knowledge: he misunderstands his own presuppositions.[30] He plays a game with masks, giving the appearance of the purity of reason, while concealing essential aspects of the issue, namely, the conditions implicit in his method and his silent borrowing of representational devices from his predecessors, whom he also criticizes. The purification of knowledge in Descartes is not a step-by-step overcoming of illusion but rather a *narrated* chain of events. Against illusion and fallacy Descartes offers the dramatic enactment of an *I* that has arrived at certainty, a position that is itself fallacious and illusory, though in a different sense than the position it replaces. Descartes is ultimately unable to escape the problem of achieving a transparent formulation of the intermediary space between the subject and the world; linguistic representation cannot be ''neutralized.'' The medium is part of worldmaking. Attempts to make it transparent, as Descartes proposes doing, merely shift the difficulty into the sphere of unspoken assumptions. Dalia Judovitz has shown how Descartes's search for clearer and more distinct knowledge draws him step-by-step into a multitude of dependencies, which he fails to take into account because his axiomatic method shields them from view.

In his *Praeambula,* Descartes formulates the idea of his New Science for the first time. The cause of all things and events is supposed to be referred back to a single ultimate cause through a kind of deduction. Logic and mathematics, as instruments by which knowledge is ordered and organized, can then be used to reconstruct the order of the world anew on the foundation discovered in the process. Descartes uses the idea of a clarified order and the metaphor of the mask to introduce and represent the new discourse: the sciences are masked and the masks must be removed so that they can appear in all their beauty. But the pronouncer of this discourse, a purportedly empirical person, is also hidden behind a mask; Descartes, rather than writing under his real name, conceals his identity with a pseudonym. ''The metaphorical structure of the Cartesian text is an expression not simply of personal style, but rather the expression of the discursive exigencies of his philosophical position . . . because the philosophical subject is represented through the bias of autobiography.''[31] The bracketing together of philosophical and autobiographical subjects is typical of Cartesian philosophizing. The *I* represented in autobiographical form is simultaneously the pure knowing subject. Just how that is supposed to be possible remains unclear throughout Descartes's oeuvre.

According to Judovitz, this fundamental opacity, this changing between the quotidian and the knowing subject is constitutive of Descartes's strategies of purification, neutralization of the medium, and the ultimate grounding of his thought. Clarity of knowledge is bought at the price of unclarity in the texts responsible for creating knowledge. It is telling that whenever the derivation of the pure *I,* its isolation from the world and its indubitability, is supposed to be represented, Descartes tells a story. Judovitz concludes that the instance of the philosophical *I* can only be constituted by means of narrative forms and is therefore necessarily bound to literary modes of representation, conventions, and traditions. This dependency appears at least paradoxical: the pure *I* is represented as if it arises ex nihilo and independently of any representation.[32]

In the *Rules for the Direction of the Mind* (written in 1628, published posthumously in 1701), Descartes delimits science from the arts. The connection of the arts to the bodily habitus, to practices and physical dispositions, prevents their results from achieving universal validity. Science, which Descartes, unlike Galileo and Bacon, conceives as nonexperimental, deals by means of universal rules given in nature, "an *a priori* representation of what defines science."[33] The "order or the standard" of the world refers to the universal language of mathematics (rule 4); the world of objects must be brought into line with the preexisting order derived from this language and thus rendered subject to knowing. The universal order becomes visible for the "mind's eye" in a supersensuous "inner" seeing, from which the light of reason (*la raison*) emanates by means of a special faculty of knowledge, "intuition." In the language Descartes uses to characterize intuition, metaphors of empirical seeing slip in, which he otherwise rejects because of their illusory qualities. The "visual space" of intuition is purified, emptied of empirical elements; it is the space of pure thinking. What is seen is represented by means of "schematic figures," which designate and summarize the essential characteristics of objects.

It is no longer an arbitrary subject that is served by the Cartesian method and its rules. The subject is the creator of the world and in this respect akin to God; its world is idealized and formulated in a universal mathematical language (*mathesis universalis*). This language makes no practical or medial reference to the world, nor is its relation to the world one of similitude; it is an analytical representation of the inner order of the world, a world for itself that is manifest in the figures of the ideal language. Another attempt would be made at the beginning of the twentieth century, in Ludwig Wittgenstein's *Tractatus,* which posited the theory that the inner relations of the world can be replicated in a logical language, to realize the Cartesian dream of a pure description of the world. In the *Discourse on Method,* the effort is based on the indubitability of the pure thinking *I.* Here as well the *I* is conceived as unmediated, solipsistic, and cut off from all trace of history—an antimimetic construction par excellence. It is a unique, bodiless subject created wholly from within itself in thought. This *I* exists not only as a philosophical conception; it is at the same time a fiction introduced, presented, and ultimately invented in a literary text. It would not be representable without literary devices, nor, following Judovitz, would it even be thinkable. Descartes must resort to the fictional to represent the pure *I*. He invents a "hyperbolic" doubt, a doubt raised beyond all bounds, and an evil spirit that leads philosophers into illusion when they think; through dramatic enactment he pursues to the absolute limit of doubt the search for a final certainty on the part of an anonymous empirical *I*.

In the *Meditations,* the literary and fictional character of the Cartesian text is yet more pronounced. The narrated *I* acquires autobiographical contours, and these characterize the philosopher himself; the literary form of the meditation has a palpable weight of its own; its situational character is emphasized (Descartes sitting by the fire in a morning gown). A stage, a textual form, narrative elements from the repertoire of literature—and it is precisely now that the *I* fancies itself free of presuppositions. The devices of rhetoric and literature are deployed, as Judovitz demonstrates, to overcome rhetoric and literature. It is even possible to push her thought a step farther: both the *Discourse* and the *Meditations* use the literary pattern of the saint's legend. Descartes narrates the story of a conversion: the purified *I* takes the place of the saint following conversion. It is the condition of an "afterward," which only makes sense in reference to a before. The indubitably secure *I* plays a role in a conversion narrative, and in this respect a literary form is inextricably involved in its construction.[34]

Cartesian philosophy, once it has arrived at the "Archimedean point," confronts another problem. It is no more than a point and it is located outside the world. How is one supposed, from this point of departure, to construct a language that amounts to more than calculation? And how can an analytical order of the world be described without reference being made to some of the experiences, concepts, and modes of speaking and understanding found in the world? What world is being described? Judovitz points out how Descartes approximates the perfection of God; the self-created subject "now controls the once divinely created order"[35]—a calculated order, not a world inhabited by human being. Descartes reduces his construction of the world to nonsensuous images, which are strictly conceived as "schematic prototypes."[36] The creation of these images proceeds from an absolutely certain point, according to an exact method, by means of strictly defined rules—while reference to the empirical world obviously remains uncertain. With the renunciation of mimesis, Cartesian philosophy suffers a loss of the world, an absence of reference to the world of human being. This is one problem of antimimetic philosophy; we have already mentioned the other, Cartesian writing, the operation of which produces the indubitable thinking of an *I* devoid of characteristics, creates an unresolvable tension between the implicit presuppositions of the text and the purportedly nonpresuppositional nature of the text through the agency of the pure *I*. A paradox emerges in all of Descartes's major philosophical works in the resulting friction between the text and thought, which originates in his rejection of the linguistic mediation of philosophy.[37]

Dutch Painting of the Seventeenth Century

According to Alpers,[38] seventeenth-century Dutch art is based on a "visual culture" (in Baxandall's term) resulting from a combination of handicrafts, the technical spirit, scientific discoveries, traditional attitudes, and pedagogical ideas, which, in comparison to that of the Italian Renaissance, represents an entirely new way of seeing. The picture in Italian art is correctly defined by Alberti as "a framed surface or pane situated at a certain distance from a viewer who looks through it at a second or substitute world. In the Renaissance this world was a stage on which human figures performed significant actions based on the texts of the poets."[39] The mimetic imperative voiced by Horace in his "ut pictura poesis" holds valid in reverse for painting. Painting was narrative, a form in which "imitative skills were bound to narrative ends."[40] Dutch painting, in contrast, founded another pictorial mode as the art of describing; it does not tell what is, but shows it.

In these terms, we might consider Dutch art to have been especially mimetic. But Alpers's work (which admittedly does not deal directly with issues of mimesis) proves that there developed in Dutch art a type of representation that, according to the contemporary understanding of the handicraft tradition, the state of experimental science, the technique of the camera obscura, and the theory of vision, relied not on mimetic mediation but rather on the direct apprehension of images taken in from the world by the eye. Dutch painters did not experience the world of images as a particular world derived from the empirical world by means of mimetic processes. Expressed in their work instead is a conception according to which the creation of images in painting is equivalent to the optical generation of images in the eye. The basis for their attempt to overcome mimesis is scientific and technical development.

A particular pictorial mode, an "attentiveness to descriptive presence,"[41] characterizes seventeenth-century Dutch art. It does not change reality but depicts things directly in terms of their visual facticity. It paints whatever is visible in the world *naer het leven* or *uyt den geest;* it creates "images of the world as they are stored mnemonically in the mind."[42] The opposition between changing reality and depicting it directly designates the essential distinction deriving from two different sources of perception. Painters in the Italian Renaissance committed themselves to the mimetic activity of creating a new order in the world: they located in the space between the world of images and the painting of images the selective, organizing, and idealizing operation of the mind. They supposed themselves to be penetrating the surface of things into their depths. The artist, in Leonardo's understanding, "rather than giving himself over to the makings of nature . . . takes that making . . . upon himself. Everything then becomes a creature of *his* eye."[43] Artistic mimesis amounts to a fresh creation of the world, which is characterized by intellectuality and a sense of proportion and has the effect of rendering the inner order of things transparent. With the Dutch, in contrast, the image assumes the position of the eye, as a true mirror of the external world. Not strongly influenced by the organization of perspective, Dutch painters tend more to regard the image as a surface on which the world is described. They arrange their *descriptio* of the world according to the model of mapmaking, which identifies the descent of Dutch painting. "The graphic use of the term *descriptio* is not appropriate only to maps—which do inscribe the world on a surface—but also to northern pictures that share this interest."[44]

What is the meaning of this intention we find in Dutch painting to replicate "pure seeing"? The answer, according to Alpers, lies in a consideration of the contemporary scientific theory of vision, which, in the form of Johannes Kepler's theory, provided the basis for the descriptive attitude of Dutch painting. There was extraordinary interest in optical instruments at the time, especially lenses, magnifying glasses, microscopes, and telescopes; the Dutch clearly originated a new visual orientation. Artists were fascinated by the camera obscura and made rich use of it. Kepler regards the eye as an isolated object and puts the image on the retina at the center of his scientific interest (first in his *Paralipomena* of 1604). "This involves an extraordinary objectivity and an unwillingness to prejudge or to classify the world so imaged."[45] According to Kepler's theory, "vision is brought about by a picture [*pictura*] of the thing seen being formed on the concave surface of the retina."[46] Pictures of the world, in that they are replicated on the retina, have the same characteristics as painted pictures. "Artist's brushes paint a picture of the world outside the eye on the opaque screen of the retina in the back of the eye"; in Kepler's words, "The retina is painted with the colored rays of visible things."[47] Kepler explicitly terms the image on the retina *pictura*. The world outside the eye also consists of images, which he designates with the expression *imago rerum*. Such an image of things is projected onto the retina, appearing there as a pictura.

In his physical reconstruction of the mechanism of the eye, "Kepler not only defines the picture on the retina as a representation but turns away from the actual world to the world 'painted' there."[48] With this isolation of the process of seeing and the eye as an optical system from concrete human beings engaged in perception and experience, it is not only seeing that becomes objectified but also the image that is seen, the pictura. Seeing becomes an act of production; what is seen is a replication of what is produced. Everything that is involved in seeing is contained in the objectified image of perception—*ut pictura, ita visio,* or ''sight is like a picture.''[49] The artist, who is engaged solely in painting what he sees, namely, the image on his or her retina (pictura), faithfully reproduces the images that make up the world: the images on the surface of the painting are equivalent to those on the retina and those in the world. Dutch painters seek to describe the world without any mediation, without positing any intermediary space between the world and the image. The images on the retina are comparable to painters' mirrors, which reflect images found in the world. In this conception, art is no longer mimetic but rather a reflex of reality, whereby reality is defined in physical terms. The things of the world are left untouched; they are not integrated into a deeper order. The artist is reproducing no invisible sensations or passions of the soul.[50] Description true to nature requires a particular bearing toward the image; the painter has no influence on the process but instead subordinates himself so thoroughly to it that he is obliterated: the creator is supposed to disappear into his work.[51]

Dutch painting of the seventeenth century opposes to the mimetic replication of the world a mechanical method derived from science, technology, and the handicrafts. A comparable theorization of the artist will be undertaken in the nineteenth century, in the context of the invention of photography; photographic replication on a plate or film will be accepted as a neutral reproduction of what is and what is seen. Just as much as the achievement of the photographer, the involvement of the medium in the process of photographic reproduction will be entirely overlooked. Dutch painting and photography both belong to the broad current of what Alpers terms an ''alternative visual culture,'' which is organized around principles other than those worked out in Italian Renaissance painting. To the extent that Dutch painting develops and deploys apparently objective and formal methods, it tends to mask the involvement of the subject, as well as the interference of artistic techniques, in the process by which images are produced.

Part IV

From Imitation to the Constitution of the Creative Subject

Aesthetic theory during the Enlightenment is devoted to an intense discussion of the nature of mimesis and the mimesis of nature. The concept of nature broadens in the first phase of the debate in France, England, and Germany, whereas the concept of mimesis becomes restricted to imitation. At the center of the argument is the question of the nature of the world produced by means of artistic mimesis: Just how is it constituted? How closely tied is it to social reality? Can this created world legitimately make reference to worlds other than the empirical one?

The eighteenth century explicates imitation, the key word in mimesis theory of the time, by reference to the concept of similarity. The approach does not prove productive; it bears scarcely any gain at all for art, and it drives the disputants into pointless subtlety and theoretical dead ends. The broadening of the concept of nature is another story: it is not only the objective world that is fit for artistic reproduction; now the possibility arises of the existence of other worlds and ways of seeing, which are perhaps what literature is most capable of representing and, in a certain sense, even discovering—the worlds of interior images and processes, or impressions, the subjective, and the strange.

The debate over artistic mimesis enters a new phase in the second half of the eighteenth century. Now the question becomes the way in which artistic mimesis comes into existence. Compared to the earlier posing of the question, the methodological slant is much more precise and leads more powerfully to technical and theoretical solutions. How is it possible by means of signs to produce symbolically constituted worlds? What rules are applied in the process? What are the limitations that must be respected? In place of a vague philosophy of mimesis invoking the authority of classical literature and poetics, there now emerges a way of thinking based on semiotics, aesthetic criticism, and judgments of taste. Aristotle remains the great authority, but the rigid neo-Aristotelianism of seventeenth-century French dramatic theory is replaced by an interpretation that strives to fulfill not the letter but the intention of the *Poetics*. It remains questionable, to be sure, whether this reanimation of the Aristotelian definition of tragedy does justice to classical ideas, but in regard to the bourgeois tragedy, it fits plausibly and effectively into the broader ideational context of the eighteenth century.

No such adaptation of old ideas fails to introduce essential changes; Enlightenment drama occupies a wholly different position in context than the drama of earlier epochs. The theory of catharsis becomes the conceptual mechanism by which the stage is made the preeminent site of the unfolding of the bourgeois cult of emotion. Drama permeates the world of actions with interior motives, wishes, and feelings; it renders the world transparent in reference to them. This emotionalization of practical life is characteristic of the rising class; it comes to expression in the theater, is rendered valuable by being made to convey an ethical quality; emotion, in particular, compassion, is attributed universal validity. These apparently universal human feelings have a political meaning. "The awakening of the bourgeois intelligentsia takes place in the private interior space to which the state had confined subordinate members. Every step toward the outside of this space is a step toward the light, an act of enlightenment. As R. Kosellek has written, the Enlightenment progresses along its triumphal march in the same degree as it expands private interiority into a public sphere."

The theatrical heroes of the bourgeois tragedy, by presenting spectators with a vision of their equals, facilitate the rendering public of private feelings. The theater represents the capacity for emotion as a defining characteristic of the bourgeoisie. Theatrical mimesis contributes to the process by endowing emotional expression with a universally recognizable scenic form and, through the codification of public modes of expression, defining the contours of interiority itself. Moreover, since theatrical mimesis helps share self-representative emotional behavior, it contributes to the bourgeoisie's symbolic self-presentation. In the sixteenth and seventeenth centuries, mimesis assisted self-authorization for individuals protesting against political authority; in the Enlightenment, it contributes to the self-legitimation of an entire social stratum and to political critique, which, in morally based theater (Schiller, in particular), becomes a court of judgment over dominant politics.

The theater formulates models of aesthetic action, and these models become increasingly important for bourgeois self-understanding as time goes on. Mimesis becomes an instance of mediation between interior life and the public sphere. It expands its influence within the emotional world, at the same time subjecting emotional expression to standards of validity derived from taste and probability. Taste is a matter of judgment; everyday probability, one of observation. The two taken together are what lend mimetic artistic productions their realistic, socially acute character. In the anthropology of emerging bourgeois society, Aristotelian concepts are recast and newly interpreted— from within the problematic circumstance that neither the society nor its anthropology exists yet in delineated form. Thus arises the singular situation of theatrical mimesis actively involved in the formation of society and its anthropology (image of man, humanity, liberality, freedom of the will, morality). The drama offers to the public, for its social interpretation and self-representation, various positions and roles of its own design and formulation: the male head of the family, the virtuous businessman, the young man struggling against his desires, the discharged officer.

The effects of theatrical mimesis are felt far beyond the stage. It transforms the world of daily life into a dramatic text, in which individuals all have a role to play. Each person is individually responsible for formulating his or her own part; each must assert a symbolic self-presentation against the others: play-acting becomes a category of social behavior. Rousseau, in his *Confessions,* stresses the dramatic character of social role-playing. At the same time, however, he represents role-playing in terms of a fate suspended above social relationships. Denis Diderot, in contrast, isolates playacting as a theme in reflections spanning both the theatrical and the social world (in his *Paradox of Acting*). Not only in the theater but also in the world of social practice the body must be cultivated, to become capable of effective emotional expression and thereby evoke desired reactions. The theater fashions models of expressive action, a task that it—in the work of its great actors—is optimally suited to fulfill.

There are ideal models available in nature, for Diderot and also for Gotthold Ephraim Lessing, and it is incumbent on authors and actors to understand them. Diderot and Lessing both hold fast to the idea of a mimesis of a preexisting universal order of nature; but both are headed for new ways of thinking. They recognize that signifying systems and media not only shape what is represented but also are critically involved in the production of it. In *Laocoön,* Lessing renews two of the essential categories of oral culture: plot and time. On the stage and when watching or reading, the plot that the writer imagined and, at the same time, himself preserved in a plot, in the writing, is brought back to mind. The mimetic process consists in a revitalization of an inner world that author, actor, and recipient all share in common.

What most interests Lessing in the literary media of speech and writing is their temporality. Temporality becomes the defining characteristic of authenticity in Rousseau. His autobiography becomes the writing down of a life to preserve the impressions of a life lived. Rousseau's novels describe a second type of mimesis, in which there is no literary world produced, but rather a self is made, a modern person with a birth, a unique individual. In the *Confessions,* Rousseau produces his own literary self, which he offers as his real one; in

Émile, the teacher creates the self of his pupil; in *Nouvelle Héloïse,* Saint-Preux forms the self of his beloved.

In Rousseau's novels, mimesis becomes the process by which an individual self is formed. The persons being formed are seduced by interior images; they desire to achieve the self that the seducer, the writer, the teacher, has shown them. Mimesis regulates the power of imagination; it evokes the desire to realize the images and thus leads to social action. In his novels, Rousseau anticipates the social mode in which mimesis will tend to operate in the nineteenth century. Toward the end of the eighteenth theory, aesthetic theorists lose interest in mimesis; it seems nearly as if the significance of the concept for art has been lost. Simultaneous with the decline in aesthetics, however, mimetic processes become increasingly important for the production of the social world. Mimesis begins to become an all-encompassing social category, if one that is barely recognized in theory.

12

Problems in the Imitation of Nature in the Eighteenth Century

The great eighteenth-century debates about the imitation of nature, especially in England and Germany, show systematically how profoundly the concept of mimesis undergoes reformulation. They are remarkable discussions—which attempt in every possible way to define art as becoming similar to nature. None of the essential concepts in the disputes is even approximately explicated or analytically clarified. What is "nature"? Under what conditions is an artifact to be regarded as "similar" to nature? What distinguishes imitation from other types of reference? It is best to adopt a cautious attitude toward aesthetic debates of such questionable philosophical consistency. If we are seeking to arrive at an overall judgment, there is little sense in reconstructing individual positions and exploring their nuances. That is the task of historical philology, and the results would obviously not tell us what the disputes were finally all about. Two positions in the debate are clear: mimesis as a concept is restricted to the "imitation of nature"; and "imitation" is understood essentially in terms of the "similarity" existing between an artifact and a natural model.[1]

Both conditions represent substantial reductions of the concept from today's perspective, and earlier interpretations of mimesis were often essentially richer as well. But, located in historical context, the interpretive narrowing of the concept can be understood as a strategic move: the stipulation that art should imitate nature frees literature from the combinational schemata of rhetoric and its descriptive conventions. Authors must now find their own individual modes of representation; they should no longer say what is appropriate and customary, what one is obliged to say about specific natural objects, but derive their descriptive expressions from the objects themselves.

How is this task to be achieved? One answer is that the path to the precise representation of nature is observation. But this response is not adequate. Those characteristics of nature that come to verbal expression are not subject to observation, and the question in the first place is one of just what can be apprehended in direct observation. Sensuous impressions, after all, cannot be inscribed directly in the text. Objects affect the senses; but in order for them to be captured in language, they must be assigned verbal expressions that are "exactly suited to them" or otherwise appropriate. How can such a relation be conceived?

The modern position maintains that observations are determined by language and that it is not possible to have objects existing independently of language. In this formulation, the whole problem of the relation between the two areas of observation and language does not arise at all. The general assumption in the eighteenth century was that a correspondence pertains between things external to observation and things internal to the observer: the objects of external reality correspond to specific representations in the mind of the observer, which, in turn, make reference to the objects. The truth of observation lies in the possible correspondence between the world existing outside the individual and the ideas evoked by the examination of that world. The call for writers to get free of the rhetorical canon and turn as observers toward nature makes sense in the context of correspondence theory, which was the prevailing theory of the time.

Hilary Putnam gives us an idealizing summary of the basic characteristics of this theory.[2]

> The oldest form of the correspondence theory of truth, and one which endured for approximately 2,000 years, is one that ancient and medieval philosophers attributed to Aristotle. That Aristotle actually held it I am not sure; but it is suggested by his language. I shall call it the *similitude theory of reference;* for it holds that the relation between the representations in our minds and the external objects that they refer to is literally a *similarity.*
>
>   The theory, like modern theories, employed the idea of a mental representation. The presentation, the mind's image of the external thing, was called a *phantasm* by Aristotle. The relation between the phantasm and the external object by virtue of which the phantasm represents the external object to the mind is (according to Aristotle) that the phantasm *shares a form* with the external object. Since the phantasm and the external object are similar (share the form), the mind, in having available the phantasm, also has directly available the very *form* of the external object.[3]

If we interpret the demand that writers imitate nature from the perspective of the similitude theory of reference, the narrowing of the concept of mimesis becomes understandable: writers, by making recourse to their ideas, internal images, and impressions of the world, emancipate literary mimesis from the representational conventions of rhetoric and open up to the individual the possibility of subjective writing. The demand that literature imitate nature, therefore, amounts to an intensification of the *subjective* aspect of literary production undertaken in reference to external objects. A new relation between subject and object comes into being, one characteristic of mimetic processes: literary mimesis expresses the internal by aiming at the external. Interiority has as yet no worldly character; the theorists of the seventeenth and eighteenth centuries continue to conceive of the inner world as a reflex of the outer world and only in correspondence with it. Only with Rousseau and Kant will this tie be broken.

The reference made by ideas to the external world is understood in the seventeenth and eighteenth centuries as a relation of similarity, so that individualization, intensification, and subjectivization are considered the results of a process by which the internal and external become similar. Internal to the writer is a mental mirror of external things, and his or her descriptions of the world are an expression of what is internal.[4] Mimesis, in this interpretation, is understood as imitation, depiction, or copy. In the modern conceptualization, a neutral reproduction, a copy of the world by means of language, even if all that is sought is a copy, is not considered possible. Precisely the contrary assumption on the part of the Enlightenment is what constitutes the difficulty of its theory of imitation.

Certain Enlightenment aestheticists, like Johann Christoph Gottsched, hold fast to a strict conceptual interpretation of imitation in the sense of an act by which nature is depicted. This relatively clear initial principle comes at the cost of insoluble problems later on over the definition of what the term "similar" is supposed to mean. It turns out, of course, that literature is by no means characterized by a copying of the external contours of things and events. Other theorists who postulate a relation of similarity between an artwork and its model move on to explicate similarity on the basis of anticipated, conventional, and probable behavior. They lose sight of the literal sense of "imitation": how can artistically represented actions or objects be considered imitations, if they fail to make reference to a genuine original? Finally, some theorists give priority to the process by which the internal comes to expression. The author, in this version, is outfitted with quasi-divine characteristics, becomes a creator of the world. The liberation from the apparatus of rhetoric finds a suitable form in this position, which takes seriously the autonomy and subjectivity of the artwork made possible by the liberation. Karl Philipp Moritz assumes what is no doubt the most progressive position.[5] On critical points, in accentuated form, he anticipates Kant's aesthetic theory and Goethe's theory of symbols prior to the publication of either. In Moritz, the creative idea and the sovereignty of the worldmaker goes so far beyond the conceptual tradition of mimesis that his theory must not be regarded as representing a modern version of imitation but rather as marking the end of that entire tradition.

All interpretations of mimesis as imitation rely on the similitude theory of reference, and their essential problems stem from a weakness that necessarily accompanies it. What these theories have not yet recognized is the difficulty inherent in the concept of similitude. It is simply not possible to maintain the similarity between an object and an idea in the way the imitation theorists have attempted to do. To what are the mental representations supposed to be similar? To things as they appear to us? If this were so, we would have to embrace all kinds of perceptual errors, sensory illusions, and subjective opinions. The reference must ultimately be a matter of things as they exist *in themselves,* independently of any individual observer, independently of their "effect on *us,* on beings with our rational natures and our biological constitutions."[6] The ideas that we actually have of objects are not copies of any reality that is presumed to exist independently of mind. "*Nothing at all* we say about any object describes the object as it is 'in itself.' "[7] We are not capable of attaining pure knowledge of objects in isolation from human modes of perception; we always perceive an object in terms of some one of its aspects. There is no way to get around this anthropocentric frame condition. The character of an object having multiple aspects raises a critical problem for the identification of similarity: whether an object appears to us to be "similar" to other objects depends on which aspect we have chosen. The number of aspects available for selection is not subject to any a priori limitation.

We can therefore produce countless similarities, so that any given objects can be made "similar" to each other; or, as Putnam expresses it, "In fact, *everything is similar to everything else in infinitely many respects.*"[8] For this reason it is not possible to found a theory of truth on the quality of similarity. That which is regarded as "similar" is a function of the aspect according to which it was observed and to that extent inseparable from the observer's subjectivity and language.

In attempting, albeit on the basis of untenable theory, to substantiate their interpretation of mimesis, aestheticists of the eighteenth century nevertheless opened the way to a future solution to the problems and difficulties in which they entangled themselves: what they are concerned with is an objective relationship between ideas and external objects; their discussion in fact promotes the subjectivity, autonomy, and creativity of the individual artist. With every step they take in this direction, they approach an idealistic position and distance themselves from the tradition of mimesis in which the internal and external existed into a balanced relation. Marking the end of this development is Moritz's pathbreaking treatise, *Über die bildende Nachahmung des Schönen.*

The transformations the concept of mimesis undergoes in the eighteenth century become evident first in English literature, which anticipated changes on the Continent. Rose Zimbardo, on the basis of detailed individual studies in the period from 1660 to 1732, depicts the transition from the aesthetics of the Renaissance to those of the bourgeois epoch.[9] Up until the beginning of the seventeenth century, the object of poetics is not yet the noumenal world subject to immediate perception. At the end of the century, writers' interests have already turned to experimentally based knowledge and a culture of interiority.

The fundamental transformation is characterized by a change in the conceptual and literary field: toward the end of the seventeenth century, the novel supplants the drama as the major and most favored genre; in dramatic literature, the comedy gains in influence. Novelistic literature is precisely suited to the development of a new way of speaking that is capable of lending expression to the contemporary developments in the conception of nature. Beginning in 1690, the novel dedicates itself to the depiction of empirical reality. People understand the drama of the time, in contrast, as an imitation of the form of an ideal reality;[10] words are taken to be images, shadows, or doubles of ideas, to which they were supposed to be similar. The dramatist's task is to glean universal substance from the familiar materials of empirical life, to abstract from there to ideas, and to grasp the latter conceptually.[11] The form of nature is presented from the viewpoint of the ideas.[12]

The development of the novel at the end of the seventeenth century gradually displaces this view; reference to empirical particularity and the ability to represent inner psychological experience becomes more important than ideational expression. A "new reality" is opened up in the novel; the vernacular is rendered suitable for literature; irony and ridicule become formative stylistic elements. With the representation of characters from daily life, first in the novel, later in the theater as well, readers and spectators are summoned to identification, to enter into the psyche of another person; this all amounts to the creation of a new representational mode, which calls on recipients to imagine the experiences and adventures of literary characters. An attitude aimed at personal interest, curiosity, and involvement develops among readers and spectators. Earlier plays, such as those of the 1660s, do not yet possess this personal and subjective dimension; they function more like tableaus.[13] The plots and events they portray are occasions for the representation of ideas.[14] These earlier works strive for ideal truth and the dramatic imitation of ideas. In the 1670s and 1680s, "truth and reality become a matter of perspective":[15] contrary ways of seeing are directly confronted with one another, heroic greatness and ideal truth, on the one hand, and base, antiheroic dimensions and mute as well as experimental "facts," on the other. The imitation of ideas appears to have become intolerable without an antithetical reduction to the actual from the other side.[16]

Toward the end of the sixteenth century, a materially oriented, naturalistic way of seeing comes to prevail over the ideal one. In a comparison between Thomas Shadwell and John Dryden, Zimbardo demonstrates the effect of the new conception in dramatic theory. Shadwell is still of the view that dramatists who imitate the empirically observable present on the stage confront their public with something "unnatural" seeming. Dryden has reasons of a completely different type for rejecting the representation of the particular: a writer could represent any specific individual but prefers not to do so for social or moral, but in any case not aesthetic, reasons.[17]

Zimbardo dates the breakthrough of the new aesthetic conception to the period between 1680 and 1690. This is when the dramatic hero becomes a character in the modern sense; the hero becomes a "fictional internal arena."[18] Writers simulate the speaking style of empirical persons and use it to characterize their heroes. Dramatic characters have the task, through action, of identifying their inner qualities; their deeds are nothing other than external manifestations of feelings and thoughts, an interiority directed outward.[19] The context of the plot in the drama, as a representation of character, increases in significance; "interior, psychological truth" is established as "the new locus of reality."[20] What drama is supposed to imitate is actual phenomenal reality; "the representational idiom of these plays refers outside the works themselves and finds meaning in the justice with which the 'reality' in them corresponds to the reality evident to our ordinary perception."[21]

The dramatic is subjected to the rules of quotidian probability: dramatic characters are supposed to produce the illusion of an inner reality; they become portraits of individuals like ourselves.[22] In temporal terms, the drama is measured according to our own experience: three hours in the theater correspond to three hours of actual life. The goal of the new conception is to effect a change in the spectators: their nature is to be improved as their affective qualities undergo formation.[23]

German poetics of the period remain strongly in the grip of tradition; "from the last third of the seventeenth century up until Gottsched's *Critischer Dichtkunst*" they present a "largely unitary entity, determined primarily by the past and scarcely open to the future."[24] Poetics theory is dominated essentially by rhetoric, which determines "the objective, structure, and methods, as well as nearly all basic concepts."[25] Mimesis is construed according to formal rules as the "imitation of nature," which has the result of expanding the concept to encompass everything "that can be taken as credible according to logic and convention"; and it extends "to the miraculous and manifestly supernatural . . . insofar as the latter is authoritatively certified by the Bible, classical antiquity, or other traditions."[26]

Christian Wolff, in the German tradition, is still characterizing the imitation of nature primarily as the "the repetition of the rational relationships of natural things in literature or works of art."[27] A revision of this concept of imitation is prompted especially by two foreign influences, Joseph Addison's *Spectator* and Jean-Baptiste Dubos. According to Addison, genius is independent of the rules of nature and capable of poetically transforming empirical reality. The beauty of representation wrought by genius exercises its effect directly on the soul of the recipient.[28] The traditional conception of objective reality, however, runs counter to this idea of addressing subjectivity directly. Imagination, as the "organ of the poetic representation of reality," devises "subjective, artistic responses to empirically recognized reality''; it becomes the ''medium of the subjective mastery'' of nature.[29] But this new concept, in its initial dissemination, falls far short of the breadth and profundity that it will later attain, especially in Kant and Moritz.

H. P. Herrmann gives us a detailed survey of the history of the concept of imagination in Germany:[30] until the eighteenth century, sensuousness is not yet understood as an autonomous psychological faculty; the poetic *delectatio* remains, in full correspondence to traditional rhetorical notions, subordinate to docere. The intuitive moments of poesie have not yet been fully discovered; inventio has not yet taken on the meaning of *creatio*.[31] From 1700, fantasy, under the rubric of imagination, begins to make a place for itself in poetics; the expression, however, initially denotes only the traditional concept of *ingenium*.[32] An objective order is attributed to nature. The historical form of this order can indeed change, but it does not lose ''the character of self-evidence and certainty in principle.''[33] Decorum, as a conventional repertoire of characteristics belonging to nature, has a self-evident validity according to rhetorical doctrine. '' 'Nature' is . . . never meant simply as matter and a field of objects, but always as an ordered form, the mutual relations of the elements of which are bound in advance by rules—which is the way the demand for mimesis can be directly reflected in the formal rules of poesie.''[34]

The rhetorical doctrine of imitation prevails until Gottsched, who attempts to anchor his poetics in the regularity of nature.[35]

> While he does indeed clarify his predecessors' system of rules and present it in the fashionable garb of Wolffian terminology, the adoption of philosophical *termini* remains external. . . . Precisely the concept which he so credited himself for introducing into German poetics, that of the imitation of nature, contains nothing that goes beyond his forerunners.[36]

Johann Jakob Bodmer and Johann Jakob Breitinger also stick to the ground of the traditional conception; according to their theory of poetics, literature renders the object itself present by means of the poetic image. Their conception of a ''painterly literature,'' however, does introduce a new accent: in order for writers to evoke images, they must themselves be impassioned; literature must proceed from experience.[37] With this idea a critical step is taken in the direction of a new conception of nature.

> As the first poeticists in Germany they no longer have a formal understanding of the demand for the imitation of nature as a regulative principle including *inventio,* but rather a substantive one as the substantial orientation of poesie toward the reality, which is presented to the individual as a given and must first of all be apprehended in its uniqueness.[38]

The literary imagination is referred to the observation of nature; nature is the mentor of poesie.[39]

The mimetic imperative in this analysis is understood as a prohibition placed on the productive activity of the writer. But, at the same time, this view brings with it a new accomplishment on the part of the knowing subject: it is up to the subject to observe nature precisely and to express in language what is given in experience. Bodmer and Breitinger "opened the horizon within which the problem of imitation can be raised in a modern sense, which, as such, is simultaneously the problem of aesthetic illusion."[40] Incumbent on the work of art from now on are epistemological and formative tasks. Still bound to the model of nature, though now empirical nature, the artwork is attributed the power to create a world on the basis of individual and subjective experience.[41]

For Moritz, "imitation" is primarily a productive capacity, a nearly autonomous act of worldmaking as an achievement of the subject.[42] The receptive side of mimesis no longer plays any role: the beautiful "cannot enter into us through imitation—but, if it is to be imitated, must necessarily be developed anew from *within ourselves*."[43] We produce and express the beautiful. External expression is necessarily the symbolization of internal processes of production. Why, then, does Moritz continue to speak of "imitation"? Because he calls for the imitation, not of objects or actions, but of the process of creation. Plastic artists re-create on a smaller scale; they make a "copy of supreme beauty in the grand entirety of nature."[44] Their formative power unfolds within themselves and manifests itself to the outer world. The creator possesses in microcosm the internal interrelations of the world and renders them visible to observers: on the surface is manifest that which "is concealed within the integument of *existence,* which itself already outweighs all phenomenal appearance." The "internal essence" that is transformed into the phenomenality of art is re-created natural beauty. This is why the "brilliant work" of the artist is "more enchanting" than reality.[45]

In cases of genius, the horizon of active power is as broad as that of nature itself.[46] Moritz marks an end to a receptive and contemplative attitude toward art: "The beautiful . . . cannot be recognized; it must be brought forth—or *felt.*"[47] These two capacities, of feeling and imagination, "encompass *more* than the capacity for thought."[48] Aesthetic production gains complete autonomy; "the bringing forth of the beautiful [is] the supreme perfection of our active power."[49] The autonomy of art is a constituent element of the autonomy of the human species as such, which possesses "in itself the ultimate purpose of its existence";[50] "our inherent essence" tends "to dissolve" in imitation, in which "that which is perfect strives once again toward perfection."[51]

To the capacity for imitation, Moritz ascribes the "formative power," which is the essential characteristic of *poiēsis.* The artwork is not understood as solely as a reference to a prior world but acquires the character of a world of its own. Closed off like this from other worlds, the artwork now represents a fundamental transcendence of its former mimetic character. As Adorno will show, the work of art will have to overcome its isolation from the social world for the latter to have a fully mimetic, while still autonomous, character. On the one hand, the idealistic interpretation of the artwork initiated by Moritz raises the creator above reality: the author of the work becomes more powerful than reality. On the other, this same author bows in humility before his or her own creation. From the point of this conceptual turn, it is only a small step to the view that reality is constituted by means of principles analogous to those of the literary world. If to this is added the view that mimesis of literature is comparable to mimesis of the social world, there develops out of the romantic conception a realistic conception of art. It is possible to see, therefore, that Moritz's innovative aesthetic prepares the way to the future theory of art—from idealism through romanticism to realism.

The tradition of mimesis is definitively broken with Kant's critique of the similitude theory of reference. Our ideas of "objects," in Kantian epistemology, are not copies of things that exist independently of mind. Kant retains as a postulate of reason the existence of a reality independent of mind; he designates it the realm of the things-in-themselves, or noumena, of which no representation exists. Kant's aesthetics makes a clean sweep of mimesis, which is left no role whatever in aesthetic processes. The new ruling concepts are those of imagination, disinterested satisfaction, and purposefulness without purpose. The subject characterized by these concepts is one that makes aesthetic judgments; it is equipped with an intellectual apparatus suited to the purpose and the gift of "the capacity to communicate," so that it makes these judgments without reference to tradition and physical behavioral practice, based on a minimum of social content. While Kant maintains the objectivity of the external world,[52] even if it is in principle unknowable in its own being, Rousseau's epistemology leads to a radically subjective self-demarcation from the empirical world. Rousseau pursues this path with utter consistency, presenting himself as a nearly autonomous self for whom it is possible "to attribute the moments of contingency in life to an invisible power of the subject."[53]

Imagination, taste, and disinterested satisfaction become the guiding ideas of the new aesthetic, which encounters a public,[54] an entire social stratum unified through, among other things, its common taste.[55] Both philosophical and social developments are critically involved in the upheaval in aesthetics in the eighteenth century. The philosophy of art of the rising bourgeoisie constructs aesthetic objects in a way that is then taken over in the social sphere. The taste in beautiful objects becomes a *social* category, possessed of validity for both producers and recipients. On poesie—no differently than on nature— devolves the task of awakening feelings and embodying them in symbolic representation. This process of awakening and representing transpires in a series of individual acts—which are quite beyond the reach of social control and capable, in principle, of encompassing the whole world.

13

Mimesis in the Theater
of the Enlightenment

Like Corneille and Racine, the writers and dramatic theorists of the Enlightenment are bourgeois in origin, but their position in society is a different one. They write for the bourgeois audience and represent bourgeois themes, though we may as well say that they are the ones who produce the themes in the first place.[1] The critical innovation in Enlightenment theater, compared to the theater of absolutism, is this newly constituted area of substantive concern. The subject about which everything revolves in social practice and in literature is professional work; everyone, spectators along with writers and theorists, pursues this theme. The authors of Enlightenment drama represent the social power of a group, of an entire class, but the class itself has fundamentally changed since the period of absolutism. Writers are no longer involved in the constitution and dissemination of actual power, the workings of which have moved to the economy. Power, rather than achieving visibility in great representational tableaus, now shuns representation.[2]

The cult of feeling is the bourgeoisie's first original contribution to literature in the postabsolutist period, the time in which the bourgeoisie first begins shaping the medium of language to serve its interests. The compassion bourgeois tragedy aims to stimulate—is it not the fulfillment of Aristotle's call for catharsis, which seems obviously to imply an emotionalization of theater? Are bourgeois dramatists not justified in claiming to have found a modern answer to the problem of the purifying effect of theater? But the new bourgeois tragedy was not born of discussions inside aesthetics. The reverse is closer to the truth. The popularity of the comédie *larmoyante* finds an ideal theoretical starting point in Aristotle's conception of limited releases of emotion as therapeutic, but it in fact designates a place where the abilities characteristic of the bourgeoisie can be played out: the ability to have genuine feelings; the esteem for humanity and compassion.

Writing in the tradition of Georg Lukács, Peter Szondi has studied Enlightenment bourgeois drama for signs of a power struggle, in particular, for signs of class struggle.[3] He finds, at most, discreet suggestions of conflict over aristocratic ideals. What Szondi fails to recognize is the political dimension of the cult of feeling. Bourgeois authors of the time are interested in genuine feelings, in concern for other people, sympathy for them, in an altruistic, philanthropic attitude. They represent all of this in terms of universal concepts, which seem to refer without distinction to the whole of humanity, which seem to contain no delimiting qualities. Political meaning must be discovered, exposed, behind the apparent neutrality. While the bourgeoisie's new conceptual terminology indeed has a universal character, it is designed for specifically bourgeois purposes. The human capacities that the terminology designates, as well as the actions through which such capacities find realization, are reserved for the bourgeoisie.

Altruism, fellowship, and philanthropy are bourgeois virtues; a man who pursues a profession, provides for a family, and arranges his life according to the bourgeois ethic is capable of these virtues. We are seeing here the emotional side of the bourgeois idea of competition: subject to relentless conflict over social position, the bourgeois reserves for himself certain spheres that are exempt from competition, spheres in which he is able to live out his emotions, the *doux commerce*.[4] Family feeling, care for one's own, love for wife and children and for fatherland and hometown, solicitude toward the young, attention to education and culture—these are not duties taken over from previous generations, as in feudalism, but one side of the comprehensive ethic of a new social class. The other side includes the professional ethic and the obligation to act in accord with an instrumental calculus. All the traits we have listed— instrumentalism, economic competition, professional life guided by ethical principles, emotionality restricted to specific spheres—characterize the bourgeoisie. These values were never those of the nobility, and the lower strata (the working class had not yet formed), so ran the judgment, were incapable of them.

Bourgeois dramatic principles—whether as the intention of individual authors or not—articulate a political theme by declaring a monopoly on these characteristics for the bourgeoisie and contrasting its values to those of other social groups, in particular, the nobility. The thematic constellation that Diderot presents as the veritable discovery of his bourgeois comedy,[5] the *père de famille,* the man of the house with his concern over the absent son and the enamored daughter, takes on a political significance in that it is addressed exclusively to the bourgeoisie. It simply passes over other social classes.

The father of the family! What a subject in a century such as ours, where it seems that no one has the least idea what the father of the family is![6]

The claim raised by Diderot's drama is this: this is our world; we created it with the feelings, the morality, and the culture that characterize it. The issue is not what is special about and particular to the bourgeois, not about what he has of value. Those who belong to the bourgeois world are invited to witness themselves on stage; everyone else is turned away. The bourgeois world is presented in the secure assumption that it is the world of tomorrow: the bourgeois household in Diderot and the merchant's office in Lillo. Expressed in sociological terms, the cult of emotion in England, France, and Germany—above and beyond national particularities—identifies a corresponding social membership: the bourgeoisie belongs; all other social groups are left aside; they are not among those included in the play. The play is written for them only in one sense, to parade their exclusion before their eyes. The capacity for feeling is a kind of entry ticket into the mimesis of bourgeois theater in the eighteenth century, a prerequisite for access to the new social and theatrical world.

Dramatic mimesis in the Enlightenment does not side openly with power, as it did in absolutist theater; it declares itself nonpolitical. It claims to be speaking for all. But, now as then, theater is permeated by power, even though it no longer stands in service to the prince and attests itself nonpartisan. Theater is not now contributing to the constitution of power but is instead exemplifying it; in every play there is an example for the eyes of the public of the rising social power of the bourgeois class. The new comédie larmoyante, the *comédie sérieuse,* and the bourgeois tragedy are all constructed according to the same principle: they summon the audience to participation and, at the same time, supervise the right to participate.

Lessing's reinterpretation of fear as "compassion directed toward ourselves"[7] is an example of the way the mechanism of identification operates. Szondi glosses the quote as follows: "Thus is the postulated similarity of dramatic characters and spectators brought into the definition of the tragic effect, and thereby into tragedy itself."[8] Diderot proposes an outright sociological barrier in *Entretiens sur le fils naturel:* it is not characters who ought to be shown in bourgeois theater but the *conditions,* the social situations of the characters, "les devoirs des conditions, leur avantages, leurs inconvénients, leur dangers ont été mis sur la scène."[9] Part of the performance, so to speak, is the spectators' recognition that the conditions being depicted before them are theirs as well.

What is supposed to be represented in theater is the social practice of the bourgeoisie; bourgeois daily life is the object of the onstage world. But the bourgeois drama is not the actual site where feelings come into being; the drama presupposes the presence of the feelings in the audience. The public goes into the theater with a particular emotional bearing; theater guides the feelings, ultimately raising them to the intensified pitch of horror or pity. The bourgeois spectators are all but forced into the play. In their imaginations they become equals among the equals standing on the stage. The representation of a social milieu onstage which compares to their own situation and status facilitates audience identification, which, in bourgeois dramatic practice, turns out to be more a socialization than a psychologization of the stage. The spectator is constantly being told, you too are a dramatic character.

The identification doctrine is in the first instance a social mechanism that functions to admit and exclude spectators. The mechanism can be exploited for pedagogical purposes, a side effect that Enlightenment dramatists never tire of citing in justification of the theater. Also in the first instance, the strategy of dramatic identification is aimed at members of other social groups: "By having Thorowgood explain to his obedient apprentices on stage the tasks and merits of the merchant class, Lillo does the same with his public."[10] The bourgeois public requires no such instruction, but the indicative gesture does have an effect on the nonbourgeois spectator. Lillo's *Merchant of London* is shown in special performances "on Lord Mayor's Day as well as during the Christmas and Easter holidays to an audience consisting largely of apprentices, for the education of whom rich bourgeois financed the performance."[11] The pedagogical stance of the bourgeois tragedy, when it confronts members of lower social groups, is the expression of a strategy of power: social inferiors are to be formed according to a specific image; they are to be brought into conformity with the newly rising society. "Lillo's *Merchant of London* serves to praise and disseminate these bourgeois virtues [the spirit of capitalism in Max Weber's sense], and it is this intention, rather than the social status of his characters, that makes the play a bourgeois drama."[12] But the *Merchant of London* is not simply a piece of propaganda; the bourgeois model of virtue popularizes and legitimizes itself in other ways more effectively, in particular, through the economic and political successes of the bourgeoisie and the power and endorsement it enjoys. As the self-representation of the bourgeoisie, the model is part of a symbolic order. It belongs to the system that constitutes the power of the bourgeoisie, especially in the nineteenth century: it manifests its virtues, which, in turn, stand in need of manifestation. The manifestation itself of virtue belongs among the virtues; thus the moral insistence of the bourgeoisie.

The capacity for feeling, understood as a kind of access ticket, has two sides. First, the bourgeois belongs among those for whom the play was written; he participates in its values and can put himself in the position of the main character. This is his path into the play. But there is also a path coming from the other direction, from inside the play out. This one is just as important as the first: spectators are meant to take something away from the theater; they are supposed to leave the performance changed. In the initial phase, this ambition amounts to little more than a declaration of will; positive pedagogy belongs among the rituals and conventions used to argue the utility of theater during the Enlightenment. With this ideology of the theater as an institution of moral betterment, however, the sphere of instrumental thinking expands to encompass art. The play supplies spectators with an image of the bourgeois and a theatricalization of his situation. Both of these things can be turned to good advantage under the conditions of social practice. Instead of being encouraged to repress vital feelings, which can be the effect of a moral didactic, the bourgeois is given an opportunity to enhance his social self-representation. Theatrical performances serve as a lesson, open his eyes, show him the way, and put in his hands new dramaturgical and choreographical devices, which will be of use in his private life.

There are dangers written on the wall: a Lady Milford, drives, unruly passions, and so on. They may threaten an apprentice, but the bourgeois has learned long since how to control himself. He can watch serenely the fate of seducers and failures work itself out. He wants to have his emotions, wants to enjoy his compassion, and, above this, wants to improve his symbolic capacity for self-representation; he wants to carry his cultural profits home.[13] He learns, by understanding, what Erving Goffman terms the "presentation of the self in everyday life."[14] To accumulate symbolic capital, he requires guidance and models of behavior. He must learn ways to represent his professional diligence, his earnestness, the love he feels for and from his family, his morality, reliability, and so on. The symbolic register of the social game that is characteristic of bourgeois society arises in the eighteenth century in close connection with the theater.

In the situation of eighteenth-century capitalism, in which economic processes are not yet understood and call for explanation, mimetic representation, which creates order, interprets interrelationships, and renders the world of competition coherent, is of inestimable value.[15] Aristotelian dramatic theory serves well in structural terms for the introduction of order into the confusion of events: theater describes what essentially happens in bourgeois society as struggle, as an opposition of forces that are not trying to escape each other, but are locked together in an *agon.* That is the one aspect, the aspect of dramatic conflict. But that imposes form only on a narrow section of society; all that is left over, the swirl of mutually countervailing, destructive, and catastrophic events, which cannot be captured in the agonistic image, must be accommodated: the leftovers are regarded as accidents, in both senses of the word. A place can be made for them in the schema of Aristotelian poetics, as *peripetie,* the change of fortune. Another structural characteristic can also be transferred from the theater to social practice: once all the stations of the tragedy have been traversed, it comes to an end, to a conclusion in the form of an incontrovertible, definitive judgment.

The bourgeois public becomes acquainted with the structure of tragic events in the theater; the device becomes available for purposes of representing other events. Several elements, such as agonistic competition and the merciless struggle of individuals against each other, quite closely approximate Aristotle's idea of the theater; other key Aristotelian concepts, such as probability, tragic guilt, and catharsis, are given quite new interpretations. The need to adapt classical theory to the present occasions many discussions, nearly all of which proceed from the false presupposition that it is possible to take over the Aristotelian theory of the theater into the present. Lessing sees more clearly than any other contemporary theorist that it is not possible to realize any Aristotelian imperatives without modification. What must be recognized, first of all, is which of the fundamental ideas in the *Poetics* can be taken over by contemporary dramatic practice. Neither the doctrine of the three unities nor catharsis occupies a central position in contemporary dramatic practice. Mimesis, however, is central, as the making of a secondary world, an epicosmos, in relation to the empirical world of social practice. The authors of tragedies under French absolutism participated in the symbolic production of social power. In Aristotle, mimesis was mimesis of myths, of a world that was transmitted orally, that was once alive and has meanwhile declined; the theater undertook to codify that otherwise lost world in dramatic form.[16] Over the course of the eighteenth century, along many false paths, in partial, insecure, and vacillating form in Diderot and ultimately in Lessing, there developed the idea that theater is mimesis of the empirical world and that the tangible existence of that world consists in social practice.

This reference to immediate reality is something quite new and far removed from Aristotle, but it is what lends the basic call for mimesis a real meaning. Mimesis is now, as in Aristotle, the making of a symbolic world with reference to a not-yet-codified reality, one that finds itself still in a "state of fluidity" and stands in need of symbolic treatment. The epicosmos of social practice is made up of signs that depict a specific order of the world. Enlightenment dramatists lend form to bourgeois society: they depict, in excerpts from the lives of everyday characters, typified actions representative of the rationality, obligatory roles, and morality of bourgeois society. The new axis and pivot of theatrical worldmaking becomes bourgeois life; not just any bourgeois life, but one that could conceivably be that of a person of a specific status and in a specific situation. This point of reference is the perspective from which the critical concepts of dramatic poetics are established. Under the rubric of the "probable," all modes of action are brought together which manifest conformity to the norms of the social situation and status of the bourgeois. The idea of the "probable" gets drawn into the same vortex that swallows up stage representation.

This shift of directions has considerable consequences: whatever is presented onstage in the bourgeois theater must be ruled by the same principle of judgment that guides the actions of the bourgeoisie. This also describes the site where the normality of social actions and actors is adjudicated. Foucault's analyses of the effect of the concept of normality in enlightened, humanitarian societies show that the judgment works by classifying deviant behavior; it represents the great disciplinary machinery that comes to cover bourgeois society with an ever-finer net of normative control.[17] Plays, however, represent not social routines but primarily deviant behavior, a particularity that has repeatedly caused confusion in the literature, for example, in the *querelle du Cid* and the reception of *La Princesse de Clèves*. Critics already demanded of the literature of French absolutism that it conform to the norms of society; they did so in the name of *bienséances*. "The identification of probability with the question of what *is* as opposed to what *should be* becomes increasingly evident as a tendency,"[18] with the "should be" comprising everything "that conforms to public opinion."[19]

Respect for behavioral norms, which was the concern of criticism in the previous century, with classical French plays not always heeding the admonition, becomes the guiding principle of the eighteenth-century bourgeois drama. How can this assertion of norms that is represented in the literature be brought in line with such expectations? Deviations from the norm must be motivated: literature accepts the obligation of revealing the causes of every important violation of a norm. Explanations usually come inconspicuously; they are incorporated in behavior that is represented so that it can be understood. It is suggested to readers that if they ask the question, why does the character behave in this or that way? they will receive an answer. The standard according to which the explanation is judged adequate is supplied by social practice. Thus do the essential principles of daily life find their way into literature. The basic attitude toward literature derives from the principle of exchangeability: whatever appears in literature must be such that it could occur in social practice. Ritual is repudiated from this point of view, and an attempt is made to find a direct style; time on the stage is measured according to the lived time of the author and spectators. An "order from below" gets put in place, based on the life of everyday people.

It seems remarkable that Enlightenment drama, referring to the authority of Homer and Shakespeare, would insist on the autonomy of the imagination and grant recognition to the supernatural; in this liberation of the imagination lie the seeds of romantic literature. There is, in other words, a complexity to bourgeois theater that allows it to escape instrumental rationality and bourgeois morality. All the important writers of the age display such tendencies running against the grain of the principles of a bourgeois way of life. The sudden intrusion of accident, a change of fortune, or slow progress toward catastrophe is used as a comic device; theater caters to the public's desire for enjoyment. The other side of the well-mannered world of normal bourgeois life is its indulgence in a representational mode whereby a shipwreck occasions feelings of pleasure. In this is manifest certain of the otherwise hidden aspects of bourgeois society, aspects that lie carefully concealed beneath tales of agonistic competition, morality, and rationality. Theater in bourgeois society is "play," just as it was in Shakespeare's time, but in a different sense: the play inhibits complete social conformity; it prompts the development of contrary forces, such as curiosity and sensual pleasure; it allows for the negation of bourgeois virtues. In theater an imaginary space is opened up, where repressed desires and drives are permitted to triumph; though they might be condemned in the end, they have at least made their appearance. Bourgeois theater displays repeated opportunities for breaking free of bourgeois society; it lets the mind play out scenarios of escape from the bourgeois world—potential scenarios, sanctioned only in the world of the imagination.[20]

The paradox by which the play is characterized[21] allows the hidden facets of society to be seen[22]—the wishes, the desires, the fears, the unacknowledged other side of a life of bourgeois diligence and professional employment. These desires and drives, rather than being repressed in the subconscious, come to expression in plays and literary texts. It will be Honoré de Balzac who brings this side of life into the full light of day; it is his insight that tabooed passions, the existence of which the eighteenth-century bourgeois did not dare even admit, must be counted among the critical driving forces that transform society: love, the desire for objects, ambition, passion for profit. Balzac represents in his novels an image of the baser energy of drives as a productive force; drives in the novels help construct a society that is both rational and awash in the intoxication of the senses, a society that becomes ever more wealthy and powerful. There existed no such interest as this during the rise of the bourgeois drama in the eighteenth century. What the bourgeoisie required at that time was above all an initial representation of itself.[23]

The bourgeois theater, still in a state of insecurity, tries out the various devices and potentialities it has at hand, at the same time involving the public in its experiments; the public, for its part, is also trying out its behavioral options in the social sphere. The bridge connecting the autonomous field of literature to social practice exists in the category of action, whether it be virtual action, undertaken experimentally, or action that assumes the form of a model. The norms of social action impose limits on the freedom ceded to action on the stage. It is only once authors have come into secure possession of the imagination as an autonomous field that they can cut the fetters of social practice and attempt to establish theater as a world of its own. By then, the historical function of the drama as the site of experimental action will have been fulfilled. Theater will still be seen as bound to social practice; but the bind will be termed mimesis and exposed to public scrutiny.

Thus it is that the theoretical interest in mimesis wanes in the historical moment when mimesis has wholly fulfilled its new function as that which encompasses the theater and the social world as a unit. Theoretical interest declines, not because there is no meaningful object for it, but, on the contrary, because mimesis has now penetrated into society and gradually permeated it. In nineteenth-century bourgeois society, social action gradually becomes mimetic: each individual subject presents its own world, with all the worlds together yielding a systematic "order from below," which is organized according to specific mimetic schemata common to all individual instances. The underlying conditions that make such a general arrangement of the world possible become one of the key problems of sociology.[24] The concept of mimesis, however, is banned from processes of theory formation. It is as if writers hold it responsible for the insecurity of early bourgeois poetics; writers continue to cling to old concepts while, having recognized that something new is coming into existence, attributing to them new meanings.[25]

What is new here is the social role played by writers and artists in developments that had their beginnings in the eighteenth century: professional work, in which all factions of the bourgeois class takes part, including the highest (excluding those who are ennobled), operates according to the laws of the economy, which does not on its own produce any symbolic representation of itself. Bourgeois society, however, is organized to a considerable extent on the basis of symbolic activities. The bourgeoisie does not simply take these activities over from the nobility; and they are not such that they can be created by professionalized bourgeois work. The sphere in which this symbolic work is initiated and carried out is art, in particular, the theater and narrative literature. The separation between professional work and the means by which social situation and position are presented signifies that the bourgeoisie is obliged to rely on specialists in symbolic representation. No one recognizes this process as a social one, though there are public discussions of mimesis in art. A reinterpretation of the "imitation of nature" in poetry gets under way, whereby it acquires the meaning of the vital processes of an individual, a social group, or an ideal type, which is to say, the symbolic production of a fictional life.[26]

Of supreme moment to absolutism is the organization of space, while the chief task of the bourgeois epoch is to codify the organization of time, to regulate the temporality of action in the life and social practice of the individual. Social behavior tends toward deritualization and the cancellation of accepted codes, as the ways and means of social control undergo fundamental transformation. The same dynamic operates in specialized areas devoted to the production and use of symbols. As Elias[27] and Foucault[28] have shown, the control of power is no longer exercised externally from a central point but becomes internalized in each individual; external control becomes self-control. The individual psyche, the way it is structured and modeled, is now the starting point of effective control. Only after the psyche has assumed its shape does the individual gain control over his or her preferred classificatory system. The autonomy of artistic production thus confronts a limit as well. Internalized control does not come out in the open; it requires individuals to present themselves as if their life had been created from the inside out. The internalization of social control can only proceed indirectly, via some access to the individual psyche as an internal instance of control; mimetic processes are critical to this access. Access is gained, for example, through stories that influence, convince, explain, praise, condemn, or disturb. Paradigms mediate between exemplary narratives and internal images in the psyche in formation.

Characteristic of the development of mimesis in the eighteenth century is the adoption of the constitutive principles of textual production as the instruments for the production of a social world, of symbolic presentations, of social distinctions between the bourgeoisie and other classes, for the formation of interior life, of the psyche. Daily life, beginning in the theater, gets transformed into a text and aestheticized. The transformation processes operate according to the model of address: one who is addressed is drawn into a text. Written dialogue is the typical form of this type of literature; it should be composed with sufficient artistic skill to make an impression of orality. It is not, however, a genuine dialogue, but an imagined one. It is a playful note among recent literary developments; literature strives constantly for seriousness but tolerates something frivolous within itself. Authors open a role in their texts both for themselves and for the public they address—two roles through which authors predetermine the interaction between reader and text. The latitude literature creates for itself in this way, the drawing of the reader into the literary world, opens the way for a textualization of the empirical world, which, in turn, expands enormously the possibilities of expression and aestheticization.[29]

14

Diderot's *Paradox of Acting*

Diderot's dialogue *Paradoxe sur le comédien* can be read as an analysis of the actor's work, as a philosophical theory of natural feelings and their theatrical representation, or as a proposal for theatrical reform. Of greatest use to us here is an interpretation that formulates the *paradox* in the sharpest and most far-reaching fashion, for Diderot seems to have attempted to use the structure of paradox to identify the fundamental nature of mimetic action in society.

Necessary first is a remark on the text,[1] the origins of which have never been fully established. It was first published in 1830, long after Diderot's death, on the basis of a copy from Diderot's posthumous St. Petersburg papers. The editor of the text, Ernest Dupuy, expressed doubts about the authenticity of the dialogue, suspecting that Jacques Naigeon, Diderot's friend and literary executor, had revised and expanded the manuscript in his own hand. These particular questions are essentially put to rest in Paul Vernière's edition, on which we rely here, and other disputed aspects about its origins are irrelevant to our immediate concerns. According to Vernière, the manuscript was composed over the course of ten years, beginning in the autumn of 1769. Commissioned by Grimm for a critique of the book *Garrick ou les acteurs anglais, traduit de l'anglais par Antonio Sticoti, acteur,* Diderot wrote to his friend on 14 November 1769 that the work had inspired a "piece that likely deserves to be brought into somewhat better order." "If I were only to give it some effort, it could turn out that I'd never written anything of such refined acuity before. It is a pretty paradox. I hold that it is sensibility that makes middling actors, extreme sensibility stupid ones; and sublime actors are made by cool reflection and their brains."[2] The text is organized as a dialogue, but only the speaker termed "the first" really speaks; "the second" serves primarily as the occasion for what is thus essentially a monologue. It is the fiction of an oral discussion—which, moreover, is not strictly coherent, leaves arguments unfinished, and takes every possible opportunity for an anecdote. The presence of the second person obliges the first to address another, to narrate, argue, and represent himself. An exclusively literal text would not allow the first discussant to make his appearance in just this way. As we have yet to see, the textual quality of orality is not at all foreign to the ideas being developed in the dialogue. The first discussant, obviously a literary representation of Diderot's own thoughts, is concerned to clarify his reflections on the work of the actor, which, he says, consists in imitative mimesis (*imitation*). The question of primary moment to Diderot, however, is what it is the actor is doing in distinction to the quotidian behavior he imitates.

The actor is obliged to study the great models all around us in nature; he observes them, learns to recognize their central unifying principles. Observational skill, precise understanding, analytical competence—it is these emotionally "cold" qualities that Diderot requires of his actor. The actor has learned to recognize a *modèle idéal* and to reproduce it in the form of theatrical representation. The second requirement of the actor is also related to intellectual insight: the actor has to represent the ideal model in a way that the audience will recognize as "true"; that is, he must know how to conform to prevailing conventions in the theater. What is "true" on stage is not the same thing as what counts as truth in philosophy. Truth on stage is the result of "the conforming of action, diction, face, voice, movement, and gesture to an ideal type invented by the poet, and frequently enhanced by the player."[3] Diderot's actor, therefore, in addition to specific practical representational abilities, needs to have derived a certain kind of social knowledge from his experience, and, finally, he has to be outfitted with a particular cognitive capacity. And present in all of these qualities is the seed of mimesis. The actor discovers a model in nature. His precise observation and analysis permit him to identify it as a model and, indeed, to reveal it in the form of a general law embodied in an individual object. "Imitation is thus revelation."[4] Nature is not capable on its own of revealing its laws, its inner organization, its center; it is "like a mind which has not yet gained consciousness of itself."[5] For the order of nature to be exposed, human intervention is a necessity.

Diderot's point, that only human being can give mute nature a voice, applies not only to art but to technology as well; it is possible to clarify the relationship of art to nature by inquiring into relations between technology and nature:[6] nature teaches us about technology; inversely, it is technology that teaches us how to see nature. Thus Diderot arrives at a doubled imitation: with technology, humanity imitates nature; the finished technological object reverses the relation, and humanity begins to perceive nature in relationship to technology; we identify a relation of similarity between the two, so that it can also be maintained that nature imitates technology. The situation with art is analogous. The artist identifies in nature the universal order; he elaborates an ideal model; what he represents is the latter. Any observer with an eye trained in art then perceives nature in a new light. The observer replaces nature by art in order to arrive at secure judgment: Raphael's Virgin Mary teaches us how to assess the face of a woman. Art renders nature typical, thus making truth accessible. Art is capable of revealing the hidden unity that nature withholds from view.[7] Ideal models are the device by which it becomes possible to look into the nature of human being and see how it really is.[8]

Imitation of nature in Diderot is a much more complex procedure than depiction of nature. Imitation is constituted within a theoretical complex comprising an epistemological procedure, the reconstruction of an ideal model, and a socially determined public embodiment of it. The actor's mastery therefore rests on three different abilities; he is a knowing subject, an artist, and a creator; he must uncover the truth of human nature, conceive his role in terms adequate to this truth, and imbue his performance of the role with artistic life. "Sensibility" (sensibilité), in contrast, is not a necessary trait in the actor. Emotionality, in contrast, is not a necessary characteristic of the actor. On the contrary, they hinder successful representation. "While the power of judgment maintains its penetrating focus on things, sensibility disorders them."[9] The work of Diderot's actor must be calm and cool, the contrary both of enthusiasm and complete surrender to a role.

The successful actor is the possessor of precise cognitive and evaluative abilities; he requires a talent for observation, must make use of his experience, exercise taste, dispose over certain technical or practical skills, and have conducted an exacting study of models. He is therefore anything but natural man, equipped with strong and direct feelings. Contrary to the common prejudice, he should be insensible, since sensibility only impedes possession of the requisite characteristics. He should not have feelings that might impose limits on the extent to which he can abstract from himself and imitate all possible characters. "He came, by intensifying the poet's ideal model of natural man, to embody it for the spectator. . . . His individuality is extinguished in the exemplary generality of the artistic figure."[10] The actor performs a certain role; for the performance to be successful he must possess it (se posséder): he is able to make his feelings seem plausible, keep his eye on the other actors, the scene, and the audience, manage the effect he produces, and enjoy his own performance. He has a doubled perspective; there is first the illusion of the character he is representing, while at the same time there is an inner distance produced by his presentation of himself as someone else: "Il est double."[11] This theory of doubling, which Diderot develops in regard to the actor, represents a great advance in the mimetic theory of human action. Romanticism will juxtapose to this idea the contrary one, namely, that the subjectivity of the I allows it to become another person.

The doubling of the actor, his distance from the character he is representing, allows him to maximize the persuasive force of his performance. Diderot's theory would have it that the actor's alienation is even the necessary condition of theatrical illusion. The alienation effect in Bertolt Brecht's theater is thus not in any direct way simply opposed to the ideas of the bourgeois theater. Brecht's innovation, the revolutionary aspect he claims for his own ideas, consists in the open display of the inner distance in the theater. Brecht no doubt moves substantially beyond Diderot's "paradox," but very much in the sense of a further development, rather than in offering a completely new alternative. Making the distance public, presenting the play in its character as a play, is what Brechtian theater does; in doing so it builds on ideas of role-playing already present in bourgeois theater.

What is real emotion against this intricate play of roles, which functions to manifest to the spectator an ideal model? Emotion belongs to nature, but it is no more than raw nature; on its own it is capable of revealing neither its internal unity nor its central informing principle. *L'émotion vraie* is something grand (Diderot confesses that he is endlessly fascinated by it); but in essence its effect is dysfunctional. It takes over his behavior, interferes with the realization of intentions, and renders him mute: "It is the opposite of play, because its object is real."[12] Conspicuous in Diderot is how little he includes genuine emotions in his thoughts; emotions seem only to offer material for personal anecdotes. His interest is devoted exclusively to effective emotions: the little stories he tells about how his own sensibility has been the cause of failure, even these he represents with such artistic power that the effect is to transform the miscarried action into the narrator's triumph. As a writer, Diderot himself so far surpasses the stage of natural feeling that he remains utterly in control of the effects his words produce.

The entire dialogue ultimately turns on its concern with role-playing, with the performance of emotions, and to this extent Diderot counts as the first theorist of social role-playing. Still wholly indebted to the rhetorical tradition in establishing effect as the goal, Diderot's theory of doubling—that which results from the internal distance implied by external representation—contains the kernel of the modern theory of social action that postulates the irrelevance of emotion for role-playing. This is not the place to pronounce on the status of emotions as such for Diderot, but it is important to note that they are not essential to social action. The attitude toward the world suggested in Diderot's "paradox" resembles the one found in *Rameau's Nephew:* it will inspire emphatic opposition from Rousseau, who, rejecting Diderot's playacting, puts emotionality and the truth of the feelings at the center of his program.[13]

The paradox Diderot describes applies not only to the theater but also to social reality. The kind of activity that calls for imitative mimesis—and with it a catalog of psychological effects, ranging from primary recognition through judgments of similarity, of familiarity, of fundamental reality—the activity that creates the impression of maximum affinity to its referent, the ideal model, this "effet de réel" (Roland Barthes), is the fruit of intellectual labor, of social experience, and of practical theatrical ability. If we assume that the direct expression of emotion is mediated over spontaneity and authenticity, this conception of the problem is counterintuitive; yet in the form of artistic technique, spontaneity and authenticity are highly valued. The social circulation of emotion, in the form of compassion, spontaneous identification, and humane sentiment, functions for Diderot solely on account of a reflexive pact entered into on the part of dramatist and audience. To be certain of the audience's feelings, it is necessary to calculate them. A representation will activate the capacity for emotion, that which, for bourgeois humanity, is specifically human, with far greater credibility if it is conditioned by knowledge and technique rather than by spontaneous emotion.

Not only are genuine emotions irrelevant to social interactions, according to Diderot, he pushes his formulation one step farther by construing between the two a relation of inverse proportionality: people who have emotion are relatively less capable of effective emotional expression than those for whom emotion is not a final behavioral factor; the converse, of course, holds as well. The insight drives Diderot to an ingenious conclusion. The point he ultimately wants to make is that the effect of an emotion on an observer is achieved by means of representation and that genuine feeling is extraneous to representation. Representation calls much more directly for the utilization of intellectual insight and technical devices. Thus Diderot does not criticize the cult of emotion but assigns it to what he regards as its proper place, namely, the site of public emotional representation, which is the theater. Theatrical action, from what we have seen so far, is the exclusive object of Diderot's considerations. The question now is to what extent and how his ideas find application beyond the theater. For the ideas we have sketched out to this point apply in general to all public acts of expression, as long as they entail representation of the typical and produce social effects. Action in the theater thus takes on the significance of a model.

Bourgeois society was in its beginnings when Diderot wrote his *Paradox*. This means that essential representational modes and manners are still in the process of being invented; they must be learned and practiced. Diderot writes for the bourgeois elite at a time when theater has become a respectable part of public life in Paris. "The golden age of the theater. Drama, from the turn of the century, begins attracting an ever-growing audience. . . . The bourgeois class—judges, lawyers, doctors—can be seen in public at the theater, a place and form of entertainment which, under Louis XIV, they would have considered beneath them."[14]

The theatrical drama has a presentative structure: it is comprised of real action of an indicative character, whether on the stage or in daily life. While "your fiery, extravagant, sensitive fellow" is always losing control of himself, acting a part while gaining no pleasure from doing so, "great poets, great actors, and, I may add, all great copyists of Nature, in whatever art," operate quite differently. They observe, recognize, and imitate; they are self-controlled.[15] Theatrical action can teach a person directly how to conduct his or her life in society—an insight Diderot's spokesman will go to any length to substantiate. He would have his interlocutor believe that Philoctetes' speech to Neoptolemus, in Sophocles' *Philoctetes,* in no way differs from what "you might address to my son, or I to yours." "And," the speaker asks, "would the tone in which this discourse would be given on the stage differ from the tone in which one would give it in society?" The answer is no; nor would the tone be ridiculous in private life.[16]

Diderot's actor has the historical opportunity to fulfill a major pedagogical function specifically for the bourgeoisie, that is, to embody onstage the ideal models and moral values built into the text by the dramatist. The actor's task is to offer to the public eye a presentation through concrete action of a specific interpretation of human nature, of what is socially typical, and of social experience. Theatrical reform, in Diderot's mind, begins with the actor: the paramount objective must be to outfit him with an appropriate professional education, income, and level of social standing and prestige. The actor is to be integrated into bourgeois society, as himself a bourgeois discharging his professional duties, which, in turn, are understood in instrumental terms. He is to be treated with a respect and seriousness commensurate with his future social office.

The character of the actor's profession is comparable to no other—it is play. It is nothing new for the specialist in theatrical mimesis to be offered an official position; that was already the case under Louis XIV. That this representative of play should be accorded, of society's professional categories, his own—this tells us as much about the importance of theater in Diderot's time as about the prevailing social attitude toward the theatrical drama. The paradoxical mimesis of play is conceived here as a constitutive element of serious social action in the public sphere.

Although Diderot occasionally elides the difference between action onstage and action in daily life, he insists on a clear distinction between the two spheres. The purpose of demonstrating something onstage and the criterion of success of theatrical action are not the same as the purposes and criteria of daily life. Diderot thus insists on a distinction between the representational devices appropriate to the respective spheres. "The actor says nothing and does nothing in private life in the same way as on the stage: it is a different world."[17] Common to both worlds, nonetheless, is the use of representational techniques that are distinguishable only in certain of their principles.

Theatrical representation always employs expressive techniques; people acting in daily life often surrender to spontaneous feeling. In this difference, for Diderot, lies the superiority of theater over social practice. He develops the idea in anecdotes, such as the one in which a sensitive man falls victim to his feelings:

> A tender-hearted and sensitive man sees again a friend he has missed during a long absence; the friend makes an unexpected reappearance, and the other's heart is touched; he rushes to him, he embraces him, he would speak, but cannot; he stammers and trips over words; he says he knows not what, he does not hear the answer: if he could see that the delight is not mutual, how hurt he would be! Judge, this picture being true, how untrue are the stage-meetings, where both friends are so full of intelligence and self-control.[18]

Diderot is purporting here to depict an excerpt from social reality; he chooses a narrative mechanism that is supposed to replicate an oral report on the emotions in a style that, with its stilted and theatrical affect, seems hardly natural to us today. Diderot's dialogue is a kind of *peinture,* painting. He offers nothing about the actual feelings the two friends are having but instead deploys emotional expressions within traditional dramatic practice to which the expressions are alien; it is this practice that Diderot seeks to overcome. From his narrative perspective, an excerpt from daily life appears in terms of a dramatic plot, which is revealing of the deeper intentions behind the *Paradox:* Diderot develops a *theatrical perspective* for the representation of actions whereby it is irrelevant whether they take place in the theater or in daily life. His primary concern is to organize his approach to his object in terms of achieving the maximum effect, which he does by representing it according to the most promising literary techniques at his disposal.

Imitative mimesis is informed here by a sophisticated theatricality that does all it can to convey an impression of immediacy, directness, and spontaneity. It should not surprise us that this hyperbolic, dramatizing representational mode is assumed to be the form in which the "natural" comes to expression: in the contemporary understanding, the natural is that which, having been properly composed by the writer in terms of ideal models, comes to effective expression in the theater. The natural is not the empirically given. Diderot regards things as they are in nature as "the commonplace," *le commun.*[19] Theatrical treatment is thus an idealizing construction that exists first in the form of writing and then in the actor's physical performance of the role. Only on the basis of such an ideal construction does it become possible, in these terms, to apprehend empirical reality; the observational mode must be theatrically structured if it is to occasion the perception of what is beautiful and moral. Empirical nature is thus a product of the mimesis of the world presented in theater.

It is consistent from this perspective that theater fulfills a formative task in relation to society. Any scene in which emotions are presented can become theater; all persons potentially part of public life can become authors and actors. Speakers make an impression when they imitate rage, not when they are enraged. The situation for them is just as it is for actors, who

> impress the public, not when they are furious, but when they play fury well. In tribunals, in assemblies, everywhere where a man wishes to make himself the master of others' minds [*esprits*], he feigns now anger, now fear, now pity, now love, to bring others to these diverse states of feeling. What passion itself fails to do, passion well imitated accomplishes.
>
> Do not people talk in society [*monde*] of a man being a great actor? They do not mean by that that he feels, but that he excels in simulating, though he feels nothing—a part much more difficult than that of an actor; for the man of the world has to find dialogue besides, and to fulfill two functions, the poet's and the actor's.[20]

Life in the public world confronts people with greater and more difficult roles than what is found in the theater; life in the world, like the theater, functions via the sensuous representation of ideal models. It remains true nonetheless that the place where role-playing emerges most clearly to view, more impressively and on the basis of superior skill, is the theater. The work of two specialists goes into the conception and figuration of theatrical action, that of the dramatist and that of the actor. Role-playing in public life may have more profound depths to it, but "the poet onstage can be cleverer than the actor in good society [*monde*]."[21]

The central concern of Diderot's dialogue is the specific function of theater in bourgeois society, which is where all the threads of his argument come together. Emotions presented mimetically are more effective than outpourings of spontaneous feelings; Diderot goes so far as to suggest that natural feelings are perceived as a mimesis of ones that are mimetically represented. Though we do not find in theater the deepest and most significant feelings, what it does present are the most polished, most technically reflected, and most exemplary cases. Thus the significance of theater for social practice: the theater is the site where the most instructive of all scenes are played out. It constructs characters such that the relations among them are clear: actors double themselves onstage; they take on identities other than their own. Things are not so clear in daily life; the identity of empirical individuals is uncertain, and it is possible to make mistakes about it. All individuals, according to Diderot, are naturally possessed of an *I* particular to themselves; this *I*, however, has never been pressed into final form through reference to an ideal model; it is thus impossible to know a person's identity precisely. It can be understood only by way of imitation, but the result of imitation is not the apprehension of the initial *I* but of another one: "One is one's own self by nature; one becomes some one else by imitation; the heart one is supposed to have is not the heart."[22]

Who we are is something we can learn by way of mimesis, and mimesis gives its best lessons in the theater, because there it is mastered and controlled. What we acquire in the theater, however, is no longer the *I* as it is given in nature. This claim points to a central theme in modern identity theory,[23] though it cannot be clearly determined whether Diderot is altogether conscious of its significance. He uses the insight to improve his chances for success in the play everyone is engaged in socially.

> What, then, is the true talent? That of knowing well the outward symptoms of the soul we borrow, of addressing ourselves to the sensations of those who hear and see us, of deceiving them by the imitation of these symptoms, by an imitation which aggrandizes everything in their imagination, and which becomes the measure of their judgment; for it is impossible otherwise to appreciate that which passes inside us. And after all, what does it matter to us whether they feel or do not feel, so long as we know nothing about it?[24]

Philippe Lacoue-Labarthe, in an essay on Diderot's *Paradox of Acting,* elaborates a modern position on the concept of mimesis.[25] The distinction, already advanced in *Typography,* between a narrower and a broader understanding of mimesis is drawn more precisely in this essay: only mimesis conceived as a productive force does justice to what an actor's interpretation of a role actually calls for; mimesis in this sense is an activity that does not so much imitate as produce something new. Mimesis is itself an imitation of *physis,* of the natura naturans, of productive nature. It is, at the same time, a form of poesis, which is to say that it is also an activity that complements nature. If mimesis is understood as passive, exclusively receptive imitative behavior, there is no way to account for the functions identified here. Theatrical presentation is a productive act based on the possession and mastery of a character; the actor decides how he should put his own person into action, which characteristics he wants to lend it. The ''person'' whom he masters in this process is empty, a ''pure person.'' It has nothing of its own; it is a person with no properties. It is precisely this lack that makes the actor capable of expressing in an active figuration whatever can be expressed. ''The more the artist (actor) *is* nothing, the more he can be everything.''[26]

Diderot's *Paradox,* in Lacoue-Labarthe's interpretation, brings to expression the law of impropriety (*impropriété*), which, at the same time, represents the structure of mimesis in general. Only the person with no properties, the being without particularity, the internally rent subject without a subject, is in a position to engage productively in the work of an actor. The actor resembles nature because he has the capability of lending things form; at the same time, he distinguishes himself from nature because what he does is not finally imitation but the bringing forth of something new. The actor's work is a gift of mimesis, a poietic talent—and it is in this talent that Diderot identifies what he terms genius.

Lacoue-Labarthe's Diderot formulates here the paradox of social existence in general, which he alludes to in other texts as well (*Rameau's Nephew,* for example). Bourdieu describes the emotionless genius, in *Le Rêve de D'Alembert,* as someone who "will rule himself and all that surrounds him. He will not fear death."[27] The political side of the theater lies in its figuration in public of the empty, active person and in its demonstration of the paradoxical structure of mimesis. "Against the Platonic tradition, against the Socratic (or in this case Rousseauistic) utopia of social transparency" based on the "rejection of mimesis as an uncontrolled alteration, an unmasterable disappropriation . . . Diderot *plays* the theater."[28] Lacoue-Labarthe finds in Diderot's text both a theatricalization of society and the extension of the paradox of acting to daily life; together they eventuate in a witting renunciation of the subject characterized by feelings and passions.[29]

There is a further extension of Diderot's *Paradox* that Lacoue-Labarthe does not discuss: what exists alongside emotional expression is that which is not expressed, the representation of which is destined to fail. Should someone attempt to express this emotional substratum that belongs immediately to character, the attempt would miscarry. Obviously there is an aspect of the individual's interior life that evades public representation, an instance of individual identity that cannot participate in expression but that establishes the conditions requisite to expression. Real feelings must exist; at least it is necessary to assume as much if it is also to be the case that the intensity and particularity of real feelings supply the measure against which emotional performances are judged. Unexpressed feeling functions as a standard of judgment.

Compared to traditional versions of mimesis, Diderot locates the concept differently in his overall scheme: it moves into the person of the actor, of the person engaging in action, and works its effects from the inside out. The free play of mimesis is deployed socially; when this happens is a question of cleverness, of the goal of a particular action, of the opportunities available for intervention. In the process, the body becomes a mimetic medium, a kind of theatrical stage.

In Diderot's conception, representations of interior states are freely disposable. It is possible to initiate the expression of emotions, character traits, attitudes, and so on, to one's own advantage. Mastery over the procedures of self-representation becomes here a kind of capital that can be invested as appropriate opportunities present themselves. Diderot, to be sure, stops short of the idea that the magnitude of this capital is a function of social knowledge and is by no means universally accessible to all people in an equal fashion. But he does recognize that the individual, regarded socially, is nothing other than his or her social existence, however much it may be the case that the production of a social existence is in part a function of an inner core that cannot finally be expressed.

The natural externalization of that unexpressed aspect of a person's interiority is not what constitutes expression; social expression, for Diderot, is natural expression. In his view, what is produced mimetically is precisely what must be regarded as natural. Mimesis gains social recognition as the criterion of the natural, with the natural recognized solely as a product of mimesis. Mimesis and the natural are not at odds in Diderot; rather, they constitute each other reciprocally.

There is no site more suited to the production of externalizations of concrete interiority than the theater. A major share of responsibility for the quality with which inner worlds are produced thus devolves on theater. Assuming a comprehensive reform, *bon goût* (good taste) and people's *moeurs* (mores) could be influenced and improved by the institution of the theater. Diderot, in a suspect formulation for a professed atheist, promises actors that once they achieve commensurate social regard, they will have become *prédicateur laiques,* or lay preachers.[30]

The ramifications for aesthetic theory of the idea of an aesthetic education, of a cultivation of one's taste, of society, will emerge more fully in Batteux, Lessing, Schiller, and Jean Paul, to name a few. It expresses from the start, however, an option open to the bourgeoisie, namely, that included in its task is the cultivation and improvement of taste. Taste, through the mediation of theater and art in general, becomes a value in bourgeois society. It is the guiding value of all mimetically produced worlds, which are understood under the rubric of disinterestedness and which range from great works of art to the self-presentation of bourgeois actors. It is Diderot's opinion, offered from the universalist perspective of the Enlightenment, that an elevation of taste in the theater would lead to an improvement in the nation as a whole: "Our playwrights would soon attain to a purity, a delicacy, a grace, that they are further from than perhaps they think. Can you doubt that it would react upon the national tone?"[31]

Taste is supposed to develop via the theater, which marks it as a theater quite unlike the one we discussed in reference to court society. That the theater becomes an institution of taste signals a critical historical turn. Moreover, taste is conceived as a faculty of cultural judgment and the capability to undertake successful action in society. Finally, it is assumed to be within the reach of everyone.

As soon, however, as we acknowledge that this last claim is a pure fiction, that the circle of those who in fact have access to the theater is restricted to the nobility and upper bourgeoisie, other of Diderot's assumptions also begin to appear suspiciously ideological. Taste is not a matter of the emotions but of a capacity to make judgments: "To have sensibility is one thing, to feel is another. One is a matter of soul, the other of judgment."[32] Taste, in this understanding, is less accessible to substantive analysis and psychologization than to analysis in terms of social factors, to factors present in the class-specific conditions of bourgeois life, which are responsible for the elevation of taste to the status of a fundamental criterion. Conversely, the everyday world of the bourgeoisie is gradually subsumed under the category of taste, so that daily life itself is perceived and arranged in terms of the social presentation of emotion, the capacity to make judgments of taste, and savoir faire, a knowledge of practical affairs.

15

The Transformation
of Mimesis in Lessing

Lessing is one of the last important theorists to retain ties to the mimetic tradition of antiquity. In this respect, he can be conceived as a traditionalist. In fact, however, the return to classical sources undertaken in his philological work amounts to a fundamental transformation of mimesis, to a radical renewal, and, precisely in Lessing's insistence on the Otherness of classical thought, to a modernization of the concept. He learns to regard, as his central categories, action and temporality. His modernity, the critical role he plays in the beginnings of modern aesthetics, is not easy to see. *Laocoön*[1] may be correctly regarded as one of the most important texts of the German Enlightenment and as a masterpiece of rational argumentation; yet it identifies itself as not modern in a number of its characteristics: its psychologistic manner of speech; the inclusion among its imperatives of imitation of nature; its reference to classical myths; and, finally, the multitude of ready judgments, which are apodictic, hasty, and sometimes falsely formed. There are reasons, that is, to date Lessing's work to the Enlightenment in the negative sense, to consign it to the museum of history under the rubric of "the poetics of effects." A careful reconstruction of Lessing's argument, however, immediately renders *Laocoön* much more interesting from our present point of view.

Perrault, in his *Parallèle des Anciens et des Modernes,* which appeared near the end of the seventeenth century, poses for the first time the question of difference among the various artistic media. While Perrault continues to use painting "metaphorically as a characterization of literature,"[2] Dubos, in his *Reflexions critiques sur la poésie et sur la peinture* (1719), recognizes that "difference among the media is explained essentially by the divergent nature of signs and variation in the usage of signs."[3] Diderot takes up the question of the medium's nature, focusing his inquiry on literary language in his *Lettre sur les sourds et muets* (1751) and formulating his answer in his doctrine of "hieroglyphs." Hieroglyphs are "motivated or natural signs" that not only designate but also represent.

A concern with the possibilities open to art, in particular, literature, from the perspective of a theory of signs also stands at the heart of Lessing's considerations. He focuses on the "boundaries" that demarcate the arts from one another, identifying them from the perspective of the various ways in which fictional worlds are constructed. How do the visual arts accomplish representation? How does literature? The theater? A comparison of representational modes among the arts will yield an answer, but the comparison must be *among* the arts, not between representation and some hypothesized original event.

Lessing's Argument[4]

Lessing begins his investigation with the material characteristics of the various arts: painting makes use of figures and colors; poetry articulates sounds. Figures, colors, and sounds are what results when the signs proper to the given artistic system are realized, and they are subject to rules specific to that system. Mimesis, for Lessing, is first of all the methodical realization of signs in the form of images, sculptures, successions of sounds, and scenes. The Trojan priest Laocoön cries out in mortal fear as he is entwined by serpents, and in doing so signals, not an event with a specific mode of existence, but a mythological theme; it can be understood as a kind of quotation. Artistic renderings of the scene do not point to an event in the sense of a referent that exists independently of language; rather, they are artistic representations of Laocoön and, as such, comparable to each other. Mimesis is not imitation here, but an act of production, a poiēsis.

The material for artistic mimesis comes from mythology; the artist takes from it what belongs to a representation of Laocoön—the priest, his children, a monster, the expression of fear and horror. The options open to the artist are therefore predetermined to a considerable degree, but what he or she does with the material at hand is not. This is the guiding idea of Laocoön—that there is a limit to our capacity for representation and that limit can be identified. A painter is capable of representing the ugly, but "painting as a fine art refuses to do so."[5] It does not want to represent the ugly because it does want to make the fullest possible use of the signs available to painting. Between representation and that which is represented there should exist a "comfortable relation"—which implies the optimum use of the expressive capabilities of a sign system. Later periods, when the fullest possible use has been made of initial capabilities, show an interest in uncomfortable relations; they no longer strive exclusively for the beauty of realization.

Lessing's aim is to convey in theoretical terms the capabilities inherent in a system of signs to produce a symbolic world. He wants to clarify how such worlds are formed out of the materials of which the signs consist. He traces the arch that spans the artist, who takes up material and renders it into signs, the work that results from the artist's efforts, and the recipient of the work. There are thus three elements in Lessing's concept of mimesis: that which is of the artist's making; the medium; and the reproduction of the artist's symbolic world on the part of one who comprehends it. It is not the individual case that interests Lessing, although he repeatedly invokes individual examples (either celebrating them as shining examples of his aesthetic understanding or dismissing them as incompatible with it), but what he finds in them is expressed in the idea of "limits": he identifies the limits of our artistic potential, which describes, not a boundary line, but a relation among the three elements, production—medium—reproduction. We see here how Lessing is forcing open the door to modern aesthetic theory; there are suggestions in his work of Charles Sanders Peirce's triadic classification of signs, of the aesthetic experience of an artistic medium, and of formalist and nominalist approaches to art.

One way to appreciate Lessing's relevance to our own time is to contextualize his work historically, projecting just a few years ahead to Kant. Lessing seeks to answer the question of the final principles governing the expressive capacity of artistic symbols: the necessary conditions of the production of fictional worlds lie in the signs out of which artworks are made. Lessing in fact composes, before Kant, the first critique in Kant's sense:[6] a *semiotic* critique. His concern in one respect is with a critique of our capacity for representation; yet he is not strictly speaking a logician but a writer guided by powerful intuitions and his fundamental interest in aesthetics. The production of the beautiful is what finally interests him, which is a category left substantively empty by Kant. Lessing focuses on our capacity for representation only insofar as it affects the potential of signs to create fictional worlds.

Prior to the Enlightenment, artistic worldmaking proceeds under the control of external factors, of the social world: authoritative sources and the schools, which identify and transmit the rules of the rhetorical tradition and supervise artistic practice. Control is exercised over the literature of French absolutism by a single institution, the academy, even while the influence of individual critics, who base their views on bienséances, the precision of the rules, and logic, begins to increase. In none of these cases is poetry autonomous; it is the object of public discussions, which are the mechanism by which external control is secured. Literary worldmaking remains a social matter into the period in which Lessing is writing, which is to say, it is never left entirely up to the actual authors. Nor does Lessing leave writers alone with their creations; in his view readers and audiences are involved in the production process, although no longer in the sense of control or pressure exercised from without. He regards the recipients of artworks as necessary for the work to be completed in the sense of an inner re-creation of the poetic world.[7]

In the eighteenth century, literary worldmaking begins to elude these external influences; at the same time, it takes on a new dynamic in that it begins to activate forces that are internal to the reader. The result is the elimination of all that is permanently fixed and final; literary production becomes processlike in a new sense. Nevertheless, it is not understood as something in constant flux, differing from individual to individual. Unlike the romantics of a later period, Lessing does not articulate a subjectivist conception of literary production and reception. On the contrary, he emphasizes the force of rules. But what precisely does he mean? Rules are the guarantors of objectivity; they are lawlike in their functioning and exert a more powerful force than did the social pressure of an earlier time. As part of the medium, they are also external to the writer; but they are first objectified and then internalized by people directly involved in literary creation. Rules arise out of external circumstances and exercise their effect, in the form of constraints, within individuals; they work their effects on the imagination.[8]

According to this new view, society no longer influences literary creation and reactualization directly; it operates indirectly, through the constraints of the media insofar as the latter retain traces of the societies (oral or literate) that created them. This amounts to a fundamental transformation of the millennia-old relationship of interdependency among the symbolic system, social pressure, direct control, authors, and their public. The new conception centers on the imagination as an interior instance to which all other forces involved in the artistic process are systematically referred. Lessing conceives the imagination as a subjective faculty, which, however, is characterized by an objective structure. The general laws of the imagination work together with the laws of the artistic medium—an idea that fundamentally distinguishes Lessing from Kant, who attributes to the expressive medium no value of its own; Kant supplies no avenue by which artists encounter directly the means of representation.[9]

Lessing's semiotic and medial critique of the imagination points toward a theory of mimesis as the representation of a world. Each medium establishes a specific representational frame that the artist is obliged to respect. Different media open up different types of frames. All social influences are kept at a distance from the process of worldmaking, with the effect that social traces are eradicated. Lessing thus declares the process of poetic production autonomous in relation to society, but at the cost of establishing the domination of the medium over artistic mimesis. The autonomy of the imagination is not coterminous with the autonomy of the subject.

How does artistic mimesis, equipped in this way with an autonomous status, establish reference to empirical reality? How can it mimetically represent empirical objects to the reader or observer? The writer—Lessing elaborates an answer only for the writer—must evoke impressions of reality in his or her readers, which makes the readers' worldmaking comparable or even equivalent to the writer's. Lessing offers his conception of "motivated signs" as the solution to the problem: the laws of the imagination and the media work without differentiation in the minds of the author and the recipient, in an interplay between the two.

In literary works, signs must bridge the gap between writer and recipient. They must trace out a connecting link that reaches from one to the other. Only a specific type of sign is capable of accomplishing this mediation, and it is precisely this capability that Lessing is concerned to convey in his critique. His ideas focus on signs whose material structure is such as to make possible the author's creation of fictional worlds, while at the same time enabling recipients to reproduce the worlds in their minds. Signs are the better suited to artistic mimesis, not the more powerfully they render the fictional world present, but the better they are at initiating a reproduction of the world on the part of the recipient. The question for us now is how signs must be constituted such that they make this reproduction possible.

Lessing, working initially from intuition, offers the explanation that effects are produced by different qualities in the various arts: the reproduction of Laocoön's torment evokes the image of a great man in the grip of misfortune. Yet it is possible for the artistic medium itself, carved marble, to inhibit the intended effect on the observer. A face captured in the movement of violent distortion will not suggest to the observer the expression of a noble soul—the presence of suffering is too great, the expression of pain too direct. At the same time, any immediate expression of pain violates the demand that the aim of art be the creation of beauty: a mouth opened in a scream appears instead as an ugly hole. The sculptor therefore dispenses with the scream; Laocoön opens his mouth only slightly in a sigh. The actual mythological model, in other words, must be treated with some license, according to Lessing; the model does not fix the requirements of representation but—precisely on the contrary—must be altered so that the operation of the mimetic process is not impaired.[10]

Lessing transfers the principle of imitative production from the artist to those whose task is to understand the work; the latter also imitate, and what they imitate is the process of the artist's production. For this convergence to be possible, the medium must be treated appropriately: first, on what Nelson Goodman terms the "syntactic level," the level of the realization of the sign (the sculptor refrains from making a hole in Laocoön's face); second, on the level of meanings, the "semantic level."[11] For the writer, things are quite different: Virgil describes Laocoön's expression of pain as an emotional outburst—which affects neither the nobility of Laocoön's soul nor the beauty of the representation. The poet characterizes Laocoön not by his scream but in other ways—by his noble heritage, his exalted priestly office, the tragic truth that he glimpses in the moment of his death. The beauty of the representation is achieved by the forward movement of the poetic action (e.g., by the representation of the writhing serpents), by Laocoön's bearing, and by the meaning of his death within the frame of the epic as a whole. Lessing juxtaposes the writer's problem to that of the sculptor: what the literary medium renders present is not the suffering of Laocoön but the figure of the sufferer; the problem for the writer is thus not, as it is for the sculptor, to moderate excess. The writer must imbue the signs with a ''charge,'' which makes it possible for the recipient to follow the author's lead.

So far in our recapitulation of Lessing's argument, he, operating as artist, is engaged in an intuitive interpretation of the example of Laocoön. Now operating as theorist, Lessing proceeds to infer the relationship between production and mimesis from the characteristics of the signs employed: very much in the sense of an antimetaphysical philosophy of reason, Lessing's critique of language is meant to formulate the rules responsible for the existence, in the artist's production and the recipient's reproduction of the work, of an identical structure: the sculptor produces signs of an immediate presence; because they are sensuous signs, they are ''directly legible.'' The sculptor's signs themselves identify the mode of existence they will have for the observer: the signs are spatial and physical, possessed of extension, and they are ''arranged next to each other.'' The body signs created by the sculptor become for the observer a sign-body.

But how do signs operate for the writer? The organization of Lessing's argument is such that the visual arts serve as the exemplary case, which prompts an analysis of literature for the purpose of identifying the principle that is analogous to spatial arrangement.

> I reason thus: if it is true that in its imitations painting uses completely different means or signs than does poetry, namely figures and colors in space rather than articulated sounds in time, and if these signs must indisputably bear a suitable relation to the thing signified, then signs existing in space can express only objects whose wholes or parts coexist, while signs that follow one another can express only objects whose wholes or parts are consecutive.
>
> Objects or parts of objects which exist in space are called bodies. Accordingly, bodies with their visible properties are the true subjects of painting.
>
> Objects or parts of objects which follow one another are called actions. Accordingly, actions are the true subjects of poetry.[12]

Lessing's argument seems to be smoothly sequential, which allows Todorov to reconstruct it as a syllogism.[13] However, it results directly in contradiction, which we shall attempt to demonstrate via a systematic reconstruction of his reasoning on the basis of Goodman's *Languages of Art*. The characteristics of painting and poetry that Lessing names refer to the *syntactic* structure of signs. He moves, that is, from the syntactic characteristics of signs directly to the representational characteristics of signs, leaving out one analytical step in the process: he fails to investigate the *semantic* characteristics of signs. This intermediary step is essential, however, because the semantic structure of signs does not follow logically from their syntactic structure. The claim that painting has a spatial and poetry a temporal representational form can be accepted as valid only if the semantic structure of the respective signs implies a limitation of either spatial or temporal representation.

The absent intermediary link sets Lessing's argument off along a false path. He fails to justify in any way his forced definition—"Objects . . . which follow one another are called actions"—which leads him to what is presumably the result determined in advance to be the desired one.[14] Actions, Lessing tells us, are "the true subjects of poetry," just as "bodies with their visible properties are the true subjects of painting." But how does he come to distinguish actions as the subjects of poetry? It seems obvious that he has actions in mind from the start and thus twists his argument to that end. His point of departure is definitional: poetry imitates in that it makes use of "articulated sounds in time"; that is, it imitates through *speech.* Yet the poet writes his poetry, meaning that what Lessing is ultimately referring to are the signs of *writing.* What the action of speaking, reading, and writing opposes to painting is the dimension of time, and herein lies the critical discovery of *Laocoön:* the mimesis of language, the author's production and the recipient's reproduction are both characterized by the passage of time, just as the central characteristic of mimesis in painting and sculpture is spatial. The world produced in literature is essentially temporal: the author's time merges by way of the work with the reader's time; the space of the painter and the sculptor is the space of the observer. Lessing arrives at this result because he views the visual arts and poetry as analogous; image and sculpture are the counterparts to epic and drama.

The question, however, is whether the difference between space and time, which Lessing identifies as the distinction between painting and poetry, is exhaustive. Are there not perhaps other important distinctions to be drawn, distinctions that Lessing overlooks, between the visual arts and literature? Goodman's analytical tools allow us to show that artistic systems of signs distinguish themselves in terms of other characteristics precisely on the syntactic level, which is the object of Lessing's analysis. Goodman regards the characters that are fixed in writing, the signs, that is, of language, as classes of written realizations, of "marks." Thus, for example, it is possible to realize the first letter of the alphabet by means of the following marks: A, *A,* a, *a.* The mark *a* belongs to the sign to which all other realizations of the first letter of the alphabet belong, such as: A, *A,* a, 𝔄, **A** . . .

According to Goodman's distinction, signs, or in his terminology, characters, bear one of two syntactic properties. They can be syntactically "disjoint" and finitely differentiated (or articulated). Characters are disjoint in cases in which "no mark may belong to more than one character."[15] Linguistic characters have this property. A specific mark, *a,* belongs either to the first or to the fourth letter of the alphabet. No such judgment is possible in regard to the signs of painting. Signs are finitely differentiated when it is possible in principle to decide whether or not a mark belongs to a character.[16] In such cases, it is possible, at least theoretically, to state whether a mark is the realization of one particular sign and not of another. In regard to a written mark, a judgment can be made, by referring to context and on the basis of experience in the reading of writing, as to the character to which the mark belongs.

A character system that is not finitely differentiated disposes over an infinite number of signs, arranged such that between any two characters a third character can always be inserted. In this case, "no mark can be determined to belong to one rather than to many other characters."[17] Such a sign system is, in Goodman's terminology, "syntactically dense." Syntactic density is proper to the signs of the visual arts; it designates their nature as "concrete." The material properties of a painting, such as coloration, brush stroke, background texture, and surface texture, are indivisible elements of pictorial symbols. They cannot, even theoretically, be isolated from their context. We shall see how linguistic characters, because they are syntactically differentiated, differ in their expressive capacity from the syntactically dense signs of the visual arts.

Syntactic density is not equivalent to the spatial dimension, although it does stand in relation to it. And the property of syntactic differentiation, for its part, is neither a characteristic of time nor involved in temporal processes. It would be more accurate to say that writing organizes time. Lessing also overlooks the fact that semantic differentiation does not automatically accompany syntactic differentiation; the two elements must be strictly distinguished from each other. Thus, in reference to Lessing, we might summarize Goodman's analysis of the semantic properties of sign systems as follows. The meanings of linguistic marks can overlap; they are semantically ambiguous. They are not finitely differentiated semantically, which is to say that meanings are arranged such that a third can always be inserted between any two others; they are semantically dense. The same is true of the marks of painting. They can also have several meanings, which, likewise, are not finitely differentiated and can overlap.

Linguistic signs, in this case, written characters, are capable of defining a literary work—as a text—syntactically on the level of the marks. Painting, in contrast, does not define a work; it *is* a work, is not replaceable by other realizations. Painting is an allegorical art; the identification of a painting is inextricably bound to the history of its production, to the time of the work.

The signs of painting constitute analogue systems; they form syntactic and semantic continua. A transition from one color to another is an example of a syntactic continuum; a semantic continuum might be the shading of light on a represented surface, such as a wall. The two continua can be distinguished from each other. The side-by-side arrangement of the signs of painting thus does not result, as Lessing thought, in the limitation of the representation to "objects . . . that exist [next to each other] in space." Because of the semantic characteristic of symbolic systems in painting, it can be stated that they are suitable to the representation of classes of objects understood as continua.

But not only spaces and bodies can be understood as continua. There is no difficulty in interpreting temporal progressions as continua and representing them on a surface in a "comfortable" diagrammatic relation. Temporal progressions can be expressed in painting, for example, in the form of processes of decomposition, corrosion, effacement, detrition, soiling, and so on.

It is therefore necessary to formulate an alternative to Lessing's definition of the representational capacity of poetry, which, in his view, hampers spatial and favors temporal representation. But does the semantic density of language allow it to represent semantic continua? In answering this question, we shall attempt to explicate the central idea of Lessing's work. The statement "A bright blue line runs across the white wall" represents a spatial continuum in writing. A painter's rendition of the same wall specifies the height of the line, how broad it is, the nuance of color involved, and the degree of contrast between the bright blue line and the white wall. The "dense" symbolic continuum of the painting's surface specifies the absolute positions of the visual elements and their relations to each other. A linguistic text, in contrast, is a discontinuous system. It is not capable of specifying absolute positions and of describing precisely (in comparison to the possibilities inherent in painting) the relation of the representational elements to each other.

The syntactic and semantic "density" of the symbolic system out of which painting is constituted allows it to represent continua. The discontinuous symbolic system of language is not in a position to do this; linguistic texts are distinguished by another representational form, which is not bound to its material and can thus surpass the representational limits characteristic of painting. In the representation of continua, linguistic texts suffer a disadvantage in comparison to the symbolic systems proper to painting, which consists in the specification of elements within the continuum. Lessing's fundamental assumptions on the level of aesthetic theory, carefully corrected and reduced, can thus be reformulated as follows. Given the stipulation that we are dealing with cases of a "comfortable relation" it can be said that (1) the subjects of painting are continua, spatial as well as temporal; and (2) continua are not suitable subjects for poetry in instances in which meaning is assigned to the absolute position of their elements and the latter's relation to one another. According to the second assumption, discursive languages run up against their representational limits when the intention is to describe, for example, a space, a face, or a landscape as a continuum.

This logical reconstruction of Lessing's position does away with the dimension of time; a succession of signs has no necessarily temporal character. Yet we have seen that time is precisely the dimension that is critical to Lessing. It may be that his entire argument serves to put the concept of action at the heart of mimesis, which suggests that our understanding of action must be differently organized. Having corrected Lessing's argument, we nonetheless have not yet arrived at an understanding of why he distinguishes two types of mimesis, one spatial, the other temporal. We can best approach this question, not by way of a logical examination, but in terms of the historical context in which his ideas arise.

Mimesis of Time

"Mimesis in space," the making of worlds by means of signs arranged contiguously, refers to the old idea of the relationship between a model and a copy of it; this is the mimesis of the mirror, which, taken over by the Renaissance from antiquity, enters into a stage of crisis during the seventeenth century. Central to the plots of Madame de Lafayette's novels, in particular, *Zaide,* are the extraordinary problems raised by mirror-image portraits.[18]

According to an analysis undertaken by Foucault,[19] seventeenth-century linguistic representation undergoes a process of detemporalization. The discourse of French classicism is based on a representational language that "names, patterns, combines, and connects and disconnects things. . . . In this role, language transforms the sequence of perceptions into a table and cuts up the continuum of being into a pattern of characters. . . . The profound vocation of Classical language has always been to create a table."[20] This is, for Foucault, only the beginning of a long development that leads to the appearance of "man" in "dehistoricized" form at the beginning of the nineteenth century.[21] History becomes empty. "Man . . . was already beginning to recover in the depths of his own being . . . a historicity linked essentially to man himself."[22]

Lessing's definition of the representational capacity of text, drama, painting, and sculpture amounts to a complete renovation of the concept of mimesis. The characteristics he attributes to mimesis ultimately cause the concept to disappear behind a modern semiotic representational mode: there are no longer any referents to be imitated; what becomes determinate are the rules of representation; what must be found is a formal method for the production of artistic worlds and a transcendental boundary that separates from each other the various symbolic systems. There are passages in *Laocoön* that suggest—though it means moving beyond Lessing himself—a conception of painting from the point of view of its syntactic characteristics. Painting can be conceived, from this point of view, as bound to a surface, a possibility the full ramifications of which will be realized only much later by Cézanne. With the concept of time, the mimesis of language acquires a new element.

Which time does Lessing mean? Whose time? Obviously he is concerned with personal time, which is the meaning of his forced insistence on the concept of action: it is the time of persons engaged in action; linguistic signs are employed in reference to these persons. It is the time of all who are involved in the overall process of artistic representation, the time of the author and the time of the reader and spectator; it is the time of social reality. Lessing supposes that the medium of poetic language "transports" a fragment of time from one person to another. Initially this idea implies nothing beyond interpretation; it is designed to demonstrate what is new in Lessing's concept of mimesis. A recapitulation of his solution to the problem of "natural signs" in poetry will allow us to see this more clearly.[23]

Words are not themselves natural signs, although they can become similar to them. Lessing writes to Nicolai, "Poetry must seek without qualification to elevate its arbitrary signs to the status of natural signs, and it is only by doing so that it distinguishes itself from prose and becomes poetry. The instruments by which it accomplishes the change from one to the other are sound, words, the position of words, meter, figures and tropes, similes, and so on."[24] Lessing's proposed elevation of the meaning of normal linguistic expressions, their organization as specifically poetic, restates a transformation that had already been implicit in the naming practice of ancient Greece: Jesper Svenbro[25] has demonstrated that a boy's given name, more rarely a girl's, was formed out of an epithet assigned to his (or her) father or ancestors. Most frequently the father's reputation (Greek: *kléos*) was taken up in the name of the son; thus the calling of the son's name always contained an echo of the father. For example, Heracles was accorded the epithet *aniketos,* invincible; his son was called Aniketos. The son of Odysseus, Telemachus, received his name from the epithet of his father, *tele-mákhos,* one who fights far away. "While Odysseus, unlike the suitors, is fighting far away, his son—who is the perfect image of his father—remains, like a memorial in Ithaca, reminding everybody of what his father is doing."[26] The name of the son effects his similarity with the father. "In a culture of mimesis, a Telemakhos who seeks to imitate his father by doing himself what his name announces will be a model son, for the best thing that could be wished for a child is that he should resemble his father."[27] The sound of the son's name brings the father to mind even after the latter's death. The Greek onomatothesis of given names, which are regarded as inscriptions, only functions if the epithet now become name is called aloud in a situation of scenic orality.

Lessing, in his letter to Nicolai, is not far from this conception, that naming signs call to mind the content of that which is named. He writes that the highest literary genre is, "however, the dramatic; for here the words cease being arbitrary signs and become *natural signs,* arbitrary things."[28] Signs in drama are "motivated" when mimetic reproduction causes the work being performed to become iconically involved in the original production. According to the idea Lessing develops here, the participation is *temporal.* It becomes possible because of the syntactic properties of poetic language, which is the vehicle that "transports" time. Lessing discovers time as the defining quality of literature. Although he refers to written literature, he repeatedly returns to the qualities of oral poetry. The condition of orality appears to him to be the typical condition of literature. Oral poetry is literature in time: simultaneity of production and reception, the consumption of time and a transitory nature that does not imply a forgetting.

Lessing is obviously concerned to recapture the oral character of poetry, which is supposed to happen by way of a language that preserves the temporal dimension in its written codification and passes it on to the recipient, a language that combines oral and literate characteristics: writing as the site at which time is preserved, combined with the oral character of actions. In this interpretation, Lessing's three principle innovations—the renewal of the oral character of literature, motivated signs, and interior reproduction—serve to convey the temporal aspects of poetry.

These ideas can be elucidated as follows. The speaking of the author takes place in time. If it is recorded on tape, precisely the same fragment of time can be reproduced when the tape is played back; for the listener, it is the time required for reception. The electromagnetic registration of the sounds serves as a qualified example of the recording of speech through writing: writing is a temporal process; time in this sense is not something imagined by the writer but a characteristic of writing. The act of writing down contains the authors "lived time";[29] writing is in this respect a repository of time, a preservation of time, an act of producing a particular memory.[30] Marcel Proust will demonstrate later how this writing is inscribed in the body and how memory is released by sense and motor perceptions. But also in Proust memories remain accessible under written "addresses"; they have names: "la petite madeleine de la tante Léonie"; "le pavé de Saint Marc"; "la petite phrase de Vinteuil."

How is it possible to imagine that time is "transported" by means of writing? If the statement is supposed to have more than a metaphorical meaning, the techniques and devices by which such a conveyance becomes possible must be made explicit. On the magnetic tape is a series of technologically created marks, which, taken in themselves without being played back, are neither words nor even sounds. But precisely in this quality, in the abstractness or emptiness that presupposes an additional procedure, lies the necessary condition of the possibility of a transportation of time. Both the sender and the receiver dispose over the appropriate technical devices and knowledge necessary for the recording to be decoded. But this is not all; the recipient has an interest in the author (for example, to hear him or her), just as the author has an interest in the recipient (for example, the wish to be heard). Thus the author-recipient relation is based on a characteristic relational structure, a central property of which is complementary interests. The processes of writing and reading are composed of analogous elements.

Let us go through the elements of the writer-reader relation in detail: written marks in themselves are meaningless, empty; they contain no sounds, no meanings, no time. They must be decoded, which requires the use of a technology that was already employed in the encoding process, but now with significant differences: reading is not only a different process than writing, if only because, if done aloud, it activates the voice and the ear and acquires, as performance, a social character. Reading also brings to the fore the fundamental difference between the role of the writer and that of the reader.

Assume that a man composes a text, a message, a description, a story, a set of user's instructions, or a poem. In the formulation, dissemination, and representation of the contents, he turns to one or several other persons on whom he focuses his expectation that they will read his text. These readers must be able to understand what is written; the author is obliged to choose his language and representational mode in such a way that readers can understand what is essential to the text; he must assess in advance their capabilities and the effort they will be required to expend. The writer thus prepares, at least in its crude outlines, the place in which the readers will be put. There are scarcely any texts that do not, at least in a rudimentary way, contain roles for the readers and bring these roles into relation with the role of the writer.

The author writes for absent readers; they read the text of an absent writer. There exists latently in a text the role of a person who wants to be read. This summons is answered by reading. But there seems to be a contradiction here: only when the reader has answered the summons to read is it possible for the summons itself to have been read. The author's desire is obviously present, not only inside the text, but in the existence of the text as such. In a form that has not yet been decoded, the desire is already expressed: the written marks have the character of an appeal. They are addressed to people who are capable of fulfilling the role of the reader that is also implicitly contained in the text; they summon potential readers to surrender their time to the author and bring him or her to speech. Contained in reading is an activity that is no longer merely the activity of the reader, namely, the action undertaken by someone else—the writer—in the expectation that the reader will take over the writer's words by internalizing them or, in reading them aloud, will speak with the writer's voice.

Since we no longer routinely read aloud, as was the custom in Greece in the first centuries following the introduction of writing, the temporal dimension of reading as well as the character of language as action remain scarcely familiar. The practice of reading silently entails the internalization of the acts involved in the reception of a text and makes them into mental automatisms. We hardly notice that we are being summoned through the text by an absent author and that we reactualize by reading that which the latter has thought at a previous time. The mental reproduction of a previously produced mental formation brings into play not only the semantic dimension of the text but, in particular, the syntactic dimension. Reading requires us to share certain things in common with the author, which do not necessarily include the interpretation of the meaning of the text. Every correct semantic interpretation has as a precondition the reading of the text and, indeed, a reading that corresponds to that of the author.

Had we retained the custom of reading aloud, it would be easier to summarize the points at issue here: the writer puts down in the text what he or she previously expressed aloud; the reader, in reading aloud, repeats exactly the same words that were originally spoken. This illustration, of course, is fictional: a writer who conceives a text for an absent reader and commits it to writing has no need to speak it aloud (and if so, perhaps only in part or experimentally). Nevertheless, a text is produced in the act of writing. There is also a fiction at the heart of writing, that is, the relationship of roles distributed among writer and readers. But what we are interested in here is not fictional at all, but thoroughly real, namely, the time that the empirical reader spends when he or she answers the appeal that comes to expression in the text. How much and whose time the reader reactualizes in the process is insignificant. What is critical is the appeal of the text to readers that they spend their time reading it, just as the author spent time writing it down. It is easy to imagine this process if we think of the time spent reading a bulky novel, the reading of which (and, presumably, also the composition) requires an unusually long time.[31]

Reading and Time

We shall be well served by a turn to the early phase of reading in our culture, when reading was performed aloud, to garner concrete information about the temporal processes it involves. Such information is available in Svenbro's investigation, *Phrasikleia,* which develops an anthropology of reading in early Greece.

In the first centuries following its introduction, Greek writing was "first and foremost a machine for producing sounds."[32] Writing was exclusively read aloud. One very early use of writing involved inscriptions on monuments, especially epigrams on grave statues. Inscriptions on the base of such statues speak in the first-person singular; they say "I." The following appears on a bronze statue from the sixth century B.C., found on the Acropolis in Athens: "To whomever asks me, I reply [*hupokrínomai*] with the same [*ísa*] answer, namely that Andron, the son of Antiphanes, dedicated me as a tithe."[33] To anyone who poses it a question, the inscription offers an answer. And, indeed, always the same answer. The statue refers to itself; the inscription is autodeictic, indeed, "forthrightly egocentric," in the correct etymological sense of the word. It takes over "the *ego* of the speech act"; it makes the statue into a "speaking object" (Burzachechi). But this statement is not comparable to normal verbal expressions; the "inscriptional first-person speech of objects" (Häusle) does not have an original speaker who would have performed it in an empirical speech situation. We would be closer to the mark in saying that the communication is "staged by an author who is systematically considered absent.''[34] An amphora from the sixth century speaks, by designating itself, of its manufacturer: ''Kleimachos made me and I am his (*eimì keínou*).''[35]

The presence of the inscription emphasizes the absence of the author. The reading of it aloud acquires its significance in the span between the present time of reading and the past time of its manufacture. What kind of *I* is speaking here? *Ego* expresses a spatial and temporal conception, which J. Brugmann designates ''hereness,'' a condition lacking in ''psychological depths.'' It belongs to the present of the statue; it comes from the producer and will be repeated later by whoever reads the inscription. The temporal dimension of the writing is the time of the respective readings, the pronunciation with the mouth of the reader in the respective presents. Every new reading and pronunciation is a repetition of a fragment of time from the past. The ''transport of time,'' as this reference back to the early history of reading shows, amounts to a reactualization of the same act of reading in the present of the reader, who lives in a different time from that of the absent author. It is the unchanging presence of the statue that the inscription contains—later it will be the unchanging presence of the depersonalized writing—and that makes the reactualization of time possible. The present of the statue in the presence of the reader inserts its inscription into the respective present, as a ''hereness'' expressed in material, in which it can disseminate its enactment in the lived time of the reader.

Early Greek inscriptions illustrate the temporal process so clearly because, reduced to their syntactic dimension, they were regarded as a kind of written-character material when they were not being read. Our automatic reading apparently comprehends at a glance both the syntactic and the semantic dimension; we assume that it is possible to see both a word and its meaning simultaneously and thus combine into a single act the decoding of the characters and the interpretation of meaning. We overlook the extension inherent in the time of reading, which realizes the appeal of the text and brings a past time into the present.

In terms of the early Greek attitude toward writing, which regards what is written but not spoken, the unread text, as incomplete, the structural linking of writing with the act of reading is constitutive for the text: ''the reading is part of the text.''[36] From this point of view, the text requires the reader's temporal investment; reading is not a private process, but belongs both to the reader and to the text. ''If he lends his voice to these mute signs, the text appropriates it: his voice becomes the voice of the written text.''[37] The words spoken by readers are not their own; they put their voices at the disposal of the text as a ''necessary instrument'' for its realization. Everything depends on the action of the voice, not on the person. The voice is an accomplice, the instrument that the author needs if the written characters are to acquire reality. ''To write is thus to demonstrate one's mortality, one's humanity. . . . The abstract Reader of the poem, however, is immortal, eternally renewable and, as such, stands as the polar opposite of the one [Sappho] who presents the proposition: 'I write, so

I shall die.' In truth, that is exactly what the majority of archaic inscriptions say.''[38]

The following inscription appears on the base of a bronze statue found at Halicarnassus:

$$αὐδὴ \ τεχνήεσσα \ λίθου \ λέγε$$

Svenbro translates the inscription "O voice that reads the stone, read!"—a self-directed vocative. This inscription "demonstrates the *tékhnē* that it is thought to possess. The inscription counts on that *tékhnē* of the reader, which suggests that the *lége* should be translated as "read!"[39] The voice, by reading the inscription, puts itself at the service of the stone. Later, once reading has become routine, texts no longer express such an imperative; but everything that is written nevertheless presses this claim by virtue of the fact that it has been written, preserved, and prepared for the absence of the author.

This expectation is most clearly expressed in the theater; written dramas demand a performance, and the text must be spoken aloud. It is hardly surprising that Lessing discovered the temporal character of literary language through his analysis of the structures of dramatic signs. A theatrical performance is richly suggestive of the transformation of a text into spoken language. At the same time, the spectator knows that it is based on a written text. It can therefore be observed to operate in both directions, from the text to the performance and from the spoken to the written. It is Svenbro's thesis that this latter movement, as it became a familiar experience to the Greek public, made possible the transition from reading aloud to reading silently. The process, however, cannot be understood simply as the consequence of frequent extensive reading; rather, it arises out of a change in attitude toward the written.

According to Svenbro, the innovation of silent reading can be traced back to the experience of the theater in Greece of the fifth century B.C. "Extensive reading seems . . . to have been the *outcome* of a qualitative innovation."[40] What are the new elements here? The text is constantly present in the theater; the actors speak it, while the spectators watch passively and listen mutely. The actors lend autonomy to the text and demand a receptive attitude from the audience. What the latter sees and hears is the speaking of the text; the performance is part of the text, a "vocal writing"[41] that is necessary if the text is going to exist in this form. These two specifically theatrical properties—the autonomy of the text and the public's attitude of passive reception toward the spoken performance—effect, according to Svenbro's thesis, the separation of writing from the voice. The mute receptive attitude of the spectator is a result of the appellate character of the theatrical performance, which no longer summons one to read aloud but charms spectators into focusing their concentration exclusively on watching and listening. The presence of the theater is all-powerful; a printed text can likewise exercise a comparable fascination on the reader, so that its

omnipotent appellate character goes unnoticed and reading becomes the equivalent of surrender to the written. The time of a theatrical performance is social
time. It is also internalized by the spectator, taken up in the form of ideas and
emotions; it is both physical and measurable as well as psychological and subjective time.

Silent reading is accomplished in a fashion analogous to watching in a
theater: it is not understood as exertion; it is an act the active character of which
is no longer prominent enough to be noticed. It is regarded primarily as a
momentary recognition of meaningful successions of words, while the idea that
the reader's time is being infiltrated by the text remains obscure. "The text that
is 'recognized' visually seems to have the same autonomy as the acting on the
stage."[42] The actor on the stage is an instrument by which the text is interpreted; his acting is directly legible to the spectator's eye. Thus, in the experience of watching in a theater, does the play become a text that one can read
in its public performance. Inversely, written characters, after silent reading has
become widespread, appear in a fashion that is comparable to the play: they
are passively read and internally "performed." The text, now become autonomous, no longer needs to be read aloud; it "vocalizes" itself.[43]

The temporal dimension of writing lies in its theatrical and scenic character
for silent reading (understood as passive); the written letters disseminate the
text as a total enactment. In reading, the reader follows the temporal succession
of written characters. The measurable time that passes in the process corresponds to the subjective time of an "internal" performance, which, though
distinct from physical time, remains always bound to it. The notion of reading
that arises with this new conception is one in which the book is inscribed in
the mind, *phrénos*. "The dramatic poet, who writes texts intended for mem-
orization by the actors, is aware in a very concrete manner of the inscription
of the text in the mind of the actor. To the dramatic poet, the actor seems to
receive an inscription in the same way that a stone or a papyrus leaf may receive
one. The mind of the actor is a space for writing, [an] inscriptional space."[44]

The performance of a play is a reactualization of time, not precisely the time
that the author spent writing, but an idealized temporal fragment measured out
of his or her lived time and reserved for the play. It was this use of time of which
Lessing became aware. We can read in the *Hamburgische Dramaturgie* how
he inserted the performance time of plays into his own time, his lived time.[45]
Spectators, by being present at the play, assume the performance time into their
lived time. The performance time takes up the lived time of the author and the
spectators; in this respect, literature cannot lie.[46]

Time on the stage is constituted by theatrical plots. It belongs to the semantic
dimension of a play and, as signified time, cannot be measured by physical
means. Lessing establishes a reference between the author's time and the
spectators' time, mediated via the temporal extension of the performance, an
observation that is restricted to the syntactic level. But Lessing moves beyond

this to note a supplemental particularity on the semantic level: every action of speaking or writing is tied to a person; every listener hears, every reader reads as a person. Ivan Illich and Barry Sanders, in their book on the interrelations between thinking and writing, show how the category of the self arises only as a function of writing: "The idea of a self that continues to glimmer in thought or memory, occasionally retrieved and examined in the light of day, cannot exist without the text."[47] "The self is as much an alphabetic construct as word and memory, thought and history, lie and narration."[48] Writing becomes a testimonial of the self; the dramatic text registers a second temporal succession, namely, a succession in the time lived by the writer.

Lessing dramatizes the time of the self: it undergoes a development that he identifies as typical in ideal terms of the bourgeois tragedy—which is divided into acts and proceeds from exposition to catharsis, with the effect of improvement. The lived time of the dramatic author, for Lessing, is his development into a refined, a purified, individual. The temporally determined mimesis of language by means of language marks the course of a personal development. In the moment of catharsis, the lived time of the author and spectator (or reader) coincide. *Laocoön* contains the kernel of a rediscovery of time (following what was probably the first discovery by Augustine)[49] as that which constitutes literature and opens the way for time to be treated thematically in literary texts and in the drama.

At this point we must recall the objection raised by Goodman in his theory of symbols: the linguistic characters of writing have no semantic differentiation. Semantic density does not allow for any necessary transmission—free of error, arbitrariness, illusion, or distortion—of the meaning of a text. In Lessing, the rules of poetry—in distinction to the entire prior tradition—serve as a guide to the imagination, not only of the producer of a text, but also of the recipient: the rules are supposed to guide the spectators' reactualization of worldmaking. Lessing redefines the role of the doctrine of the unities in regard to the poetic tradition; the unities are responsible for mediating between the productive and the reproductive imagination. They have meaning only in terms of this process, of their effects in the mind of the recipient. They cannot, therefore, be understood as external prescriptions, as had been customary in the time prior to Lessing.

Beginning with Castelvetro's commentary on Aristotle (1570), which formulated the doctrine of the three unities for the first time—that is, formulated it in a way that cannot be found in the *Poetics*—the unities had been imposed on drama from without as a formal regulatory apparatus.[50] For Lessing, however, only the principle of the unity of action is important; for it is the product of imagination, which concentrates on what is essential among things dispersed in time and manifests their inner coherence. The two other unities, of place and time, the imagination has no difficulty simply passing over. That the imagination is capable of effecting the unity of action, that it is endowed with a synthetic capacity, cannot, according to Lessing, be disputed—a position that differs fundamentally from the socially promulgated rules of the Italian Renaissance and French classicism, which are finally nothing other than social conventions even if they appear in the guise of universal concepts: bon sens, necessity, raison, *jugement.* In Lessing, rules serve to guide the imagination, to control it, to stimulate it to an extreme and drive it to catharsis.

Lessing ascribes to rules—if in completely changed, modernized form—the task of controlling literary texts. While this aspect of his work is not taken up by future theorists, his reflections on the syntactic dimension of language leads poetry in a new direction. Lived time flows into the act of writing something down: writing becomes a testimonial on the part of the author. On the syntactic level, there can be no talk of development, but instead only of authenticity. And, contemporaneous with *Laocoön,* there appears the textual model of authentic writing in Jean-Jacques Rousseau. He is also working on a connection between the oral and literate character of literature, but the issue for him is how to shape linguistic material and slip into it traces of life. Lessing and Rousseau realize two possibilities of textual formation on the syntactic level, both of which become important to modernity. Lessing chooses a more philosophical bearing, which uses writing as the site of the preservation of time; Rousseau seeks to find a place in writing for the traces of an authentic life and to impress transitory existence onto the surface of the text.

Lessing shifts the action in which writing and reading (or watching) have a part in the drama; Rousseau demonstrates that the real drama is the life of the author himself or herself: the lived-time dimension of his writing functions to dramatize his literary inspiration. The surface, the sensuous quality of the writer's action, makes visible the true *I.* Rousseau uses metaphors from painting to identify this process; in his letter to Dom Deschamps of 12 September 1761, he writes, "I am convinced that we are always well painted when we paint ourselves." Starobinski continues in reference to the letter, "A self-portrait is not a more or less faithful copy of a subject called 'the self.' It is a vital record of a search to discover the self."[51] Rousseau definitively abandons similarity as the principle of mimesis, replacing it with the idea of the trace.

Rousseau seeks the authenticity of the artist in the material traces of his or her poetic action—an idea that will be realized much later in surrealism, frottage painting, "action painting," "land art," and so on. Textual traces, in distinction to the traces found in painting, are organized in time; they are temporal traces. "Authentic speech," Starobinski writes about Rousseau, "occurs when the immediate impulse takes control." What is thus maintained in reference to speech is valid on the syntactical level of signs: "Words and essence coincide at once in the affirmation of a self. . . . The coincidence of words and essence is no longer a problem but a given. . . . It is unnecessary for the self to seek its source in the past, for that source exists here and now, in the surge of present emotion. . . . The essential task is therefore not to reflect upon or judge myself but to *be myself.*''[52] Mimesis does not disappear; thoroughly stripped of its pictorial character, it becomes a method of actualizing time, in which the author forges a connection with the reader or spectator. The drama becomes the model for Rousseau's writing.

Not only does Rousseau outline the first great model of subjectivity and self-mimesis, he also opens up the dimension in which modern individuality will be realized, the dimension of time. The authentic traces of the artist mark his or her individual lived time. It is a time unique to the artist, organized by personal events; it no longer feeds off the great flow of public time. Lived time constitutes a dynamic dimension in which the individual has the possibility of developing according to his or her own rhythm. Unlike private space, individual time is from the beginning a category of interiority, a sphere into which public power does not reach. It promises every individual a space in which to be entirely himself or herself. This particular, individual time is part of a mimetic construction of a world; having withdrawn into private time, the individual sends out manifestations of the self, authentic traces of life, into the space of the public sphere.

16

Self-Mimesis (Rousseau)

The majority of Rousseau's texts are written in an action-oriented style suggestive of orality and have the fundamental structure of a drama. No other example of modern literature gives the reader such a distinct sense of how a dramatic structure can be used as an enactment of right—of justification and of being in the right. Each of Rousseau's texts bears the mark of his life; thus the impression of temporality and of process, in the temporal sense but also in the juridical sense of a process of justification. Although Rousseau's *Confessions* evidences this characteristic most clearly, autobiographical justification determines the fundamental structure of his thought in general and his perception of the world. The juridical standpoint finds expression in Rousseau's self-authorization to reproduce his life before the eyes of his readers; he draws them into a process of self-mimesis. It is not, however, disinterestedness that supplies the basis for Rousseau's literary maneuver; rather, he seeks to seduce those to whom he exposes his life into becoming similar to him. The process of becoming similar inclines the reader to believe Rousseau, to acknowledge the correctness of his views. His autobiography is thus much more than a description of a life or even the production of his own life. The world of his literary production is the actual, real world for him as well as for his readers. It comprises the valid interpretation of the world. As a support for his interpretation, Rousseau needs the reader, who shares his view and defends it along with him.

With Rousseau, literature begins to draw the reader into a world created by the author as a kind of higher reality. To this purpose Rousseau summons the arts of seduction, and, when necessary, he uses force—the thunder of his words and the powerful undertow of his narrative stream. We shall go into this aspect of his work below, after we have demonstrated how Rousseau's autobiography contains a kind of user's manual, which is to be put into the hands of his readers for their own use.

The *Confessions* marks the beginning of the adoption by the individual over against both the public sphere and himself or herself of a *self-representational* behavioral form: it is a turning outward of an intimate interiority.[1] The dissemination of autobiography defined in this way sets into motion a cycle of self-observation and self-consciousness.[2] Rousseau convinces his readers that society has done damage to the individual. To this social corruption, he counterposes "the ideal of authentic personal being."[3]

Self-Formation

With reckless love of truth and in unadorned, "natural" language, Rousseau lays bare his *I*, exposes his ego to public view. Layer by layer he strips away the skins he has grown in the air of society: lies about his life, his own pretenses, other people's distortions, prevailing conventions, and so on. What emerges is an *I* about which no one had really been able to speak before, which no one, even in the most intimate conditions, could have perceived in another. Rousseau's words trace the contours of this *I*, which, far from "grand," is extremely vulnerable and morally inadequate. This *I* expands nonetheless to breathtaking dimensions, because it goes so far in its honesty as to desire only to be itself, to oppose itself in its raw condition to social conformities of all sorts. Rousseau's aim is to represent his *I* as honestly as possible, to render his heart "transparent comme le cristal." "Rousseau lets his emotions speak and agrees to write from dictation."[4] He accepts errors into the bargain, thereby giving rise to "a more complete truth, but one that escapes the usual laws of verification. We have moved from the realm of (historical) *truth* to that of *authenticity* (the authenticity of discourse)."[5]

The authenticity that Rousseau's *I* undertakes to realize—perhaps for the first time—is essentially the product of the elimination of all socially imposed falsifications. These include, first of all, falsifications on the level of the representational mode; Rousseau, in the preface to his *Confessions,* promises to deliver the only existing portrait of an individual that is "painted in every way true to nature and in all of its reality."[6] Then come the falsifications of the represented *I:* once all social elements have been subtracted, as it were, from the portrait, there emerges a unique *I,* the *moi seul,* which is separated from others by a multitude of differences. "I may be no better, but at least I am different."[7]

It would be difficult to sustain a charge of naïveté against Rousseau's project. He sees clearly that representation is inseparable from social conventions, as, for example, those of the vernacular language. And he stresses the social influences worked on his true, unfalsified *I:* growing up in Pietist Geneva without a mother, leaping early into life, and so on. The idea is that underneath social institutions like language and other forms of influence are to be found elements of personality that resist social pressure; it is a kind of presocial substratum of the personality that bears distinctly subjective characteristics. This true personality lies concealed under a mask; Rousseau says of himself that he was "soigneux d'écarter mon masque" (intent on discarding my mask).[8] Once the mask is gone, there appears "un modèle intérieur," which the subject is capable of recognizing clearly. But to describe it, Rousseau had to "invent a language that is just as new as [his] project."[9]

The solution to the problem Rousseau sets himself consists in a new form of writing: he surrenders his most intimate feelings and memories to language, to the freedom of the *parole* and to "the movement of language."[10] The subjective principle of an *I* running counter to society is the most significant philosophical "invention" of the *Confessions*. The claim entails an assumption that all subjectivist authors find irresistible, that of an intimate *I* substantially removed from social existence, which is present beneath the public part of the personality and is latently antisocial. In exceptional circumstances, this *I* can break through the social overlay, for example, in an act of literary production or through intoxication or insanity, or otherwise in chance moments.

The society in which such an *I* exists necessarily appears repressive from this point of view, with the *I* getting caught up in a destructive conflict with oppression. The desire for an authentic existence becomes a political call for opposition to that which impedes the development of the intimate *I*. Only by developing gradually out of its individual subjects can a society arise which offers the individual a chance to realize his or her potential. Rousseau draws this political conclusion, a radical critique of society, in two of his discourses, on the arts and sciences and on the origin of inequality (1750 and 1755, respectively) and in the pedagogical conclusion to *Émile*.

By moving so directly to a call for political action, Rousseau glosses over an important problem: how, from an ontogenetic perspective, does knowledge about the intimate *I* come into existence? From a genetic standpoint, the first knowledge an individual develops comes via the body, which is to say that knowledge about one's own person and interiority is constituted from the perspective of the body. The individual gains knowledge of what is transpiring within through his or her behavior in public, or, more precisely, through processes of verbalization, through language. Given that language and concepts are socially formed, it is tempting to assume that it would be impossible on this account to gain knowledge about the intimate *I*. But why should it not be possible to deploy social instruments to a thoroughly personal, highly individual end? The intimate *I* is not necessarily a "private" *I* in Wittgenstein's sense. Moreover, language and concepts are not the only means by which this knowledge is constituted for Rousseau, a point that he overlooks in general. Since the *I* does not exist as an object accessible to public perception, it requires a *medium* in which to represent itself.[11] In order for the *I* to be able to depict itself faithfully, this medium must be a neutral one, a "mirror medium."

The initial formation of the ego, according to Jacques Lacan, takes place in the so-called mirror stage[12] of development, in front of a mirror that reflects an image to the child of the child's own body. But Lacan's mirror is not a passive medium; it not only portrays but also contributes in a certain sense to the production of the one who is portrayed. The mirror is not a dead object, but partner in a dialogue that goes on outside the awareness of the person being reflected. The mirror emphasizes certain features and characteristics, identifies interrelationships, provokes comparison to other mirror images; it produces a coherent image and conveys the incontrovertible conviction that the person being reflected is as he or she appears to be in the mirror. This conviction is determined by the mirror; the person being reflected can mount no resistance to it.[13]

It is necessary here to draw a distinction in regard to two aspects of the mirror. First are the characteristics of the medium itself: like all expressive media, the mirror exercises a formative influence over that which is expressed through it. Second is the user of the mirror, who holds it up in front of the person being reflected and retreats behind it. The user deploys the formative power of mirror. The child, which has as yet no fixed ideas about its *I,* is led to a specific form of the *I* by the person who controls the mirror. It is always others who—intentionally or not—occasion the child's look in the mirror, and these others thus participate in the formation of the child's *I.* To the mirrored child, this circumstance remains concealed; the mirror is doing nothing but reflecting reality. The adult who holds a mirror up has long since lost faith in the mirror's truthfulness.

The mirror has two seemingly countervailing effects. First, it persuades the child to accept a specific image of itself, to regard as real that which the mirror shows it. Second, the mirror represents a barely palpable constraint that is being introduced into the child's life, by reason of the fact that it always repeats the same image. It forces the child to submit to its reflected identity. Endless repetitions submit the child to a specific discipline that fixates its thinking on the mirror image as an image of the self. These two effects of the formative and fixating image—persuasion and discipline—both aim in the same direction: the mirror enables the person holding it to choose a specific type of mirrored reflection as the real image of the child, to persuade the child to accept this *I,* and to fix it as its own, because of the child's disciplined perception of the evidence of the mirror, as its real self-image for the future. The medium of the mirror and its user, as constituent elements of society, are both so deeply entangled in the constitution of knowledge about the intimate *I* that they must ultimately be regarded as the essential constituents of self-knowledge.[14]

Given this analysis of the mirror, the question arises as to how we might justifiably apply it to Rousseau's autobiography. If we acknowledge that the latter is a mirror medium, then we also have to assume that Rousseau displays to us his (presumably) intimate *I* in terms of a representational structure reserved for biographical purposes, a structure, that is to say, that preexists Rousseau's representation of his *I*. The particularity of his *Confessions* would then lie in the impression of freshness it conveys, in the immediacy of the representation. If this is the case, then we are dealing here with an aesthetic effect, while Rousseau's exploration of his own person amounts to the utilization of a conventional structure of representation. A more precise analysis of what this entails presupposes a treatment of the structure of self-representation and an examination of the structure of the *I*.

However much it might seem that Rousseau's autobiography resembles a novel, the self-representation it offers us bears essential characteristics of the drama.[15] Its dramatic structure is constituted by the following compositional elements. The readers are addressed directly; they are put in the position of an audience, as simultaneous witnesses and judges of Rousseau's *I*. The fundamental structure of the text is thus dialogical. Moreover, the justificatory character of the *Confessions* shows that Rousseau intends to exercise an effect on his audience. He represents events with the aim of exhibiting, of manifesting, his *I*. We observe biographical circumstances as if we were watching a peep show. The text is arranged as a series of sequences. Each sequence represents an event, acquires a particular meaning, and fulfills a function, as an individual scene within the overall set of events, in the construction of a biography. The scenes are arranged in larger segments, comparable to acts.[16] In their procession, they constitute a dramatic process leading to ever more complex situations. They culminate in collisions between the *I* and the external world, which are not rationally comprehensible and which reach their climax in an unresolvable conflict that completely separates the self from society. Each collision, including the final and greatest of them, leads to an affirmation of the self, which, because of the intensity of the experience, becomes the equivalent of a formation of the *I*.[17] The *I*, in the experience of the conflict, is created anew. The dramatic purpose of Rousseau's report of a linear succession of external events thus lies in the representation of the increasing compartmentalization and complexity of Rousseau's *I*. He interprets an external set of events, which are accessible to perception, as the expression of an inner development.

The depiction of scenes from a life, taken to be the expression of the *I* of action and experience—this representational mode is much more than a dramatic artifice. Revelation exposes nothing that exists independently of the strategy of revelation. Rousseau's intimate *I* acquires its dramatic structure from the dramatic structure of its representation. The enactment of the *I*, by way of its dramatization, produces an impression of authenticity: the revelatory character of the work, the collisions it depicts, the differences between the self and milieu, the isolation, and its aggressively unconventional openness appear to make it possible to have speech in the absence of artifice. This authenticity is produced within a literary world; it is *mimetic;* the *I* is artificial and at the same time genuine for the purpose of illusion. The dramatic conception of the *I* fulfills the hope placed in it by Rousseau and his successors only within the confines of an *aesthetic* project.[18] The *I* is not an instance of behavior undertaken in resistance to society. Constituted mimetically, the *I* belongs in this sense to the category René Girard terms *mensonge romantique,*[19] romantic lies. Resistance to the falsification of the *I* is transformed, in the process of a mimesis of authenticity, into an unnoticed reconciliation with society.

Pedagogy and Seduction[20]

The *Confessions* provide us with an example of a new type of worldmaking, which is centered on the individual and presented by an artist skilled in the uses of the emotive and anticipatory powers of language to act on the imagination. The seductive force of Rousseau's approach may not be fully apparent in his autobiography, but it appears in full strength in the two novels that have as their protagonists an educator, *Émile* and *Julie, ou la nouvelle Héloïse.* These books develop, discuss, and test a new discourse and new techniques of human development. They begin the history of strategies of seduction presented under the mantle of pedagogy. The new educational knowledge on which they are based has the inestimable advantage of renouncing the old style of seduction as immoral and creating for the seducer the role of helper and educator, whose job it is to set free the potential slumbering in the hearts of his pupils.

The transformation of the old art into the new science of seduction, which can no doubt be tied to the decline of the ancien régime, is nowhere more evident than in the novel by Choderlos de Laclos, *Les Liaisons dangereuses.*[21] This old art of seduction relies on the careful separation of truth and falsity: the seducer wears a mask that conceals his true face; his apparent moralism dissimulates his absolute separation from any and all laws of man and God; his alleged motives are pretenses, behind which lies the real goal, which is seduction, the enjoyment of the seduced, and, yet more sublime, the enjoyment of the enjoyment via confidential letters telling a third person of how the last and highest obstacle was overcome.

The old strategies of seduction, as can easily be seen, have two main failings: the play with falsity necessarily appears highly immoral; and the object of desire is in principle not to be had, for the desired person, once possessed, loses his or her value. The events in Laclos's novel differ from the old seduction strategies on both of these points: at the end Valmont, the inveterate seducer of the old style, falls into the trap of the profoundly moral being of the Présidente; captivated by the surrender of innocent female being, his strength, which has been fed up to that point by cynicism and calculations of power, fails him. This fatal victory of innocence, the first victim of which is innocence itself, can be read as an ironic twist on Rousseau's lesson of the victorious power of virtue in *Julie*. Laclos has the Présidente pursue a pedagogical strategy, if, as befits her character, timidly, in the intention of improving Valmont's character. Precisely her worthy aim becomes her ultimate doom; Valmont overcomes her resistance by pretending that her strategy has succeeded. The pedagogue becomes the victim of her (apparent) pedagogical success; she becomes the possession of and is possessed by the object of her teaching.

We see in this development a reversal—even a twofold reversal—of the ideas Rousseau expressed in *Émile*. Here the pedagogue succeeds in truly and comprehensively shaping the character of the pupil, in this way taking over the latter's thoughts and will. What Rousseau offers may seem like a technically expert and innovative pedagogy, with only a few incidental remarks suggesting otherwise (and they do not fundamentally alter the educational conception on which it is based). Laclos's parodistic twist of the ideas in *Émile,* however, throws a completely different light on the educational project: the formation of Émile's character becomes the central element in a new strategy of seduction. Laclos seems to repudiate the strategy ironically—the inflated moral language, the nobility of his characters' souls, and their renunciation of pleasure for its own sake prompt the representative of the ancien régime to vigorous pro-test[22]—but the universal applicability and the certain success of the new methods escape him.[23]

Other bourgeois theoreticians of seduction also make use of the devices of pedagogy. The life of Søren Kierkegaard's seducer[24] is based on an aesthetic attitude toward pleasure that likewise approximates the immoralism of the ancien régime. But he too prefers not to return to a game of mere pretense. The point for him is not the possession of the body of the one he desires: "I can imagine," writes the fictional publisher of the diary, "that he knew how to excite a girl to the highest pitch, so that he was certain that she was ready to sacrifice everything. When the affair reached this point, he broke it off without himself having made the slightest advances and without having let fall a single word of love, let alone a declaration, a promise."[25] That is, no falseness, but also none of the rhetoric of love; rather, a new discourse that operates on the imagination of the object of seduction: once the victim has finally been forsaken, she struggles with her doubts as to whether the whole thing was not simply her own fancied invention.

The abandoned Cordelia writes to her seducer, "Flee where you will, I am still yours." She is inspired by no other thought than "being [his] slave."[26] The seducer has forsaken the person, but her soul remains in his possession. "But what enjoyment can there be in love if there is not the most absolute self-surrender, at least on one side?"[27]

The faculty of imagination, the central point of attack for the Rousseauian educational system, is stimulated by pedagogical techniques. "What am I doing? Do I fool her? Not at all; that would be of no use to me. Am I stealing her heart? By no means. . . . Then what am I doing? I am creating for myself a heart in the likeness of her own. An artist paints his beloved . . . a sculptor fashions his. I do this too, but in a spiritual sense."[28] Seduction depends on lending form; the seducer's weapon is an image. It represents the object of desire, but not as she is or as she sees herself. It is a fantasy image that reveals one potential development of her person, that shows what she could become. As soon as the object of seduction becomes fascinated by this possible image she falls under the power of the seducer. Each step in her development renders her more dependent on the figure in the image. Only because the object of seduction desires herself does she let herself be seduced. In retrospect the seducer will say, "Her development was my handiwork."[29]

In the final and highest stage of seduction, the imaginative world permeates the girl's real world; the seducer has constructed a dream world. The reconstruction of Cordelia's normal surroundings, her apartment, "everything is the same, only richer," "the illusion is perfect."[30] The seducer himself enters along with her into the fantastic reality. "Everything is symbol; I myself am a myth about myself."[31] He rises to ultimate levels: the creator of an image and an environment that are taken as one's own special world. "How vigorous is my soul, sound, happy, omnipresent like a god."[32]

The pedagogical strategy of seduction gains a certain independence over against the desired object in comparison with the strategy of the *ancien régime.* The latter does not indeed require a beautiful person, but at least she must belong to a rich, aristocratic, highly regarded family—all of these are conditions that must be fulfilled not only by the desired woman but also by her husband. Desire, the magnitude of which depends on the status of the husband, is aimed ultimately at consuming the prestige of the man. It places almost no demands on the object of desire aside from the one, that it must be a suitable object of erotic affection. Kierkegaard's seducer demands that it be a young girl, no matter which; instead of Cordelia, it could also have been one of the many girls he is constantly observing. Don Juan's Zerline is as insignificant as possible; and Faust's Gretchen acquires meaning for him only through her love.[33]

Rousseau demands nothing but a completely normal child, although the latter might have to fulfill one further condition to become the object of the seduction: it cannot be his own biological child. This idea might appear highly speculative, but it explains why Rousseau would depict in fictional form the raising of a stranger's child, while sending his own children to an orphanage. One already has one's own child and cannot want to possess it (unless in the sense of a projection). All of this, of course, has very little to do with the educational practices of a traditional schoolmaster.

Personality formation is expected of a pedagogue; it thus allows the seducer to assume a normal social role. Given the skills of a pedagogue, it is pedagogy that has the best chances of success: the seducer develops an image that represents a possible future stage of higher development in the child. A persuasive discourse is capable of capturing the imagination of the child and causing it to desire its own image. In the process, the position of the educator becomes ever more firmly established; the child will do everything possible to achieve the promised state. The path to that state—as is repeatedly made clear to the child by indirect means—is indicated by the educator. Even the details of the image, which the child does not yet know, but wants to, are supplied in the educator's step-by-step depiction. With the image, the pupil takes over the ideas, goals, and ultimately the will of the educator. Everything that the child wants, conceives, and strives for, the educator has already made part of the image.

The educator not only watches his power increase over the object of desire but also his desire.[34] Because the child desires itself, it becomes a rival; the cycle of mimetic competition, the imitation of desire, is set in motion. It is sufficient now for the educator to continually stimulate the pupil's own self-love to secure for himself a constant affective attraction. What he must by all means avoid is the penetration into his closed system of a third person, such as one with whom the pupil falls in love.

Rousseau chooses a compelling solution in *Émile:* he prepares the place in the mind of his pupil for a potential lover of his own. The educator supplements the image he has defined, at the proper time, just prior to the completion of physical and psychological maturation, with the figure of a fictional lover. The real person whom Émile will later love thus steps into a precisely prepared position. Does Émile really love Sophie? This question, in the frame of Rousseau's seduction strategy, has a distinct meaning. Émile imagines himself to be in love; his imagination is guided by his teacher. What really is and what is the product of his imagination cannot be separated. The fictional world contains no line demarcating the true from the false.

Rousseau's *Julie* describes a structure of seduction referred back on the person of the seducer. The point of departure here, as in the modern seduction of an Other, is the wish to desire a person in which the wish is directed toward the seducer's self. Self-seduction is ultimately the consistent development of a line that was already established in the old style of seduction. Madame de Merteuil[35] knows precisely how one's gaze at the object of seduction is subject to the multiple formation of mirrorings and imaginative fancies. In one's perception of the desired person there is scarcely an element existing independently of the desiring observer: "For, let us not deceive ourselves, the charm we think we find in others exists only in ourselves, and it is love alone that confers beauty on the beloved."[36] In *Julie,* the imaginative system has been developed to the highest stage. Love is talked about constantly, but it is not allowed to unfold: the plot of the novel consists in the prevention of love. Thus is *Julie,* though easily experienced as a love story, actually the antithesis of one.

According to the customary way of reading, the tutor Saint-Preux and his pupil Julie are hopelessly in love with each other. The girl's father refuses her tie to the lover, who lacks both means and a name, and marries her to his aristocratic friend Wolmar. Many years later, Saint-Preux, whom Julie has had to abandon, is taken in by Wolmar and charged with the education of the children who have meanwhile been born; he gains the privileged position of an intimate friend of the mistress of the house. Saint-Preux knows how to appreciate the generosity of the husband and lives at Julie's side, if tormented by a certain temptation, without deceiving his benefactor. It is a ménage à trois after Rousseau's taste. The specific effect, however, is that what at least appeared to be a burning love is transformed into an intimate tie of friendship and with the approval of the third party.

There are, to be sure, serious questions as to whether Saint-Preux's love at the beginning of the novel is ignited by his pupil. One might sooner have the impression that an overheated sort is seeking an object of desire anyway, whereby Julie, the person who is immediately present and his pupil, has only to take over an already established role. Three successive letters from Saint-Preux, two of which go unanswered, form a kind of accelerated foreplay to a desire that grows constantly larger in proportion to the obstacles set in its path. Julie is less the focus of discussion than himself. Saint-Preux, at the beginning of the novel, is more a rhetorician of love; he becomes a lover only through Julie's response, in which she reveals her own love to him. Julie is not the person who releases his passions but the one who puts him in the role of the lover. She enables Saint-Preux to experience himself as inflamed. What prompts Saint-Preux's seductive activities is Julie's capacity to reciprocate love. Claire, Julie's intimate friend and cousin, writes to her, "There is no surer way to win the affection of another than to give him your own."[37]

Julie loves Saint-Preux, and Saint-Preux loves himself. The relationship has an obviously triangular structure: two persons love the same object, and each desires because the other desires; the two desiring persons enter into competition with each other. The sharper the competition, the more intense the feelings produced. The triangle has the particular characteristic that its apex— the loved, idealized Saint-Preux—exists only in the imagination of the two persons. For neither desires the empirical Saint-Preux; both desire the image that he has made of himself and that represents the passionate lover of Julie.[38]

The husband, Wolmar, despite his intellectual superiority, never has a chance to penetrate the triangle. But he controls the object of his desire, Julie, whom Saint-Preux's love makes all the more desirable. As the one who is in control and who loves, he becomes the equivalent of Émile's teacher; he prevents feelings from becoming overpowering. The means of control, which he instills in both actors, is self-education: they may experience themselves as lovers but must behave as friends. Wolmar informs the trusted Claire of his exact diagnosis of the emotional state of the couple: "that they burn more hotly for each other than ever before, that there is something between them beyond an honorable affection; that they remain lovers and are not friends; that is something, I venture, you scarcely expect and will believe only with some difficulty."[39] Saint-Preux, for his part, writes to Milord about his state of well-being: "C'est celui de se plaire avec soi-même";[40] it is the state in which one is appealing to oneself.

Part V

Mimesis as the Principle of Worldmaking in the Novel and Society

With the turn of the nineteenth century, the rhetorical tradition is left definitively behind. Old conceptions of mimesis can no longer be enforced because there is no longer any recognition of an obligatory canon according to which the literary language can be codified. We also find at this time a marked retrieval of the oral elements of language, which expresses a turn toward social practice as registered by the senses.

The changes are particularly evident in the rehabilitation of images in the sensuous representation of reality or of the imagination. Since images are ill-suited to science and the acquisition of a knowledge of essences, since they may even impede the type of cognition necessary to both, Plato regarded them as dangerous. But, with the Renaissance, images start to play an increasingly significant role in thought and expression. The cosmos, the social milieu, and the human body are brought into mutual reference and classified in the form of images. In the eighteenth century, they take on a new actuality, which is legible in the general cultural resonance of physiognomy, that is, of a decoding of physical phenomena that is at once mystical and scientific. Images of social life come to the fore in the nineteenth century, as is most clearly expressed in the social novels that begin to appear in France. Particular to this shift is the *affective* nature of images in the nineteenth century: authors see themselves as also involved in the world they represent; their task is to lend expression to an internal perspective, to an individual way of seeing as regards social relations, social opportunities and expectations, and the densely articulated context of action in which novelistic characters take part.

Nineteenth-century literary mimesis serves to isolate individual cases within the social totality; in this regard, it distinguishes itself from the great models of sociological, political, and economic theory. Literary mimesis comes now to be founded on methodological individualism, with new codes—which are expressive of the characters' interior circumstances in the form of precisely defined social indexes—laid out over the surface of social action. Literature treats external social appearances as a way to open up access to interior realms; it authorizes itself to convey a version of reality that, according to authors' claims, is superior to all other possible interpretations. There ensues a competition among the various modes of empirical description—scientific, philosophical, theological, and literary. The codes employed in literary mimesis are aesthetic; they are "translations" into the medium of the novel of codes that find application in social practice.

Nineteenth-century bourgeois society insists on the representation of social rank. The play of social action entails the production of worlds on the basis of principles that are analogous to those underlying novelistic construction. Balzac, for example, in order to create affectively charged images of society that enchant author and reader alike, makes use of the entire range of possible artistic devices stemming from the worldmaking of social practice. Himself desirous, he sets his readers off on the tracks of his characters with the intention of making them desirous as well. His novels help charge social practice with emotional energy and contribute to the fortification of customary patterns of normative judgment. Literary mimesis of social mimesis, of the modes of worldmaking current in society, as presented by the novelist—an expert in aesthetic representation—works to intensify readers' experience of social reality and to dramatize and justify it. Fascinated by the written world of Balzac's invention, they are cast under a spell, rendered virtually powerless to resist the authority of the author.

A number of other novelists, however, choose not to delve into social mimesis. Following Girard, we designate this approach "antiromantic," juxtaposing it to the "romantic" approach of Balzac. The antiromantic orientation is shaped by the authors' knowledge that their own worldmaking takes place only under the pressure of social forces operating both on the narrator and on his fictional characters. On the basis of this insight, they self-consciously distance themselves from social mimesis, thereby achieving a certain remove from society and developing an alternative authorial orientation in which literature is regarded as the free and splendid play of creativity. The understandings these authors, among them, Stendhal, Flaubert, and Dostoevsky, have of their roles diverge sharply from one another, but they share one thing in common: they are conscious of the inescapable social pressures that weigh on both their writing and the literary worlds they produce. Girard has worked out the defining characteristics of the work of these antiromantic authors. The extraordinary importance of his studies for our own analysis of mimesis in the nineteenth century stems, in particular, from the emphasis he places on the connection between literary and social mimesis at that time. The theory that he develops in the process amounts to a reconstructed version of the conception of mimesis implicit in the antiromantic novels; that is, it is not solely Girard's own theory that he presents, but one he also attributes to the antiromantic authors. It seems sensible to us to separate his literary analyses from his general theory of mimesis, which will be presented and discussed on its own at the end of Part V.

The antiromantic novels depict social actors, perceived from an external perspective, in the course of constructing their worlds in the medium of social action. At the same time, they show us action taking place in an interior medium, which is accessible only to an internal perspective. From within this internal perspective, characters produce interior images, choose models for their own action, and conceive their goals. It is here, always in reference to the Other, that desires, wishes, and goals come into being. The combination of external and internal perspectives in these novels makes it clear that what the characters are doing is searching for their own individual *I*. While they experience their own existence as empty, in the interior medium they attach themselves to another *I*, with the aim of becoming equivalent to this Other. The form of their relation to the Other is imitation, which can quickly turn into competition. Girard's antiromantic authors produce their novels through their efforts to overcome this rivalry.

Literary work offers the antiromantic authors the chance to free themselves from the power of the interior medium and to effect a catharsis of desire, rivalry, and violence. The *I* of both the fictional character and the author is relieved of the compulsion to follow the Other. This liberation is accomplished in the novel by way of a withdrawal from social life and the renunciation of mimesis. Individuals authorize themselves over against society in terms of a nonmimetic existence that is radically their own.

On the critical points, the antiromantic authors surpass their seventeenth-century predecessor, Madame de Lafayette: they do not content themselves with discovering the power of mimesis, but show it to be a driving force of social life whose grip they themselves, as representatives of their time, do not necessarily escape. They find a solution in writing. As authors, they make use of the world-producing power of mimesis in their representations, while attempting simultaneously to distance themselves from it. What makes this possible is first of all the formal construction of the novel, in particular, the play of perspectives, which exposes the quality of the social world as a mimetic composition and the role in that process of the individual imagination. Second, the novels reflect on their own mimetic constitution. This reflexive thematization of mimesis occasions a breakthrough to a modern aesthetic conception: worldmaking, that is, the process that produces both the social world and the antiromantic novel, becomes the object of literature. This representation of representation refers back to the medium and to the activity of both author and reader, to writing, reading, and imagining; it amounts to a reflexive approach to the constitutive processes of literature. In the visual arts, impressionism represents an analogous transformation (one that drew especially vigorous notice for having been so spectacularly enacted); impressionism takes as the foundation of its conception of art the making of worlds from the materials of light and seeing.

Antiromantic literature liberates the novel from social mimesis. But can it also overcome literary mimesis? What we in fact find in this period is a tendency toward the self-dissolution of the novel, of the representation of representation. Once mimesis is made fully visible, the novel falls silent; as long as it continues the project of depicting, the novel remains mimetic. Thus only silence can put an end to literary mimesis. In the twentieth century, Marcel Proust will offer a way out of this quandary: he develops the idea of the internal book offered to each reader for self-composition. But neither is this book ultimately a material product; rather, it finds completion only as an intellectual procedure that takes place beyond the written word.

The Mimetic Constitution
of Social Reality

Mimesis undergoes a fundamental transformation in the aftermath of the aesthetic debates over the imitation of nature in the Enlightenment and in German classicism and romanticism, a change that is particularly evident in the French social novels of the nineteenth century. These novels no longer focus on fashioning behavior, as did the bourgeois tragedy, claiming instead to be involved in the mimetic composition of reality itself. It is not, as Auerbach maintains, a situation in which literary representations come to approximate social reality ever more nearly; rather, it is that they make up an essential aspect of social life itself. Reduced to a concise formula: the aesthetic principle of mimesis is generalized far beyond the sphere of art into a constitutive characteristic of class society. Inseparable from this expansion is an initial decline in theoretical interest in the concept of mimesis; only in the twentieth century does an intensive preoccupation with the concept return. To understand the thoroughgoing functional transformation of mimesis, we must begin with the symbolic dimension of nineteenth-century bourgeois society.

Images of a Society

Social reality does not exist independently of linguistic representations and, in a certain sense, is itself constituted linguistically. Literary descriptions advanced with the authority of a figure of Balzac's stature lay claim to an essential role in the symbolic aspect of society. Balzac characterizes this (purported) accomplishment on the part of the novel as a form of science.[1] In doing so, however, he fails to do justice to the particularity of his literary writing. He begins with the description of the outward appearances typical of members of a specific social class. To these belong the ways in which they present themselves in public, their self-representational modes, their life-styles—everything that indicates social membership, which, in turn, is perceived and evaluated by other persons.

Balzac's "tableaus" and "scenes" show how a social rank is literally produced. It is possible to recognize in such simple things as clothing a person's primary social characteristics: "Why should clothing not always amount to the most eloquent of styles if it were not truly the whole of the individual, the individual with his political opinions, the individual along with the text of his existence, the individual rendered in hieroglyphs? The individual is contained in the style of his clothing." This is the position Balzac offers in *Traité de la vie élégante*.[2] "*Vestignomie* has today nearly become a branch of the art founded by Gall and Lavater. Although all of us now dress in approximately the same way, it is easy for an observer to pick out in the crowd the proletarian, the property owner, the consumer and the manufacturer, the lawyer and the soldier, the man of words and the man of action."[3]

It is an old idea, one that can already be found in classical antiquity, that it is possible to draw conclusions about a man's internal state from his external aspect. The presumption is that a truth about the nature of an individual is legible in the form and surface of the body: the body speaks an "all-meaningful language for the eyes."[4] Johann Lavater's influential work, *Physiognomische Fragmente, zur Beförderung der Menschenkenntnis und Menschenliebe* (1777–1778), is taken to have disclosed to view the interiority of the individual in a quasi-scientific way. The first outline of a systematic psychology, in Moritz's *Magazin für Erfahrungsseelenkunde,* also seeks the path leading from the external sign to internal fact. The external appearance of the individual betrays images of his or her real circumstances, which do not exist on their own but stand for something else, for something internal. This view changes in the nineteenth century: to the pictorial level of external social appearance is once again attributed the autonomy and affective content that was once, before being reduced by the critique of the Platonists, regarded as constituting the particularity of the image.[5]

In the Balzacian novel, images are no longer regarded as symptoms or indications but are themselves among the elements out of which society is constructed. They comprise one of its aspects—which is not theoretical truth but the perspective of a social individual in which the affective condition of bourgeois society is brought into relief, a reality that includes the interests of the actors, their passions and desires, as well as their relationships to social surroundings and the sensuousness of social life. Their truth is preconceptual, a doxa;[6] it lies in the concentration and intensity of literary representation. Social reality thus becomes an epicosmos of the realistic novel. The novel does not simply illustrate reality; rather, it is the means by which the truth associated with the sensuousness and substance of reality is rendered accessible to experience. To understand this point of view, we must turn briefly to the social theory of Pierre Bourdieu.

The differentiation of class societies, as they arise in France and England in the first half of the nineteenth century, is accomplished on the basis of the possession of capital. In distinction to the Marxist understanding of social classes, which Bourdieu draws on, he includes symbolic types of capital among the central criteria of class formation.[7] Class action is culturally coded.[8] The possession of economic capital on its own secures neither the legitimation of a higher social rank, nor the prestige associated with a rank, nor the lifestyle on the basis of which classes and subclasses differentiate themselves.

> Alongside specifically economic distinctions appear symbolic differences that relate to the type of utilization or, if you will, the type of consumption, in particular, that of symbolic or ostentatious consumption, that works to double the commodities, to transform them into signs, or, as linguists put it, into values. A *manier,* the form of an action or of an object, comes to the fore at the expense of function. For this reason the distinctions that carry the greatest prestige are those that symbolize most clearly one's position in the social structure, such as clothing, speech or accent, and above all "manners," taste, and education.[9]

Social differences between classes and subclasses, which Bourdieu terms "distinctions," are more or less discreetly expressed in the struggle over recognition, prestige, and the relative superiority of the respective types of symbolic capital. In the public and performative character of the cultural coding of class affiliation is found the connection between the symbolic dimension of society and the tableaus and scenes in Balzac's novels. The linkage between economic and cultural power is the central theme of the *Comédie humaine.* "Economic power is first and foremost a power to keep economic necessity at arm's length";[10] it offers the possibility of preferring style "at the expense of accomplishment."[11] Balzac is fascinated by the distinction of the leading class, by the "caractère d'élegance, de noblesse et de bon ton,"[12] by a person's virtuoso disposal over the means of style. Class society is a cultural society, a capitalism of taste; economic being is doubled via the devices of aesthetic appearance.

Balzac describes these interrelationships and at the same time is involved in them in the conduct of his own life. Trapped inside the illusion of a person rising through the social ranks, he imitates the behavior of the leading classes, makes models of them, undertakes propaganda in their favor, and creates prestige for them by having them appear aesthetic and desirable. How does it happen, he asks himself, that an individual exercises the effect of elegance? Wealth can be gained, but elegance is a function of birth. It is not enough to acquire the right articles of clothing; rather, elegance consists "in a certain way of wearing them."[13] It is necessary, in other words, to manifest a certain familiarity with elegance, a material and psychological naturalness, expressed all the way down to the level of a person's physical bearing. The effort that the concern with external appearance has exacted must not be visible: "Whatever gives expression to an economic point of view is inelegant."[14] It is in principle possible for every member of society to possess the requisites of an elegant appearance; however, for reasons of living conditions, socialization, and access to economic and cultural capital, it is reserved to a tiny minority, the elite class, to have the effect of unaffected, seemingly natural elegance.

Not only does Balzac have an unerring sense of the symbolic codings of class action, he is also an unqualified admirer of the dominant class in terms of its cultural capacities to represent its social rank. Having married the Polish Countess Hanska, he supplements newly gained wealth with an appropriate arrangement of aesthetic details, in imitation of his aristocratic and haute bourgeois models. He "translates" into literature the attitude of a social climber that he himself adopts in the social world: he is the author who gives literary representation to social distinctions, transforming his fascination with the elite class into the power of literary persuasiveness. Balzac represents the culture of the economically superior as the superior culture by transforming it into a novelistic aesthetic.

In the *Comédie humaine,* Balzac develops a system of aesthetic signs[15] that organizes the social world of fiction. To his contemporary reader, the sign system represented in the novels, which Balzac conceives in reference to the empirical social world, must have appeared the literary codification of the tastes of the elite class. The *Comédie humaine* aestheticizes French society of the first half of the nineteenth century as if it were itself a novel; the stylistic devices of the novels are also the ones we find being deployed in society. Balzac initiates an exchange between the literary and social worlds, which transforms the social usage of aesthetics into an aesthetic usage of the social and in this way lends an artistic sanction to the lifestyle of the elite class.

The aesthetic of the *Comédie humaine* has yet another social purpose—to incline readers to recognize the distinctions of the elite class as guiding social values. Reading stimulates their interest in what happens in the novel; the stories continue in a fantastic dimension the lived reality of bourgeois society; readers are flattered, all but forced to cultivate a belief in the values promoted in the novel. Balzac's literary recipe combines magic and authority: the magic is in the words, a function of the "authoritarian speech" (Bakhtin) that characterizes his narrative attitude; receptive readers become involved in a process of mimetic worldmaking, so that they come to share the desires of the protagonists as they follow them through the stories.

Balzac represents the social world, the economic and political processes of which confront the individual as an external power, in such a way that it seems possible, on the symbolic level, for the subject to shape it. This (subjective) perspective encompasses solely that aspect of class society that we, following Marx, can designate "illusion"; it takes no heed of objective social conditions.

Given this involvement in the symbolic dimension, the author and the readers who go along with him close off the possibility of becoming enlightened as regards the constitution of society. Balzac's tableaus and scenes do not offer a description of what is objectively the case; they are rather images of other images that society makes of itself.

Any examination of the nineteenth-century novel and its "proximity to reality" must consider the relationships that necessarily pertain among author, readers, and fictional characters. A key characteristic of these relations is an interpretation of society from the perspective of those who participate in it. The point is not how reality is—how it constitutes itself, what forces are active within it, the role played by the bourgeois subject, and so on. Rather, readers are intended to understand and aestheticize social reality, to engage themselves in it emotionally, in the same way the creator engages himself in relation to the world of his novels. Understanding has here a stronger sense than the customary hermeneutic one, as is clear to Nietzsche: "But to understand— Balzac, that typical man of ambition, has revealed it—*comprendre c'est égaler.*"[16] Readers are supposed, at least for the duration of their reading, to become just as ambitious as the fictional characters and the author.

Balzac's *Illusions perdues*

It is a defining characteristic of nineteenth-century French novels that they occasion a confrontation between the fictional and the real social world, a collision organized within the fiction that leads to the destruction of essential elements of the fictional world—a mimesis of *illusions perdues.* In the process of this autosubversion, the ideas, values, and attitudes of the old world of tradition fall to pieces. There is no need for us to decide whether that which is suggested by tradition ever really existed. Traditions are, in any case, products of glorification or invention and as such exist in the present in the form of narratives told about the past, thus, in the form of fictions. What we find in Stendhal, Balzac, and Flaubert, beyond the great differences that separate them, are essentially such disenchantments. In a wholly new context and with very different results, disillusion will also play a major role in Proust.[17] All of these authors construct the novel as a laboratory situation. They set up an *experimentum crucis,* a critical experiment, in which an understanding of the world is put to the test. This understanding is not, to be sure, a purely theoretical product, but a generalized view of social reality, and this view is decisively involved in the construction of aspects of the fictional social world, such that what ultimately is tested, and potentially discarded, is a preexisting realm of represented reality.[18]

In the novels *Lost Illusions* and *A Harlot High and Low,*[19] Lucien de Rubempré is the test character who arrives in Paris from the provinces; he is a stranger in the capital, isolated in his new surroundings, characterized by a blend of his tender poetic endowment and his ruthless desire for social bet-terment. In Paris he meets up with, in Balzac's sense, reality, which will offer the hero a merciless demonstration of what it is all about. It may be that everything in the novel is invented—except the constitution of the critical reality and what the test reveals. The fundamental situation characteristic of Balzac's novels has an analogue in science: the person to be tested represents a certain way of seeing the world and a specific moral constitution; he is reduced in nearly elementary form to his critical limiting quantities and subjected to examination under controlled conditions. The world of the novel has a harder and more precise structure than does intricate and often hazy reality, and it serves as an instance of judgment. Balzac inserts into his novel the kernel of reality, which is structurally equivalent to social practice but more clearly seen within the fiction. The worlds that are tested in a novelistic experiment are mimetically constructed, here in the traditional sense of "mimesis" as the making of a world according to an extrinsic model. There are thus two forms of mimesis: first, the social world as the instance of judgment; second, the tested construct. The first form is holistic, encompassing the whole of reality; the second is a social mimesis, which designates the specific relations of imitation within that reality.

Balzac's heroes proceed through a drama of stations, with judgments ren-dered one after the other at the end. So long as this final station has not yet been reached, the novel represents a series of opportunities for the reader to be drawn into the mimetic design of the fictional world. The whole aims at the loss of illusions; Balzac constructs a multitude of new illusions in order to arrive at that end. Lucien Chardon, the son of a pharmacist and a noblewoman by the name of de Rubempré, allows his ambition and his love for a grand lady, Madame de Bargeton, to sweep him off to Paris with her, where she abandons him.[20] The first lost illusion: all that he took at home in Angoulême for a sign of his stunning beauty is socially denigrating and ugly in Paris. His suit has a ridiculously old-fashioned cut; he has a tie like an errand boy's; his shoes, his haircut, his whole outward appearance, which not long before had astounded refined society in Angoulême, makes him on the streets of Paris, in his own eyes, a figure of ridicule.

Lucien's traditional bearing and appearance, which was so highly respected in the provinces, bring him a woeful lack of success in Paris. The test to which he is subjected in the capital is devastating in its results, but we are interested here in the instance, the matter of the test itself. Balzac does not call it into question: Lucien's appearance is represented in the novel as unambiguously wrong; the novel establishes the verdict without qualification. That which is meant as a metaphor, " 'I look just like an apothecary's son,' he told him-self,"[21] is the truth. Equally true are Lucien's further observations about

> the graceful, smart, elegant young men of the Faubourg Saint-Germain: all of
> them having a special cachet, all alike in their trimness of line, their dignity of

bearing and their self-confident air; yet all different thanks to the setting each had chosen in order to show himself to advantage. The best points in all of them were brought out by a kind of *mise-en-scène*. . . . Lucien had inherited from his mother invaluable physical traits which, as he was fully aware, lent him some distinction, but this was only the ore from which the gold had to be extracted.[22]

Lucien's internal conversation seems to express the truth. But Balzac also destroys this illusion under the experimental conditions of an even severer, indeed life-threatening, test. Lucien's ultimate development is suggested as early as the description of the first lost illusion on his arrival in Paris. Lucien sees "that a great gulf separated him from such people and was wondering how to cross it, for he wanted to be like these slim young dilettantes of Paris."[23] Making oneself similar is the strategy of the Balzacian social climber: to acquire the necessary cultural signs; to gain access to nobility on the surface of appearance—which, however, is to some extent part of the substance of the matter. Thus, though Lucien is partially successful in his undertaking, at the decisive moment it fails definitively. The power of his desire allows him to make himself similar in a certain sense. On the basis of desire he overcomes social barriers, gathers together some of what is required in the way of investments, transforms his outward appearance; it inspires his longing and even love, gains him entry to the highest social circles, and secures for him a prominent place in society. But all of this overdraws his account. He lacks not only financial capital but also other of the social conditions of access into the highest stratum: Lucien's similarity is built on nothing more than mimesis in the narrow sense. This is the decisive defect in Lucien's career, which will lead him ultimately to founder on the hard rock of the social reality the novel represents.[24]

We are now in a position to inquire into the core reality that the world of the Balzacian novel shares with social practice. It is, first of all, the plethora of symbols that organize the world. But lying beneath this one is an additional and much more recalcitrant layer of social behavior: the dispositions, the mental forms, acquired over long periods of time and embedded in the history of the family and socialization, the stable, transsituational patterns of action that can be summarized under the concept of habitus (Bourdieu). By way of social mimesis, the Balzacian hero tries to appropriate the habitual forms of the social elite—a futile enterprise; against the background of the genuinely acquired habitus, the fragility of mimetic desire becomes apparent. Amid all the circulation of objects, values, and wealth, the *Comédie* leaves the principles ruling the empirical social world intact.

Social mimesis structures and values the social perception of the characters in the novel. It is extraordinarily dynamic and highly sensitive; it constantly takes sides by issuing judgments of revalorization and devalorization, which are not independent judgments of the individual but ones taken over from others. The perception and judgments of the protagonists of *Lost Illusions* are not anchored in habitus; they take shape in reference to model characters. The great lady of Angoulême, Anaïs de Bargeton, née Nègrepelisse, called Louise by her intimates, appears shortly after her arrival in Paris at the opera with her famous cousin, the Marquise d'Espard: "Louise had remained the same. Proximity with a woman of fashion, the Marquise d'Espard, a Parisian Madame de Bargeton, was so prejudicial to her, her Parisian brilliance set in such strong relief the imperfections of her country cousin that Lucien . . . at last saw Anaïs de Nègrepelisse for what she was and as she was seen by the people of Paris."[25] There follows an avalanche of unkind adjectives, such as big, haggard, faded, pretentious, which culminate in the reproach that she enacts herself badly. Lucien is immediately ashamed that he ever loved her and swears to abandon her at his first opportunity.

Lucien sees Louise through the eyes of the elegant Parisian public, but above all through the eyes of the Marquise d'Espard, an arbiter in questions of elegance; her judgment therefore speaks the truth for him. A short-lived truth, which the object of judgment, with the aid of her elegant cousin, is quickly able to correct. This judgment born of social mimesis contains a certain aspect of the truth, which, however, is neither lasting nor any more than a partial truth (a charge to which Balzac admittedly makes himself subject often enough). Both Lucien and his former beloved take over the judgment of the Marquise d'Espard and mutually destroy each other: "Madame de Bargeton intercepted one of these glances; she watched him and saw that he was more interested in the Marquise than in the performance."[26] She guesses what is going on with Lucien: "She became jealous, though less for the future than because of the past. 'He has never looked at me like that,' she thought."[27]

Both Madame de Bargeton and Lucien imitate the perception and the judgment of the Marquise d'Espard; both desire her social position, so that their gazes at this object of their admiration cross, causing them to devalue each other reciprocally. His gaze at the marquise signifies Lucien's disqualification for Madame de Bargeton; for him, it signifies the woman whom he will love from now on. "Losing his illusions about Madame de Bargeton while Madame de Bargeton was losing hers about him, the unhappy youth, whose destiny was a little like that of Rousseau, imitated him in this respect: he was fascinated by Madame d'Espard and fell in love with her immediately."[28]

Lucien's sudden affection for the marquise prompts Madame de Bargeton to imitate her cousin down to details; she lets her cousin dress her, cut her hair, and apply her makeup, and she takes over her gestures, her habits in society, and her sitting posture. Shortly after the episode in the opera, Lucien, whom Madame de Bargeton has meanwhile dropped, sees her driving down the Champs-Élysées with her cousin.

> She had adopted her cousin's gestures and deportment; sitting in the same posture as the latter, she was toying with an elegant perfume-box attached by a tiny chain

to a finger of her right hand, which enabled her to display her shapely and daintily-gloved hand without seeming to do so deliberately. In short, she had modelled herself on Madame d'Espard without aping her; she was a worthy cousin of the Marquise, who seemed quite proud of her pupil.[29]

Reciprocal mimesis characterizes the deep structure of the social universe represented in the *Comédie:* in all its essential spheres, society functions as an agon, in a form of oppositional cooperation that is affectively charged, a mixture of desire, struggle, and economics. In the Balzacian universe, the mimetic has an agonistic structure and the agonistic a mimetic one. On the surface of events, relations in the *Comédie* are unbelievably mobile; there is no tableau of any duration; all social signs are just as much in flux as conditions of personal fortune. But this impression comprehends only the mimetic constitution of the processes of social exchange. Only in reference to the latter is what Christopher Prendergast maintains applies to the whole of the *Comédie* really applicable, namely, that "money is the universal measure of value."[30] While it is true that "virtually everything is for sale," the critical values cannot be had with money. Esther gives her love to Lucien, and Nucingen, the banker, cannot buy it for all the money in the world. Lucien requires money in order to improve his social position; it is paid for with Esther's life, as Lucien ultimately sacrifices his life for having speculated badly in his bid for social betterment. The final and hardest currency is one's own life, which is the condition of participation in social mimesis. Julien Sorel and Madame de Bovary have to pay the same price.

The circulation of values is ultimately a dubious affair in the *Comédie,* a betrayal of deeper, of genuine values, a kind of prostitution, as Balzac shows most vividly in the trade and commotion of the Galéries-du-Bois: boutiques, bookstores, and prostitutes offer their goods for sale right next to each other; luxury items, the mind, and the body are traded in utterly the same fashion. Having become a journalist, the writer Lucien sells his mind here no differently than the prostitutes their bodies. Balzac is not sparing with moral condemnations (Lucien receives "a terrible lesson" here); his intensive description of the *galérie* betrays a fascination that he is barely able to resist: "It was horrible but gay. The gleaming flesh of shoulders and bosoms stood out amid the almost invariably sombre hues of male costumes, producing the most magnificent contrasts . . . which affected even the most insensitive persons."[31]

According to Prendergast, the significance of the episode in the Galéries-du-Bois lies in its formulation of a political and aesthetic assessment of the dangers "incurred by an uncontrolled and degraded *mimesis.*"[32] At the same time, however, this claim identifies one of the weaknesses of Balzac's representation, namely, that he often reduces mimetic processes to the level of swindle, charlatanry, fraud, and caricature. Stendhal and Flaubert, in much subtler fashion, make it clear that even those interactions that seem most intimately and purely affective are influenced by mimesis. Their representation does away with the possibility, which remains one potential avenue of flight in Balzac, of searching for a better, unspoiled social reality. Prendergast finds a conservative nostalgia for the old values in the *Comédie:* earlier, under the ancien régime, there was not yet any confusion of appearances; the signs of social distinction were semiotically stable. Under the ancien régime, every social class had its specific dress; clothes still allowed everyone to recognize the lord, the bourgeois, and the craftsman.[33]

What threw society into confusion and effaced distinctions is the ideology of equality, the consequences of which Balzac represents with regret. Against the backdrop of a conservative ideology like Balzac's, the modern conviction that it is possible to simulate all social signs appears a pure illusion. A model instance of this is Lucien de Rubempré: newly outfitted with his mother's title of nobility, catapulted on his course in life by the master criminal Vautrin, living in dubious luxury on misappropriated funds, supported by a courtesan looking for her big chance, he is absolutely artificial, a pure creature of signs. Lucien will become the tableau created so carefully in such detail by Vautrin. As the latter says of Lucien, ''I want to love a creation of my own, shape it, mould it to my purposes so that I may love it as a father loves his progeny. . . . I shall say: 'This handsome young man is myself! This is Marquis de Rubempré, I made him and set him in the aristocratic world. His greatness is my work; he speaks or keeps silent at my prompting and consults me on every matter.' ''[34]

The narrator observes this transformation of the unstable but talented and handsome young Lucien with unconcealed delight. His novelistic worldmaking assumes for itself the same authority that Vautrin evokes in his fashioning of Lucien. Balzac makes his protagonists into puppets of his descriptive will; he dresses them up and sends them off on adventures, using them to test his truth about society. Prendergast notes, ''The desire of the narrator to establish himself as a centre of authority within a discursive hierarchy is thus seriously compromised by a process of fluctuation in which the meanings and values of words appear to change from one context to another.''[35] But, contrary to Prendergast's supposition, it is wrong to suppose that there is no solid ground in the relativity of things and exchangeability of values and concepts. The *Comédie* is founded on an absolutely firm foundation, on the authority of mimetically constituted worldmaking. What remains fixed and incontrovertible here is the mutual opposition of forces locked in a struggle conducted at great expense, and finally paid for with the foundering of the character's life.

The agonistic structure of the story of Lucien becomes clear in the meeting between Vautrin and the head of the French criminal authorities, Monsieur de Granville. Is the Balzacian narrator really no longer able to recognize, as Prendergast thinks, the distinction between ''the genuine and the fake''?[36] We see a different set of differentiations at work in the *Comédie:* ''the fake'' is the challenge raised by society and, at once, one of its pillars. By having made itself independent, falsity threatens society. Social institutions of surveillance declare war on falsity. It is not destroyed—because it is ultimately not possible to do away with it—but, instead, is integrated into the apparatus of social control. The key and final scene of Lucien's story reveals what is ultimately at issue here: social power, the nerve center in the novel's construction. Social power creates a correspondence between the *Comédie* and the construction of reality. Power consists of maximum manipulation, of one's maximum disposal over social signs, over a high degree of both economic and cultural capital together with a fitting social lineage.

The efforts of Vautrin and his creature Lucien fall short. What they lack is money and birth. Lucien has a chance only so long as his and Vautrin's true nature remain concealed, that is, only until Corentin's spies reveal their true nature, the effect of which is fatal. Knowledge about the two conspirators' actual resources is the immediate cause of their downfall, leaving genuine social power a good chance of emerging strengthened from the battle. It is capable even of enhancing its control. And who is more suited for the job of surveillance than the great manipulator himself, the creator of the impressive fake character? Monsieur de Granville offers to make Vautrin the chief of the Sûreté. No one can expose society's counterfeits better than the master counterfeiter. Thus political power becomes more penetrating in its gaze than ever before: it consolidates control over the social production of symbols. Everyone who, like Lucien, attempts to outwit society by means of self-representation would from now on be immediately discovered and revealed by the greatest expert of all, Vautrin. The kingdom's premier spy, Corentin, who has pursued Vautrin relentlessly, admits in their final meeting, "You are the most extraordinary man I have encountered in my life."[37] Vautrin responds that he does indeed possess all the qualities necessary for the position; he has both manners and an education in rhetoric. All the antagonisms of society come together in the person of Vautrin, alias Jacques Collin: he works against honorable citizens as a criminal, as a counterfeiter against genuine values, under cover against the visible, as a creator of a character against the stratum of social climbers who work on themselves, as a banker to convicts against the official financial system. But in one point he is the same as the elite class, in his will to power. The social mimesis of desire, pursued with the utmost energy and deployed with unscrupulous ingenuity, finally manages to have a part in real power.[38]

So far, we have described Balzac's view of society, a seductive view in which social relations are antagonistic forces, represented and conducted, respectively, by outstanding characters combined into a secret ensemble ruled by mimesis. Its silent concurrence in society's more glamorous side and the presence within social power of dark forces cause the *Comédie* to appear sometimes cynical and acquiescent in the inadequacies it criticizes. But Balzac also offers a deep insight into the constitution of society, its class structure, into movements up and down in the social space, and the role of capital. He relinquishes essentialist thinking in all its forms, conceiving social values and positions in differential and dynamic terms. This is the principle of the Balzacian codification system. The authoritarian narrator of the *Comédie* exerts pressure on his readers that is disguised as a striving toward the truth about society; it presses toward exposure and revelation.

A detective's perspective on society, adopted in the aim of manifesting the ceaseless and total flux of which society is comprised, expands beyond all limits, mystifies perseverance, the nobility, and its habitus; it glorifies dynamic forces, money, desire, energy, deception. Social mimesis is raised to the level of the destiny of bourgeois society. It is the principle of the devaluation of all values. In his attempt at a universal interpretation of society, Balzac naturalizes social movement and its opposite, stability. His authoritarian and emotional mode of representation subjects readers to the pressure of truth, which leaves them scarcely any chance for alternative interpretations. The Balzacian narrator makes his appearance with the presumption of being a boss himself—the boss of symbolic power.

Balzac never calls into question the mimetic constitution of literary representation itself. The legitimacy of representation is the truth that forces itself violently on the reader. The narrator is not free in relation to mimetic desire, which he represents as the motive force of social reality. Is it not his desire to fashion the reader in a manner altogether comparable to Vautrin in his dealings with Lucien? Balzac outfits his readers with masks of their own, which draw them ever again into the events related in the novel. They are offered mimetic models, only to have them taken away in an act of revelation; readers are seduced and enlightened, but never given a chance to assume a perspective outside the novel. They become players in their own right, who never escape their role-playing. Lucien loses his illusions, but not Vautrin, not the Balzacian narrator, and, possibly, not the reader.[39]

While Balzac's attitude toward the social mimesis of desire remains ambivalent—on the one hand, critical and distanced, but, on the other, itself involved in it—other authors, in particular, Stendhal and Flaubert, develop in this regard a purer conception. The grand authoritarian gesture of the *Comédie* asserts the utter authority of the narrator. But since, at the same time, it in no sense possesses any power over social reality, but takes over and helps model the societal constitution, it reflects nothing more than an illusion of a freedom. Balzac failed to understand fully the conditions to which his artistic mimesis is subject. He did not see the extent to which he himself functions as a catalyst of mimetic desire, the extent to which his own authorial bearing is born, on a grandiose scale, of the social mimesis of creativity.

18

"Mimetic Desire" in the Work of Girard

In his first major work, *Deceit, Desire, and the Novel,* René Girard develops a theory of nineteenth- and twentieth-century literary mimesis.[1] He traces a line of development running from Stendhal through Flaubert to Dostoyevsky and Proust (finally to Camus). Common to the novels he examines is a specific structure: the protagonists find themselves desiring an Other, whereby they are focused emotionally on a third person, a mediator (*médiateur*). This person, whether real or imagined, always directs the protagonists' attention toward the object of desire; it is clear that he desires the same object, which has the effect of endowing the Other with a special value.

Girard sees Cervantes as having provided the initial model of this representational mode, insofar as Don Quixote allows Amadis to define what he wants and what he seeks to accomplish. The introduction of printing and the dissemination of books to a mass audience meant that this mode would be a powerful legacy to later periods, with Cervantes remaining the first to represent the mediation of desire and wants and the goals of action as a kind of mechanism. The approach is fully developed only in the nineteenth century, with Stendhal providing an illuminating example. "In most of Stendhal's desires, the mediator himself desires the object, or could desire it: it is even this very desire, real or presumed, which makes this object infinitely desirable in the eyes of the subject."[2] The preferred victim of the mechanism is a character possessed by vanity (*vanité*): "A *vaniteux* will desire any object so long as he is convinced that it is already desired by another person whom he admires. The mediator here is a *rival*."[3] In Stendhal, the mediator is an actual character in the novel, a person distinct from the hero. The hero ultimately becomes more or less aware of his dependency on an Other.

Proust internalizes this "external mediation" (*médiation externe*), collapsing the distance between mediators and heroes—which had previously been great enough for the two to be clearly set off from each other—sufficiently to bring the two characters into the closest possible contact with each other. In this "internal mediation" (*médiation interne*), the hero becomes irresistibly subject, often without achieving any consciousness of the fact, to the influence of the Other, whom the hero himself, given the right circumstances, can influence in turn.

For Girard, the desire represented in the novels he examines is a function of dynamic social relationships. The object over which the rivals compete does not in and of itself possess the high value attributed to it. Rather, it is rendered valuable by the mutual entanglement of characters who come to understand themselves as competitors. The competition of Others accepted by the protagonists as models confers on the object the character of uniqueness. The mediator becomes the hero's competitor, which has the effect of effacing the distance between hero and Other, toward whom the hero assumes a status of equality in principle, with the result that the hero ends up imitating the Other's desire.

Girard's view is that an anthropological mechanism underlies the social relationship of mimetic rivalry, such that desire is created relatively independently of historical situation and of the type and nature of the persons involved and can be directed toward nearly any goal whatever. It is no more necessary for the mediator to be possessed of particular value than it is for the desired object to have intrinsic worth. It suffices if he disposes over a certain prestige. Girard thus conceives desire as a form of struggle that comes into being and is maintained by one person's imitation of an Other; the dynamic informing desire is in principle unlimited and the goal toward which it aims empty. The only satisfaction that can be achieved stems from one person's success over rivals and not from the attainment of the goal. Over the long run, the hero, if he indeed manages to achieve his goal, faces only disappointment and the feeling of emptiness.

Girard's analysis reduces the hero's interpersonal relations with the mediator and the object of desire to struggle and reduces the latter, in turn, to mimetic rivalry. It is not necessary for the mediator to fulfill the function of a model in a strict sense, because hero and mediator can be much too close to each other for that to be possible. The mediator can be assumed into the hero, through the latter's imagination, enlarged and rendered more powerful than would otherwise be the case. As the distance separating the two is reduced, so is the distinction between them; the rivals become increasingly the same. Girard speaks of "triangular desire": the object of desire at the apex, hero and mediator at the two remaining points on the base. This triangular configuration undergoes a change with the passage from Stendhal to Proust, with the distance separating the two base positions diminishing and the corner points all but coinciding. Just as the triangles can take on different shapes in various novels, so can they appear in various constellations; for example, in interlocked succession, so that the mediator in the first triangle becomes the desiring hero in the second, and so on. Or there can be a "doubled mediation," in which the desiring character himself takes on a mediating role in relation to the original mediator. Underlying Girard's examination, however rich it may be in individual interpretations, is just such a triangular schematic: it isolates personal constellations from their contexts.

The effects of mimetic rivalry on the protagonists in the novels Girard examines are so enormous that they lose sight altogether of the mediator and the role he is playing. Stendhal's heroes still have flashes of clarity in their self-perception, whereas the self-estimation of all of Proust's characters is subject to falsification—until the narrator finally achieves certainty in *Temps retrouvé* (Remembrance of Things Past).[4] The protagonists Girard considers are characterized by a quality he terms "romantic": they believe themselves to be defining the goals of their action as autonomous and self-determined persons and assume that the goals are possessed of inherent value. The novels, however, overcome both of these fundamental positions of subjective autonomy and value essentialism. They discover a form and level of "novelistic" representation, which exposes the mediated structure of their desire to view. In Stendhal and Proust, the heroes all but renounce their persons by the final stage: Julien, in the solitude of imprisonment; Marcel, in the great concluding meditation in Geurmantes's house. At the end of both novels stands death; but in death, the hero is healed of his errors. "He comes to life again as a novelist. He reappears *in person* in the body of his novel."[5] All of the novels Girard examines are "antiromantic"; they end with an insight into the error of mimesis. Girard identifies mimetic rivalry, which dominates the social life of the protagonists, as a principle that comprehensively informs the driving forces of the nineteenth century—the struggle of desire in love, in the economy, and in politics.

Girard maintains of mimetic mediation that it is a general principle of society. Mimesis has taken leave of art to become one of the active factors in a new ordering of nineteenth-century social relationships. "Romanesque" literature attempted to overcome mimesis as a "romantic" principle. Art begins to articulate itself in fundamentally antimimetic fashion.[6] But if this is the case, what is it that makes a world of mimetic mediation so worthy of critique? There have always been mediators of conceptions of the world; people have never "spontaneously" created "their" world. What the Other in the antimimetic novels mediates is something transpersonal, something that also exists independently of the mediator: an internal medium. Girard's discovery of this internal medium deserves a clearer elaboration than it receives in his hands, due to his excessive interest in fundamental transhistorical anthropological mechanisms. We wish now to separate out from Girard's speculations those of his ideas that bear specifically on our own examination and to express them in a different, more analytical language.

The internal medium is not easy to discover, because the messages it carries are generally regarded as pertaining to an intersubjective reality independent of particular persons. What allows Girard to find it is his precise investigation of the role of the mediator, who reveals to the protagonist a special world, one symbolically constituted out of inner images, affects, ascribed values, and designations, which are not the usual ones. It is an *inner* world; the mediator causes them to be seen from the perspective of the person who belongs to and is emotionally involved in it. The inner world is constituted in speech, in stories, by means of hints, descriptions, and names. The hero for whom this inner world is being mediated regards it as social reality. In fact, it is produced out of the subjective view of the mediator and is perceivable only from that angle. It is the model world according to which the hero organizes his own world, such that it should also be his reality.

Put philosophically, the model worlds provide interpretations of the world of the subject. It is customary for every individual to undertake an interpretation of the world, but here we are concerned with interpretations of a particular type—those that are produced mimetically under the influence of a medium and function to determine action. What exists as the instance prior to interpretation is not experience, practice, reflection, or similar cognitive instances recognized by philosophy, but rather an Other's verbally mediated interpretation. It is even possible that the interpretation is only ascribed, or that the Other is imaginary. The medium is the prior instance; it is comparable to a film, expressing the hero's ideal images and dream narratives, including situations, constellations, and projections by which the individual is attracted. Under the influence of the medium, wishes and fantasies, which the hero has already formed in one way or another even if he has not yet articulated them, are respectively actualized and set free. The critical elements required for a mediated interpretation of the world have already been put into place, but they are activated and combined with each other only under the influence of a mediator.[7]

Girard's reductionist treatment restricts the various complex and differentiated contexts of action to the mimetic relation between hero and mediator. But it seems to us that he is speaking more of a constellation that varies from novel to novel. Rather than searching for a fundamental anthropological mechanism and conceiving formulaic variations on the fundamental schema, we find it more appropriate, given the multiple and historically differentiated nature of the object, to examine the interrelations among the respective novels and the protagonists depicted in them as individuals typical of their respective epochs. On the assumption of this qualification, it is possible to grant the correctness of Girard's view, that the mimesis of interpretation of the world, via internal media and the organization of perspective, plays a central role in the antiromantic novels. The issue, however, is not solely desire, but in general the interpretation of that which is the reality of the protagonist in action and the role played in this interpretation by mimesis.[8]

The literature Girard examines represents a settling of accounts with mimesis. In the nineteenth century at the latest, the interpretation of reality slips from the grasp of great social institutions—the church, the monarchical state, ideologies, schools, and authorities. It becomes increasingly the work of social groups, which establish how reality is to be interpreted. The characters described in the novels are simultaneously individuals and representatives of specific social groups. The power mimesis holds over them is a discovery by novelists in opposition to the general assertion of self-determination and subjective autonomy. The mimetic mediation of interpretations of the world is not particular to the characters described in the novels but is typical for the role played by mimesis in the nineteenth century. Mimetic processes have become generalized by this time, have been fully adapted to social life, and have become all but unrecognizable. The accepted habits of social behavior are acquired under the decisive influence of mimesis; in this it fulfills a wholly different function than it did in the seventeenth and eighteenth centuries. The new role of mimesis is characterized by the ever-increasing contribution of the imaginary.

The antiromantic novels present us with a paradoxical situation: they both discover mimetic mediation and attempt to overcome it by means of the novel. They take aim, in other words, at mimesis itself, which is their own central principle. The novel is a mimetic medium; it assumes a form, in the hands of Stendhal, Flaubert, Dostoyevsky, and Proust, such that it is directed back against its own constitutive characteristics as a genre. What these writers criticize in society, they find repeated in literature. They discover in society a fictional principle; they recognize that the formation of the social world proceeds in the same way as the formation of a novel. Society, in important aspects, is constituted in terms of the same principle as the novel. Put the other way around, this claim reads as follows: the novel is constituted in terms of a principle that informs and dominates the social reality of its time. The social world and the novel, on account of the principle of mimetic interpretation and worldmaking, are bound together; they exist in constitutive reference to each other.

The antimimetic critique leveled by the authors Girard examines rocks the foundation of the novel; mimetic writing, if the critique is pursued to its conclusion, is no longer possible. Stendhal and Proust cut through the mimetic tradition in the conclusions to their novels, deciding in favor of a nonmimetic statement of truth. They turn against one dimension of the concept of mimesis, which extends far into the history of the European literary tradition—against the production of fictional worlds. The great break in art in favor of an antimimetic attitude, the onset of which is usually identified as the beginning of the twentieth century, already took place in the first half of the nineteenth century. It began, if Girard's interpretation is justified, with the first modern novel, *Don Quixote*. In precisely those great examples of the novel in which the reproduction of the social world seems to have been achieved with technical perfection, an interior movement turns against mimetically conceived reality and against mimetic writing—against the principle that renders society aesthetic and the novel social.[9] What is gained thereby is a dangerous aestheticization of the social and a bad—on account of being delivered up to an illusory reality—sociologization of literary texts.

It has become possible to reflect in this way about mimesis only since the nineteenth century, the period, that is, in which individuals begin to have a relatively free hand in interpreting the world within the frame of their own social experience. Mimesis now takes on a different meaning than it had in earlier times. It is bound to the mediating perspective of an Other. In this *perspectival mimesis,* a world is produced in conformity with the interpretation of an Other. The fact that this can occur at all marks a particular historical situation, in which the power to interpret the world individually devolves on the subject; but the subject misses its chance to realize individual interpretation by subjecting itself to an already existing interpretation, which is present in an inner medium. A certain affinity for the interpretation already exists within the individual; but once the interpretation is accepted and realized as purportedly the subject's own, the subject is rendered vulnerable to alien compulsions.

The medium and the interpretations mediated by it are largely detached from specific persons and can function independently. There exist established forms, patterns, and techniques, which organize the medium independently of the individual. Whoever has control over the internal medium—which has the power to guide wishes, fantasies, desires, and dreams, which is to say, to control extensive areas of the imagination—exercises power over the individual. Not the least involved in this play of power are the writers of literature who represent a "romantic" conception of art. Antimimetic novels, in contrast, are the primary opponents of the internal medium and the interpretations of the world transported by it. This medium, in its structure and effect, is related in essential points to modern mass communication. In distinction to the latter, it functions via relays from person to person, via speech, and not yet via the nineteenth-century print media of journals, newspapers, and magazines.[10]

Girard's work on antiromantic novels generates a multitude of new insights. In two points, however, it calls for critique: the depiction of mimesis represented in the novels as a fundamental anthropological mechanism is an oversimplification, the result of a reductionist procedure that leads to the postulation of mimetic processes as independent of context and historical situation. There is more to be gained from an emphasis on the differences to be identified in the ways in which the internal medium is utilized and the effects that it produces and from integrating these differences into the investigation. The novels Girard examines are concerned with perspectives on and interpretations of the world, which is a significant nineteenth-century theme. In Nietzsche, the power of interpretation that the antiromantic literature learns to recognize is raised to the level of a philosophical object.[11]

The mimesis inherent in the internal perspective by no means loses its force under the assault of the antiromantic novels. On the contrary, as a relationship between model and imitator, it is firmly established in the nineteenth century: mimesis identifies that which a school, model, exemplar, or a master or teacher is for a pupil. In the form of academies, schools, and educational institutions, of the enactment of the state, and of "great men," this dimension of mimesis becomes a standard of the nineteenth century. According to this standard, society is to be read like a novel, a circumstance that is usually overlooked in the discussion of literary realism. Antiromantic art at the onset of the twentieth century discharges its energies like an explosion: it draws conclusions from its reflections about its own truth, which endures only in the form of negation, and calls for an end to mimetic worldmaking.

19

Violence in
Antiromantic Literature

Antiromantic literature might resist social mimesis, but it is itself based on a mimetic principle. The author supplies the reader with an obligatory interpretation of the social world and is, to this extent, also consolidating influence over an Other, over the reader. The relationship of author to reader is characterized by the transmission via writing of an interpretation of the world, which in essential respects is equivalent to relations among the author's characters. The heroes of antimimetic novels, whose interpretation of the world they have taken over from a model, are all readers. Antimimetic authors create themselves as authorities who, while escaping external influence, produce worlds designed to exercise an effect on Others.

The Authorial *I* and Others

What moves directly in the images created by the antiromantic authors is their gaze, an expression of abandonment and loneliness. These writers seem to have plumbed the depths of suffering, of emotion and creation; they are cut off from the Other. Writing is for them a form of defense against the Other; their bearing is that of an isolated individual for whom solitude functions to exclude anyone who might interfere with the action of the authorial *I*. There is, in other words, a fundamental antagonism between author and Other, a defensive posture on the part of the former, designed to preserve and protect the author's self. But the writing *I* can be successful in keeping Others out only to the extent that they are made of flesh and blood. Transformed into images and ideas, they surround the author: they are the targets of his or her plots, which, indeed, are invented for precisely the purpose of targeting.

Every text begins with the author establishing relationships to Others, to readers. Since readers are only imagined persons, it seems that the author disposes freely over them. But even as imaginary beings Others retain certain freedoms, above all, the freedom to refuse the text. These author-Other relationships are by no means arbitrary. For Others' reactions to the text, however indifferent the author might be in relation to individuals, are important; the author demands from them something in return, something he or she needs. If it appears that Others are completely dependent on the author, so is the author dependent on them, who are nothing more than products of the author's own imagination. Thus does the solitude of the author turn out to be an attempt to master Others with the greatest possible degree of security.

In a situation in which Others play such an important role, it can scarcely be said that the author is free in relationship to them; the author considers Others for the sake of his or her writing. Stendhal seeks to enchant them with his lightness and refinement, to draw them, apparently voluntarily, over to his side so that they share with him his hatred of the father and the reactionary clerical milieu, his sensuous pleasure in the unfolding of life, and his admiration for its passion and energy. For Flaubert, the book is a terrifying instrument of domination: "It is utterly gratifying, one can do everything, can be king and people at the same time," he writes to Louise Colet. And further: "It is very nice to be a great writer, to put people into the frying pan of a sentence and set them hopping about like chestnuts."[1] Even the apparently so composed work of Proust obligates the reader to take his side against the snobs, the social climbers, the Verdurins; Parisian society is declared the enemy, with the exception of its cultural elite centered around the Duchess of Guermantes. These relationships transform Others into facets of the authorial *I*. Others are compelled by the text to become a part of the author himself or herself. But the author as well, dependent in turn on Others, becomes one with parts of them.

Many people penetrate the author's silence: first of all, Others whom the author has influenced, readers of whom the author demands something and to whom the author has simultaneously bound himself or herself; second, the protagonists of the novels, on whom the author has also imposed something, namely, that they exercise influence over Others, in this case, over other characters in the novel. The author thus establishes relationships on two different levels; first, among protagonists in the text; and then, between his or her own *I* and the real or imagined milieu.[2]

An *I* exists in a relation of domination over Others on both levels. The strategies are the same, only the persons (or characters) are different: protagonists are not identical with the author; they do not have the same antagonists and they do not act in the same way as their authors. Nearly everything that concerns individual persons can differ on the two levels. Nevertheless, authors obviously create specific ways of regulating relations between *I* and milieu: they are distanced, yet aim their work at Others; they perform autonomous gestures, in the expectation of a verdict being rendered; they concentrate on analyzing other persons, but it is ultimately their own *I* that fascinates them.

If authors were as they pretend to be, then they would write about objects without regard for their own person. Authors would assume a fixed perspective in relation to Others, one that remained unperturbed by their own emotional states, partisan preferences, or presuppositions. If authors were occupied with a study of their own person, they would assume the same perspectival immobility toward themselves, with an inwardly directed gaze. What they would have to say, in either case, they would say from an unchanging point of view and out of a concern for objectivity. Authors would, beyond self-directed compulsions, make use of the freedom of their gaze.

But this is not the way things are done among the antiromantic authors: constraints do limit the freedom of their gaze, and these constraints can by no means be ascribed exclusively to milieu; Others do not compel the authors' insecure attentiveness, their listening for resonances, their self-enclosure in solitude. That authors, however, have voluntarily committed themselves to such an attitude can scarcely be doubted. They submit to compulsions that inhere in the way they order experience. They adopt a perspective toward Others that operates as an ordering structure—first, in the way they perceive situations, and second, in the way they represent situations in the text.

Perspectives, as ways of seeing and markers of experiential horizons, belong to the individual. Like language, they betray individual variations and habitual particularities, but they are neither individual nor even subjective creations. The fundamental features of perspectives are shared by many, and they possess an established, if hard to identify, form that orders experiences and texts; they are mediated essentially through language. Textual perspective must be distinguished from the perspective of pictorial representation; the former does not function as a peephole, is not limited to a specific representational extract conveyed by the succession of events, and is not characterized by a vanishing point. It can, in contrast, jump from one person to another, allowing us to see the narrated material simultaneously through more than one set of eyes. In the antiromantic novels, perspective is distinguished as the point of view of a potentially real person. To this extent, it imposes certain constraints on both author and fictional characters, which can be understood as perspectivally determined necessities that foreclose specific freedoms.

But what relationships exist between the perspectives of real events and those of fictions? What are the constraints, and what absences of freedoms bind the two together? Can there be any path at all leading from fiction to reality?

Perspective is a prearrangement employed by author and character to produce a specific "version,"[3] their version, of the things they describe or perceive. Art's capacity as a worldmaking activity makes it comparable to other such activities, including the sciences, which comprise the classical spheres of worldmaking. Art, too, is capable of expanding or advancing knowledge.

Fictional worldmaking can serve, in a fashion similar to nonfictional cognitive procedures, to order the actual world. Modes of worldmaking, in particular, the prearrangement of perspective, may be equivalent in the case of a given author in both empirical reality and in fiction.[4] Worlds produced by different authors are not mutually translatable, although they belong to the same family of worlds.

In contrast to pictorial perspective, which expands the observer's knowledge, perspective in literature, with the exception of the omniscient narrator, has the effect of limiting knowledge.[5] Reading is a way of gathering information about a fictional world; perspective organizes the way the information is conveyed. Readers learn about certain aspects of the world, but about other aspects they learn nothing. The information they are allowed to receive can be expressed explicitly or suggested by implication. It can be transmitted by means of two types of perspective, which are often combined with each other within the frame of the text. First is *internal* perspective: it is bound to a specific character and serves to produce a particular world; it can "leap" from one to another character over the course of the novel. Second is *external* perspective: it conveys a way of seeing "over and above" the individual characters which is no longer bound to the specific point of view of an individual; it conveys information about characters, often doing so in a concealed rather than openly declared fashion in the text. Antiromantic authors suggest models or guiding ideas in a concealed external perspective, according to which—if, as is often the case, unwittingly— the protagonists act, in that they imitate them unconsciously.

Perspectives and the interconnections that pertain among them are formal elements in the framework of a text. However, because they also contribute to the delimitation and production of a world, they are also carriers of substantive content. It is therefore impossible to maintain a distinction between what is said and the way it is said. A world is produced out of the concrete versions of itself, and all of the constitutive parts of these versions are also parts of the world.[6] The strict differentiation between form and content presupposes a world existing independently of language.

In many antiromantic novels, the external perspective communicates a common quality shared by the main characters: they are readers who believe in the superior reality of literature. Sometimes the parallel between their own persons and that of a literary model is explicit: Julien Sorel knows the world according to Rousseau's *Confessions* and has made the *Mémorial de Sainte-Hélène* into his own internal logbook; Frédéric Moreau, as a young man fresh out of college, has an academic's knowledge of literature and ambitions for a career as a writer; Madame Bovary, as the most ardent of readers, waits, like all of her sisters in suffering, for something to happen, waits to achieve great happiness; Jean Santeuil and Marcel have consumed whole libraries; even Dostoyevsky's cantankerous inhabitant of the "underground" is capable, according to his own protestations, of demonstrating a comprehensive knowledge of literature. Literary models function simultaneously as an Ariadne's thread and a safety rope, along which protagonists feel their way through the world.

In *Scarlet and Black,* Julien Sorel takes leave of his paternal home with the model of Napoleon, the man of action, before his eyes. He declares the inhabitants of the haute bourgeois milieu of the provinces, where he plans to become a private tutor, to be enemies—who hold in their hands the key to his career. But when he is moved by a meeting with another character, so that he, as if suddenly amnesiac, forgets his model, his imperious bearing disappears to reveal a tender, nearly feminine young man. Julien's soft side is represented in the internal perspective in his direct contact with Madame de Rênal; the concealed external perspective gives expression to his antagonistic attitude. The combination of the external and internal perspectives of the two main characters prepares a shock, which supplies the energy for what Stendhal calls "truth." Manifestations of the truth, to be sure, are short-lived: Julien recovers quickly from the shock to fall back under the thrall of his transpersonal model.

Madame de Rênal is awaiting the arrival of the new tutor, whom she imagines will be a crude, badly dressed fellow, when "she noticed a young peasant, still almost a child, whose face was extremely pale and bore the mark of recent tears."[7] The thought occurs to her that it is a girl coming to her for a favor. As she approaches to offer assistance, Julien gives a start. He had not heard her coming "when a gentle voice said close to his ear: 'What brings you here, my boy?' Julien turned around sharply and, struck by the very gracious look on Madame de Rênal's face, partly forgot his shyness. Very soon, astonished by her beauty, he forgot everything, even why he had come."[8]

As if having fallen into a deep dream, they move toward each other with utter security, innocent of models, values, and preconceptions. They have not been seized by passion—on the contrary, the scene emanates calm—but the seed of a great passion has been planted. With no sense of constraint, both of them gain direct access to their feelings. Both have had imprinted in the language of pure emotion an image containing the truth about the other.

There is no compulsion, no violence, raised between or against them, only an astounding freedom in the meeting of two persons of different gender, age, and social status. Julien quickly recovers his composure; his "normal perspective" re-forms the situation, sees in Madame de Rênal his enemy, and compels him to an audacious deed; for, as he says to himself, "It would be cowardly of me not to perform an action which may be of service to me, and lessen the disdain this fine lady probably feels for a humble workman."[9] He kisses her hand. He regards this act of bravado as an expression of his freedom, while, in fact, it is simply the product of a constraint to which he subjects himself. To Madame de Rênal's mistaken impression, Julien responds with a particular form of violence; the supposed child puts on the airs of a conquering man. The violence, however, is directed primarily against himself: he destroys the original emotion he felt for Madame de Rênal and deforms his tenderness for her; the result is coldness, haughtiness, and rejection. Julien dons a uniform and his metamorphosis from worker into tutor is complete. "Finally Julien made his appearance, an altogether different man. It would have been incorrect to say that he was grave: he was gravity incarnate."[10] Nothing in his thoughts or feelings any longer belongs to him. Everything has been adopted, imitated; it is all alien to his original *I*.

The Relationships of *I* and Other in the Novel

Perspectives are the representational forms of situations in which an *I* establishes or maintains specific relations to others. They are available to be used both in fictional worlds and on the level of empirical life. The way the hero of a novel arranges his relationships with Others can correspond to the way in which the author sees his or her own relationships to Others. Perspectives are points of view adopted toward Others, but also authorial points of view toward the self. They encompass the authorial *I*. The author's way of seeing in regard to novelistic characters corresponds to his or her way of seeing in regard to the self. But perspective oscillates around an empty center, the site of the *I*. This, in a certain sense, is the defining point of reference of the antiromantic novel.

Perspective enables the author, without a word having been explicitly pronounced on the matter, to become present in the text. Already in Rousseau, who in this sense is an antiromantic author, authorial presence becomes the guiding subterranean theme of his fictional and autobiographical texts: Saint-Preux is, of course, no simple replica of the author, but he does arrange his relations with Julie like Rousseau arranges his in reference to his milieu and his readers. All three types of relationships are based on a certain relation of Rousseau to himself: Saint-Preux pretends to reveal to Julie the reality of his feelings, whereby Julie serves no other purpose than to assist in the constitution of this reality. A comparable role falls to the reader of the *Confessions*. Others, whether in a novel, in biography, or in life, are Jean-Jacques's objects of seduction and love, his audience, confidants, and accomplices. All of his texts take the form of a search in which the object searched for is only constituted in the first place by the text. The object is found in those Others who bear the brunt of the search and are obliged to open themselves to penetrating interrogation. The truth that Rousseau claims for himself he finds in them. Although he is constantly opening his heart to allow the reader to look inside, it is the fact that the reader sees, directs his or her gaze onto that which is offered to sight, that produces the truth according to Rousseau. It is an exhibitionism that would remain impotent if no one looked, as Saint-Preux's love would vanish if Julie did not read his letters. The truthfulness of the disclosure would not come to light had the *Confessions* not been published; his asseverations of friendship would remain emotionally empty if no one heard them. Rousseau is in this respect radically modern, a person who intrudes into the interiority of Others in order to extract from them his *I*.

The search for the authorial *I* in literary texts directs the perspective of the author onto Others. This gaze, which seeks in Others what cannot be found in the self, can be best recognized in autobiographical works, which is to say that perspective takes clearer form in Stendhal's attempt at an autobiography, *The Life of Henry Brulard,* than in *Scarlet and Black.* Perspective betrays how completely Henri Beyle sees himself in terms of an imitation of his mother, who died when he was six years old. He withdraws into his mother's room as he begins to write (a *matrice-tombeau,* as Béatrice Didier notes);[11] he hates his father; he is delighted by the story told by a servant girl that his mother once cried out at his father, "Leave me alone, you horrid ugly thing."[12] The imitation of refusal is also directed at the mother's sister, Aunt Séraphie, who got on perhaps a little too well with the father. But the sister, who looks extraordinarily like the mother and becomes her—posthumous—rival, suddenly, when the young Henri Beyle steals a glance at her uncovered leg, becomes an object of his desire. Stendhal even lends his own body feminine characteristics (resistance to the masculine is quite clear at the beginning of *Scarlet and Black*): "the surface of my body is like a woman's. Thence comes, perhaps, my insurmountable horror at everything that looks *dirty* or *damp* or *blackish.*"[13]

Stendhal, in contrast to his characters, is aware of his problem; it is the difficulty he has getting hold of his own ego: "At heart, dear reader, I don't know what I am: kind, unkind, witty or foolish."[14] As the author informs us at the beginning of the book, he began *Henry Brulard* to gain clarity as to who he really was; finally, at nearly fifty, it was getting time for him to answer the question. Imitation had determined his life, imitations of famous men ("ces *hommes illustres* dont j'aurais voulu imiter la vie et lire les écrits"; those *famous men* whose lives I wanted to imitate and whose writings I longed to read)[15] and of literary models ("moi qui me croyait à la fois un Saint-Preux et un Valmont"; I who thought myself a combination of Saint-Preux and Valmont).[16] Stendhal diagnosed, as the result of his attempts to imitate others, a disappearance of the ego: "mon moi avait disparu en présence de la personne aimée, j'étais transformé en elle" (my self disappeared in the presence of my beloved; I was transformed into her).[17]

Still worse is the condition, of which he is aware, that every time he strives through imitation toward a desired goal and reaches it, he meets disappointment rather than fulfillment; it recurs throughout his entire life, an "étonnement: Quoi! n'est-ce que ça?" (astonishment: What, was that really all?). He refers these terrible moments, which at bottom cheated him out of that which he strived for, back onto himself: "Je crois que cela tient à l'imagination" (I think it is due to imagination).[18] The world is reduced to a bad mimesis of his interior images. At least his autobiography is to be duty-bound to truth; his goal is "peindre *ressemblante* la nature" (painting a *faithful likeness* of nature).[19] He gave it the title *Confessions,* which should have made him cautious, for he thereby names the model, although he distances himself emphatically from it. He fears "being insincere and artificial like J.-J. Rousseau."[20] In vain—the literary modes of worldmaking, the model of the novelistic narrative, are more powerful than his love of truth. The great novelistic beginning, direct and, so it seems, of lifelike immediacy, is contrived and, in terms of the facts of the matter, even false: Henri Beyle, at the time he claims to have begun writing, was not in Rome at all, but on a trip through the Abruzzi mountains. The writing starts two years later than he maintains.

The fullness of the ego, on careful examination, proves artificial; the life of Henri Beyle is shaped by great compulsions, which for him attain the rank of necessities, while they are overlooked by his biographers. The will to become an Other, which he both concedes and describes in its effects, determines his life. Only in a radical, unreserved confession of the facts of the case does he succeed in distancing himself from it.

The general conclusion to be gained from our reading of *Henry Brulard* may be stated as follows: the moment the authorial *I,* in his textual production, assumes parts of others into himself, he enters into his text. He forfeits his freedom in relation to his own creation—over both the novel's representational mode and its characters—and is constrained to submit to their compulsions. Insofar as the representational mode of texts constitutes a portion of their content, perspective is part of what determines the content represented. Until now, it has been possible to answer the question of what substantive content necessarily accompanies perspective in the antiromantic novel in general terms: perspective produces specific comparabilities between the world of the text and the world of the author. Thus are individuals formed in a certain way, made comparable to each other and referred to each other, and depicted according to analogous points of view. There arises in this process a specific type of relationship between *I* and Other.

Yet if we examine the *I* 's attitude toward itself and Others in antiromantic novels more specifically, we find everywhere the motif of violence. It is not an open violence, as in Greek myths or the Old Testament, where it appears unconcealed, brutal, and transpersonal. In comparison to these older ones, antiromantic texts seem to have expelled violence; but once we discover the trace of violence here as well, its operation becomes evident. Desire assumes in antiromantic texts the form of self-desire; the central character sets off on a search for himself. The mainspring of these novels is the wish for self-possession, but it goes unsatisfied in the normal conditions of the protagonist's life; frequently, he is not even aware of where his desire leads him. "Good Heavens, what a disappointment! What is there to hope for?" cries Stendhal as he finally escapes Grenoble and has arrived in Paris.[21]

Among the authors examined here, Flaubert has the most complex and instructive relationship to his narrative texts. His problem is also desire, but in his case desire takes the form of possessing, of increasing power and fortifying pride. The fictional texts he writes shield him from life.[22] Since, however, what is recognized as "real love" ultimately issues out of literature, he transforms feelings of love back into literature, into the novel. Flaubert's writing solves for him the problem that besets his fictional characters: their inability to possess the desired person. Flaubert renounces love and instead describes the aimlessness of desire on the part of characters he himself invents. His self-hatred is turned productively, as hate, against his fictional characters, and his striving for power develops in opposition to the reader. The compulsion of wanting to possess the Other to which the main characters in the *Sentimental Education* are subject remains ineffectual because of their affective impotence (Marthe Robert), while Flaubert realizes his own desire through writing.

In general it is possible to identify in antiromantic novels a specific succession in the genesis of violence between two or more characters. The hero seeks out a concrete person as a model, toward whom various kinds and degrees of relationship can be established: the *I* makes contact with the model, wants to become like it, wants to become one with it. If the model resists the *I*'s endeavor to become similar or equal to it or even to replace it, if, that is, the model perceives in the *I* an enemy, the result is competition. A cycle of violence is set into motion in which each, the model and the *I*, becomes the rival of the respective Other.[23] Violence, which so far in our considerations has been understood as actions undertaken in the intention of establishing a relation with the Other, takes the form of action designed to prevent the Other from possessing the desired identity.

Ego constitution is usually understood in social scientific theory as the process by which an identity is conceived and realized in interplay with the social environment. Beyond all the variations that can be identified in individual theories, the dominant idea remains that ego constitution represents, within more or less narrow limits set by milieu and social origins, a relatively free act. Antiromantic novels, in contrast, depict a process driven by a remarkable necessity, which runs counter to the characters' will and outside their knowledge. The freedom that the protagonist believes himself or herself to possess proves illusory: the fictional character is fixated on a model and forces on his or her own action a kind of necessity, which is, indeed, self-produced but obviously subjectively unavoidable.

While individuals begin already at a young age to develop abstract schemata for objects and actions,[24] they remain in their relationships to their own kind much more subject to the sensuous and the concrete. Where they have access to examples and models, abstraction is neither necessary nor especially useful. The generalized Other (G. H. Mead), which plays such an important role in interactionist sociology, seems no more important than the concrete Other, of whom it takes no notice whatever.

Language, Violence, and the Internal Perspective

The internal perspective of the antiromantic novel produces the conditions that frame relationships between *I* and Others. The way these relationships develop in individual cases depends on further conditions, above all, on the language system common to the partners in them. If the shared language disposes over a very limited reservoir of signs, or if it tends toward silence, the exchange between *I* and Other will be disturbed, blocked, or even broken off. The fewer areas of latitude given to communicative interaction, the worse the chances for equal exchange among the active partners and the greater the probability that relationships to Others and to the self will be informed by violence. We want now to consider examples of each: for the reduction of language to too few signs, *Lucien Leuwen,* and for a language tending toward silence, the *Sentimental Education.*[25]

Language sets up a form of iron compulsion over the pairs Lucien and Madame de Chasteller, on the one hand, and Frédéric and Madame Arnoux, on the other. But it would be too simple to assume that language itself is the source of this type of necessity and that it would suffice for some kind of positive resolution to wrest additional latitude from language, as surrealism, for example, attempted to do. Language belongs, no doubt, among the great mechanisms productive of necessity in relation to the *I;* it exemplifies this above all in the symbolic arrangement of perspective. But the constraints to which the individual is subject are generated in the production of his or her world.

The external perspective tells us about Lucien Leuwen that he, like his author, is searching for his *I,* for his path in life. At bottom he desires himself as one who desires, so the search for his own *I* amounts to nothing other than a search for an object of desire. In Nancy he suddenly finds his passions directed toward Madame de Chasteller, a beautiful and still-young widow. Stendhal equips both characters, in the internal perspective, with a language reduced to a few signs, which has, on the one hand, great expressive power but, on the other, contains no possibility for development. The first sign is a failure of Lucien's motor skills—he falls from his horse under Madame de Chasteller's window—which is stripped of its accidental character in that it is repeated several times. The second sign is made up of their mutual gazes, a classical symbol, here of extreme intensity and directness. The single intimate encounter between Lucien and Madame de Chasteller in the novel is dominated by the shock expressed in her eyes. Just as he has spoken of the fright her eyes inspire in him and of his love, her expression changes—again it is as if by accident—for a fraction of a second, and before she has time to think about it her eyes answer:

"J'aime comme vous" (I, too, am in love).[26] The third sign comes in the period in which the development of their relationship has ceased and is bound to fail. The only true connection, in Stendhal's sense, between them is the glimmer of Lucien's cigar: in the evenings he sits on a stone across from Madame de Chasteller's window, where, without his knowledge, she knows to expect him: "Now and then, in the intense darkness, Madame de Chasteller could make out the lighted tip of Lucien's little cigar. She loved him madly at this moment."[27]

The three signs occasion no real dialogue between the two characters: the constraints to which both are subject, and which are represented in the external perspective, are more powerful than the microscopic instants of truth. The body's failure in the face of a higher power—the fall from the horse—is rendered ridiculous; the momentary immediacy of Madame de Chasteller's gaze is quickly corrected by social propriety—she leaves the ball; the nightly colloquy dies without result. The three signs are highly charged; they reach the Other but remain intimate signs, accorded validity only in the internal perspective between two persons, left impotent in relation to the necessity represented on the level of their thought. The tiny margin of freedom that the internal perspective makes manifest in flashes is of no use to the fictional characters. Lucien proceeds through the entire plot pursuing these moments of truth, without ever capturing one again. Stendhal, who realized at a certain point that he would not be able to turn the novel onto a different path, left it a fragment.

The necessity that confronts the fictional characters releases a self-destructive force that seems to come from society but is really generated by the two main figures; it is directed against the Other in the form of suspicions and rejections, exaggerated mannerisms, and a fanatic concern for propriety and etiquette. Ultimately, however, necessity turns back to strike the self, leaving behind an open wound.

In the *Sentimental Education,* there is no longer any intimate language in which an *I* can explain itself to an Other. Relationships between characters can no longer solidify into moments of truth. In the internal perspective of *Lucien Leuwen,* the three signs produce images that capture these complex relationships in palpable ideas. They are images of passion and violence; they arrest us, to borrow an expression from Wittgenstein, not because they include us, but because they transform our way of seeing.

Flaubert's protagonists have no important models; they are searching for many things at once: success, prestige, artistic expertise, and so on; in short, they are dilettantes of desire. For Frédéric Moreau, a chance acquaintance with the art dealer Arnoux takes on a certain exemplary character. In any case, he pays court to Arnoux's wife. Aside from their first meeting, at which she in his eyes acquires a nearly numinous quality ("une apparition"; a vision),[28] the two never find a common language; over the course of the plot they become strangely unable to act. There are ever-lengthier intervals of silence in their dialogue: their behavior becomes increasingly reserved the more they reveal their love for each other; the constant lie on the surface of their dialogue finally exhausts their sensibility.

Silence is no doubt the result of an attempt to avoid unreliable speech, to regain freedom, and to find access to the very soul of the Other. But unspoken feelings endure only for a short while; then, especially once they have been infiltrated by social concerns, they collapse helplessly into themselves. Feelings need language, but language imprints them with the marks of its social formation. Emotion flares up briefly in moments of silence and is then extinguished; feelings without words grow dull. The movement of the emptying out of perspective in the *Sentimental Education* is also supposed to be accomplished, according to Flaubert's idea for the novel, on the level of syntax, with increasing "blancs," white spaces that finally come to dominate the final pages: a novel that resolves itself into nothing.

Frédéric's feelings become increasingly untenable, until, at the end of the novel, they flow together into a motherlike image: when Madame Arnoux, after years of promises and missed rendezvous, finally takes the decisive step and seeks out Frédéric in his rooms, he suspects that she wants to give herself to him. "He felt something inexpressible, a repulsion, and something like the dread of incest."[29] Nothing happens. After a long period of silence and paralyzing inactivity, she stands up. "And she kissed him lightly on the forehead, like a mother."[30]

The internal perspectives of Frédéric and Madame Arnoux have diverged sharply from each other. There is no place left for her in Frédéric's perspective of social success and brilliant *amours;* she is left only the place of the mother, which, though unconscious and lustful to be sure, was already there on their first encounter. Madame Arnoux, from her perspective, has finally cast off her marital submission and renounced her maternal quality. Both, through their respective perspectives, do violence to the Other without having been able to take possession of the Other.

The changing perspectives of the protagonists in the antiromantic novels first produce desires, then rivalry and violence. The latter emerges toward the end of the novels in resolutions that lead to actual or symbolic death, arrive at metaphysical dead ends, or, as in the *Sentimental Education,* refuse resolution altogether.

The mutual movement of desire and violence in the world of the narrative is constituted by the fluctuation of narrative perspectives, which represent the view of the *I* toward the Other and toward the self, whereby the *I*'s central experience of the Other is as a rival. The author has precisely as much knowledge of the perspective of the Other as he does of the narrated *I,* not because he sits atop the Olympus of an auctorial narrator, but because that which is imitated and resisted is part of his own person. The author orders his own world in terms of situations of imitation, desire, and the exercise of violence; the biographical evidence left by Rousseau, Stendhal, and Flaubert leaves no room for doubt here. One's own person, as imagined or remembered, can also become the model of desire and the target of a violence directed against the self.

The mechanism of violence is grounded in the intention of becoming the Other, in the taking over of the latter's aims and wishes. The Other becomes the object of a comprehensive process of empathic understanding. The mimetic empathy that is manifest in the antiromantic novel intensifies the principle of the romantic hermeneutic and discovers in consistent identification with the Other a source of an extremely explosive—for being socially effective— violence. The world of a person whose understanding is structured mimetically is organized according to such a perspective: the Others stand, on the one hand, opposed to the *I* and, on the other, are regarded as the standard of a sought-after equivalence between the *I* and Other. This process of comparison would not be possible in the absence of the normative effect exercised by language. The antiromantic novels allow us to recognize, in the process of acquiring an understanding of the Other, both violence and the role played in it by lan- guage.[31] In the intensified form of fiction, this process leads to a competition between the imitating *I* and the imitated Other. Friedrich Schleiermacher's hermeneutic maxim—that the interpreter can better understand the person being interpreted than the latter can himself or herself—is an unconscious expression of this relation. Wherever desire comes into play in the relation to the Other, understanding can assume the form of competition.

According to Wittgenstein, the relationships between a model and an im- itator are already marked by violence in their (ontogenetic) origin. Every mimetic relation presupposes that the imitator is capable of producing results equivalent to those of his or her model. The pupil is given a model, the imitation of which occurs under force (*dressur,* training). At the beginning of it all is the reproduction of the model; and Wittgenstein leaves no doubt that reproduction is no spontaneous act of imitation: "For here I am looking at learning German as adjusting a mechanism to respond to a certain kind of influence."[32] Witt- genstein's own biography allows us to recognize that the violence of the violent teacher, mediated over the "intermediary station" of the pupil, is ultimately directed at the self.[33]

The understanding subject, in its extreme type, is one that is excluded from all social life, one for which others are scarcely real at all, but exist primarily in imagination, where they are woven into the subject's imaginary dialogue. Understanding in this case is no longer receptive; it no longer fol- lows on an experience of Others but instead constitutes them itself in order to possess them. Dostoyevsky's underground man[34] is a powerless person. His ideas about Others take form in his overheated imagination and are filled with resentment; they almost never accord with reality. Thus the underground man's constant disappointment with the real behavior of Others as it diverges from his expectations and the incessant reapproximation to events in his fantasies. In *Notes from Underground,* the reader discovers an implicit external perspective: Dostoyevsky makes it understood that the underground man makes a model of every Other who appears superior to himself, no matter what the nature of the superiority or the personality of the Other might be. The more powerfully the underground man experiences the superiority of the Other, the more valuable becomes the latter as his model. In the internal perspective, in which all superiors are declared enemies, the underground man is simultaneously organizing his competition against them: he gathers all the violence of which he believes himself capable to attack them. The external perspective reveals that he manages to do nothing but imitate their actions; to actions he understands as violent, he responds mimetically with violence.

The inhabitant of the underground is also on a search for his *I;* but he has not the slightest notion of what the latter could look like. He has only a terrible inner emptiness and the wish to be loved, no matter as what: "In the most powerful paroxysm of cowardly fever, I had visions of having the upper hand, of winning, carrying them along with me, forcing them to love me."[35] Only if others love him can he love himself. If they do not love him, he wants admiration. If they do not admire him, he wants them to fear him. And when, finally, they do not even fear him, they should hate or despise him. In his eyes this latter is also a solution: those who despise him are those who love themselves; since he imitates them, he becomes like them and thus achieves at least a conception of himself as a self-loving *I.* Only those who cannot despise him, who therefore do not love themselves, are beneath him and unworthy of imitation. Only as medium do the Others play a role for the underground man; the violence that he exercises against them serves to prompt violence from them in response. For him, positive relationships to others, love and admiration, are also forms of violence. "To me love meant tyranny and moral supremacy."[36] "I always began with hatred and ended with moral subjugation, and I could not even imagine what to do with the subjugated object afterwards."[37]

The particularity of Dostoyevsky's novella lies not only in its extreme form of self-desire. It differs from the novels we have otherwise cited also in its structure, in the interweaving of the internal and external perspectives. Written in the first person, connected to the figure of the underground man, it reveals in the form of self-analysis the impossibility of self-desire's fulfillment. The protagonist analyzes his attempt to gain power, knows in advance the senselessness of his action, abjures in advance, even while in the process of engaging himself, the results of the engagement, in order then to behave accordingly after all and to triumph in the negative consequences.

The underground man, despite the most acute self-analysis, fails to understand the problem of his *I*. He slides into cynicism and overwrought self-absorption:

> And so, long live the underground! I did say that I envied the normal man with all my guts, but under the conditions in which I see him, I don't want to be him (though I will not stop envying him. No, no, in any case, the underground is more advantageous!). There at least one can . . . Aw! But here I am lying again. I am lying because I myself know, like two times two, that it is not the underground at all that is better, but something different, entirely different, something I crave but that I just can't find![38]

20

The Mimesis
of Violence (Girard)

In a succession of interrelated works, René Girard has argued the existence of a close, all but necessary, connection between mimetic action and violence in interpersonal relationships.[1] We have become familiar in an earlier chapter with his thesis of mimetic desire. Girard's first work, *Deceit, Desire, and the Novel,* is focused strictly on literary works, specifically, on works of the nineteenth century, and deals exclusively with the details of the constitution of the self and interactions between the *I* and its social environment. Already apparent in this early work is a tendency to postulate transpersonal connections between mimesis and equally mechanically isolated modes of action and to develop these ideas as a general sociopsychological schema adapted to the nineteenth-century context. The decisive points at which the purported mechanism is articulated, that is to say, is conceived, in *Deceit, Desire, and the Novel* are specific in terms of time and place: the body of texts Girard discusses stems from a precisely defined literary epoch and makes sense only in relation to that context; the literary figures he discusses can be regarded as representatives of their respective national bourgeoisies, with the intellectual constitution corresponding to the respective cases (which is especially true of Stendhal and Flaubert). The desire Girard constructs in relation to these figures expresses a specific psychohistorical situation and does not pertain to periods prior or subsequent to the one in question. Precisely what he discovers is the existence and operation of an internal medium, which mediates emotional models and prompts mimetic modes of action in regard to the Other.

In his later works, beginning with *Violence and the Sacred,* to which we turn now, Girard expands his view of mimetic processes beyond a restricted historical and social context in an attempt to develop a general theory of human social action based on his understanding of the mimetic structure of consciousness. Girard generalizes his initial hypotheses to all human societies and constructs the mimetic as the fundamental anthropological structure as such, as a social mechanism that is all but completely autonomous in its operation. He refers all human action to models established by Others; these models both generate the goals of action and release the psychic energies that motivate the accomplishment of the goals (independently of whether there is any realistic chance of success).

Girard conceives the mimetic structure of consciousness as a blind mechanism that, given the irreducibly mimetic nature of human action, constrains people to orient themselves according to models. Mimesis, interpreted in this way, becomes an inescapable fatality, a determining factor of human history. Specific instances of mimetically generated action are interlinked, on the basis of what Girard terms "acquisitive mimesis" (*mimésis d'appropriation*). In accord with his agonistic image of human being, the linkage of mimetic actions begins with one person's appropriation of goals that are deemed valuable and worth striving for solely because they are desired by an Other—who may already have achieved the goal or may be seeking to achieve it. But the point of acquisitive mimesis is ultimately that an object becomes the goal of an action because the Other, either previously or at the same time, is either really or presumed to be bent on the same goal. This triangle of mimetic action appears to Girard as an elemental figure from the perspective of which the order characteristic of all human endeavors can be explained.

The problem raised by triangular action, in the first instance, consists in the way it inevitably produces mimetic rivalry and thus a relationship of violence between rivals. All human appropriative actions, according to Girard's assertion, automatically generate violence; this becomes the great problem of human societies for which some resolution is imperative. In distinction to animals, human beings are not protected by instincts that prevent them from striving for the same goal as other members of their community. Among humans, according to Girard, situations are inevitable in which two or more individuals desire the same object and seek to appropriate it. The attractive force of the object does not lie in its inherent value; nor is it rendered valuable by the libido of the competitors. Rather, it is the dynamic of the competitive situation that confers value on the sought-after object and prompts rivals to affective engagement. Mimetic conflict is therefore subject to resolution neither on the level of objects nor on that of the competing individuals.[2]

Only in exceptional circumstances, Girard argues, is the violence that arises out of the mimetic character of individual human action subject to amelioration. We might object that functioning societies dispose over an entire arsenal of inhibitory mechanisms: prohibitions, hierarchical orders, and social institutions such as the legal system, morality, and ethics. But the problem is not solved by these means, because they too must at some time have been brought into being, founded, that is, and instilled with authority. Prior to the foundation of order, following Girard, there must have existed a situation of lawlessness; the social institutions responsible for curbing violence, in short, were themselves necessarily established through violence (*violence fondatrice,* founding violence). Every social order is the termination of a condition of lawlessness, of anomie, within a grouping of individuals, which threatens to erupt in violent, annihilating action whenever the opportunity arises. If we were to go back to a time prior to all order, we would find a point at which the disorder and violence generated by acquisitive mimesis is transformed into order, an order that interrupts the operation of the mimetically produced mechanism of violence.[3]

This originary order—every new order in general—must come to terms with a particular problem that arises out of the violence that characterizes relations between competitors: supposing that mimetic rivalry has eventuated in murder, vengeance will have been the response, which then results in a chain of violent acts, each new one representing vengeance for the previous one. The prohibition against killing cannot be fundamentally distinguished from revenge; on the contrary, it threatens death to whomever violates the injunction and kills. A potential act of violence is supposed to be prevented by the threat of an act of counterviolence. Fear of violence produces the commandment against vengeance and thereby sets in opposition to violence the principle of violence. "Inevitably the moment comes when violence can only be countered by more violence."[4] The only antidote to violence is violence; thus the endlessness of the cycle. Having established to his own satisfaction the operation of mimesis on this anthropological level, Girard conceives of the violence inherent in social institutions as a dynamic force that, momentarily stilled, can break out again at any time. The cessation of violence is always only provisional; every overcoming of violence is in effect a delusive condition.

According to Girard's anthropology, there can be no effective defense against violence as long as the mimetic mechanism continues to function. Cyclical patterns are ever-recurring: from utter anomie to temporary conditions of order, then to a weakening of order, and finally to a crisis and a new period of lawlessness. Typical of the process is the escalation of violence. The number of competitors involved and the intensity of the conflicts rise in proportion to the erosion of the effectiveness of structures of social order. In conditions of extreme social crisis, according to Girard's analysis of ethnological and classical texts, there appears a typical solution: the identification of a scapegoat, a weak, marginalized individual to whom others attribute responsibility for the crisis. Once a consensus has been reached by the remaining members of the community as to the attribution of guilt and the explanation of the ultimate cause of the catastrophe, all of the violence inhering in society is turned against the single individual. The attribution of guilt becomes the occasion of collective vengeance.

In this sacrifice of an individual, who is ostracized, ritually abused, or even killed, society overcomes the mimetic rivalries among its separate members, who join together in common action. The result is not the disappearance of violence from society; but it is given a causal explanation, aimed in the same direction by agreement of all the members, pushed to the point of a cathartic discharge, and, following the sacrifice of the scapegoat, used to erect a new order, to establish prohibitions and regulations intended to prevent a new outbreak of violence.

In the aftermath of such a succession, which Girard posits as a hypothetical scenario, it can seem as if violence has been eliminated from society. Society, however, remains unaware of what Girard regards as the "true cause" of violence, namely, unmastered mimetic rivalry. Its solution to the crisis, in other words, runs in precisely the wrong direction, although the error—peace having returned to the community as a whole—appears to be the truth. The great narratives depicting a scapegoat's guilt and the community's reestablishment of order are records of the historical existence of this perspective. The interpretation of the crisis becomes the founding act of a new order; it is inscribed in myths representing the origins of culture from the point of view of the newly constituted community of survivors.

The single victim is the representative of all who share responsibility for the situation of social crisis. In principle, each and every person could be chosen. The selection of one person (or group of persons) is justified in retrospect by a multitude of factual, imaginary, or attributed particularities: the evil eye, physical deformities, peculiar habits, the status of an outsider. Often the scapegoat is figured as a foreigner who has come into society from the outside. "Scapegoat indicates both the innocence of the victims, the collective polarization in opposition to them, and the collective end result of that polarization. The persecutors are caught up in the 'logic' of the representation of persecution from a persecutor's standpoint, and they cannot break away."[5]

The Oedipus myth, in Girard's reading, is just such a retrospective, rationalizing myth of sacrifice and founding: Oedipus, a stranger arriving in Thebes, is declared guilty for the great crisis besetting the city. His guilt is confirmed by the heinous crimes attributed to him in the myth. After he has been identified as the scapegoat and driven out of Thebes, prosperity returns to the city. This revitalization of a society following a severe crisis is the source of a remarkable opposition that typically appears in the figure of the scapegoat: sacrificed as the one responsible for the misfortune of the community, he is then regarded as the cause of the positive changes. His violence—in the mythological attribution—brought about the crisis, but it also gives it a happy turn. Accorded tremendous power as a stranger, held responsible for extraordinarily dangerous but also ultimately fortunate effects, elevated to transcendent, superhuman status as the savior and founder of a culture, his person is graced with saintliness in later tellings of the story.[6] Oedipus in Colonos remains a dangerous, fear-inspiring figure, but he is also regarded as extraordinarily valuable. The saint is possessed of both aspects of violence, the malignant as well as the curative effect. It is this ambivalence, which has long been noted in the scholarship, that Girard feels able to explain through the mechanism of the scapegoat.

The phenomenon of religion arises in the context of order-establishing violence. The goal of religion is to prevent the occurrence of violence; its great paradigm to this end is the mythical figure of the saint. "Primitive religion tames, trains, arms, and directs violent impulses as a defensive force against those forms of violence that society regards as inadmissible."[7] Its primary means is the preventive victim, the selection and sacrifice of whom, as a violence-inhibiting mechanism, is essential to the survival of societies that lack a judicial system.[8] Religion thus has the congenital defect of having arisen through the sacrifice of an innocent victim and being permeated by ambivalent violence. Violence is the condition of its possibility, and it can never repair the deficiency. "If the god is nothing more nor less than the massive violence that was expelled by the original act of generative unanimity, then ritual sacrifice can indeed be said to offer him portions of his own substance."[9] The religious is "nothing other than this immense effort to keep the peace. *The sacred is violence,* but if religious man worships violence it is only insofar as the worship of violence is supposed to bring peace."[10] The abolition of violence—this is Girard's conclusion—is possible only by way of the abolition of the religious. The danger of religion lies in its misunderstanding of the sacred; it tells a false version of the story of the sacrificial victim, and it must tell the story falsely because only if what is really happening remains unknown can the sacrifice be effective.

The religious represents the violence that exists in society as a principle external to individual human being, as allied with external powers. "Violence is the heart and secret soul of the sacred."[11] The function of religious rituals is "to 'purify' violence; that is, to 'trick' violence into spending itself on victims whose death will provoke no reprisals."[12] The sacred is malady and remedy in one. For it to be effective, it must be as similar as possible to bad violence. It repeats and renews the effects of the scapegoat mechanism. In this way it keeps violence external to the community. Girard's key example here is the Greek rite of the pharmakos. The city of Athens maintained a range of social outsiders, such as beggars, for use in a ritual observance; in the context of a religious ceremony, they were led through the city, treated like kings at a festival, and finally driven out, stoned, or killed in some other way.[13] A comparable example, in yet more drastic form, can be found in the pageantry of the so-called African monarchies: the king is treated as "a catalyst who converts sterile, infectious violence into positive cultural values."[14] Girard regards rituals of this sort as the most precise possible reproduction of an initial spontaneous lynching. The sacrificial ritual and religious ceremonies and festivals are for him a repetition, a simulation of an original act of collective violence.[15] "These rites permit the participants to play out all the roles performed by their ancestors during the original crisis."[16]

The ambivalence of the sacred is designated by the Greek term *katharma*. In its first meaning it indicates a malevolent object that is expelled in the course of a ritual act; its second meaning is that of a human victim in a ritual sacrifice, a variant of the pharmakos. "The word *katharsis* refers primarily to the mysterious benefits that accrue to the community upon the death of a human *katharma* or *pharmakos*."[17] There is also a specifically medical usage of the term "katharsis": "The illness and its cure are often seen as one; or at least, the medicine is considered capable of aggravating the symptoms, bringing about a salutary crisis that will lead to recovery."[18] (*Pharmakon* also connotes simultaneously poison and remedy.)

The religious, according to Girard's thesis, is permeated by violence; its ultimate purpose is to channel violence, its basis nothing other than a distinction between good and bad violence and the repetition of an original act of murder. It can only remain effective if its true structure and the devices by which it functions remain an undiscovered secret, if, that is, the truth about humanity's mimetic disposition is not understood. An analogous procedural schemata is evident in the widest possible array of myths. "The extraordinary number of commemorative rites that have to do with killing leads us to imagine that the original event must have been a murder."[19] According to Girard's fundamental assumption of the operation of a blind mimeticism, all societies must have been founded on the basis of and by means of violence. All of them have the same congenital defect, consisting in rivalry, crisis, and sacrifice, on which the cultural order is raised. "In all primitive cultures the institutions and rituals surrounding death, marriage, hunting, child rearing, and initiation present themselves as a 'mimetic crisis' that concludes with the sacrifice of a victim."[20] In Girard's understanding, all of the myths of cultural origins are encoded representations of real events in which order is established as the result of originally violent acts. In his book devoted exclusively to the issue of sacrifice, *The Scapegoat,* he summarizes his essential assertions in abbreviated form:

> 1) the acts of violence are real; 2) the crisis is real; 3) the victims are chosen not for the crimes they are accused of but for the victim's signs that they bear, for everything that suggests their guilty relationship with the crisis; and 4) the import of the operation is to lay the responsibility for the crisis on the victims and to exert an influence on it by destroying these victims or at least banishing them from the community they "pollute."[21]

Girard considers this schema to be universal.

Human societies into the present have yet to manage to free themselves entirely from the originary context of order-establishing violence. From this perspective, Girard's enterprise is aimed against the sacred, the sacrificial victim, and the religious, insofar as they never escape their bond to violence, vengeance, and the concealment of the way they function. His goal is to demystify and expose blind mimeticism and the mechanism of violence. Girard's theses derive their force in particular from his coherent, often quite original, and surprising readings of myths. How is it possible to read myths—which in Girard's own estimation remain an essential instrument in the concealment of truth, of the rewriting of history from the point of view of the victor—such that they reveal the original founding events? Girard attempts to answer this question, the decisive one for his theses, by means of a procedure he terms the "deconstruction" of myths. We shall illustrate this method on the basis of an example, but first the following points must be made. In his attempts to decode the myths, Girard makes reference to, among other things, rites that in his opinion represent the initial crisis in less dissembled and thus more accessible form. The transcultural comparability of myths, on his assumption, makes it possible to transfer insights gained in the decoding of one myth to the corresponding myths of other cultures.

The Greek myths that supplied the content of dramatic tragedies, in particular, the Oedipus story, offer a good example of Girard's method.[22] The tragedies themselves already contain the beginnings of a disclosure of the hidden content of myths since they were written at a certain distance from the original narratives. They neither coincide entirely with the mythical story told from the perspective of the victor nor do they, without further treatment, accept the judgment of guilt imposed on the victim or the multitude of charges with which it is justified. Sophocles' *Oedipus Rex* makes it clear from the beginning that the drama is set amid a crisis in the religious institutions of Thebes. The city is threatened by hunger and pestilence, an epidemic spread by contagion, which has the effect of rendering all people equal. The search for the guilty party gets under way, but genuine guilt cannot ultimately be ascribed; all that can be found is a scapegoat. The tragic plot consists in a gradual polarization of the violence of a few, then of the many, and finally of all against one. The central literary device of which the tragedy makes use is stichomythia, speech and counter-speech, whereby two protagonists answer each other in alternating lines. It creates an absolute symmetry between opposed positions, a kind of substitute through the word for real physical conflict. Constructed on the basis of the equality of the two positions and thus the leveling of social distinctions, the tragedy is a continuation of hand-to-hand combat through the medium of language.

In the moment of crisis, all the essential differences between the protagonists are canceled; everyone is caught in the grip of violence. Oedipus, as the story proceeds, becomes increasingly similar to his father, Laius, just as hot-tempered and unrestrained. At the peak of the crisis, the differences that distinguish him from Tiresias and Creon vanish. All of the major characters contribute to the destruction of their own order, while they act as if they are doing everything possible to preserve it. The "symmetrical reading" reveals that all of the protagonists assume a comparable position: each one believes himself the master of violence, but it is violence that successively masters all of them. The only guilty character to be found in the crisis is Oedipus; the crimes he is accused of, parricide and incest, are characterized precisely by the way they efface differences. The fatal moment of Oedipus's selection comes in the course of a dramatic exchange between the three protagonists, a tragic debate corresponding to a confrontation in battle. In the myth, Oedipus's guilt is represented as truth; this is the version of Tiresias and Creon, the victors. In Girard's interpretation, the tragedy leaves the question of Oedipus's guilt hanging for a long time, revealing a shifting procedure of searching and attributing guilt, which hesitates to choose from among the main characters the guilty one. The spectator is able to recognize in this extension of the question of guilt that, in principle, another outcome would also be conceivable.

This impression is also conveyed by the medium of the theatrical drama, which moves almost like a trial, that is, begins in uncertainty and stretches ever more tautly the dramatic arch of suspense. From this point of view, Girard's observation seems less an indication of the distance gained by the tragedy from myth than an effect of the medium. But here we arrive at a general difficulty with Girard's "deconstruction": the analysis of the mythical series of events as a crisis of the religious institutions is undertaken in regard to a text that does not exist, but must first be produced. The extant mythical texts are systematically distorted; they must be read anew with the distortion filtered out. Only on the basis of this (hypothetically) correct text is it possible to recognize the distancing of the tragedy. At least two hypotheses are always considered in an assessment of this method: one concerning the correct version of the mythical events and one about the intentional deviation of the tragedy in the sense of an approximation of the truth. Methodologically we are led into a precarious situation in which it is impossible to determine which of the individual hypotheses is correct. But Girard does not argue that he is proceeding hypothetically; on the basis of his anthropological postulates, he construes both the right version, in his view, of the originary events and the distortions contained in the founding myth and, finally, the deviation from the latter in tragedy. It requires a great deal of faith in Girard's anthropology to accept these steps in his reasoning.

The tragic form itself favors a departure from myth, with the change consisting in the way tragedy depicts the process that leads to the expulsion of the scapegoat. The scenic presentation of tragedy likewise operates to demystify the victors' story by penetrating the protective veil of ignorance responsible for opening up a narrative space for the myth. Nevertheless, rather than take the side of the victim, tragedy ultimately reproduces the accusations found in the source. It does indeed denounce violence, the cancellation of differences, and the selection of a scapegoat; but it does not turn the whole story around and tell it from the perspective of the victim. Such a transformation would have been utterly foreign to tragedy, incompatible with the finality of its pronouncement.

In Girard's interpretation, tragedy takes over the place of the victors' myth, but it remains within the tradition of ritual sacrifice, which it continues in a distanced fashion. This standpoint is laid down in particular in the Aristotelian idea of catharsis. Aristotle established that "tragedy can and should assume at least some of the functions assigned to ritual in a world where ritual has almost disappeared."[23]

Theater operates like a ritual. It has functions analogous to the act of sacrifice: catharsis is the expulsion of an evil by means of an antidote. Aristotle examines the tragedy above all from the perspective of the order to which it contributes. Plato, in contrast, had a more acute understanding of the crisis of social order. He notes that tragic disorder and tragic violence can become one and the same. He firmly renounces both. More clearly than others, Plato recognizes the ambivalence of the tragic solution, which is itself created only by means of violence and preserves the ambiguity of the pharmakon as both remedy and poison. Derrida shows that the modern translations of Plato efface ever more completely the traces of the founding events, in that they use different terms to designate pharmakon-as-remedy and pharmakon-as-poison.[24]

Girard's goal is to enlighten us as to the nature of mimesis and violence—an enlightenment that transcends ignorance about the sacred and the religious to reveal the truth about violence. It is necessary, he suggests, to know the nature of violence if we are to defend ourselves against it. There is no form of the religious, however consecrated, that can break the cycle of mimetic violence. Every instance of the sacred is nothing other than a polarization, a channeling, and a preservation of violence. Only the passion of Christ[25]—in the Old Testament the Book of Job[26]—is subject to a reading that departs from the pursuit narratives of mythology (and also the other books in the Bible). The murder of Jesus is condemned, but it is not avenged. The change of perspective is already evident in Judaism: the texts sometimes take the side of the victim, insist on his innocence, and denounce the guilt of the murderers.[27] New Testament texts move definitively beyond the victors' narrative; they are not the mythological expression of founding events seeking to claim and delimit the sacred. In Girard's interpretation, the evangelists finish what was left unfinished in the Old Testament. Jesus is represented as an innocent victim in a society in the throes of crisis,[28] but he does not become the object of a ritual sacrificial act that reproduces his death. It is, for Girard, a complete misunderstanding of the passion of Christ to interpret it in sacrificial terms.[29] The evangelists absolutely reject any thought of vengeance; in their view of the matter, Christ's sacrifice is supposed to bring the mechanism of violence to a definitive end. By insisting on the innocence of Jesus and on forgiveness for the murderers, the New Testament narrative sublates the ambivalence of the sacred.

In distinction to the Old Testament, no trace of a positive assessment of violence remains among the evangelists. The passion of Christ relieves the divine of precisely the function that is central to primitive religions, namely, "that of polarizing everything mankind does not succeed in mastering, particularly in relationships between individuals."[30] Jesus dies "not as a sacrifice, but in order that there may be no more sacrifices."[31] New Testament texts underscore the naturalistic character of his death; his death is not made into a guarantor of life.[32] The sacrifice of Christ turns back against the scapegoat mechanism: the sacrificial victim is sacralized as an innocent rather than a guilty figure; violence is not constructed as a characteristic of the divine.

In Girard's interpretation, the story of Christ's passion signifies the renunciation of violence: only the unconditional renunciation of violence, unilateral if necessary, can bring mimetic rivalry to an end.[33] With the sacrificial death of Jesus, which is supposed to prevent all further sacrifice, mythology is also brought to an end.[34] The meaning of the Christian narrative lies in its demystification of "founding violence," of the scapegoat, and of social order based on violence. The Christian God, as a god of the innocent victim, stands as a polar opposite to the gods of Olympus.

Girard's texts aim at offering his readers a forgotten message or one that has not been understood, and they increasingly take on the tone of revelation in the process. The problems of violence, desire, social disorder, and the founding of cultures, in his interpretation, are to be referred back to a final principle, whereby he traces the multiplicity of mythical and ritual forms back to analogous events that he maintains are empirical. By reducing the meaning of every society to its essential origin, however, Girard raises truth claims in regard to his readings, even while he fails to consider alternative interpretations. The emergence of society conceived in terms of an originary event, the assumption of a presocial condition ruled only by relative physical strength, the definition of society as a mechanism for channeling violence, and finally the contrived consistency of a chain of events leading necessarily to the establishment of a cultural order—these elements of Girard's anthropology are neither directly obvious nor lacking in interpretive alternatives, as the author's truth claim would have it.

It is beyond dispute that Girard has developed a powerful instrument of interpretation. He argues essentially on the *meta*level of narratives about social origins and crises. Yet the texts that speak of a founding of society through violence do not offer us any knowledge about empirical events; the structure in which they are themselves organized has been influenced by violence. While Girard's theses are quite capable of giving new impetus to textual hermeneutics, the objective level, that of the events in question, remains completely in the dark. To render textual structures transparent, to look through them as if they were not there—these are the principles of Girard's hermeneutic.[35] But it is a futile endeavor that seeks to penetrate through the structures constitutive of texts to empirical events. Girard overlooks the possibility that the verbal references in the texts he examines can be instances of "null denotation."[36]

It is not at all Girard's intention to tell an origins story about human societies. But must we assume that there ever was an identifiable origin of the social? Nelson Goodman relegates the search for an initial world to the realm of theology; in his view, every world arises out of *another* world, and there is no more to be said about it.[37] Theological thinking is, to be sure, not foreign to Girard. But the question of the origin has perhaps yet another meaning: the anchoring of a culture in an originary event ultimately points to a repetition of the founding of culture in a new event. Many of Girard's considerations on the end of violence speak for such an interpretation. The founding of our society through violence, which from then on remains embedded in its foundations, must be understood as a defect and must awaken desires for a new founding, one that would return to individuals the greatest possible freedom and make clear the imperative of renouncing mimesis. In regard to these idealizing thoughts, the question may be raised as to whether violence against the Other is not constitutive for the individual in the context of antagonistic personal relationships. The texts Girard examines do indeed manifest analogous forms according to which the relationships of *I* and Other are arranged, perceived, and represented. The reason for this is in the first instance a perspective that opposes the Other antagonistically to the *I*. The question, however, is whether this perspective is not being imposed on the texts by modern interpreters and whether it is appropriate for the reception of myths and texts prior to the modern period.

Girard makes successful use of the antagonistic perspective in his interpretation of antiromantic literature. These texts are characterized by a number of family resemblances, which are to some extent overlapping, in that they represent their characters' problems in their relationships with Others and emphasize mimetic action, desire, and violence. These characteristics are grounded in the constituted nature of the modern individual: empty and lacking in substance, the individual is left to fashion himself or herself in opposition to Others. Seen in these terms, the relationship of *I* to Other is all but necessarily charged with violence; but only in the modern period does there arise the antagonistic *I* in reference to the self.

If we impose the modern constitution of the *I* onto mythical struggles for a social order, then we obviously attribute to the individual *I* a sense for establishing order. This sense produces an order in which the *I* allots specific positions to itself and to Others. The *I* thus becomes an originator of order, like the author of a novel is the originator of a world produced by literary means. Girard uses techniques of literary and artistic worldmaking and accords them the character of empirical events, which he then postulates as the beginning of culture. In this way, he projects the problematic of the modern individual back onto the beginnings of history. What Girard is finally saying, in summary form, is that the problems of the modern *I* began with the history of society. Girard seems to have taken up a position outside the world, from which point he thinks it is possible to observe the beginnings of time. The movement back to origins, the symbolic repetition of the beginning, aims—as a new myth—to take up history once again from where it began in order to repeat and renew it.

In Girard's "mythical narrative," the mimesis of desire and violence becomes a question of human existence and society. It attempts to offer us information, derived from an anachronistically constituted origin, about who we are. By representing the inexorability of the mimesis of desire and violence, it offers us hints as to what we should do. The narrative fashions a mythical understanding of the *I* that enters compulsively into competition whenever it is offered the opportunity to compete. And finally, the narrative supplies answers to the questions it raises, answers that must not be regarded as worthless simply because they have a mythical character. Perhaps it is only mythical narratives that have a chance to offer answers to such questions.

Part VI

Mimesis as Entrée to the World, Language, and Writing

There are two sides to human mimetic capacities. On the one hand, they open up an entrée to the world and to Others. They fulfill the preconditions of understanding and allow for a partial overcoming of the subject-object split. Without mimesis, understanding fails and experience is impossible. Through mimesis the world is "translated" into images, put at our disposal in the form of memory and ideas. It produces similarities between nature, society, and human being, between adults and children, between inner and outer. On the other hand, mimesis can lead to a collapse into nature and to an assimilation to an ossified environment; it can occasion subordination, alienation, even the dissolution of the self. Examples include the adaptation of prehistorical humans to a hostile nature and a reified environment, in which the individual encounters nothing but more of its own self.

The human body has always served, in dance, gestures, language, and imagination, to produce similarities. In this process, representation and expression emerge as two inextricably intertwined aspects of mimesis. The gradual suppression of the mimetic relationship to the world, to Others, and to the self leads to a loss of immediacy. This development also entails a reduction of the expressive side of language in favor of its semantic content and instrumental function. Aspects of the mimetic relation to the world have been made over into writing and language as an "archive of nonsensuous similarities." The individual uses the mimetic powers at its disposal to decode and revitalize these aspects to avoid an impoverishment of the relation between the self and the world.

Walter Benjamin illustrates the ontogenetic significance of mimetic processes in *Berliner Kindheit,* which centers on childhood development as the result of mimetic interaction with the environment. The child becomes similar to the many places, objects, and constellations that surround him; in the process he expands his subjective boundaries. In "breakthrough situations" the child develops needs in interaction with the external world, needs that eventuate in important lifelong dispositions that themselves will shape the future. By way of language and imagination an interior exterior world takes shape, which is enriched by further mimetic processes.

Mimetic capacities make possible what Theodor Adorno calls "vital experiences" (*lebendige Erfahrungen*), as well as the opportunities for happiness associated with them. These experiences operate as a corrective for identifying thought and conceptual knowledge, which entails to some extent a sacrifice of the self. With the triumph of human being over nature comes a repression of both nature in the human self and the possibility of "self-illumination without the self," which that aspect of human nature includes. The mimetic faculty is not capable of sublating this development, but it can make it bearable by enabling the self to undergo other experiences and to acquire "nonconceptual knowledge." The predominance of the object together with the nature of the subject beyond the boundaries of the *I* determine aesthetic experience. They become a refuge of mimetic behavior and a generalized form of vital experience. It is not that art should imitate reality, but that reality should imitate art. Thus does it become possible for reality to absorb into itself the utopian promise of art and change itself.

Writing and reading are mimetic (Derrida). They refer to prior matters: writing to what has already been written; reading to what has already been read. Texts are never originals, always "doubles"; they come into being through acts of collation and supplementation, through entanglements in other texts. They have no origin, but rather begin in situations that are already mimetic. Every origin is a repetition. What is written can be imitated at will and is open to divergent interpretations. Texts are produced and then scattered; their dissemination and the use to which they will be put is beyond anyone's control; they remain always ambiguous; they have to do with play, simulacrum, concealment. The mimetic treatment of texts and writing marks itself off from imitation and simulation through an element of difference. The goal is not the production of the same but the generation of the similar; it makes difference possible and, with difference, productive freedom.

21

Nonsensuous Similarity

**On the Linguistic
Anthropology of Benjamin**

Walter Benjamin, like few other writers in this century, understood the anthropological significance of mimesis. It is central to the relation between the individual and the world, to the Other and to the self. It makes it possible to discover meaning and have experiences. The mimetic faculty leads us to perceive similarities and invent correspondences with surrounding nature. It articulates itself in early forms of dance, in the practice of expressive naming, in an interpretation of the world in reference to central human needs.[1] Meaning is apprehended in the correspondence between the individual and the world. Sensuous apprehension takes place through the perception and production of similarities. The ability to generate similarities belongs, according to Benjamin, to the earliest of human capacities. Similarities can be discovered in various ways. They are obvious in the case of phenomena that correspond to each other in sensuous terms. They can appear in regard to two faces or in processes in which one person imitates the actions of another. Forms of similarity can also be discovered across the divide of animate and inanimate things, for example, children spinning their arms in imitation of a windmill.

The human body has always been used to produce and express similarities, obvious examples being dance and spoken language, both of which are intimately bound up with the mimetic faculty. In neither dance nor speech, however, do representation and expression name two different abilities. Rather, they make up two aspects of the mimetic faculty, which, in mimesis, do not diverge but are combined in a single act. If it were the case that such activities involved two different abilities, the subject-object split would already have established itself here, while in mimetic action there occurs a ''sublation'' of the split between *I* and object, subject and object. In the face of all the separations and differentiations, there pertains between nature and human being a commonality that finds verification today in natural scientific conceptions of the origin and evolution of the earth and life.[2]

Searching for, discovering, and creating similarities is the defining characteristic of the magical relation to the world in human consciousness. In Benjamin's view, people of earlier times noted a similarity, for example, between a particular stellar constellation and the destiny of the individual; we are simply not able to perceive it today. Even though there is no question of there ever having been a sensuous similarity between the stars and individual fate, it was plausible at that time to assume a correspondence. Benjamin speaks of ''nonsensuous similarity'' in reference to this nonsensuous experience of the world on the part of magical cultures. The term designates similarities that are not directly legible but must be decoded, which suggests that the whole cosmos is permeated by similarities, the sense of which is always there to be exposed to minds capable of decoding it in an act of reading. Human being and nature, far from being strictly opposed as subject and object, are bound to each other. The sense of the world is revealed to the individual by way of the individual's adaptation to the world.

As we have seen, this particular relation between the individual and the world and knowledge disappears with the transition from the Renaissance to classicism.[3] Up to that point there had existed a mimetic continuum in which human being had not yet made itself an object of knowledge and reflection. The mind did indeed cast its gaze at nature and at human nature, yet it was not able, because of the way it was seeing, to apprehend itself. Only as the human relation to the world began to undergo a fundamental change in French classicism did there arise a new form of the perception of the self. Since knowledge had not yet been separated from nature in the Renaissance, the signs of nature remained legible; irremovable similarities appeared to determine the relation between nature and human being.[4] The signature on the surface of things makes it possible to apprehend similarities and recognize the world. To know means to recognize the natural signs of similarity, to discover the unity of the world, and to read the correspondences. As classicism destroys the mimetic continuum of knowledge, there opens up a space for a kind of thinking that proceeds outside the mimetic faculty. The result is the transition from a ternary to a binary structure of the sign.

In the ternary structure, which predominates at least from the time of the Stoics, the significant and the signified are bound together in a conjuncture, which produces a nonarbitrary relation between language and the world. This relation is based in the sixteenth century on similitude, but ''from the seventeenth century . . . the arrangement of signs was to become binary, since it was to be defined, with Port-Royal, as the connection of a significant and a signified.''[5] The transition to a binary structure of the linguistic sign becomes particularly clear in the dualistic worldview of Descartes. Language and the world are no longer bound together by conjunctural similarity; they have been separated. Restricted to its arbitrary representational function, knowledge of the world loses the sensuousness it had in the mimetic cosmos of the Renaissance, the reconstruction of which is one of Benjamin's central ambitions. The quantification of knowledge and the development of the scientific order advance the loss of sensuousness and give rise to a new episteme. Mimetic sensuous experience is devalued, comes to be regarded as a fantasy world, and is relinquished to literature. "The new order of linguistic knowledge is constituted inside the closed space of representation itself; meaning arises through the dominant logic of representation. Nature falls silent. Knowledge no longer connotes interpretation (dialogue), but the organization of order (disposal)."[6] There develops a representational system that conceives objects instrumentally. An ordering according to differences and identities takes shape; the manifold nature of the singular, the sensuous-concrete disappears. The subject-object split, to which the rising sciences all contribute their share, is consolidated. This new logocentrism supplants the old mimetic order and its conception of language, with the premodern conception surviving only in literature, where language counts as something more than just an instrument of knowledge and human mastery.

Against the background of such considerations as these, Benjamin's works demonstrate that the dissolution of the mimetic relation to the world through logocentrism entails not only a gain in reason, enlightenment, and autonomy but also a loss of immediacy. A reduced conception of language sacrifices its expressive aspect to semantic content and instrumental function, which accompany the disappearance of the mimetic relation. This loss becomes more painful as the reduction of language contributes to the reification of the world and to the alienation of the individual. "It is to writing and the spoken word that the clairvoyant powers [of earlier people] are ceded in the course of history."[7] Writing and language have become "an archive of nonsensuous similarities, nonsensuous correspondences."[8] In this view, some part of the magical mimetic relation to the world found in earlier cultures has transformed itself into language.

Benjamin's conception of mimesis leads him to a theory of language, reading, and experience. The reading of writing preserves something of the abilities people formally possessed to read destiny in the stars or from viscera. Reading is more than the taking in of information; it includes the task of decoding the appearance of nonsensuous correspondences, of finding out what it is that comes to expression in writing. Also part of this operation are unconscious processes of which the writer is not aware. Benjamin sees graphology as a kind of research into such connections: it "taught us to recognize in handwriting images that the unconscious of the writer conceals in it."[9]

Reading, therefore, must discover the mimetic procedure that "expresses itself ... in the activity of the writer."[10] Writing always contains more than the writer is conscious of expressing.

These considerations confirm the existence of a close relationship among mimesis, orality, and literacy. The mimetic faculty undergoes profound changes in the course of the civilizing process in connection with the transition from orality to literacy at the time of Plato and from writing to printing at the beginning of the modern period. The rise of writing and, even more, the spread of the art of printing transform the relationship between the individual and language. Without the spread of book printing, the transition from a ternary to a binary language sketched above would not have been possible. Binary language calls for precision, clarity, and discursivity, which necessarily entail a decline in forms of analogous and allegorical thinking. Depending on the perspective we adopt, this development is either a gain or a loss. The universal spread of writing promotes the development of binary language. Writing and reading enhance processes of linguistic abstraction. The rudimentary pictorial elements retained in the gestures of a speaker become the universal image of script. Readers, by means of their mimetic faculty, analyze the abstractions of writing, concretize them, and fill them with "life." Imagination and the fictions contained in it allow readers to produce the necessary supplement to writing, so that writing and image work to complete a logically structured rationality and imagination.

The loss that we suffer with transition from a ternary to a binary language is intensified, according to Benjamin's view, because the mimetic faculty represents the origin of writing, of reading, and even of language. Benjamin relies on Jean Piaget, who sees the origin of language in mimesis, to elaborate his own ideas. The "articulation of the gesture, of the vocal apparatus," according to Benjamin, "is among the aspects of bodily mimicry. The phonetic element conveys a message, the original substratum of which was expressive gesture."[11] Benjamin connects this expressive character of the gesture with the physiognomical character of language, without being precise about the connection. As in the case of writing, where graphologists are able to recognize traits of the inner person, or in the legibility of emotions in a person's countenance, language is an individual expression bound to the body and the senses. Language is a mimetic transformation of perceptions and sensations, the mimetic aspect of which requires something on which to anchor itself. "This bearer is the semiotic element. Thus the coherence of words or sentences is the bearer through which, like a flash, similarity appears."[12]

If, however, the object world has dried up and is no longer itself an "archive of nonsensuous similarities," if, instead, language and writing have become the archive, then the corresponding mimetic experiences can only be had in language. With this change language acquires a contrafactual element over against social-historical reality, with which it can surpass the particular contours assumed at any particular moment by reality.

> This results only in a tendential restitution of the historical structure of the experience of nonsensuous correspondences—namely, the discovery in objects of a meaning that refers to human being—in that physiognomical expression illumines the object represented semiotically in language. The meaning discovered is mimetically relevant, and thus the full dimension of the "overall linguistic energy" contained in the full semiotic potential, in the potential of language for meaning, reactualizes itself as a unity of expression and objective reference, of subjectivity and objectivity (insofar as these concepts are at all appropriate).[13]

Seen in this way, language becomes the "highest level of mimetic behavior and the most complete archive of nonsensuous similarity."[14] It is a "medium into which the earlier powers of mimetic production and comprehension have passed without residue, to the point where they have liquidated those of magic."[15] This is the course by which there emerges an unexpected universalization of mimesis in "modernity."

In this anchoring of language in the mimetic faculty, expression and representation become the foundation of discrete experiences (*Erlebnisse*) of sensuous correspondence that are no longer bound to magic. The experience of nonsensuous similarities becomes tied to the reciprocal permeation of human needs and objects in the world. If mimetic abilities disappeared altogether, there would no longer be any way of interacting with the environment and experiencing it; for it is by means of the mimetic faculty that the objective world metamorphoses into the Other for human being. Experiences are had "in the state of resemblance."[16] With Benjamin's theory of language, with the concepts of nonsensuous similarity and nonsensuous correspondence, the foundation is laid for a theory of human experience (*Erfahrung*), within the frame of which it seems that the subject-object split characteristic of modernity can be overcome.

Benjamin's mimetic theory of language and experience has a predecessor in Johann Gottfried Herder.[17] Arnold Gehlen's theory of language, based on the principled openness of human being to the world, goes in the same direction.[18] In Herder's view, "Man has language already in his animal nature. All strong sensations, and among the strong the strongest, the painful sensations of his body, all of the intense passions of his soul, are immediately lent expression in screams, tones, in wild unarticulated sounds."[19] Every acoustical utterance is an expression of an interiority; human beings and animals express sensations in the same way. In distinction to animal expression, however, which is pressed into a certain condition of conformity by instinct, human language has a further function: it names and designates the objects with which the individual has to deal. By means of this linguistic function, objects are identified, fashioned, and made subject to an overview. Moreover, human communication precisely about this functional aspect of language becomes possible. The expressive and the significatory functions of language are therefore based on its mimetic character.

Hearing, for Herder, plays a critical role in the mediation between language and the world. Sounds become properties of objects through the ear. Thus does bleating become the aural sign of the sheep. "He (man) recognized the sheep by its bleating: it was an understood sign, by which the soul has a clear apprehension of an idea—what is that, but a word? And what is the whole of human speech if not a collection of such words."[20] These "aural *verba*" comprise the earliest linguistic behavior that designates something. "The first dictionary was thus collected out of all the sounds of the world. Every being capable of sound sounded its name: the human soul stamped it with its image, conceived it as the identifying sign."[21] Herder extends these considerations, according to which words, by virtue of their sounding quality, are taken to be linguistic signs, to nonsounding phenomena, a generalization that seems justified in light of our present-day knowledge about synaesthesia: the senses are interconnected in such a way through the sensus communis that they can substitute for each other.

By way of hearing as the mediating sense, even objects that do not address the ear directly can be accorded aural characteristics. By way of hearing, all the senses, since they are all based in sensation, become capable of speech. Thus there is no opposition between the expressive and the designative aspects of language. "The position of human being in the world is reflected in language. As a natural being, the individual's perception of self and of others is grounded in sensory impressions, which are rooted in feeling as an expression of overall psychological and existential competence."[22] Sensory perceptions prompt emotional responses out of which there arises meaning. Language is assigned a mediating function between the world of objects and the responses of the individual to those objects, which is also necessary insofar as the nondeterminacy and openness of human being and its surplus of impulses (Gehlen) require that it also forge ties to the objective world via needs. The relation between the inner and the outer world is thus no arbitrary one; through language a world is constituted for the individual that is both sensual and sensible. Language is therefore not merely functional; it not only designates but is also expressive. "As soon as man makes use of language to create a living relationship to himself or to his fellows, language is no longer merely an instrument, no longer a means, but a manifestation, a revelation of our inmost being and the psychological ties that bind us to ourselves and our fellows."[23]

Herder and Benjamin are at one in their emphasis on the *expressive character* of language. Differences between them arise in their understanding of its mimetic aspects. For Herder, linguistic mimesis is strictly onomatopoeic; he generalizes this characteristic to phenomena that bear no association with "aural *verba.*" While Herder derives mimesis from sensuous correspondences, language, for Benjamin, is "an archive of nonsensuous correspondences." For Herder, meaning appears in language when words are referred to instances of sense perception bound to emotional sensation. Benjamin, in contrast, finds little in Herder's onomatopoeic theory of the origins of language that persuades him, and his theory requires no mediation through the immediately sensuous expressive qualities of language; language, for Benjamin, is in every instance the expression of the deepest, most intimate self.

Gehlen also begins with a critique of Herder's theory of the origin of language, but he retains its central insight on the unity of expression and meaning. "Language brings the internal and the external world together on its own level."[24] This understanding is tenable only on the basis of anthropological assumptions, central among them the idea that human being is characterized by an impulse structure that is open to the world. In distinction to animals, human being is not bound and restricted by instinct to a single environment. Its nonspecialized impulse structure is directed toward the external world and crystallizes itself only in interaction with the world, through the images, sounds, smells, and touch sensations of its perception. The external world penetrates into the internal one and establishes itself there, causing wishes and needs to take shape in the process. They blend irretrievably with phenomena coming in from the outside. In this reciprocal opening up of the outer and the inner, instances of human need and impulse take shape. There arise specific arrangements, structurations, and hierarchies, which, to be sure, can develop only in and through language, in which outer and inner are seamlessly mediated. Gehlen's anthropological conception of language overcomes the Cartesian split between subject and object, with the distinction it implies between the expressive and the representational function of language.

Only in interaction with the outer world does the individual come to acquire his or her subjectivity. Only there can the unspecialized surfeit of impulse take on the form of wishes and needs, the interpretation of which requires language. The development of the human individual's complex of impulses takes place in language, which is also responsible for conducting interaction with the world. Thus does there arise within a single system both the formation of the self and discrepancies between the self and the outer world. External and internal worlds are continually approximating each other and are comprehensible only in terms of this reciprocal movement, in which similarities and correspondences between inner and outer are also formed. And here we arrive again at a mimetic relation: individuals make themselves similar to the outer world, changing themselves in the process; in this transformation, their perception of both the outer world and of the self change. The result is a mimetic developmental spiral.

In terms of ontogenetics, the acquisition of language is completed in breakthrough situations (Gehlen), in which a need comes into being in the interaction between an individual and external objects. This process finds representation in language, and in the course if its being represented there occurs a "growing-into" the semantic and pragmatic aspects of language. At the same time, the individual's inner world becomes comprehensible, expressible, and interpretable in language. Experiences become possible and begin to accumulate and guide behavior. Wishes and needs become tangible and subject to linguistic definition only in reference to external objects. As experiences recorded in language, they refer back to empirical experiences but can just as easily occasion new experiences. Thus do the dispositions acquired in the course of a life history acquire significance as factors that shape the future. New situations call for mimetic behavior toward earlier situations and the dispositions that evolved on account of them. There pertains between the new and the old situations a relation of similarity or correspondence, without it necessarily being the case that the relation rests on a sensuous similarity or correspondence. Thus the precise identification of this relation, which is mediated largely through language, in Benjamin's concept of nonsensuous correspondences. The experience of the breakthrough situation is preserved in language, without this preservation implying the end of the potential for mimesis in regard to the new and unknown. The experience of a correspondence among breakthrough situations corresponds to the mimetic relation of the individual to the world. As Benjamin points out on the basis of numerous examples in his autobiography, *Berliner Kindheit,* an inner outer-world and outer inner-world take shape by way of mimetic processes supported by language.

The mimetic faculty is at the center of Benjamin's autobiography, distinguishing it from conventional instances of the genre. If the latter take as their theme the reconstruction of the texture of a life and the representation of private commitments and confessions, the goal of which is to lay bare the interior motivations of the person, his or her struggle to define an identity and shape a life, then there emerges from Benjamin's depiction of these processes in *Berliner Kindheit* no comparable subject with a solid sense of self. It would be more fitting to say that the author is and remains unknown to himself; he plays with the incognito, with concealment. His origins reach all the way back into the mimetic processes of his early childhood, through which he becomes similar to his environment, his milieu, and through which he fashions himself in language by simultaneously expressing himself and naming the objects in the world. In the linguistic reconstruction of his early years, Benjamin recapitulates processes of approximation and experiences of nonsensuous correspondence. The attempt to remember becomes an effort to read the objects of childhood in their constellations, to understand them and render them emotionally accessible. The reading becomes difficult when incidents and events, such as the experience with an otter in one episode, manifest themselves only briefly and then disappear in a flash. Many of the objects and events of childhood behave in this way; they surface for a moment, then sink back into forgetfulness; in this moment of appearance, they achieve great intensity and can even occasion a shock before they disappear again. They are fleeting traces, difficult to retrieve from forgetting, which are bound to the breakthrough situations of childhood.

In his autobiography Benjamin attempts to recapture these processes of finding and losing the self. He frequently identifies them in the rooms of his Berlin childhood, which become the organizational units of his memory. Particular spaces—corners, hiding places, caves, window alcoves, wardrobes, cabinets, and thresholds—become the sites of sudden memory.[25] The opening and closing of a cabinet is suggestive of the back and forth, the movement from outside in, of concealing and revealing, of the principle of compartmentalization. The interiors of boxes and wardrobes become the most intimate and intense aspect of a bourgeois childhood; they mark the great familial sanctities. The collecting of butterflies, stamps, and the like, and the putting away of objects in boxes refer to connections with the sacred, which becomes manifest only through a reading of spaces, collections, signs, and complexes of meaning. To write an autobiography means to read and decode the correspondences found in memory.

The section entitled "Die Mummerehlen" relates a story focused on the boundary between image and reality, on a threshold that separates a space of images from a bodily space.

> It comes from China and tells of an old painter who gave his newest painting to friends to look at. The painting was of a park, a narrow path along the water and through some foliage, to end at a small door offering entry in the back to a little house. The friends looked around for the painter, but he was gone and in the picture. He walked along the narrow path to the door, stopped in front of it, turned around, smiled, and disappeared through the crack. So was I, with my little bowls and brushes, suddenly in the picture. I became similar to the porcelain, into which I moved with a cloud of color.[26]

Here we have the (mimetic) approximation of painter to picture, which ends in a mediation of real space and the space of the picture. The incident can be understood as a metaphor for the mimetic relation between the individual and the world. Benjamin reports other similar experiences from his childhood, in which real space and imaginary space so interpenetrate each other that they become one space. The child becomes similar to things, so that it becomes a part of them.

In other scenes, things look back and seem to be making themselves similar to the child. Thus the passage, for example, in connection with the butterfly hunt.

> The old rules of hunting took over between us: the more my being, down to its very fibers, adapted to my prey (the more I got butterflies in my stomach), the

> more the butterfly took on in all that it did (and didn't do) the color of human resolution, until finally it was as if capturing it was the price, was the only way I would regain my humanity.[27]

The mimetic character of the child's experience, the way incidents are expanded by the mimetic faculty, is clear. The child gets butterflies in his stomach, and at the same time the butterfly takes on human traits. The capture of the butterfly makes it possible to erect boundaries again and to secure the child's form of human being. On the level of appearances, only in overcoming the object can the child preserve the constitution of its self-consciousness.

Berliner Kindheit relates many similar experiences. Some are charged with anxiety and fear, such as the encounter with the "Little Hunchback," who can be regarded as a symbol of preservative forgetting, because he takes from the child his unconscious experiences and preserves them, thus preparing the way for memory.[28] Things shrivel up; they enter memory in distorted form. The fright that the encounter occasions is a moment of self-awareness and at the same time an obstacle to and repression of more far-reaching self-experience. The child, on the one hand, approximates himself completely to the environment, which is comparable to mimicry, and, on the other, experiences his power over spaces and objects through the mediation of his magical interaction with them. For spaces and objects "look back," without completely subordinating the child. Or, we should say, things gaze at the child, providing him with an experience in which to develop self-consciousness. The accumulation of similarities and correspondences between the self and the world makes the world familiar to the child; the child makes a home for itself in the world. Yet, at the same time, the world is full of mysteries. The child is forbidden entry in the parents' dining room and thus has an intensified experience of both the anticipated pleasure of eating and what it means to transgress moral strictures. Many memories have an erotic tinge, as, for example, the momentary experience of the "cozy warmth" on the inside of a sock. Breakthrough situations appear in the spaces of childhood; they harbor memories, moments of fate, in which the being similar and the becoming similar of the child can be focused as a theme; meanwhile the child is developing its faculties of language and memory.

Benjamin is conspicuously shy about being identified. As he writes in "Materialien zu einem Selbstporträt," the "solution to the puzzle, why I recognize no one," is that "I don't want to be recognized."[29] Not the revelation of his inner life, the goal of Rousseau's *Confessions,* for example, but the wish for an incognito stands at the center of *Berliner Kindheit.* Objects and the experiences gained from objects are the critical interest here, as Benjamin explains that one undertakes the mimetic act of reading to decipher what is emblematic about everything, to understand the allegorical level of experiences and objects. Reading sets in motion a play of correspondences, even when the references made are to nonsensuous similarities. The otter becomes the symbol of surfacing and disappearing, of invisibility and the sacred, of waiting for an unknown future. Noises, sounds, and words take on added meaning in this play of signs and references, with the aural, because it is anonymous, corresponding more than the visual to the goal of a biography, the aim of which is to reveal and conceal. Benjamin creates acoustic spaces, in part by recasting visual emblems in auditory terms, in part by opening up new experiential spaces altogether. He offers a striking example in a passage about the telephone: an acoustical incognito is created by the "cancellation of the image and the effects of the telephone. . . . There thus appears on the level of autobiographical writing the effect of the telephone: the hallucination of a secular reverberation that wells up like the noise in a seashell."[30]

Benjamin coined the term "aura" to designate the experience of magical enchantment. In "A Small History of Photography," he defines aura as a "strange weave of space and time: the unique appearance or semblance of distance, no matter how close the object may be."[31] Another passage reads, "To perceive the aura of an object we look at means to invest it with the ability to look at us in return."[32] Benjamin's answer to a letter from Adorno points in the same direction: "But if in fact we may consider an aura as having to do with a moment of 'forgotten humanity,' it is nevertheless not necessarily that which is present in the work. A tree or a bush, which are invested, are not made by human hands. There must therefore be something human in things that is not put in them by work."[33] The experience of the aura presupposes a similarity between the world and human being as well as the human mimetic faculty for making the self similar to the world and the capacity for the things to "look at" people. Auratic experience leads to unmediated communication, made possible by the similarity between human being and the world constituted in language, between phenomena and individuals who open themselves to them. Communication here takes place via a physical-sensuous, prelinguistic, and preconscious approximation of the individual to the world, which seems, at least in the moment of the experience, to overcome the separation between subject and object. If auratic experience is conceived as the "unique manifestation of a distance, no matter how near it might be," it refers as well to a loss. Something has disappeared, the name of which is "aura." Since all doublings of the unique result in its disappearance, the technical reproduction of things annihilates their aura. The process of loss is accelerated by the instrumental and bureaucratic way of treating things. Going hand-in-hand with this loss is the feeling of mourning for some "forgotten humanity." Aura designates the memory of a cultic reverence, of something sacred, that flashes in the temporal dimension of an instant and resists localization. What is experienced is the reference to something lacking, to the poverty of experience in principle, and to an unsurpassable emptiness.

The flash of this other knowledge in an instant (*Nu*) contains a moment of hope for reconciliation, in which nonsensuous correspondences that are not accessible to perception over any extended period become visible. Bound to the mimetic characteristics of language, they make their presence known only in the form of accelerated movement. They make up the aura of things, that fleeting other knowledge, which can be experienced only through a kind of mimetic behavior that renounces an instrumental approach and the assertion of the self against the outer world and breaks through the domination of language restricted to semantics. Experiences of this sort transcend the momentary events of daily life in their stereotyped and ritualized form. As such, they become the foundation of religious and aesthetic experience. Thus the following passage from *Illuminationen:* ''I made my way up the slope and lay down beneath a tree. The tree was a poplar or an alder. Why have I not retained which? Because, as I looked up, following the movement of the foliage, it so seized hold of language within me that language, for an instant, repeated in my presence its archaic marriage with the tree.''[34]

The individual is bound to the world by language. The ''word of man'' gives names to things. It translates the nameless into language. This is only possible because human language and mute things correspond to each other in God, originate in the same creative word of God. ''God's creation is completed when things receive their names from man.''[35] This experience of language and the world is religious. It contains the hope for a paradise in which there exists a single meaning secured in God that connects people with things through language and a corresponding experience of happiness. The transition from this Adamic experience of language and the world to an instrumental utilization of language appears to Benjamin as the Fall of Man in his relation to language, of which the religious and aesthetic experience of an instant, or an aura, are reminders. The hope for reconciliation and redemption attaches itself to this memory of other experiences of the mimetic side of language. Aesthetic and religious experience in particular become the carriers of such hope.

22

Vital Experience (Adorno)

Since the mimetic faculty denotes abilities that are among those definitive of human being, it offers promising ground for historical-anthropological analysis. Max Horkheimer and Theodor Adorno made a major contribution to such study by focusing on the role of mimesis in the civilizing process, in the genesis of individual being, of the subject, in the development of human cognition, and in art and aesthetics.[1] The point of departure in their considerations is an insight into archaic character of mimesis, which they see as closely connected to human self-preservation. According to Horkheimer and Adorno's analysis, self-preservation in early times was secured by means of the mimetic adaptation of human being to nature; known in regard to animals and plants as mimicry, it is a process through which adaptation to the environment can be so complete that difference appears to vanish. The goal of this adaptation in human beings was to escape the terrors of nature, which represented a threat to the gradually developing "self." The fear of transforming back into nature, "from which it had estranged itself with so huge an effort, and which therefore struck such terror into the self,"[2] leads to an adaptation to death. "Protection as fear is a form of mimicry. The reflexes of stiffening and numbness in humans are archaic schemata of the urge to survive: by adaptation to death, life pays the toll of its continued existence."[3] This paralysis, the adaptation of the human being to the inorganic, that is, to inanimate nature, represents a defense reaction against the dissolution of the self.

Yet these forms of ossification, hardening, and estrangement signify more than the complete subordination of human being to the overwhelming power of nature. They also represent initial, if inadequate, means of self-preservation over against nature. The adaptive process itself makes it clear that human being is no longer mere nature: the self is an expression of a difference in relation to nature, although it is nature that simultaneously makes the formation of the self possible and threatens it with dissolution. Mimesis, as mimicry, is the expression of these early forms of self-empowerment and self-consciousness. Insofar as the process of adaptation, which is to say, the process by which the physical existence of human being is preserved, takes place on the level of intention, it is already an expression of human self-preservation. But adaptation does entail submission to nature, suggesting that the drive toward self-preservation finds its limit in the tendency of living beings to surrender altogether to the natural environment. Adorno and Horkheimer speak of a deeply internalized tendency in all living things to deliver themselves up to their surroundings, whereby the overcoming of that tendency is the mark of all development. This inclination to let oneself go, to sink back into nature, is what Freud terms the death instinct and Roger Caillois, "le mimetisme."

The most extreme form of ossification and estrangement and the loss of a unified consciousness stems, according to Caillois, from the adaptation to space.[4] By being delivered up to space, life, which manages to achieve order in time, petrifies into an extrinsic coexistence of dissociated individuals. The "unity of the inner sense," which is given in temporal consciousness, with its experience of continuity between past, present, and future is destroyed at the same time. Space reduces the three temporalities to an interval of simultaneity in which neither past nor future nor historical development is possible. The time-space that results from the overall process represents the schema of timelessness and the absence of history found in all mythology.

Freud also assumes that a tendency toward self-dissolution, anchored in the instinctlike aspect of human being, is inherent in all living things. He defines instinct as "an urge inherent in organic life to restore an earlier state of things."[5] The restoration is experienced as pleasurable, for it leads to a lessening of tension, which is unpleasurable. It also recapitulates an earlier state, which can be understood as imitation, as a mimetic process on which the individual depends to overcome feelings of unpleasure and which, therefore, contains an element of compulsion. Such an element is also found in the mimicry of early humans, which was based on a compulsion to escape, by adapting, the threat of hostile nature.

The drivelike "reproduction of an earlier state" and the consequent discharge of tension can also, following Freud, be designated regression: regression, or the return to an earlier state, seems here to be the goal of all life. There "must be an *old* state of things, an initial state from which the living entity has at one time or other departed and to which it is striving to return by the circuitous paths along which its development leads. . . . *The aim of all life is death* and, looking backwards, . . . *inanimate things existed before living ones.*"[6] From this perspective, the pleasure principle and the death instinct aim in the same direction, toward the transcendence of tension and discontent and toward the return of living being to the inorganic from which it developed. The compulsion to repeat earlier experiences and the death instinct work counter to the progress of civilization and the repression of instinct and passions, which has the effect of relativizing notions of the possibility of continuous advance. Death, regression, destruction, and happiness are all related and together make up an important dynamic in the civilizing process.

In the course of mimesis toward hostile nature, mimicry of the ossified and death, and in the compulsive ''reproduction of an earlier state,'' of regression to a situation free of tension, there occurs a subordination of human being through adaptation, or repeated adaptation, which supplies the basis for the formation of a gradually more controlled interaction with nature and with drives. As long as the process concerns adaptation to dead nature, it remains impossible to draw a distinction between mimicry and mimesis. Once, however, this process becomes subject to conscious guidance, then a distinction does arise between mimicry of inanimate things and mimesis of nature. Once mimesis of nature becomes intentional and subject to organization, a doubling takes place. This form of doubling through an intention and its realization represents a mode of rational interaction and a corresponding optimization of nature.

While in the early phases of human development, adaptation to nature is comprised largely of physical imitation of external nature, in the magical phase there develops an ''organized control of mimesis.''[7] To the extent that we designate the employment of appropriate means in the realization of a goal as rationality, the ''organized control'' of mimesis contains a form of rationality, of which magicians and shamans make use in their interactions with nature and mimesis. The function of rites is to trace out prescriptive scenarios in the expectation that nature will follow the prescriptions. Instead of imitating something in the past, magic copies something in the future. Magicians and shamans create rites and sacrifices that are supposed to bend nature to goals set by human beings.

The precondition of the effectiveness of such intentional behavior is the laws of magic, as formulated by Marcel Mauss to designate contiguity, similarity, and opposition.[8] The principle of similarity is above all the precondition for the effectiveness of mimesis. If the particular is the whole and the whole is in the particular, then there exists a mimetic relation among things, which makes it possible to influence the one by means of the other.[9] Affinity among things and mimesis, which rests on the affinity, are responsible for the universal character of magic. The mimetic relation to things entails a ''stance toward reality that is different from the rigid juxtaposition of subject and object.''[10] Nor does the relation imply the complete separation from one another of thought, idea, and reality. Their final separation occurs only in the natural sciences, in which the subject makes the world into an object and proceeds according to objective preconditions. What must not be overlooked, however, is that the truth claim of magic is illusory; the assumptions implicit in magic as regards relations between the universal and the particular are products of the human imagination, a circumstance that makes it imperative for us to relativize its claim to truth. A corresponding reservation applies to the laws of contiguity, similarity, and opposition. Adorno recognizes this himself when he writes, "Art is magic delivered from the lie of being truth."[11]

While the "precivilized" phase is marked by a mimetic relation between human being and nature, which originates in the affinity between human being and nature and realizes itself via physical, ritualistic, and magical processes of adaptation, this archaic form of mimesis declines in significance in the historical period. The phase of "organic adaptation to others" and the "organized control of mimesis" of the magical phase are replaced by "rational practice, by work, in the historical phase."[12] The rational practice of the historical period is simultaneously based on mimesis and a substitute for it. Rationality, as instrumental rationality, develops out of the organized form of interaction with mimesis and operates to control the latter's negative side, thus serving the interest of self-preservation. The goal is no longer the organic adaptation to others and surrender to nature but the rational self-assertion of human being over against nature.

If nature is dominant over human being in the precivilized phase of mimesis, in the course of the civilizing process human being takes over the place of nature. Human domination extends to both inner and outer nature. Instead of the general subordination of all things to magical-mythical forces as in early times, there results a new subordination to the abstract universal of a form of rationality, the power of which is ultimately totalitarian. Rationality becomes a power comparable to the mythical powers of the magical period. It becomes a myth that assumes the place of prehistoric myths. The constraint once imposed on human being by nature is continued in the form of *work on the civilizing process.* Human history comes to aim "at liberating men from fear and establishing their sovereignty."[13] To replace the domination of nature by the domination of human being appears, from this perspective, to be the goal of all development. Obviously, human life without reference to domination is not possible. Human being appears to be restricted to the choice between subjecting itself either to the domination of nature or to its own domination.

Sacrifices are necessary in both cases. Attempts are made in the mimetic-magical phase to influence natural powers through sacrifices. The calculi that prove effective in the process represent forms of rationality through which human being asserted itself historically against nature and gradually came to dominate. That rationality takes over the place of the mythical powers and becomes the instrument of self-assertion, however, does not mean that the shift is accomplished without sacrifice. Lost in the transformation of mimesis into rationality is precisely a nonrational interaction with outer and inner nature, which is to say, the possibility of maintaining a mimetic relationship with nature. Rationality does indeed enhance security, but it deprives human being of the opportunities for happiness that otherwise inhere in outer and inner nature. Thus does the self-constituting *I,* bent on control and self-assertion, forfeit chances for sensuous fulfillment. The human self removes itself from nature and takes up a juxtaposed position; two substances, separated from each other, come into being. Descartes's differentiation between a self-sufficient *res cogitans* and an opposing *res extensa* is the clear expression of the emerging dualism. The distinction implies an abstraction from the physicality of thought. It makes it possible to identify a res cogitans that is identical with itself and independent of nature. Only total difference is able to create total identity.

The domination of the self over inner nature leads not only to its suppression but even to its dissolution. The sacrifice now is the vitality of the self, along with the sensuous fulfillment it contains.

> Man's domination over himself, which grounds his selfhood, is almost always the destruction of the subject in whose service it is undertaken; for the substance which is dominated, suppressed, and dissolved by virtue of self-preservation is none other than that very life as functions of which the achievements of self-preservation find their sole definition and determination: it is, in fact, what is to be preserved.[14]

The subject, which constitutes itself through its domination over a nature that it has rendered objective, itself becomes an object. Subjective self-empowerment entails a commitment to universal disposability; the subject succumbs to its own will to domination, which ultimately turns its sights on the self. The operation of faculties that make the human being a subject eventually causes the ruin of precisely that subject. The strict separation between subject and object, the split between mind and body, intuition and concept, the overcoming of a mimetic relation to outer and inner nature and to Others, all lead to isolation and to an intensification of the processes of abstraction and objectification, as well as to diminished opportunities for happiness. Domination and rationality, which owe their existence to the subject, come to permeate and reify all human relationships.

With the disenchantment and demythologization of the world, human being no longer makes sacrifices to mythical powers, but it does sacrifice its affinity to nature and thus a part of its self. The result is an introversion of the sacrificial victim. In order that self-sacrifice not be experienced as painful, the mimetic relation to the world is repressed, rendered taboo—and the desire to recapture what had been lost becomes a central theme in art and aesthetics. Repressed mimesis survives as the longing for sensuous proximity, for immediate expression and nonidentifying cognition. A simple regression into conditions that have been overcome in the process of civilization, however, is ruled out; even the juxtaposition of mimesis and rationality is problematic, since the latter developed out of the former in historical terms and because mimesis itself always contains rational elements, which stand in the way of a complete assimilation to the inorganic in the sense of mimicry. There remains always a certain distance and thus as well a memory that "finds mimetic assimilation falling short of true identity; that finds mimesis falling short period."[15]

Mimesis conceals within itself an unresolvable ambivalence, which is manifest in the relation of human being to outer and inner nature. On the one hand, it is a point of departure for a form of rationality that detaches itself from its origins and for which "all that remains of the adaptation to nature is the obduracy against nature."[16] On the other, it makes the complete unity of human consciousness impossible and introduces to the subject something that eludes the latter's domination, that cannot be domesticated or controlled. Mimesis raises a resistance, of a sort shared in by the body, to reification and secures the "primacy of the object" against the subject's claims to domination; it refers to the ultimate indeterminacy in principle and the enigmatic character of things, which is what offers human being the chance to undergo "vital experience."

No less than in the civilizing process is mimesis important in the formation of the individual, the emergence of the subject. "The human is indissolubly linked with imitation: a human being becomes human at all by imitating other human beings."[17] The child acquires its capacities for self-preservation and self-assertion through mimesis of the environment and other people. It adopts gestures, representational forms, and patterns of action and makes of them its own expressive forms. Values, attitudes, and predispositions are acquired in this process, to help the child orient itself in the world. By assimilating to others, the child acquires the practical competence to live its life. Mimesis allows the child to grow into language and establish a sensitive connection to its inner nature. The young person makes himself or herself similar to externalities, not vice versa. Mimesis is a movement from inside out; it establishes a bridge between the subject and the outer world. "Mimesis imitates the environment, but false projection makes the environment like itself."[18] An essential quality of mimesis lies in this movement toward the world. The goal is to bridge the gap between inner and outer, between sensory data and objects. To establish this bridge, the subject must order the multitude of impressions and sensory data, consider them in reference to their preconditions, and construct them independently. "The subject creates the world outside himself from the traces which it leaves in his senses: the unity of the thing in its manifold characteristics and states."[19] Mimesis is not merely a receptive but also an active process, the results of which manifest singularly subjective aspects. At the center of the process stands a reference to the Other, who is not to be incorporated, but rather approximated. In this movement there is a moment of passivity, a pause in activity, which is characteristic of the "mimetic impulse."

Mimesis, accordingly, is a precondition of fellow feeling, compassion, sympathy, and love toward other people. It is imitation, assimilation, surrender;

it leads one to copy in experience the feelings of others, without objectifying or becoming hardened toward them. "Love you will find only where you may show yourself weak without provoking strength."[20] Love encompasses a moment of fellow feeling, of the duplication of the individuality of the Other, and of mirroring. The point is now to allow the Other the possibility of seeing himself or herself, now to see oneself in the mirror of the Other. In view of objectification, such possibilities of reciprocal reference are few. The principles of identification, of the *I*-identity, and of exchange all work against them. While love drives lovers to lose control of themselves, to surrender themselves to someone else, the *I*-principle emphasizes the autonomy and sovereignty of the *I*. Self-surrender, the consignment of the self to the Other, appears as a danger to the *I*, which is secure only within its own boundaries. The *I* is not prepared to give itself over to another, to cancel itself; it has a much greater need to assert itself. Love thus leads the subject to exceed its capacities to control its feelings and drives, to domesticate its inner nature, and to engage in the world in ways that cede precedence to the outer, in this case, to the Other; the goal of love is the broadening of the self, the assimilation of the self to a counterpart. Mimesis, sympathy, and love are movements that transcend the subject, in which the principles of identification and self-assertion lose in significance, while the nonidentical, the unintelligible and mysterious aspects of the world and the Other come into view.

It becomes possible to have vital experiences that lead to a "self-illumination without the self."[21] Adorno termed the human spirit in the grip of the fetish character of commodities "semicultivated"; its access to the world is deformed by the commodity character of society such that the only mediation it knows rests on an end-means calculation. To overcome the implicit reduction, the subject must, in the course of its cultivation, reflect on the conditions responsible for the degeneration of cultivation to semicultivation.[22] One's relation to the world and the Other must not be structured solely by the principles of the economy and instrumentality; the greater need is for mimetic access outside the self that proceeds independently of questions concerning the potential advantage of giving such a relation priority. The appropriate criteria are not instrumentality and utility but the intrinsic value of the Other. To do justice to the latter, the subject must free itself from forms of the desire to know better, from semicultivation, and open itself to what is not immediately as-cribable, to what is not identical. These experiences come in special moments; the manifold and the heterogenous become concentrated in such experiences to the point of impenetrability; nonconceptual knowledge is gained, which supplements the conceptual knowledge of science. Only by means of the mimetic faculty can such subjectively decentering, complementary knowledge be gained, which is to say that only the mimetic faculty makes it possible to gain such access to the world and the Other. In this movement of subjective transcendence toward the world, the fixed *I*-identity dissolves, reason itself is held in abeyance, and the subject is disempowered, whereby there arises a presentiment of what does not yet exist. This type of thought, which opens up the boundaries of the self, appears as a transgression, a stepping beyond the individual given in sense experience. It is like a labor of Sisyphus; it cannot succeed, it necessarily misses its object. "Thought must aim beyond its target just because it never quite reaches it. . . . It extrapolates in order, by the over-exertion of the too-much, to master, however hopelessly, the inevitable too-little."[23]

The precondition of a mimetic movement toward the world is the otherwise irreducible separation from the world bound to language and consciousness. The separation is the origin of the unhappy consciousness, of which Adorno writes, "Conscious unhappiness is not a delusion of the mind's vanity but something inherent in the mind, the one authentic dignity it has received in its separation from the body."[24] Pain, negativity, and the ability to wish have a somatic side to them; they refer to the unovercomeable lack that is given in language. The attempt to overpower the world by means of language cannot succeed and must end in the experience of deficiency. For human needs and wishes have been split up and scattered over many different linguistic signs, whereby gratification becomes impossible. Embedded in these conditions of language and consciousness is the origin of the longing for reconciliation articulated in religion, art, and utopia. Hope aims not at a mimetic sublation of differences but depends instead on the possibility contained in mimesis that differences can be made bearable.

Mimesis assumes the function of a corrective for identifying thought and conceptual knowledge, the domination of the abstract and the reified and the self-identical (*Mit-sich-Identischen*). Mimesis, by fostering assimilation to the world and to Others, makes it possible for sensuous access to the world to be opened up. Sensuous access, in turn, is the point of departure for vital experience, in which the focus is on the priority of the manifold and uninterpreted, on what extends the subject beyond its boundaries and enriches it. These experiences pick up on incidents from early childhood, that is, on such as preceded the formation of the subject and thus the fully formed subject-object split; the child continues to have a partial experience of the nonseparation and correspondence between self, world, and Other that wholly determined its prenatal experience in the womb. Absent the development of a self with an autonomous orientation, there exist none of the critical boundaries between inner and outer, so that the child experiences itself as similar to the world and the world as similar to it. These early experiences of nonseparation are the basis on which expectations of future happiness take shape, a process that depends on the self's mimetic ability to assimilate to Others and the world. The goal is not regression into a presubjective, prerational state, or the repression of wishes for surrender or the elimination of hardenings, but rather the broadening of the subject through openness to the world, to Others, and to the wishes for surrender. Much of this is manifest in aesthetic experience.[25]

Aesthetic experience consists in the apprehension, beyond the boundaries of the *I*, of the precedence of the object and the nature of the subject, the unity of *I* and not-*I*. Both from the outside in and the inside out, the settled arrangements of the *I* are transcended. The result is a release from the constraints of self-preservation, which, however, only becomes possible if the subject does not have to see to its self-preservation by means of work and instrumental rationality, if, that is, that which is responsible for the separation of the world into subject and object can be suspended at least temporarily. This suspension also causes the reality principle, to the extent that it is a product of the subject and the ways the latter constitutes the world, to decline in significance. The critical precondition of aesthetic experience is not the separation of subject and object, which corresponds to the scientific epistemological ideal, but the affinity between the artwork and the recipient of it. In aesthetic experience there forms an ''active passivity'' that allows the subject to make itself ''similar'' to the artwork. And it is not only the recipient but also the artist who behaves mimetically; the work of the artist includes not merely the imitation of the objective world, but aims at bringing objects to speech. Similarity with the products of nature is not the aim of art; rather, it is similarity with the natural force that brings them into existence. When Adorno emphasizes the similarity between nature, the artist, and art, he has in mind, not natura naturata, but natura naturans. If artworks, freed from the obligation to posit identity, are equivalent to themselves, then this self-equivalency can only be grasped mimetically. For it is by ''assimilating'' the observer, reader, or listener to the self-equivalent artwork that mimesis is able to forge the connection. The recipient does not subordinate the work; rather, by way of his or her active-passive assimilation to it, the work crosses into the inner world and enriches the subject.

As in the experience of love, mimetic movement invokes ''the power to see similarity in the dissimilar.''[26] By making this assumption, Adorno also takes a position in the old epistemological dispute concerning the question ''whether like is known by like or by unlike,''[27] taking up the position shared by Parmenides, Plato, and Aristotle against Heraclitus. In these terms, no knowledge is possible without the production of similarities, without mimesis. It is certainly taken as true for scientific knowledge that mimesis is indispensable in the process of knowing. ''Cognition itself cannot be conceived without the supplement of mimesis, however that may be sublimated. Without mimesis, the break between subject and object would be absolute and cognition impossible.''[28] If a mimetic element is indispensable to scientific knowledge, it is at the heart of aesthetic experience. Mimesis makes it possible to comprehend the self-equivalency of the artwork and occasion a ''knowledge from within,''[29] which exists independently of theories and concepts. Aesthetic experience arouses "a sense of being overwhelmed in the presence of a phenomenon that is nonconceptual while at the same time being determinate,"[30] and this sense is largely beyond the reach of planning and resists precise localization. In the sudden density of a moment there occurs an "aesthetic shock," which can rock the foundations of the *I*.

The mimetic impulse leads to momentary contact with what is nondeterminate in the similar-to-itself artwork.[31] The work's similarity is not referred to something outside itself, which is why mimesis in this context cannot denote the imitation of something that preexisted the work; rather, mimesis is similar to the self-referential creative force of the *natura naturans*, the nonobjective aspect of nature. In the ideal of *l'art pour l'art* of artistic modernism, this self-referentiality on the part of art becomes programmatic. Great artworks are similar to nature; they are without identification, without intention, and thus self-sufficient. Their self-referential similarity does away with the significance of outer and inner as reference points. What remains to art in this view is clearly not some "beautiful illusion" that can be referred back to something else but the possibility of making visible something that does not yet exist, that refers rather to something that might sometime be. "The being-in-itself of art is not an imitation of something real but an anticipation of a being-in-itself yet to come."[32] Artworks refer to utopia. They occasion a reversal in the direction of mimesis: "in a [sublimated] sense reality ought to imitate art works, not the other way around."[33] Art points to the possibilities contained in the general and the particular and stimulates the development of both; it refers to areas of inner nature that are "free from immediate desires," with which the subject in mimetic movement comes into disinterested and selfless contact.

The mimetic impulse of the recipient is similar to the spontaneity of the artist. The similarity lies not in the productive aspect of the artist's work, which the concept is often used to designate, but consists in the circumstance "that this ability is nonintentional, is not identical with the conscious will of any individual."[34] Spontaneity and mimesis are similar to each other in respect to the quality of being automatic, immediate, and unconscious, which is prior to the *I* and cannot be squeezed into the narrow corset of the self. Mimetic movement encompasses these pre- and nonrational elements, which represent the essential aspects of art that are anchored in the ambiguity of the somatic. In aesthetic experience, these elements are immediately complemented by the rationality contained in mimesis; for without rationality mimesis would degenerate into a bearing toward art that is comparable to mimicry, which would not be adequate to genuine aesthetic experience.

Aesthetic experience arises in the "fine distance" between recipient and artwork and represents a nonscientific form of knowledge. "The continued existence of mimesis, understood as the non-conceptual affinity of subjective creation with its objective and unposited other, defines art as a form of cognition and to that extent as 'rational.' . . . Art expands cognition into an area where it was said to be non-existent."[35] Art is "a refuge for mimetic behavior,"[36] "the organ of mimesis."[37] It emphasizes the "precedence of the object, which acquires its validity in mindfulness of the nature in human being."[38] Art itself appears as the historical voice of suppressed nature and in this function as a form of cognition, the truth of which can be apprehended as a "movement against the subject"[39] and as mimetic. "Art moves toward truth. It is not directly identical with truth; rather, truth is art's content. Because of this relation to truth, art is cognitive. It knows truth insofar as truth manifests itself in art. As cognition, however, art is not discursive. Nor is its truth the reflex of an object."[40] Truth is therefore not "in" art but rather becomes manifest in art. Truth is not discursive and is not simply a reflex; it appears. It comes into existence between a work and its recipient in the two mimetic impulses that connect them. These impulses make up the core of aesthetic experience, which is the occasion for mediation between *I* and not-*I,* which leaves all definition of purpose, consideration of utility, and instrumentalization behind, and in which the precedence of the object, the nature of the nonidentical, is grasped by the recipient.

From an anthropological perspective, Adorno thus accords aesthetic experience a significance similar to that of work and interaction, since it refers human being to areas of experience not available either in work or in interaction. He goes so far as to claim to see in aesthetic experience a generalizable form of vital experience, which makes it possible to perceive objects, works, and other people nonintentionally and thus refrain from stripping them of their enigmatic quality. Those who approach art with an excess of understanding, like a "slick connoisseur," turn art "into a completely transparent thing, which it is not. Trying to grasp a rainbow is the surest way of making it vanish."[41] It is possible to recognize the enigmatic character of art and to grasp the inexplicability inherent in it as "the determinacy of the indeterminate."[42] The enigmatic quality of the artwork derives from the operation of mimesis inside it. "The configuration of mimesis and rationality is the enigmatic image of art. It is a product of history."[43] At the same time, however, the enigma outlasts and defeats all striving after cognition, every effort to attain to the truth.

If aesthetic experience contributes, by way of its reference to truth, to the positive gains of cognition, then it cannot be described solely as a subjective experience. As Adorno stressed repeatedly, it is necessary to recognize the significance of elements that exist objectively in the artwork. This objectivity is what distinguishes the artwork from the products of the culture industry, which Adorno and others were at constant pains to critique. Artworks have to offer more and something other than a satisfaction of consumer expectations that arise as compensation for the deficiencies of the world of work and of prevailing relations of domination. If the task of art consisted merely in compensation, the effect would be its functionalization in favor of goals that are extrinsic to it. Yet aesthetic experience does not yield to adequate analysis in terms of such categories and the categories of the subject. Concepts like "pleasure" and "displeasure" have only limited explicatory value. "It is one of the grave defects of past aesthetics to have started with the subjective judgment of taste, thereby selling out art's claim to truth,"[44] which is founded on the precedence of the object and the evocation of the inner nature of the recipient. This character of art runs counter to the wishes of the *I* to reduce every counterpart to its own ego boundaries; art demands much more that the subject surrender to aesthetic experience, which means allowing art to refer it to Others. In a mimetic act directed toward the artwork, the subject is "forced open" and broadened. The shock leads to a partial suspension of the subject. In the flashes of aesthetic experience is contained a promise of happiness, which presupposes an affinity between the work and the recipient of it. This is the condition of a successful aesthetic experience, the possibility of which is furthered by interpretation, commentary, and critique. There are specific preconditions required of both the artwork and the recipient in order for, in aesthetic experience, the dominance of the subject and its objective constitution as a dominator of nature to be overcome and for an encounter between sensuousness and spirit, on the one hand, and the disinterested, the nonidentical, and the enigmatic, on the other, to take place.

Aesthetic experience refers mimetic movement beyond works of art and beyond the subject to possibilities of historical development. It can thereby become the carrier of hopes, expectations, and promises. Its central concern is a nonfunctionalized, improved relation between rationality and sensuousness. Because mimetic movement can open up a perspective on changed life conditions and provide a foil against which hope for change can be measured, it can become a model for the formation of social reality. With this step, aesthetic experience emerges from the "realm of necessity" into the "realm of freedom"; it reveals possibilities for overcoming the "chronocracy" and gaining a new relationship to time.[45] It relativizes and criticizes the idea of progress gained at the expense of human domination over nature and continual increases in productivity and thus abandons its faith in the emancipatory dynamic of the productive forces. The ecological crisis has made it impossible not to doubt the possibility, via a subsequent reconciliation with nature, of correcting the domination and destruction of nature by industrial society. What seemed to be the progress of rationality turns into the opposite. Aesthetic experience thus brings the following to consciousness: (1) human being replaces the domination of nature with its own domination; (2) the validity of natural scientific claims must be relativized and supplemented by other forms of cognition; (3) technology is not merely possessed of emancipatory potential, but also sets in motion a dynamic that leads to eschatological and apocalyptic visions and to the destruction of the world; and (4) it is no longer tenable to trust in the dialectic of social development to lead to amelioration. The mimetic faculty is an integral component of culture; it will have increasing significance for humanity in the future, since it can effect a fundamentally different relation between the individual and the world, and Others, and his or her own inner nature.

The mimetic movement inherent in aesthetic experience begins with the precedence of the object and leads to a broadening of the subject. The subject encounters the world through sense perception, which makes it possible for subjective experience of outer and inner nature to enter into a relation of exchange. Mimetic impulses traveling from the inside out set the inner being of the subject into motion; drive potentials overshoot their objects in the world, with the resulting collisions introducing tension into the relations between the *I* and the not-*I;* inner and outer are then integrated anew in transformed constellations; which, finally, is the origin of the cathartic and moral effects of art. The possibilities for such aesthetic experience, in which the splits between outer and inner are temporarily transcended, making it possible to experience new forms of unification, were also available in the ecstatic festivals, the cultural and religious rites, of earlier times. ''Memories'' of such intense mimetic experience are yet to be found in the various arts.

This analysis suggests the necessity of relativizing the ideas of autonomy and maturity that have long been critical to the self-conception of the Western individual. It focuses attention on the limited nature of human action and the mortality of human being. The consciousness of the physicality of all experience renders the subject powerless. Death, language, and desire become visible as the inescapable conditions of human life; they refer to what cannot be disposed over, which is also central to aesthetic experience and of which the subject is so reluctant to become conscious. The result of these insights is a decentering of the subject and a dissolution of anthropocentrism in aesthetic experience, which can then become the occasion for the realization of other possibilities. Human being withdraws itself as the center and measure of being and becomes free for an intensive mimetic relation to the world, to the Other, and to inner nature, all of which take on new importance. In the momentary experience (*Erlebnis*) of beauty and the repeated experience (*Erfahrung*) of beautiful illusion, art recalls suppressed nature.[46] Art and nature enter into a new relation to human being, reminding it of unredeemed forms of human life.

23

The Between-Character
of Mimesis (Derrida)

Jacques Derrida radicalizes Benjamin's view of the mimetic character of texts and intensifies Adorno's emphasis on mimesis in aesthetics. For Derrida, every text stands in a mimetic relation to other texts, even if it is not always possible to define the relation unambiguously. Texts as such refer to non-identifiable other texts, to inheritances for which there are no names or models. Texts repeat prior texts; they are networks of differences without identities of their own. Writing and reading as well are mimetic. There is no first writing and no first reading; every beginning is actually a doubling. In every act of writing, there is already given a reference to something past. Thus writing has a permanently testimonial character.

Writing produces differences to past statements and words, with the body of the new text growing in reference to what it is not; it is open to what is Other than itself, assumes the Other into itself, and delimits itself against further instances of Otherness. Every text has an "unending" density. Not only does it reveal its openness to logocentric conceptual analysis but it is also open in its syntactic dimension, that is, in the context in which concepts are located in it. While the meaning of the concepts is conveyed via hermeneutic reception, the context opens itself only to a mimetic act in which heterogenous elements are referred to each other, without this referentiality implying that ambiguity can be overcome. It is not by way of direct analysis that writing and reading produce (or reproduce) texts; they often enter laterally into the production (or reproduction) of texts. The mimetic impulse requires no center; it gains entry to textuality in multiple sites and locations.

Texts do not open themselves up as delimited bodies of words; they have a history, are the result of "grafts" in the course of which parts of texts of various provenance are joined together. Texts are thus the outcome of citations, of unknown references, and, seen in this way, never have the character of originals. Every sign in the text is a unit in its own right and, as such, is repeatable in divergent contexts. The "citationality" and contextual dependency of the sign opens itself up to logocentric analysis and to an act of mimesis. This act is not bound to meaning; nor does it aim at the opening up of meaning. It can accommodate contradiction or even meaninglessness without having to stipulate new meanings in the process. In the mimetic act, author and reader are capable of creating the silhouette of a text, of perceiving it and putting it into motion.

Texts exist in the form of additions or supplements; the nature of textual production is such that meaning is negated, which calls for an end to thematic criticism; texts affirm the play of words, statements, and meanings. A mimetic approach to the text puts its elements and positions into motion; it disperses and disseminates them, renders them fruitful in a new way. The mimetic approach deconstructs texts, combines their elements with others into new texts. In the play of words, new effects come into being. Every text, in its referentiality to other texts, is a game that operates according to rules. A text is multiplied in the play of contingency and necessity, a circumstance the inalterable condition of which is the written character of the text. The meanings of all texts are in principle indeterminate and immune to closure. They constitute and displace themselves in the process of dissemination. Derrida provides examples of this process in his reading of concepts—*pharmakon, supplément,* and *hymen*—taken, respectively, from the works of Plato, Rousseau, and Mallarmé. Every expression has, for Derrida, a germ, which, comparable to semen, swarms out, fructifies, and leaves behind its traces.

It is impossible to identify the origin of or model for a text, since every text begins as a double. There is thus no beginning without something having preceded it, with precedence contained in the structure of the double. The structure, however, is vulnerable to reductions, which gives rise to a mimesis with no original model. Concepts like "key," "hinge," and "bridge" maintain reference to the initial double structure of mimesis.

Within the frame of an image, in the parergon, the inner and outer of an artwork come together in a "between." In this between-structure of parergonality lies a summons to mimetic play, which moves on the boundary from outside in and from inside out and comes to completion in the search for and identification of *différance*. Différance is a force constitutive of the text; it demonstrates that traditional hierarchies of meaning can be deconstructed. The concept has lost its function as a sign for something; the reference that remains is to the possibility of its own deployment and to the structure of the idea as repetition, as well as to the unspeakability of the absolute. The traditional opposition between difference and identity therefore loses meaning. The intertextuality of writing and reading becomes increasingly important. As aesthetic activity, the act of reading decodes the unspeakable like hieroglyphs. There arises in the relationship between text and context a free play of substitution and doubling. In this displacement lies an attack on the metaphysical assumption that meaning produces itself in a straight or circular line.[1] The result is that both textual elements and the reading of them are decentered, which is what lends them their disseminative character. Without repetition texts could be neither produced nor read. Only a moment of repression allows us to understand the double as the replication of a complete and self-assured original. Mimesis occasions a counteroccupation of the text, which allows the original to persist through the change. When every beginning is a repetition, every arrival at a text comes "too late." Reflection thus becomes possible only in retrospect. What comes later, however, also constitutes the present; for every present is reconstituted, rather than original. Every reading is a writing-once-again, a supplementation of a definite text. Every text, however, refers to the text of a subject; it is both the trace of and the difference in relation to an individual. Like a dream, it is—itself pure surface—both decodable and unfathomable.

Mimesis has played a critical role in Derrida's works on textuality from the start, as is apparent from his contribution to *Mimesis des articulations* (1975). His goal is not to investigate mimesis in the "great discursive or cultural figurations."[2] Nor does he attempt to approach the concept by translating it into another. Attempts to render mimesis as "imitation, reproduction, simulation, similarity, identification, analogy, etc.," fall short of the mark for Derrida.[3] While they may indeed capture respective dimensions of the mimetic, these concepts do not add up to an exhaustive definition of mimesis, for an unambiguous concept of mimesis would be a contradiction in itself. Derrida's goal, accordingly, is to examine mimesis itself, to show how it is manifest in "theoretical and practical formations."[4] He finds mimetic processes both prior and subsequent to mimesis. These processes consist in play with unveiling, concealing, and masking. "Mimosa" oscillates between plant and animal and in Derrida's hands becomes an image for a mimesis that crosses the boundaries between science, literature, art, and the social world. Not the elimination of ambiguity, but difference is the principle of mimesis, which contributes to the multiplication of images, words, thoughts, theories, and actions, without becoming tangible itself.

In his early essay "Plato's Pharmacy" (first published in 1968), Derrida referred to the connections between pharmakon, writing, and mimesis. The Greek concept of pharmakon is untranslatable; its characteristic significatory ambivalence cannot be conveyed in other languages. Pharmakon means poison, drug, and remedy all at once. Its ambiguity and ambivalence cannot be sublated. Only in reference to a specific context can the appropriate meaning be determined; but even then it retains the resonance of the other respective meanings. In an immediate sense, pharmakon is something that comes from the outside, like a disease, but produces its effects within the body. It can bring about harmful, curative, or curative-harmful effects; it represents an addition, which, lacking an unambiguous character of its own, instead reveals its effects in the space between the curative and the harmful.

Writing presents a similar case. What is written can be repeated at will, whereby it always means the same thing; writing is an enactment, a play, and retains for Plato its unsublatable difference from truth. In the *Phaedrus,* Theuth, who is also the god of medicine, makes a present of writing to the king. Writing and pharmakon suddenly appear to be closely connected. Is writing a remedy or a poisonous gift? Here too the ambivalence is maintained. In distinction to the spoken word, which issues from a speaking subject who is simultaneously father of the word, writing is a poisonous gift. The living speaker, the subject of the speech, is no longer present in it; the logos of the speech is not contained in it; it becomes a commodity. It is the effect and the cause of faulty memory (*hypómnesis*); and it does not make knowledge possible in the Platonic sense of a product of memory (*mnéme*). Writing offers only the repetition of knowledge, not its production through an act of remembering, of *anamnesis.* Insofar as it invites people to make use of it, it seduces them into ceasing to remember, that is, into ceasing to produce true knowledge. Because of this effect, what initially appears as an aid and a remedy is more like a poison that weakens people and prevents them from acquiring true knowledge. Writing can therefore only imitate true knowledge; it can mimic but not produce it. This conclusion finds clear expression in the opposition between mnéme and hypómnesis.

In the *Phaedrus,* Plato depicts the mimetic relationship between pharmakon and writing in the character of Theuth in the Egyptian myth. He is the god of writing and the god of medicine. ''Medicine'' includes both healing and poison. Theuth obsequiously offers writing to the king as a drug, which brings pharmakon and writing into a mimetic relation with each other. The pharmakon is taken into the body, where it is related mimetically to illness insofar as it, as in homeopathy, aims at a cure by means of producing something similar to the illness. The illness is ''imitated'' by the pharmakon and therefore cured. When, however, as in the case of writing, the pharmakon pretends to be an aid and a remedy but is neither, it becomes part of the world of illusion and mere appearance and is therefore mimetic once again. For Plato, it is writing's written character, which is always only productive of the same thing, that causes it to appear unsuitable to the comprehension of truth. Writing, in his conception, produces nothing but dead knowledge; for it does away with speech and the speaker and, with the latter, the living subject from whom the words issue. While words are the expression of logos and carriers of something living, written characters are merely doubles of the words and logos. Words issue from the father as a form of power, while written characters pertain merely to a secondary order and its effects.

In his interpretation of the *Phaedrus,* Derrida elaborates a mimetically self-constituting series: father / logos / sun / cause / life / commodities / capital. This series leads to further development in its juxtaposition to a second series: son / writing / effect / death. Derrida then builds significatory pairs around the oppositions: word/writing; life/death; father/son; master/servant; first/second; son/orphan; soul/body; outer/inner; good/bad; earnestness/play; day/night; sun/moon; and so on. Thus the complex significatory field of the dialogue: between individual contrasts and the multitude of oppositions are mimetic movements that result in assimilation and repulsion, in repetition and the creation of new meanings. Such significatory fields compose the background of Platonic thought, out of which arises a momentary cancellation of ambiguity, which then dissolves back into the background.

Pharmakon and writing become the point of departure for ever new chains of thought that emerge out of the Platonic text, or, in other words, can be identified in it. The Sophists and sophistic knowledge are located in reference to writing and written knowledge, a context in which writing has no value of its own but amounts to a simulacrum. People who come to be dependent on writing cannot, for this reason, be wise. Like the Sophists, who only imitate the possessors of real knowledge and sell the signs and insignias of knowledge, they deal only with the appearance of things. In Plato's understanding, the concern of writers and Sophists alike is not the production of knowledge in memory but exclusively the reproduction, dissemination, and alienation of knowledge. They therefore lose all access to truth and remain at the level of quoting, copying, and compiling already known knowledge; they create simulacra and mime the property of knowledge.

The designation of Socrates as Pharmakeus gives rise to another chain of meanings. This one refers to the noninstrumental use of logos, *Socratic magic.* Socrates calls familiar knowledge into question, thus destabilizing otherwise secure orders. At the same time the Socratic pharmakon is a poison, which, like a snakebite, produces paralysis, which, that is, leads to doubt, dead ends, and aporia, situations that occasion fear. The ambivalence of the pharmakon, its vacillation between remedy and poison, becomes apparent, and "repetition" reveals its double character. Repetition in the form of writing is the repetition of dead knowledge; in the form of anamnetic dialectics, in contrast, it aims at the re-representation of the *eidos* and thus at the retrieval of knowledge from memory. Only after the insecurity and aporia stimulated by the Socratic pharmakon has been overcome is it possible to arrive at true knowledge. "The *pharmakon* is the movement, the locus, and the play: (the production of) difference. It is the differance of difference."[5] In itself it is nothing; it refers us to the background out of which interrelations are constructed—to "Plato's pharmacy." "It is in the back room, in the shadows of the pharmacy, prior to the oppositions between conscious and unconscious, freedom and constraint, voluntary and involuntary, speech and language, that these textual 'operations' occur."[6] It is here that chains of association and meaning arise. This is where *pharmakos,* which is inseparable from *pharmakon* and *pharmakeia,* also belongs.

Since *pharmakeus* also designates the "scapegoat," who, by being killed or expelled from the city, offers the means by which social crises are overcome, there arises another constellation of meanings. In Athens, "scapegoats" were regularly identified and ritually sacrificed as a practical measure to preserve civil order. Socrates, whom Plato explicitly designates Pharmakos, was also made into a "scapegoat." His death was the sacrifice that served to establish social peace in the city. Socrates and his philosophy become the "pharmakon" by means of which the true (Socratic) philosophy distinguishes itself from its Other. The Other of philosophy is represented by the Homeric world and the Sophists. True philosophy constitutes itself in a displacement in relation to both; its father is Socrates, after the death of whom its son, Plato, begins writing down the dialogues. This rendering of philosophy in written form is mimetic; in the course of mimesis the thought of Socrates is represented. The Platonic Socrates, who is distinct from the historical Socrates, comes into being. For his students and for the city, he is the father from whom philosophical logos issues; Plato belongs among his "sons," who preserve this logos by committing it to writing. But only the logos of the speaking father is really alive, so Plato, to come as close as possible to the philosophical speech of Socrates, chooses the form of a dialogue. Still, the difference between speaking and writing is not to be transcended: "Writing is the miserable son."[7]

Writing is based on the death of the father; it is itself the "lost son." It cannot finally succeed in bringing the absent father back into the present; it remains forever a simulacrum of the father. Only when Plato speaks of inscribing truth into the soul, that is, when he refers metaphorically to writing, does he assess it positively. At issue in that case is a "true writing," rather than the "simulacrum-writing" which has as its precondition the death of the father. His death is therefore the condition for the rise of writing in general, which is accompanied by the loss of truth. "Nontruth is the truth. Nonpresence is presence. Differánce, the disappearance of any originary presence, is *at once* the condition of possibility *and* the condition of impossibility of truth."[8] This inability to distinguish between truth and nontruth corresponds to the impossibility of distinguishing between pharmakon as the remedy, the good, the true, the living, from pharmakon as the bad, the false, the dead. "The *pharmakon* is the *same* precisely because it has no identity. And at the same time (is) as supplement. Or in differánce. In writing."[9]

Derrida, in his analysis of Platonic texts, succeeds in demonstrating that no cognition is possible in the absence of mimesis. Even anamnesis consists in the imitative remembering of knowledge previously possessed but then lost. For Plato, the quality of this knowledge is attained through the degree of intensity of the mimetic memory. To this extent the knowledge of truth depends on Plato as well on mimetic processes. He attempts to delimit mimesis as *methexis* (participation), which he values and which is indispensable to his epistemology, from mimesis as the production of beautiful illusion in the arts, to distinguish conceptually between a positive and a negative form of mimesis. If, however, one asks about the processes of which methexis is made up, it becomes clear that the distinction fails; for methexis rests on mimetic processes. Plato marks off the sphere of beautiful illusion from the mimesis of eidos entailed in Platonic cognition, which is achieved by the individual in the course of re-membering. Writing, painting, and poetry, for Plato, fall into an area in which cognition is not at issue, in which, rather, seduction, delusion, illusion, ap-pearance, and the simulacrum are determinate.

The ambivalent character of the mimetic becomes especially palpable in the concepts of the pharmakon and the pharmakeus. Every concept unifies a significatory multitude, which sets contradictory aspects into play simulta-neously, abrogates existing orders, and calls forth crises in the episteme and society, which can only be overcome through the violent expulsion of scape-goats. Mimesis refers also to the dynamic of socioeconomic processes.[10] It is not adequately conceptualized when it is pressed into a binary classification, in which the value of the double depends on the value of the model, which, in turn, is forever beyond the reach of mimetic processes. The criterion of agreement between the model and the result of the mimetic process implies a reduction of mimesis. What is not taken into account here is the side of mimesis that leads to the development of the new and the Other. Mimesis takes place prior to Plato's philosophical distinctions and evaluations. That which seemed objectionable to Plato is what makes mimesis resonant today: its reference to play, to masks, to the simulacrum, to apocryphal textuality.[11]

In a second essay, "The Double Session" (1970), which is devoted pri-marily to the work of Mallarmé, Derrida elaborates his ideas on the "between-character" of mimesis, which comes only inadequately into view in Plato and in the subsequent history of mimesis. For the concept of mimesis remains tightly fettered by its supposed reference to truth. Either mimesis leads to the emergence of a double in the place of the existing or, as methexis, it serves truth, and thus knowledge, through the similarity of double. Fundamental to each is a metaphysical understanding both of being and of mimesis in reference to it. For Mallarmé, there no longer is any truth or any metaphysical constellation of being as a reference point.

What becomes clear in "Mimique" is that the mime is no longer imitating anything, neither a thing nor an action nor a reality nor a text. What he represents does not exist outside of his representation; it has no reference of similarity or truth to something outside the representation of its gestures. Nothing is prior to it; the mime opens up something, initiates a "white page," without submitting to the authority of a book. "The mime ought only to write himself on the white page he is; he must *himself* inscribe *himself* through gestures and plays of facial expressions. At once page and quill, Pierrot is both passive and active, matter and form, the author, the means, and the raw material of his mimodrama."[12] There is nothing prior to the page, nothing alongside and outside it. By writing on it the mime is not imitating something that already exists in the world, and in the process of writing he attends to no external rules or prescriptions. His miming does not disappear in an identification with the truth. Rather, it calls for a doubled marking, for the generalization of the miming and the miming of the generalization, that is, a generalizing doubling. In the mime's representation, the distinction between fiction and reality also collapses. For Mallarmé, "there is only the equivalence between *theater* and *idea*."[13] The scene, to be sure, is more an illustration of the idea than a real action. From this definition of the mime, who has no model and makes no reference to an outside, it is but a short step to find in the "between-character" of the hymen an essential feature of the mimetic. The presence of the mimetic is guaranteed; it no longer needs to be defined as either antecedent or subsequent.

The hymen offers a fitting image for the character of the "between." In the initial meaning of the hymen, it is a sign of virginity; but then it also becomes the expression of marital union. It marks the "between-two" and the disappearance of difference. The hymen is located between desire and fulfillment, between duration and memory.

> [It] stands *between* the inside and the outside of a woman, and consequently between desire and fulfillment. It is neither desire nor pleasure but in between the two. Neither future nor present, but between the two. It is the hymen that desire dreams of piercing, of bursting, in an act of violence that is (at the same time or somewhere between) love and murder. If either one *did* take place, there would be no hymen. . . . With all the undecidability of its meaning, the hymen only takes place when it doesn't take place, when nothing *really* happens, when there is an all-consuming consummation without violence, or a violence without blows, or a blow without marks, a mark without a mark (a margin), etc., when the veil is, *without being,* torn.[14]

> Within this fusion . . . there is no longer any difference between desire and satisfaction. It is not only the difference (between desire and fulfillment) that is abolished, but also the difference between difference and nondifference. Nonpresence, the gaping void of desire, and presence, the fullness of enjoyment, amount to the same. By the same token [*du même coup*], there is no longer any textual difference between the image and the thing, the empty signifier and the full signified, the imitator and the imitated, etc.[15]

The hymen becomes a sign of a mimesis that has nothing before or after it, that is not merely the present referred to the future or the past. There is no repetition, no imitation, no reality, no right or wrong similarity, no truth outside of the mimetic. What the mimetic is, it is through itself and in itself and not by way of reference to something outside itself. The hymen illustrates the temporary exclusion of all reference points outside the mimetic and the temporally bounded sublation of distinctions. In the hymen as the image of the mimetic, the mimetic is a world for itself, comparable to nothing outside itself. It is a world of play and appearance, which is not reducible to anything else. The mime also makes nothing, imitates nothing; he produces appearance; he plays a game of the between, a game that is like writing with the body. The between of mimesis encompasses its own time, its own form of representation, which is neither real nor imaginary.

It is also possible to grasp the mimetic in other metaphors: in the fold, in the verse, in the white of the unwritten page, in the quill. Instead of truth being a reference point for mimesis, mimetic movement furthers the *dissemination* of individual elements and meanings, in the course of which new interconnections, figurations, and simulacra come into being. Mimetic structures simultaneously take shape on a canvas in the play of various forces and resist our longing for nonambiguity. Lost are certainty, truth, and a claim to revelation; what exists instead is the play of signs over the abyss, a game with emptiness, contingency, and necessary structures. Analogy, metaphor, metonymy. Chains of images, the compositional principles of which conceal themselves in the invisible. Drama, ballet, miming. Various sites of mimetic movements, which concentrate and accelerate themselves, displace each other and in their play dissolve truth—into individual aspects that, in their mutual reference, compose themselves into thematic complexes, only to dissolve anew. Dissemination of images, words, and abyssal energies, sheets of glass, membranes, filters, white pages, and so on.

Derrida expands the concept of mimesis once more, in the concept of economimesis, by identifying the connection between mimesis and production. First, mimesis should no longer be limited to the imitation of objects, that is, to reproduction. For mimesis also encompasses the imitation of processes and the production of processes and objects. Second, Derrida wants to make it clear that mimetic processes must not be examined in isolation from the political and the economic, that, in fact, mimetic processes cross over boundaries drawn between culture and economy. This is the more true if one understands, under the rubric *oeconomia,* not only an economy of circulation but also a universal economy, which is concerned not only with the circulation of capital and signs but also with the regulation of the community and processes of multiplication and publication.

On the basis of these presuppositions, Derrida develops a fascinating critique of Kant's theory of free art and of parts of the *Critique of Judgment.* He casts doubt on the validity of the distinction drawn in §43 between ''free'' and ''mercenary'' art as well as the argument advanced in §51, according to which the mind must engage in the beautiful arts without any mercenary purpose.

Derrida rejects Kant's attempt to define art on the basis of this distinction; he does not recognize free and mercenary art as opposites. Derrida problematizes the higher status of free art on account of its lesser economic value in comparison to mercenary art. If the former were free play and the latter work, then the former would be the result of the activity of the free individual in the form of the artist, while the latter, in its similarity to bees making their honeycombs with their legs, the result of the creativity of *Homo oeconomicus.* To answer the question of what art is and what comprises artistic creation, Kant initially takes up the distinction between *techné* and *physis,* defining nature as mechanical necessity and art/techné as the play of freedom. But, by referring to the genius as the producer of art, Kant quickly overcomes his own distinction. It is true that genius must not imitate nature, yet it remains nature's mouthpiece; genius refers nature back onto itself, and nature reflects on itself by means of art. While, at first, imitation is rejected as a principle of art, with emphasis falling on the meaning of doing (*facere*) in distinction to acting (*agere*), mimesis mediated over genius, whose doing is guided by rules given in nature, is then defined as a necessary condition of art. Mimesis here refers less to the imitation of nature through art than to a violation of physis, to a self-reference on the part of nature. With this definition, the opposition between physis and mimesis, and, accordingly, also that between physis and techné, is dissolved. But how can art be both mimesis and "production through freedom," through free will? For Derrida, this is possible by way of analogy, by way of the "as-if." Works of the beautiful arts must resemble nature to the same degree that they are products of freedom. The less dependent they are on nature, the more they have to resemble it. Mimesis means here, not imitation, that is, the representation of one thing by another, that is, a relationship of similarity between two things; mimesis means much more the "production of a product of nature by a product of art. It is not a relationship between two products, but two productions and two freedoms. The artist does not imitate things in nature, for example, in *natura naturata,* but the actions of *natura naturans,* the operations of *physis.*"[16]

If one assumes such an analogy between the natura naturans and the art of a subject, of a divine artist, mimesis then refers to the identification of human and divine action. The communicability of judgments of pure taste—the universal, unlimited exchange among subjects in reference to their evaluations of beautiful art—points in the same direction. "Genuine mimesis takes place between two subjects of production and not between two products."[17] Such an understanding of mimesis, which is implicit in the *Critique of Judgment,* implies the rejection of an understanding of mimesis as passive imitation. The "anthropological-theological mimesis" developed here is the guarantor of the political economy of the beautiful arts, of a distinction between free art and mercenary art in the sense of a hierarchy. Economimesis embraces references among the instinctive work of animals, the mechanical arts, mercenary art, the free arts, the aesthetic arts, and the beautiful arts. The structure of mimesis causes the opposition between nature and art, between *agere* and *facere*, to disappear. Mimesis is a special human faculty; in Aristotle, it is the common origin of knowledge and pleasure; in Kant, the commonality is given up. Beauty exists only as the beauty of productive nature. Art is beautiful to the extent that it produces in the way productive nature produces, that it is production and not product.

Mimesis is bound to freedom. How can human freedom resemble divine freedom? The poet, the genius, can relate mimetically to God only by not imitating God. "Genius is the innate mental disposition (*ingenium*) *through which* nature gives the rule to art . . . ; i.e., beautiful art is only possible as a product of genius."[18] In distinction to the orator, who makes many promises and breaks some of them, genius promises nothing, but, because of its many talents, of its surplus value, it surprises. Genius is not compensated in the human economy for its surplus value; it owes its abilities only to God. "God commands, nature speaks, in order to convey something to the genius."[19] The genius does not imitate, does not learn; genius reproduces the productive freedom of God, the production of the production. "The analogy between the free productivity of nature and the free productivity of the genius, between God and the poet, is not only a relation of proportionality or a relation between two subjects, two origins, two productions. The analogous process is also an ascent to *logos*."[20] Insofar as art imitates least, it most resembles divine production. Genius, in its similarity to God, can create the beautiful and the sublime, the two of which can fall into mimetic relation to each other. The sublime in Kant is indeed not the complete Other to the beautiful, yet it does refer to the possibility of pleasure in the negative, of "negative pleasure." Kant's well-known distinction between the sublime and the beautiful runs as follows:

> And the latter satisfaction is quite different in kind from the former, for this [the beautiful] directly brings with it a feeling of the furtherance of life, and thus is compatible with charms and with the play of the imagination. But the other [the feeling of the sublime] is a pleasure that arises only indirectly; viz. it is produced by the feeling of a momentary checking of the vital powers and a consequent stronger outflow of them, so that it seems to be regarded as emotion—not play, but earnest in the exercise of the imagination. Hence it is incompatible with [physical] charm; and as the mind is not merely attracted by the object but is ever being alternately repelled, the satisfaction in the sublime does not so much involve a positive pleasure as admiration or respect, which rather deserves to be called negative pleasure.[21]

The negativity generates disharmony and disorder in the unity of the subject, whereby unity is productive of pleasure. It is not condemned to silence, but can come to expression through art. In this is manifest one characteristic of mimesis that was already clear to Aristotle: to represent the terrible in such a way that it becomes possible to confront it. Only disgust represents for Kant the aspect of the ugly, which cannot be overtaken by mimesis, which remains incomprehensible and therefore represents "the transcendental of the transcendental." For, in the face of the disgusting, the distinction between the artistic representation of an object and its objectivity in nature is no longer tenable. Thus is the disgusting not subject to artistic representation; it produces the physical reaction of vomiting. Now, Kant rejects the possibility of a substitute figuration of disgust in art. This nonexistent possibility of substitution (and not the disgusting itself) is what cannot be represented or named, what is the absolute Other of the system, which calls the "hierarchical authority of the logocentric analogy, its power of identification into question,"[22] and identifies an important limitation of the Kantian critique of judgment.

After the loss of a secure point of metaphysical reference and of certainty about the origin and goal of human development, mimesis takes on a new significance that is inseparable from writing. Both are presupposed by every act of human thought and action, which implies that all cultural processes contain a mimetic dimension. Mimesis becomes a central moment in the processes of deconstruction. Existing orders and hierarchies are dissolved, their components set in a mimetically determined relation to each other, and new structures composed and deconstructed. Thereby, as yet, only elements conceived in connection with each other can be referred playfully to each other and introduced into a newly generated mimetic relation. The renunciation of the secure orders of logocentric thinking opens up perception of analogous forms of composition—mimetically comprehensible new constructions in view of which logocentric thinking fails.

Playing a central role in these processes is the impenetrability and indeterminacy in principle of texts. They supply the point of departure for the thinking of difference, without which deconstruction is not possible. Difference, too, based on distinctions, delimitations, and new combinations, can only be defined in reference to mimetic processes. This component of difference distinguishes mimesis from processes of mere imitation and reproduction and secures for it its specific character. The central concepts of Derrida's thought, such as "pharmakon," "supplément," and "hymen," but also "between," "threshold," "trace," and so on, make it clear that only a mimetic approach brings to expression their specific character of gliding, of ambiguity, of indeterminacy, which, in distinction to the logocentric approach, allows them space for their between-character and their oscillation.

If texts are understood as combinations of signs, then mimetic processes take place, not between texts and a reality existing external to them, but only inside texts. Texts and the signs that constitute them come into a mimetic relation. They refer to each other. Sign worlds and simulacra come into being, and there is no longer any fixed point from which to judge them. What results is a play of absence and presence. It takes shape in metaphors, metonymies, signs, and images. The continuity of meaning is destroyed. Meanings displace each other in the alternation of similarity and difference. "Hinges," "keys," "patches," and "parerga" are metaphors for this mimetic play. In this conception, mimesis has the essence of poiēsis and, as such, names the activity of a demiurge, which, however, does not admit of being fixed and identified. Like the mimosa, mimesis resists approach. Mimesis resembles truth insofar as truth never resembles itself, can never resemble itself, and never ceases retreating and donning masks. The reduction of mimesis to assimilation is an inadequate abbreviation. Mimesis is, on the one hand, deformation, descent, eclipse, and, at the same time, uneven assimilation, dissimilar similarity. On the other hand, it generates desire and thus aims at assimilation and doubling. Mimesis inscribes signs, images, and language in human beings and is in that sense typography. Mythical fictions in particular combine with the subject, which becomes a product of fiction and language.[23]

Mimesis itself has nothing proper to itself; Lacoue-Labarthe has made this clear in his analysis of Diderot's *Paradox of Acting.*[24]

> In order to do everything, to imitate everything—in order to (re)present or (re)produce everything, in the strongest sense of these terms—one must oneself be nothing, have nothing *proper* to oneself except an "equal aptitude" for all sorts of things, roles, characters, functions, and so on. The paradox states a *law of impropriety,* which is also the very law of mimesis: only the "man without qualities," the being without properties or specificity, the subjectless subject (absent from himself, distracted from himself, deprived of self) is able to present or produce in general.[25]

What this means for actors, artists, writers is that the less they are confined by their own properties, the more they are in a position to become productive. In this they resemble nature, namely, in the act of productivity; they distinguish themselves from nature in that their act does not imitate nature but brings forth something new. Their work is an offering from mimesis; it is a poietic gift. The less actors, artists, writers are captive to their own feelings and objects, the more they are "not," the more capable they are, like nature, to give form to everything. A differentiated concept of mimesis resolves this paradox, resulting in a relation between paradox and mimesis that can be conceived as follows: "the logic of the paradox, the hyperbologic, is nothing other than the very logic of mimesis."[26] According to this view, the logic of the paradox

> is always the logic of *semblance,* articulated around the division between appearance and reality, presence and absence, the same and the other, or identity and difference. This is the division that grounds (and that constantly unsteadies) mimesis. At whatever level one takes it—in the copy or the reproduction, the art

of the actor, mimetism, disguise, dialogic writing—the rule is always the same: the more it resembles, the more it differs. The same, in its sameness, is the other itself.[27]

The movements of mimesis are characterized by breaks, concentrations, and displacements; they run up against empty spaces in which there is neither subject nor properties; they flow into paradoxical constellations in which contradictions combine with each other in mimetic play.[28]

Results

The studies in this volume do not answer the question, what is mimesis? Rather, they demonstrate that such a posing of the question leads to error. It presupposes that mimesis is a largely homogenous concept that undergoes continuous development in a historical space. We regard this presupposition as invalid, seeing in mimesis instead a highly complex structure in which an entire range of conditions coincide: it is a theoretical and practical bearing toward the world; it encompasses cognition and action, symbolic systems and communications media, relationships between *I* and Other. And to this we must add a final determination, that the relevance of mimesis is not restricted to the aesthetic, that its effects press outward into the social world, taking root, as Plato saw it, in individual behavior like a contagion. There is no doubt that the examples we have discussed here do display signs of apparent linear development. Nevertheless, we maintain that each new historical period is characterized by an interplay of complex conditions specific to that period, out of which emerges a particular conceptual constellation.

The question arises of why we designate all the individual cases by the same term. Is there something that lends a "family resemblance" to the whole? It is in fact not a case of pure terminological caprice: the red thread running through all the cases is woven out of an ongoing thematic complex that winds in its many variations through history. Each historical instance of mimesis has its own constellation, even if, for hundreds of years, all appealed to the same authority, Aristotle. The concept of mimesis has repeatedly provided the ground in which disputes could be carried on about questions of the relation of a symbolically generated world to a second world that has been claimed to be the fundamental, exemplary, significant, or real world. Thus Shakespeare's drama is focused on the empirical world of politics, power struggles, and political order; classical tragedy is concerned with the myths of prehistorical foundings; the drama of the fin de siècle is concerned with language and gesture, at a time when the capacity of both to gain access to reality is being questioned. Each historical position taken up by mimesis is a particular construction of a larger thematic complex, which can be formulated in general, but has meaning always only in the context of a specific constellation. In what follows, we provide a brief summary of the most important positions we have treated in the book.

Historical Positions of Mimesis

The first great conflict over mimesis that has been preserved in the record is found in Plato in the form of a juxtaposition of mimetic and antimimetic attitudes. The dispute proceeds in the context of a reordering of thought, cognition, and action, on the basis of the gradual spread and general accessibility of written culture; Plato takes aim against the old form of mimetic thought, which is rooted essentially in oral traditions. In doing so, Plato fundamentally reconceives the received notion of mimesis. "Mimesis" in pre-Platonic times denoted the direct re-creation of the actions and utterances of people or animals. Characteristics of other beings were re-created in the form of a "do-as-if," woven into music, organized as rhythm, and performed in public. Plato distinguishes several aspects of mimesis: he means in the first instance such recitation as overwhelms the senses, the moment of seduction entailed in the practice, and the effects exercised on the audience; he also focuses on claims that what is being said is right and true and, finally, on the emergence of the rhapsodist as pedagogue. Against these positions, he maintains the following: mimetic processes are such that they proliferate wildly; they are apt to go astray from the truth into a world of illusion; the rhapsodists are outfitted with no objective pedagogical competence. His attack is aimed primarily at the performative mimesis of oral recitals, with their religious roots and educational aspirations. But Plato also makes room for mimetic processes in his system—in his re-creation of the Socratic dialogues, in a methexis in the movement of thought, and, though in a strictly limited sense, for educational purposes as well.

Plato opens up an area, aesthetics, that is entirely mimetic. Aristotle goes a decisive step farther by transforming mimesis into a technical concept, then building it into his philosophy in terms of the representation of the possible and the general. In the *Poetics,* Aristotle elevates mimesis, as the mimesis of myth, to the rank of an organizing principle in artworks. The synthesizing, imitative, and creative power of mimesis for Aristotle is analogous to the generative mode of nature, the natura naturans. Inherent in this creative force is a fundamental characteristic of human being, which is a source both of enjoyment and the capacity to learn. Aristotle is no longer involved in the same conflict as Plato; his philosophy has completely adopted the written form. In Aristotle, mimesis becomes a theoretical concept and, in this way, is domesticated, tied in to a larger systematic context. But the attempt to render mimesis theoretical, to make of it an accommodating philosophical concept, does not proceed without difficulties: mimesis refuses to become a ''proper'' concept; it does not accommodate itself; it resists theory formation, like a wild element loosed inside otherwise disciplined thought. This resistance comes to expression in the ways in which the concept has been indefinitely applied, in the absence of a strict definition of the term, and in the way mimesis tends to be pushed back into a pretheoretical realm of human preconditions that do not admit of discussion.

Mimesis, under the name *imitatio,* plays a critical role in medieval thought. The Middle Ages constituted itself in mimetic confrontation with the late classical period, operating, of course, with ideas of antiquity and Christianity of its own making. Mimesis aims at that which exists concretely and immediately as material; it takes it up and transforms it, displaces received traditions into new contexts, amalgamizes and reinterprets it. An important aspect of mimesis in the medieval period is mimetic reference to God; this metaphysical mimesis takes up a central position in nearly all areas of literature, art, and music; its effects are evident in the way the heraldic insignias of medieval kings are formed, and in the justification of political power. Human action is placed in relation to God, who stipulates the relevant norms. In comparison to God, all human things are bound to time, provisional, imperfect. The fruitful life must be lived inside a mimesis of God, of Christ; otherwise it lacks both meaning and worth.

In the Renaissance, mimesis appears inside the highly developed written culture of an intellectual elite expressing itself in a foreign language. It makes its way into the scholarly communities by way of philology and translation. Its application this time is relatively restrained, but once again it plays a role in the development of a new culture. Mimesis, used now to express a relation of subordination to a model, is treated in a less authoritarian manner than had been the case with Plato. But the comparison of new and old authors stimulates a complex and multilayered discussion centered on the process by which a foreign culture is appropriated in the copying and studying of texts created by a foreign way of thinking. The procedure leads to substantial gains: authorities are reconstructed in the form of rules, norms, and the identification of a canon. The new culture that develops in the Renaissance is not equivalent to classical culture: it creates for itself a margin of freedom that makes it possible to say ''I''; it opens a space in which to bring antiquity, its own antiquity, into the present. In the reproduction involved, self-consciousness takes shape; the new time speaks its own name in the language of antiquity. Mimesis is simultaneously a learning to speak and a mastering of a code and implies, finally, a virtuoso's disposal over a universal language. On the one hand, mimesis generates a pressure to conform and obligations, but, on the other, it allows one one's own expression and a consciousness of the self, which works to create a distance from antiquity.

The Renaissance never gives up the reference to antiquity; it was bound to old models of style even on the level of its rhetorical dimension. But in the course of time the distance, under the altered conditions of printing and the rise of a reading public, grows ever larger. The treatment of the texts becomes freer and more confident and carves out for itself here and there—in all seriousness—a playful side. Readers of literature are also drawn into the production of texts. Authors such as Montaigne, in the making of their literary worlds, anticipate the process of reading, which is undertaken in mimetic reference to other texts. Mimetic constellations are used to describe the social world. With the expansion of mimesis into social relations, the theater in the seventeenth century becomes a model of social reality.

At the court of Louis XIV, mimesis organizes a gigantic interpretation machine. Through effects of mimesis political reality is transformed into a universal history revolving about the portrait of the king at the center. Historiographers transform royal acts into objects of wonder at the moment of their execution, while the king is himself obligated to enter into transformative circulation. Mimetic processes make use of all the media at their disposal. The person acting mimetically becomes a "great simulator," one of whose effects is to lend political reality a fictional character, condensing it into a kind of hyperreality. Protests are raised against such tendencies: Jansenist authors reject the concept of representation for religious reasons; Cartesian philosophy lowers the value placed on sensory impressions, searching for truth instead by means of ideal, methodically produced illustrations; Dutch painting devotes its entire concentration to what it regards as a faithful reproduction of what the eye sees. Each of these renunciations of mimesis, each in its own way, ultimately relies on mimetic processes, in changed and unacknowledged form.

While mimesis contributes to the production of an intensified fictional world under French absolutism, in the dramatic theory of the Enlightenment it becomes a weapon in the bourgeoisie's struggle for power. Changes in both the nature of power and in mimetic worldmaking in the field of literature render it suitable for the new role. The bourgeoisie's claim to the leading role in society is manifest in its culture of taste and emotion, which not only exemplifies but is simultaneously one of the constituent elements of power. Good taste and lofty emotion are the distinctive characteristics of a society in the process of transforming itself on the basis of the individual's disposal over both economic *and* symbolic capital. The bourgeois drama is an apt site for the representation of emotions as universal human characteristics, which, however, can be ideally realized only by the bourgeoisie and no other class. Thus assuming the function of moral guidance, theater offers its audience interpretations of behavior and models of self-representation. Mimesis turns, as part of the overall call for the imitation of nature, to the inner world, as an external representation of psychological and mental events.

In a way that is similar to the workings of nature, the writer materializes a creative force. In the eighteenth-century discussion of the imitation of nature, increasingly insistent attention is turned to the liberation of the power of the imagination, a development that culminates in the assertion of the autonomy of the artwork. Moritz and Kant put an end to the automatic reference of artistic creations to the model of a prior world. They give up the projective relationship of the mimetic to another world, and mimesis seems, as a principle of art, to have reached its end.

The contributions of Lessing and Rousseau, who, each in his own way, open up new paths for mimesis, force that idea to be revised. Lessing is the first to analyze artistic media systematically, with the consequence that he definitively abandons the similitude theory of reference in favor of another assumption: that mimesis in the plastic arts takes place in space, and mimesis in poetry in time. In the first case, it is the spatial, and in the second, the temporal dimension of the existing world that is "transported" into the mimetic world of art. The reality content of art consists in its actual involvement in both dimensions. The result of this conceptualization in literature is the retrieval of the sensuous aspect, of immediacy, and directness—which are characteristic of situations of oral communication. Rousseau takes the retrieval of sensuousness a step farther by introducing the category of authenticity in writing. He extends mimesis beyond literature to the life of the author. In another way as well, Rousseau expands literary mimesis: he discovers the seductive effect that an author can exercise by conveying images of an Other (or of himself or herself) that show the reader what kind of person he or she is or could become.

Put perhaps somewhat too neatly, mimesis disappears from eighteenth-century aesthetics to reemerge in the form of social mimesis as an object of literature. We recognize the new role of mimesis particularly clearly in Balzac's novels: one of the essential driving forces of society, aside from the economic, is the mimetic desire generated in relationship to other persons. Social actors are taken captive by images; society acquires its specific physiognomy from the multitude of legible social signs. The generation of signs and images mediates the production of relative social position. While Balzac was not able to distance himself from the affective disposition of his fictional characters, instead sharing it with them, the view of the antiromantic authors regarding the mimetic composition of action is acutely critical. The desire of their fictional characters has no truth to it; it is desire in conformity with an Other.

The antiromantic authors subvert the obligatory self-interpretation of society, depicting affective social forces from both an interior and an exterior perspective. Social mimesis orients the *I,* which is internally empty, toward Others and charges interpersonal relationships with violence. Mimetically generated violence becomes, for antiromantic authors, one of the main problems of human life in community. It dominates not only the relationships of the fictional characters among themselves but also those between the author and readers. Girard takes the rise of violence out of mimetic competition as the object of a comprehensive anthropology, with which he attempts to explain, in particular, the origin of the sacred, of religion, and of social orders.

The inhabitants of worlds organized according to the principles of magic are characterized by their ability, residing in the mimetic faculty, to discern similarities. These similarities—correspondences—are not always obvious, but, rather, a matter of "nonsensuous similarities" (Benjamin), which are perceived initially in the relation of objects to each other. In the context of an increase in processes of desensualization and abstraction, nonsensuous similarities are displaced into language and writing. The mimetic faculty, in many of its most central aspects, now establishes itself here, with the result that extraliterary mimesis loses force, while literary mimesis becomes the site of potential experience; without mimesis no connection to the outer world can be forged successfully. The initially nonspecific life of human drives assumes individual shape in the breakthrough situations of childhood, as mediated over language. These processes, which occur in the child's encounter with its environment, are mimetic; they allow the child to grasp sensuously given similarities and nonsensuous correspondences in the same way.

For Adorno, mimesis represents a bridge to the world. In the form of mimicry, it is an early form of physical assimilation to external nature, a mimicry of ossification and death. Within a magical orientation toward the world, mimesis takes the form of the organized action of the individual; processes of "presentiment" are invented by means of which nature is prescribed to behave in certain ways. The assimilation of human being to nature takes on an organized form, with the goal increasingly becoming the self-assertion of human being against nature. With growing security, however, the chances for human happiness decline. The abstraction from the physicality of thought leads to a sacrifice of the vitality of the self. By disenchanting the world, human being forfeits its affinity with nature; self-sacrifice becomes unavoidable. The separation between subject and object leads to the isolation of the individual and to an intensification of the processes of abstraction. Mimesis survives as a form of physical resistance to reification and a guarantee of the precedence of the object. Repressed mimesis is articulated as a longing for sensuous intimacy. It prompts a movement toward the world and other people; it seeks similarity and opens up the prospect of a temporary overcoming of separateness; it offers a corrective to identifying thought; it opens itself to the nonidentical and thus leads to a broadening of the subject. In aesthetic experience mimesis allows for a mediation between *I* and not-*I,* an active passivity. It makes it possible to experience the "similar in the dissimilar." Mimesis leads to intensified moments of aesthetic interaction with the world, that is, to a generalizable form of "vital experience"; it eventuates in the opening of the subject to the precedence and nondisposability of the object.

Derrida's treatment of mimesis centers on the concept of the text. Texts are nondisposable; they exist in reference to what has preceded them; the silhouette of a text takes shape in a rule-bound play of reference to other texts. Texts never represent an origin, are never inner, never outer, but always doubled. Their intertextuality calls for deconstruction. As in the case of hieroglyphs, the point is to decipher that which is unspeakable in them. Texts are traces of individuals; each one is a beginning and a repetition; it is impossible not to arrive at them too late. The theoretical comprehension of texts presupposes a prior mimetic approach; it plays with revelation, concealment, and masking and oscillates between extremes. In Derrida's view, mimesis has a doubled- or "between"-character; it is like a hinge, yet also like a pharmakon; it remains ambivalent; there is no cognition without mimesis; it actualizes itself in play, in the simulacrum of apocryphal textuality. Truth is not a reference point for mimesis; at the same time there is no truth in the absence and outside of mimetic movement. Mimesis is like the hymen, stretched between desire and gratification. It drives the process of dissemination of individual elements, resists nonambiguity. It is an expression of human freedom, articulated in interaction with texts and signs, in the play of presence and absence. Mimesis is like a "mimosa," which withdraws from contact; it has nothing of its own; the more similarity there is, the more the similarity renders itself distinct.

The Dimensions of Mimesis

The issue of the specific historical forms taken on by mimesis concerns the making of symbolic worlds by means of media. Mimetic worlds have an existence of their own; they can be understood from within in their own terms. But, rather than being closed systems, they make reference to another world. Viewed historically, these references can be of the most varied sorts. In each case the mimetic world is possessed of its own particular right in relation to the one to which it refers; by virtue of this characteristic, mimesis is fundamentally distinct from theories, models, plans, and reconstructions. It entails a mimetic process of transformation of the elements of a prior into a symbolically produced world. The first is a world of Others, the second, the world of the *I*, of an ego acting mimetically.

The aspect of production expresses the nature of mimesis as activity undertaken by actors, as a deed. This acting, which was originally rhythmic, a performance with a strongly marked physical component, is articulated variously with the passage of time: as an act of painting or writing, as a making with one's own hands, as a generation of sounds with the voice or with musical instruments, or in reading aloud, or, ultimately, in reading silently, which retains scarcely any physical component at all. But there remains always a physical residue, which makes its presence felt in typically physical processes of depletion, such as fatigue, as well as in the way in which mimetic actions are learned and, above all, in the way they are executed. Mimesis brings into play a practical knowledge, a sens pratique; it makes available models of behavior that are seemingly immediate and require no consideration; and, on the perception of a situation, it supplies an interpretation and suggests ways to react, which in turn allow subsequent behavioral steps to be anticipated. Mimesis is the answer objectified in a symbolic world of a subject seeking and finding orientation in a world of Others. In this involvement of the body, in its reference to the *I* of the actor and to Others, lies the essential difference between mimesis and purely cognitive ways of knowing. Mimesis aims at influence, appropriation, alteration, repetition; it operates by means of new interpretations of already existing worlds.

The results of our discussion allow us to identify the following dimensions of mimesis.

1. Involved in mimesis is practical knowledge and, in most cases, the body; it is bound to an active practice. When we attempt to comprehend this practice conceptually and logically, we confront, as in all theorizations of practice in general,[1] the difficulty of attempting to attribute unequivocalness, one-sidedness, and logic to relatively open and indeterminate practice. Practical actions not only do not possess such characteristics but are actually stripped of essential characteristics they do possess if a false attribution is made. We mean here the capacity of practical actions to interpret, their temporal structure, and the internal relations among them as various instances of practice. Mimesis eludes theory formation. It is a product of human practice and must always be regarded as the issue of a deed, as a part of practice.

The origins of mimesis lie in oral cultures. Mimetic actions on this level incorporate the whole body of the speaker and the participation of his audience. They are characterized by rhythm, gestures, and sounds. With the general use of writing, the sensuous elements of mimesis diminish. Since the eighteenth century, tendencies in the direction of recapturing the characteristics of oral cultures have become clearly evident, in particular, the striving after directness, the interest in an addressive relationship to Others, and authenticity. These tendencies are intensified and accelerated by the technical means of the modern communication media.

2. Mimetic processes put into operation that which the actor has already acquired, that which has already been formed through action. Thus, in imitation, are preexisting motor schemata set once more into motion. Nevertheless, in repetition, the actor constitutes something of his own, which must by no means correspond to prior realizations of the schemata. The repetition of a gesture gives prominence to qualities that originally played no special role in the action being imitated, qualities of time and space, of rhythm, of the

execution of the movement. At issue here are recognizable, habituated schemata, rather than ones that have been discovered accidentally. Mimesis is an
act of freely releasing behavioral schemata into operation and, on higher
semiotic planes, of techniques of naming, meaning, and representing.

3. Mimetic processes are not founded on similarities. Only once reference
has been established between a mimetic and another world is it possible to make
a comparison of the two worlds and identify the *tertium comparationis.* Similarity is an outcome of mimetic reference. Imitation is only a special case of
mimesis. In general terms: an object or event can only be regarded as an image,
replica, or reproduction of another one when there exists between the two a
mimetic reference.[2] The latter is the generator of images, correspondences,
similarities, and reflections and of connections of replication, which produce
relationships between events and objects on the sensuous surface of appearances.

4. In mimetic reference, an interpretation is made from the perspective of
a symbolically produced world of a prior (but not necessarily existing) world,
which itself has already been subjected to interpretation. Mimesis construes
anew already construed worlds. This applies even to repetition or simple
reproduction. Thus, in the course of repeated executions, a gesture creates
structures of meaning that are different from those that attended its first
performance. It isolates an object or an event from its usual context and
produces a perspective of reception that differs from the one in which the prior
world is perceived. Isolation and the change of perspective are characteristics
of aesthetic processes. They are responsible for the close kinship that writers
since Plato have maintained exists between mimesis and aesthetics. Mimetic
new interpretation is at the same time a new perception, a seeing-as (Wittgenstein). Mimetic action involves the intention of displaying a symbolically
produced world in such a way that it will be perceived as a specific world.

5. Mimesis is by nature intermediary, stretched between a symbolically
produced world and another one. In this relation, the determination is made as
to which world counts as the true world and which is apparent, illusionary, a
game, an exaggeration, a caricature. Plato regards the world of the ideas as the
true one, and the mimetic world, in contrast, as that of imitations. For Aristotle,
the relation is nearly the reverse: the mimetic world of tragedy is present,
corporeal; it renders what is told present as if it had just happened, and it does
so with a higher degree of presence than the world to which it refers. Out of
a merely possible present, mimesis is capable of creating an immediate one,
which, as living memory, stands out prominently in the flow of time. It makes
presence and reproducibility possible by laying hold of the sensuous aspects
of appearances.

6. The power of mimesis lies essentially in the images it evokes. It generates
a world of appearances, of semblance, of the aesthetic. Images do indeed have
a material existence, but what they represent is not an integral part of empirical

reality; mimesis belongs to a nonempirical order of knowledge. Images produce connections between the individual and empirical reality, but they also have about them an aspect of illusion, simulation, fiction, or deception.[3] They bear a recognizable tendency toward autonomy; they can become sensuous events lacking in reference to the real, can become simulacra and simulations; there then arise images and texts without a subject. In such cases, mimesis becomes self-referential; as the images become autonomous and enclosed within their own system of reference, there is no longer anything behind them to be sought for. In this case of automimesis, the references between mimetic and other worlds become fictional; they close themselves off in intertextuality or inter-figuration.

7. When the actual meaning comes to be attributed to the mimetic world as opposed to historical reality, the power of signs is increased and the (political) power that relies on signs intensified. Signs then represent, as is demonstrated in the example of the court society of Versailles, a kind of higher reality. They establish a stage on which the world can be represented as it should be. Thus the range of mimetic effects extends into the sphere of practical action: as models of behavior, an enactment of power, the definition of reality. Authoritarian regimes use mimetic procedures to construct fictional events to take over the place of reality. In the images of power there arises a world dominated by power; in this world of fascinating appearance, politics is aestheticized.

The power of mimesis grows with the historical development of the individual psyche, in particular, since the eighteenth century. Verbal representations and ascriptions generate interior worlds and open up access to the psychological life of Others.

8. As the product of social fictions, mimesis presses beyond the realm of aesthetics, where it had been confined since Plato, and becomes effective as a social force. In this aspect it becomes the object of critical literary analyses at just the time when the theory of art is giving up mimesis as an aesthetic principle and society is at the point of reconstituting itself on the basis of competition and rivalry. "Social mimesis" designates the process in which rivalries arise between individuals and groups sharing the same goals of action. The approximation of individuals to each other, their becoming similar, favors the development of equivalent valuations and equivalent perceptual modes, assessments, and aspirations, while at the same time the rivals sharpen their sense of self-delimitation in regard to each other. The mimetically generated correspondence in goals of action and the desire that, arising out of the correspondence, is experienced in reference to Others contain the seeds of violence against—real or supposed—competitors, who simultaneously impede the realization of a goal and intensify its desirability. Mimetic conflicts, the consequences of which are real indeed, have their origin in a fictional world in which objects are lent value by competition itself. Social mimesis is part of the process by which value is bestowed in modern society on social distinctions.

9. From an anthropological perspective, mimesis can be regarded as a capacity that distinguishes human beings from animals. A kind of pleasure is taken in mimesis, which Aristotle designates as the specific characteristic of human being. Especially among children, a great deal of education is accomplished mimetically. Already in preverbal stages, perceptual abilities and motor skills are formed via mimetic processes; the same is true of learning language and appropriate social behavior. Many aspects of childhood development proceed via mimetic models, regardless of whether they manifest desirable or undesirable behavior. If pedagogy is to accomplish a categorical integration of the individual into the world, it must make sufficient room for the operation of mimetic abilities, which has the added benefit of avoiding desensualization and abstraction. Mimesis is a movement of approximation between things and people, which allows people to retain their uniqueness. It contains hope for an enriched interaction with the world, even if, in the form of mimicry of the dead, it also leads to paralysis and a loss of vitality.

10. Mimesis is distinguished from mimicry by essential characteristics,[4] which are precisely those that concern the constitution of both the mimetic and the prior world. The world that mimesis encounters is itself constituted symbolically. The human symbolic systems used in mimesis are not the result of organic adaptations, but, despite all the material pressure encumbering their development, are free human creations. Beyond all individual differences, mimesis allows the elements of the empirical environment to be processed, reshaped, generalized, and removed from their concrete situation and made generally reproducible.

All important new media share the characteristic in common that they take dimensions or fragments of empirical reality and "transport" them in the form of images or sounds. Art, since the first decade of the twentieth century, has itself made use of traces of empirical reality (thus collage, frottage, pop art, land art, ready-mades, etc.). Evident over time is an ever-greater utilization of the elements of empirical reality in the making of symbolic worlds. Also evident is the countervailing process: symbolic systems are ever more intensely involved in the constitution of empirical reality. This tendency is recognizable in historical developments such as the rise of new media and forms of communication, the constitution of the individual psyche, the transformation of political power and the way it is exercised, and the construction and functioning of society in terms of distinctions in the area of symbolic capital.[5] Mimetic processes enter into the empirical world by way of its nature as a constructed world.

11. The commensurability of two worlds is a function of one's symbolic disposition over the prior world, which itself implies a moment of mastery; mimesis is the appropriation of another world. Produced simultaneously with the mimetic world is a general, reproducible model, a possession that is preserved beyond the initial situation. Operative in this procedure on a sub-

terranean level (often unwittingly so) is a declaration of unreality on the part of the creator and the recipient: this world is not real. With the spread of mimesis into regions that were not previously in its possession, the realm in which such a potential sublation of reality can be undertaken is also expanded. In all areas of mimetic operation there are to be found fluid boundaries among representation, illustration, rendering, and reproduction, but also among deception, illusion, and appearance.

The pessimistic thesis advanced by some, according to which we are suffering an increasing loss of reality in our culture, does not stand up to close examination; it is based on a naive understanding of what reality is. We observe a twofold movement in process: the growing involvement of mimesis in the symbolically constituted empirical world, on the one hand, and the increasing integration of elements of empirical reality in mimetic media, on the other. The joint operation of the two processes intensifies the effects of mimesis. The increasing sensualization of the daily world in our own time is, from this perspective, only the other side of the progressive development of mimesis.

12. Our customary notion of empirical reality identifies it in sharp distinction to mimetic worlds. When the gap between the empirical and mimetic worlds narrows, empirical reality loses its autonomy over against interpretive mimetic worlds: it comes increasingly to approximate itself to them; events become indistinguishable from interpretations and quotations. There is then no reality beyond interpreted and quoted worlds; mimesis no longer represents any other world. It becomes a self-illustration, a self-presentation.

It is impossible to overlook the contemporary tendency for everything to be turned into an image.[6] The electronic character of video images both makes them ubiquitous and allows for their acceleration. Images are mixed, come into relations of exchange with other images, and are referred mimetically to still others. Parts of images are picked out and recomposed differently; fractal images are produced, which each time form new wholes. Different images, because they are flat, because they are electronic and miniaturizable, become similar to each other across their substantive differences. They are all part of the fundamental transformation of contemporary image worlds; they dissolve things and transpose them into a world of appearance. Moreover, increasing numbers of images are produced which have only themselves as a point of reference. The ultimate result is that everything becomes art, becomes a play of images that no longer refer to anything, that no longer function as models, but are equivalent to nothing but themselves. The distance between the mimetic and the prior world, the intermediary space, ceases to exist once mimesis has become all-encompassing, and the mimetic and the other world collapse into each other. The total extension of mimesis is simultaneously its end.

Notes

Chapter 1. Point of Departure

1. Erich Auerbach, "Epilegomena zu *Mimesis*," *Romanische Forschungen* 65 (1954): 1–17.

2. The concept of style has once again become an object of current discussion in Hans Ulrich Gumbrecht and K. L. Pfeiffer, eds., *Stil: Geschichten und Funktionen eines kultururssenschaftlichen Diskurselements* (Frankfurt am Main: Suhrkamp, 1986). This book, however, by no means treats the history of style in Auerbach's sense. In the latter's own estimation, his mimesis book is "conceivable in no tradition other than that of German romanticism and Hegel" (Auerbach, "Epilegomena," 15).

3. Erich Auerbach, *Mimesis: The Representation of Reality in Western Literature,* trans. Willard R. Trask (Princeton: Princeton University Press, 1953), 47.

4. The concept of the *figura* designates "the creative-formative, the change in the residual essence, the play between the likeness and the original; and it is not surprising that *figura* was the term used for this most frequently, most generally, and most distinctively" (Auerbach, "Epilegomena," 14).

5. Auerbach, *Mimesis,* 94.

6. Ibid., 202.

7. Ibid., 220.

8. Ibid., 554.

9. Ibid., 220.

10. Ibid., 31.

11. Ibid., 555.

12. The idea that European intellectual history has a structure and a specific course belongs among Auerbach's preconditions for the reconstruction of universal historical continuity. The present investigation does not proceed according to such premises.

13. Luiz Costa Lima, "Historie und metahistorische Kategorien bei Erich Auerbach," in Gumbrecht and Pfeiffer, *Stil,* 307.

14. Ibid., 308.

15. Ibid., 309.

16. Auerbach, *Mimesis,* 23.

17. Ibid., 7f.

18. Ibid., 5.

19. Ibid., 23.

20. Ibid., 12.

21. Ibid., 15.

22. Ibid., 16.

23. Ibid., 45.

24. See Jack Goody and Ian Watt, "Consequences of Literacy."

25. This research hypothesis has been developed by Milman Parry. His work has been continued and elaborated on, in particular by Albert B. Lord, *The Singer of Tales* (Cambridge: Harvard University Press, 1960).

26. Auerbach, *Mimesis,* 19.

27. Opinion has meanwhile turned against the thesis of any unmediated restriction on the possibility of expression by the medium. Newer publications, particularly those by Goody and Ong, offer a differentiated view. For our purposes, it suffices to assume that the medium is not neutral in relation to the view of the world expressed. Such a perspective seems to us thoroughly tenable on the basis of the results of the research presented here.

28. Auerbach designates rhetoric as an important area in which stylistic qualities are united with medial characteristics. In our approach, breakthroughs in the rhetorical tradition are renovations of style and the medium. At the same time they represent an enrichment of the medium with syntactical and semantic possibilities, which, in turn, are integrated into stylistic forms. The impetus for such a change can be that social obligations that were a burden to the medium diminish or are repressed by stronger counterpressures. Auerbach's analysis of the mixture of styles in Christian texts provides a good example of this.

29. In this way the concept of mimesis is made more complex and grounded more deeply in social processes, in the exchange between the individual and society. Thus it becomes more completely a social and medial category than it was before; it makes it possible to identify both social and literary change.

30. Auerbach, *Mimesis,* 14f.

31. See Robert Weimann, *Shakespeare und die Macht der Mimesis: Authorität und Repräsentation im Elisabethanischen Theater* (Berlin: Aufbau-Verlag, 1988).

32. See Michael Nerlich, *Apollon et Dionysos ou la science incertaine des signes: Montaigne, Stendhal, Robbe-Grillet* (Marburg: Hitzeroth, 1989).

33. See Dalia Judovitz, *Subjectivity and Representation in Descartes: The Origins of Modernity* (Cambridge: Cambridge University Press, 1988).

34. See, for exemplary purposes, the discussion of German art under fascism, especially Klaus Wolbert, *Die Nackten und die Toten des "Dritten Reichs": Folgen einer politischen Geschichte des Körpers in der Plastik des deutschen Faschismus* (Giessen: Anabas, 1982); and Dieter Bartetzko, *Zwischen Zucht und Ekstase: Zur Theatralik von NS-Architektur* (Berlin: Mann, 1985).

35. See Norbert Elias, *The Court Society,* trans. Edmund Jephcott (New York:

Pantheon Books, 1983); and Elias, *The Civilizing Process,* trans. Edmund Jephcott (New York: Urizen Books, 1978).

36. Mary Douglas, *Ritual, Tabu, und Körpersymbolik: Sozialanthropologische Studien in Industrie—Gesselschaft und Stammeskultur* (Frankfurt am Main: Fischer, 1970), 42. In reference to considerations to come, we shall also refer to this work by Douglas. The discussion initiated by B. Bernstein has become bogged down in certain of its points in the meantime and, especially given its political theme, may have been surpassed. It did, however, yield important findings regarding the connection between the linguistic code and social structure.

37. Eric A. Havelock, *Preface to Plato* (Cambridge: Harvard University Press, 1963), 140. Jesper Svenbro, in *La parole et le marble aux origines de la poetique grecque* (Lund: [S.A.], 1976), emphasizes, on the contrary, the social compulsions weighing on the singer (p. 18). He supports his argument on the suggestion of a systematic deformation suffered by Mycenaean society in Homeric discourse and which he refers back to social control exercised by the audience over the singer of the *Iliad* (p. 29). The singers knew how to make their songs conform to the interests of their listeners.

38. Douglas's considerations retain close connections with Bernstein's sociological works, which restrict the investigation of codification systems to issues of psychological genesis. They are to be removed from that context here. Important to our work is the assumption that general models preexist individual acts of speaking and writing, that these models also determine the attitude toward language, and that the latter not only makes possible, but to a considerable degree determines, a specific view of the world.

39. Nelson Goodman, *Ways of Worldmaking* (Indianapolis: Hackett, 1978).

40. Ibid., 2.

41. Ibid., 14. Emphasis in original.

42. Ibid., 6. Emphasis in original.

43. Ibid., 106.

44. Ibid., 102.

45. In *Languages of Art: An Approach to a Theory of Symbols* (Indianapolis: Bobbs-Merrill, 1968), Goodman demonstrates that a picture can be regarded as similar to a person without any prior reference having been made to an entity existing independently of language or image. He subsumes representation in images under denotation. "Representation is thus disengaged from perverted ideas of it as an idiosyncratic physical process like mirroring, and is recognized as a symbolic relationship that is relative and variable" (43). "To represent, a picture must function as a pictorial symbol; that is, function in a system such that what is denoted depends solely upon the pictorial properties of the symbol" (41–42). Goodman designates the denotation characterized here as a "null-denotation."

46. See Nelson Goodman and Catherine G. Elgin, *Reconceptions in Philosophy and Other Arts and Sciences* (Indianapolis: Hackett, 1988), 66–82.

47. See, especially, Tynianov, Shklovsky, Eichenbaum, and Jakobson. The concept of difference quality is too formal and too narrow. Given a change in the codification system, the entire system changes, so that no direct comparison between them is possible. The phrasing taken over by Goodman when he speaks of worldmaking includes the claim that various codification systems produce different worlds that cannot be measured against each other.

48. In graphic representation taken in modified form from Douglas (*Ritual, Tabu und Körpersymbolik,* 36ff.), the two types of control can be arranged on a single axis, with the midpoint indicating zero, from which position they diverge and take on added weight. Zero designates a condition of no pressure.

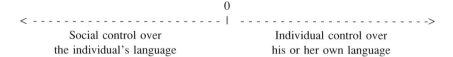

0

Social control over
the individual's language

Individual control over
his or her own language

Left of zero, the literary language finds itself in agreement with the overall ideas of the society; right of zero, it increasingly diverges from them and develops a codification system of its own. We have not adopted Douglas's further considerations on the verbal codes.

49. In cases of individuals, it is difficult to say whether the pressure comes from the author or whether the author assumes the role of a spokesperson who effectively formulates existing pressure in language. With this problem is raised the question of the role of the intellectuals in general, to which group one can as a rule assign literary authors.

50. Auerbach, *Mimesis,* 71, 72.

51. Ibid., 74.

52. Ibid., 258.

53. Ibid., 487.

54. Ibid., 486.

55. Wolfgang Iser, *The Implied Reader: Patterns of Communication in Prose Fiction from Bunyan to Beckett* (Baltimore: John Hopkins University Press, 1974).

Chapter 2. On the Origins of the Concept

1. See Hermann Koller, *Die Mimesis in der Antike: Nachahmung, Darstellung, Ausdruck* (Bern: A. Francke, 1954); G. F. Else, "Imitation in the 5th Century," *Classical Philology* 53, no. 2 (April 1958): 73–90; and Goran Sörbom, *Mimesis and Art: Studies in the Origin and Early Development of an Aesthetic Vocabulary* (Stockholm: Svenska Bokforlaget, 1966).

2. On the discussion stimulated by Koller, see especially, P. Moraux, "La mimesis dans les théories anciennes de la danse, de la musique et de la poésie," *Les Etudes Classiques* 23 (1955: 3–13); J. Tate, "Mimesis, a Review of Koller's *Mimesis, Classical Review* n.s. (1955):258–260; Albin Lesky, "A Review of Koller's *Mimesis,*" *Gymnasium* (1956):442–444; W. J. Verdenius, "A Review of Koller's *Mimesis,*" *Mnemosyne,* ser. 4 (1957):254–258; T. G. Rosenmeyer, "A Review of Koller's *Mimesis,*" *Erasmus, Speculum Scientarium* 10 (1957):293–296; H. Schreckenberg, *Drama: Vom Werden der griechischen Tragödie aus dem Tanz* (Würzburg: K. Tviltsch, 1960).

3. Mimesis phonais kai schemasin.

4. See Koller, *Mimesis in der Antike,* 25.

5. Else, "Imitation," 79.

6. See Sörbom, *Mimesis and Art,* 19–21. If Else's distinction between types 1 and

2 means that the development runs from the imitation of concrete persons and phenomena to the imitation of general characteristics, then a reading of the relevant passages makes this interpretation seem doubtful. If, however, this is not what is meant, then the sense of the distinction is questionable. The third type is also vulnerable to objection. For *mimeisthai*—and not only *mimema* (the result of mimesis)—is used in reference to material things. *Mimema* is also used in the sense of the shadings of meanings in the first two categories.

7. See on this point, Sörbom's *Mimesis and Art,* in particular, pp. 41ff., in which the following passages are discussed:

Aeschylus: P Oxy. 2162.

Aeschylus: Frag. 57 Nauck.

Homeric hymn to the Delian Apollo 156–164.

Pindar: Pythian ode, XII, 18–21.

Pindar: Parthenia, II, 16–20.

Pindar: Frag. 107a Snell.

Herodotus: 2.78.

Herodotus: 2.86.

Herodotus: 2.132.

Herodotus: 2.169.

Herodotus: 3.37.

Euripides: Iphigeneia in Aulis 573–578.

Euripides: Ion 1429.

Democritus: Frag. Diels 154.

Aristophanes: Clouds 559.

Aristophanes: Plutus 290–291.

Aristophanes: Thesmophorizusae 850.

Aristophanes: Wasps 1017–1020.

Aristophanes: Thesmophorizusae 146–172

8. See Xenophon, *Memorabilia III,* 10.1-8. The exact dating of the *Memorabilia* is disputed. It is roughly contemporaneous with Plato's works.

9. See Sörbom, *Mimesis and Art,* 97.

Chapter 3. Imitation, Illusion, Image (Plato)

1. See Christoph Wulf, "Mimesis und Ästhetik: Zur Enstehung der Ästhetik bei Platon und Aristoteles," in G. Treusch-Dieter et al., eds., *Denkzettel Antike* (Berlin: Reimer, 1989).

2. On this classification, see Ulrike Zimbrich, *Mimesis bei Platon* (Frankfurt: P. Lang, 1984), 75.

3. Plato *Laws* 817B.

4. Plato *Timaeus* 39D–E, 48E, 50C.

5. Ibid., 37D–38A.

6. Ibid., 19D–E.

7. Ibid., 28A–29D.

8. Plato *Crito* 107B–D; see also *Laws* 897D–E.

9. Stephen Halliwell, in his study of Aristotle's poetics on the basis of Plato's use of the concept of mimesis, attempted the following systematization; *Aristotle's Poetics* (London: Ducksworth, 1986), 121.

a. Linguistic: Language reflects the essence of things.

b. Philosophical: The philosopher's thought aspires to provide a copy of truth—the mimesis of an eternal model.

c. Cosmic: The material world may in various ways stand in a mimetic relation to eternal models.

d. Visual: The painter's mimesis pictures the appearances of things.

e. Mimicry: The voice and the body can be used to reproduce certain properties of the animal and natural world.

f. Behavioral: Ordinary imitation or emulation.

g. Impersonatory: The (nonartistic) acting out of a role (but see [h] below).

h. Poetic: Apart from unspecified references to poetic mimesis, Plato usually treats poetry either as an art of verbal image-making, comparable to the painter's, or (in some of its forms) as a special case of (g) above, i.e., dramatic impersonation.

i. Musical: Musical modes and structures can give expression to certain human actions and experiences. (It is sometimes impossible to disentangle music from poetry in Plato's references to *mousikê*.)

j. Choreographic: Dancers can act out representations of human life.

10. Plato *Republic* 393C.

11. Ibid., 394C–D.

12. On this point, see Gerard Genette, *Figures III* (Paris: Seuil, 1972), esp. 183ff.

13. Plato *Republic* 395B.

14. An insight is formulated here which became the point of departure for socialization theories of the 1960s, 1970s, and 1980s. See, among others, Dieter Geulen, *Das vergesellschaftete Subjekt: Zur Grundlegung der Sozialisationstheorie* (Frankfurt am Main: Suhrkamp, 1977).

15. *E kata phonen e kata schema.*

16. Enigmatic and therefore controversial is the relation of art to the Ideas, to being and to the world of appearance. For Hart and Zimbrich, the tenth book of the *Republic* offers a consistent development of the thoughts presented in the third book, though appropriately modified, to be sure, following the analogy of the line and the allegory of the cave, as well as the development of the Platonic conception of the soul. Gadamer and Koller see here a sharp critique of poetry, which ends in the exclusion of poetry from the state. Koller, in contrast to other interpretations, emphasizes the singular

character of the critique, which in his judgment does not agree with general linguistic usage. Müller and Grube's critique of Plato culminates in the contention that Plato did not understand the essence of art. Adam finds the basis of this misunderstanding in the reduction of art to the procedures of photography. He stresses the importance of understanding the pedagogical foundations of the critique.

17. See Zimbrich, "Mimesis bei Platon," 270.

18. See Jean-Pierre Vernant, "Naissance d'images," in Vernant, *Religions, histoires, raisons* (Paris: F. Maspero, 1979), 105–137.

19. Plato *Sophist* 265B.

20. Plato *Republic* 373B.

21. Plato *Sophist* 240A–B.

22. Plato *Cratylus* 432D; see also 332B.

23. See Jean-Pierre Vernant, "De la présentification de l'invisible à l'imitation de l'apparence," 347.

24. Ibid., 351.

25. See Christoph Wulf, "Der Körper der Götter," in Dietmar Kamper and Christoph Wulf, eds., *Transfigurationen des Körpers: Spuren der Gewalt in der Geschichte* (Berlin: D. Reimer, 1989), 11–22.

26. Vernant, "De la présentification de l'invisible à l'imitation de l'apparence," 351.

27. Vernant, "Naissance d'images," 112.

28. Plato *Sophist* 235E–236C.

29. Ibid., 266C.

30. Plato *Cratylus* 123D–E, 431D.

31. Quoted in Vernant, "Naissance d'images," 117.

32. See Gernot Böhme, *Der Typ Sokrates* (Frankfurt am Main: Suhrkamp, 1988).

33. Vernant, "Naissance d'images," 137.

Chapter 4. The Break in the History of Mimesis

1. The following relies essentially on Havelock's *Preface to Plato*. Jacques Derrida came to similar conclusions in reference to the transformation of thought under the influence of writing in his essay "Plato's Pharmacy," in *Dissemination,* trans. Barbara Johnson (Chicago: University of Chicago Press, 1981), 173–286, originally published in 1968. See chapter 23, below.

2. Milman Parry developed his research hypotheses in his doctoral dissertation at the Sorbonne, "*L'Épithète traditionelle dans Homère*" (1928); in English, "The Making of Homeric Verse," in *The Collected Papers of Milman Parry,* ed. A. Parry (Oxford: Clarendon Press, 1971). See also Lord, *Singer of Tales.* Walter J. Ong provides a good overview in *Orality and Literacy: The Technologizing of the Word* (London: Routledge, 1982).

3. See the overview of this issue by Harald Haarmann, *Universalgeschichte der Schrift* (Frankfurt: Campus, 1990). Greek writing has its origin in Semitic consonant alphabets. These are the result of a long maturation process in the techniques of writing (268) and "the borrowing of foreign cultural models" (278), systems of consonant writing, the organizational principle of which is based on the phonographic method

of writing individual sounds'' (280). In accord with more recent discoveries, Haarmann regards as certain ''that the alphabet is more likely to have been taken over by the Cretans than by the Aramaeans and that the representation of historical diffusion should begin with the relations between the Celts and the Greeks'' (282). The Greeks obtained an alphabet via direct phonetic mediation (282). ''In the adaptation to Greek of a system of writing created for a foreign Semitic language, an Indo-Germanic language, there came into being in a unique developmental leap the world's first complete alphabet'' (282). The Greek alphabet, in addition to a few other improvements, took into consideration the writing of vowels.

4. Haarmann states that the ''classical alphabet'' developed ''only gradually to become the central carrier of ancient Hellenic culture'' (289). Regional alphabetic variants remained in use for centuries. A decisive step in the diffusion of writing is the standardization of the alphabet in the year 403 B.C., geared to the needs of the administrative language and school instruction. On the process of the diffusion of writing, see also Eric A. Havelock, *The Literate Revolution and Its Cultural Consequences* (Princeton: Princeton University Press, 1982).

5. A second case is that of Hesiod, who, working with oral material, nevertheless developed a linguistic organization that depends on alphabetic writing (Havelock, *Preface to Plato,* 129 n. 7). The third case is that of the pre-Socratic philosophers; the oral form is particularly recognizable in Heraclitus.

6. See Jack Goody, *Literacy in Traditional Societies* (Cambridge: Cambridge University Press, 1868); *The Domestication of the Savage Mind* (Cambridge: Cambridge University Press, 1977); *The Logic of Writing and the Organization of Society* (Cambridge: Cambridge University Press, 1986); *The Interface Between the Written and the Oral* (Cambridge: Cambridge University Press, 1987). See also Alaida Assmann and Jan Assmann, *Schrift und Gedächtnis* (Munich: W. Fink, 1983); Walter J. Ong, *Rhetoric, Romance, and Technology* (Ithaca: Cornell University Press, 1971) and *Interfaces of the Word* (Ithaca: Cornell University Press, 1977). An excellent overview is Paul Zumthor, *Oral Poetry: An Introduction,* trans. Kathryn Murphy-Judy (Minneapolis: University of Minnesota Press, 1990).

7. The discovery of this problem led Ludwig Wittgenstein to the conception of language games.

8. See Marcel Jousse, *L'Anthropologie du geste* (Paris: Gallimard, 1974–1978), 3 vols., which offers a detailed examination of the relations between rhythmic-gestural physical movements and language.

9. See Havelock, *Preface to Plato.* The performance is a form of ''doing'' in which the body becomes a kind of rhythmical instrument. Through movements, the singer confirms the memory of the model he is following (150). The dancing movement of the reciter in Havelock's interpretation fulfills the conditions required for remembering the song. The audience actively participates in the performance (78). In this way there arises ''a sort of drama of rhythmic doings in which all shared'' (167).

10. Ibid., 75.

11. Ibid., 76.

12. Ong, *Orality and Literacy,* 37–57.

13. See Lord, *Singer of Tales,* 100. The singer is ''at once tradition and an 'individual creator' '' (4).

14. Lord, *Singer of Tales,* 30: "The formula" is "a group of words which is regularly employed under the same metrical conditions to express a given essential idea"; see also p. 49. When the singer takes up a major theme, he has in mind a plan for ordering all of the elements (92). See, for a contrasting view, the critical extension of the concept of the formula by Goody, in *Interface Between the Written and the Oral,* 89f., 100. On the basis of new research, Zumthor, in *Oral Poetry,* makes the following points. The formulaic style "must be described as a discursive and intertextual strategy, rather than as a transitional type. The formulaic style gradually interpolates rhythmic and verbal fragments into the prevailing discourse and integrates them by giving them a function. These fragments are borrowed from other, already existing texts which belong in principle to the same genre and refer listeners to a semantic universe that is familiar to them" (104). Given the current state of research, Parry's and Lord's definition of the "formula" has been made more flexible: "One insists today not so much on the lexical sequence as on the structuring factors, such as prosody, syntax, and the distribution of key concepts" (105). "In and by means of the formula, epic re-recognition is accomplished over the course of the poem" (107).

15. See Lord, *Singer of Tales,* 5: "What is important is not the oral performance but rather the composition *during* oral performance." "Only in performance can the formula exist" (33).

16. Havelock, *Literate Revolution,* 41.

17. Havelock, *Preface to Plato,* 59. Havelock calls Homeric poetry "a body of instruction" (64). Goody doubts this thesis, see his *Interface Between the Written and the Oral,* 294.

18. Havelock, *Preface to Plato,* 116. He takes this idea from Jean-Pierre Vernant.

19. Havelock, *Preface to Plato,* 93.

20. Ibid., 41.

21. Ibid., 57–58 n. 22.

22. Ibid.

23. Havelock, *Literate Revolution,* 26.

24. Ibid., 22.

25. Plato *Republic* 267A.

26. Havelock, *Preface to Plato,* 261.

27. Ibid., 180.

28. Ibid., 189.

29. Ibid., 140. "Control over the style of a people's speech, however indirect, means control also over their thought." "Plato . . . seems to have been convinced that poetry and the poet had exercised a control not merely over Greek verbal idiom but over the Greek state of mind and consciousness. . . . He describes [this control] as though it were monopolistic" (142).

30. Ibid., 271.

31. Ibid., 305.

32. See the overview of the history of the individual by Jean Pierre-Vernant, "*L'Individu dans la cité,*" in Vernant, *L'Individu, la mort, l'amour: Soi Même et l'autre en Grèce ancienne* (Paris: Gallimard, 1989).

33. One form of this reappearance is the literary "memory" of a postulated original state of oral culture. See Jean-Jacques Rousseau, *On the Origin of Language,* trans. John

H. Moran and Alexander Gode (Chicago: University of Chicago Press, 1966). Rousseau's theory of language, which Derrida rediscovers in *Of Grammatology,* trans. Gayatri Chakavorty Spivak (Baltimore: Johns Hopkins University Press, 1976), bears the revealing subtitle, "Où il est parlé de la mélodie et de l'imitation musicale."

34. Jesper Svenbro, *Phrasikleia: An Anthropology of Reading in Ancient Greece,* trans. Janet Lloyd (Ithaca: Cornell University Press, 1993).

Chapter 5. Poetic Mimesis (Aristotle)

1. See Sörbom, *Mimesis and Art,* 176; also see J. Walter, *Die Geschichte der Ästhetik im Altertum ihrer begrifflichen Entwicklung nach* (Leipzig: Reisland, 1893), 715; Georg Finsler, *Platon und die Aristotelische Poetik* (Leipzig, 1900), esp. 11–40; J. Bywater, *Aristotle on the Art of Poetry* (Oxford: Oxford University Press, 1909). These authors represent the view that Aristotle took over most of his concept of mimesis from Plato. In contrast, the following authors emphasize the differences between Plato's and Aristotle's concept of mimesis and the independence of Aristotle's thinking: Uberto Galli, *La Mimesi artistica secundo Aristotele: Studi Italiani di filologica classica* (Florence, 1925), 281–390, esp. 373ff.; S. I. H. Butcher, *Aristotle's Theory of Poetry and Fine Art* (London: Macmillan, 1932); K. Gilbert and H. Kuhn, A *History of Esthetics* (New York: Macmillan, 1939).

2. The *Politics of Aristotle,* 269.

3. Ibid., 329.

4. *The Poetics of Aristotle,* 34.

5. See Halliwell, *Aristotle's Poetics.*

6. We choose this latter term for the translation of the Greek word *mythos.*

7. Halliwell, *Aristotle's Poetics,* 68.

8. Ibid., 48.

9. Ibid., 35ff.

10. *Aristotle Physics* 199A/B, 193B.

11. Aristotle further states in the *Metaphysics:* "Art has to do with the production of made things" (1034A).

12. See, in this regard, H. D. Goldstein, "Mimesis and Catharsis Reexamined," *Journal of Aesthetics and Art Criticism* 24 (1965–1966): 567–578, esp. 570.

13. Paul Ricoeur, *Time and Narrative,* trans. Kathleen McLaughlin and David Pellauer, 3 vols. (Chicago: University of Chicago Press, 1984).

14. See Dietmar Kamper and Christoph Wulf, eds., *Die Sterbende Zeit* (Darmstadt: Luchterhand, 1987).

15. Iser, *Act of Reading.*

Chapter 6. Mimesis as Imitatio

1. On this, see Christoph Wulf, "Mimesis," in Gunter Gebauer et al., *Historische Anthropologie* (Reinbek: Rowohlt, 1989), 97ff.

2. See P. E. Schramm, *Herrschaftszeichen und Staatssymbolik: Beitrage zu ihrer Geschichte vom 3. bis 16. Jahrhundert* (Stuttgart: A. Hiersemann, 1954), esp. vol. 2, chap. 25.

3. See M. S. Brownlee, "Autobiography as Self-(re)presentation," in John D.

Lyons and Stephen G. Nichols, Jr., eds., *Mimesis: From Mirror to Method, Augustine to Descartes* (Hanover, N.H.: University Press of New England, 1982), 71–82.

4. See Robert Hollander, "Imitative Distance," in Lyons and Nichols, *Mimesis,* 83–99.

5. See Stephen G. Nichols, Jr., "Romanesque Imitation or Imitating the Romans?" in Lyons and Nichols, *Mimesis,* 36–59.

6. Kurt Flasch, "*Ars imitatur naturam:* Platonischer Naturbegriff und mittelalterliche Philosophie der Kunst," in Flasch, ed., *Parusia, Festgabe für J. Hirschberger* (Frankfurt am Main: Minerva, 1965), 266.

7. Ibid., 270f.

8. Ibid., 275.

9. Ibid., 277.

10. Ibid., 280f.

11. *Supersubstantiale pulchrum.*

12. See Dietmar Kamper and Christoph Wulf, eds., *Der Schein des Schönen* (Göttingen: Steidl, 1989).

13. On this, see Umberto Eco, *The Aesthetics of Thomas Aquinas* (Cambridge: Harvard University Press, 1988), 83–101. We also base our further discussion of the theory of art in Thomas Aquinas on Eco.

14. Ibid., 104.

15. *Conveniens est sacrae scripturae divina et spriritualia sub similitudinae corporalium tradere.* Quoted in Eco, *Aesthetics of Thomas Aquinas,* 150.

16. "*fictiones poeticae non sunt ad aliud ordinatae nisi ad significandum.*" Quoted in Eco, *Aesthetics of Thomas Aquinas,* 152.

17. *Recta ratio factibilium.* Thomas Aquinas, *Summa Theologica* I-III, 57, 4c.

18. Ibid., 117, *Obj.* 4.

19. Thomas Aquinas, *Truth* III, I, 7[SA].

20. Ibid., III, V, Reply.

21. *Ex speciebus primo conceptis alias formare possunt,* in Aquinas, *Summa* I, 12, 9, *Reply Obj.* 2.

22. Ernst H. Kantorowicz, *The King's Two Bodies: A Study in Medieval Political Theology* (Princeton: Princeton University Press, 1957).

23. Ibid., 47.

24. *Monumenta Germaniae Historica, Libelli de Lite,* III, 667, 35ff.; quoted in Kantorowicz, *King's Two Bodies,* 48.

25. Kantorowicz, *King's Two Bodies,* 97.

26. *Pater et filius justiciae.*

27. Kantorowicz, *King's Two Bodies,* 141.

28. *Lex animata.*

29. Kantorowicz, *King's Two Bodies,* 141.

30. Ibid., 143.

31. *Rex infra et supra legem.*

32. *Nihil enim aliud potest rex, cum sit Dei minister et vicarius in terris, nisi id solum, quod de jure potest;* quoted in Kantorowicz, *King's Two Bodies,* 155 n. 201.

33. Kantorowicz, *King's Two Bodies,* 180.

34. Ibid., 189.

35. Ibid., 192.
36. Ibid., 194.
37. Ibid., 197.
38. "Item, sicut membra coniunguntur in humano corpore carnaliter, et homines spirituali corpori spiritualiter coniunguntur, cui corpori Christus est caput . . . , sic moraliter et politice homines coniunguntur reipublicae quae corpus est: cuius caput est princeps." Lucas de Penna, quoted in Kantorowicz, *King's Two Bodies*, 216 n. 67.
39. Kantorowicz, *King's Two Bodies*, 223.
40. Ibid., 272.

Chapter 7. Poetics and Power
in the Renaissance

1. On this, see Hippolyte Rigault *Histoire de la Querelle des Anciens et des Modernes* (Paris: Hachette, 1856); Hubert Gillot, *La querelle des Anciens et des Modernes en France* (Geneva: Slatkine Reprints 1968); Hans Robert Jauss, "Ästhetische Normen und geschichtliche Reflexion in der 'Querelle des Anciens et des Modernes,'" in Charles Perrault, ed., *Parallèle des Anciens et des Modernes* (Munich: Eidos Verlag, 1964).

2. In *Europäische Literatur und lateinisches Mittelalter* (Bern: Francke, 1954), E. R. Curtius describes it as "a constant phenomenon in the history and sociology of literature" (256), which is also supposed to have existed in Arab literature. The following treatment of this context relies primarily on A. Buck, "Aus der Vorgeschichte der Querelle des Anciens et des Modernes," in *Bibliothèque de l'Humanisme et de la Renaissance* 20 (Geneva, 1958).

3. "Ut . . . nostris temporibus videatur antiquitas decentius innovata." *Variae* 4, 51; Migne P.L. 69, col. 644C.

4. See Heiric d'Auxerre, M. G., *Poetae latini aevi Carolini III,* ed. L. Traube (1896) 429, 23; see also Curtius, *Europäische Literatur,* 38; and Heinrich von St. Gallen, *Gesta Caroli,* I, 2; M. G., *Hist. Script.,* II, 731.

5. "Quare sicut nec illi [the ancients] omnia dixerunt, ita nec isti [the moderns] omnia tacere debent. Adelard of Bath, *Traktat: De codem et de diverso,* dedicatory texts, ed. H. Willner (Münster, 1903), 3 Beiträge zur Geschichte der Philosophie des Mittelalters, IV, 1.

6. *Joannis Saresberiensis episcopi Carnolensis Metalogicon libri III,* ed. CC. I. Webb (Oxonii, 1929), Prologue, 3f.

7. *De nugis curialium. Quinta Distinctio,* Prologus, ed. M. R. James (Oxford, 1914), 203.

8. See Giuseppe Toffanin, *Il secolo senza Roma* (Bologna: N. Zanichelli, 1943).

9. See Benjamin Nelson, "Die Anfänge der modernen Revolution in Wissenschaft und Philosophie: Fiktionalismus, Probabilismus, Fideismus und Katolisches Prophetentum," in Nelson, *Der Ursprung der Moderne* (Frankfurt am Main: Suhrkamp, 1977), 94–139.

10. See, among others, Peter von Blois Migne P.L. 207 313; Hugo v. St. Viktor, *Didascalion,* Migne P.L. 176, 739–809; Henri d'Andeli, ed., *The Battle of the Seven Arts: A French Poem,* trans. L. J. Pactow (Berkeley: University of California Press, 1914).

11. See, in this regard, P. O. Kristeller, "The Modern System of the Arts: A Study in the History of Aesthetics," *Journal of the History of Ideas* (October 1951): 510ff.

12. John D. Lyons and Stephen G. Nichols, Jr., eds., *Mimesis: From Mirror to Method, Augustine to Descartes* (Hanover, N.H.: University Press of New England, 1982).

13. Cf. Kristeller, *Modern System of the Arts*, 511ff., esp. the comprehensive references to further information.

14. See the extremely rich materials considered in the investigation by Bernard Weinberg, *A History of Literary Criticism in the Italian Renaissance* (Chicago: University of Chicago Press, 1961).

15. "Non inventori, ma trombetti e recitatori delle altrui opere," in Leonardo, *Uomo sanza lettere: Scritti con introduzione e commento di G. Fumagalli* (Florence, 1938), 39; quoted from Buck, "Aus der Vorgeschichte der Querelle," 534.

16. "La veritá fu sola figliola del tempo," in Leonardo, *Uomo sanza lettere,* 324. The statement can be traced back to the *Noctes Atticae* of Aulus Gellius, XII, 11, 7: "Alius quidam veterum poetarum, cuius nomen mihi nunc memoriae non est, veritatem temporis filiam esse dixet." Here the saying means that time brings the truth to light, so that it becomes possible to distinguish between the guilty and the innocent and thus arrive at a just verdict.

17. See Herbert Dieckmann, "Die Wandlung des Nachahmungsbegriffes in der französischen Ästhetik des 18. Jahrhunderts," in H. R. Jauss, ed., *Nachahmung und Illusion* (Munich: W. Fink, 1969), 28–59.

18. "Differunt autem, quod alterius fides certa veru et profitetur et prodit, simpliciore filo texens orationem: altera aut addit ficta veris, aut fictis vera imitatur, maiore sane apparatu. . . . Hic enim finis est medius ad illum ultimum, qui est docendi cum delectatione. Nanquet Poeta etiam docet, non solum delectat ut quidam arbitrabantur." In J. C. Scaliger, *Poetices libri septem, Faksimile. Neudrück der Ausgabe von Lyon 1561 mit einer Einleitüng von A. Buck* (Stuttgart: F. Frommann, 1964), 1.

19. Weinberg, *History of Literary Criticism,* 2:819ff.

20. See, among others, Francesco Patrizi, *Della poetica: La deca disputata* (Ferrara: V. Baldini, 1586); six dimensions of the Aristotelian concept of mimesis are distinguished here, but so imprecisely that they are scarcely worthy of further consideration.

21. See Weinberg, *History of Literary Criticism,* 2:801.

22. On the present-day discussion of the concept of style, see Gumbrecht and Pfeiffer, *Stil.*

23. See Weinberg, *History of Literary Criticism,* 2:819ff.

24. "Nos, quasi nani super gigantium humeros sumus, quorum beneficio longius, quam ipsi speculamur, dum antiquorum tractatibus inhaerentes elegantiores corum sententias, quas vetustas oboleverat, hominumque neglectus, quasi iam mortuas in quadam novitatem essentiae suscitamus." In Peter von Blois, *Epist.* 92, Migne P.L. 207, col. 290.

25. Alexander Neckam, *De naturis rerum* I, 78, ed. T. Wright (London: Longman, 1863), 123. "Et, ut ait philosophus, nos sumus quasi nani stantes super humeros gigantium. Praeclecessoribus itaque nostri ascribere ea quae in gloriam laudis nostrae nonnunquam transferre audemus, similes parrae quae levi labrare, immonullo, ouiaquam vicisse protestata est."

26. "Que nous sommes comme l'enfant qui est sur le col du géant: c'est-á-dire que leurs escrits nous voyons ce qu'ils ont vu, et pouvons encore voire et entendre davantage." Quoted in Buck, "Aus der Vorgeschichte der Querelle," 539.

27. Luis Vives, *Satellitia* 90, Opera Basileae 1555, II, 102: "Falsa est enim atque inepta illa quorundam similtudo, quam multi tanquam acutissimam, atque appositissimam excipuint, nos ad priores collatos esse, ut nanos in humeris gigantum: non est ita, neque nos sumus nani, nec illi homines gigantes, sed omnes eiusdem staturae, et quidem nos altius euecti illorum beneficio: maneat modo in nobis, quod in illis studium, allentio animi, uigilantia, et amor ueri: quae si absint, iam non nani sumus, nec in gigantium humeris sedemus, sed homines iustae magnitudinis humi prostrati."

28. See Pigray (see n. 26, above); Pascal, "Préface pour le traité du vide"; Newton, letter to Robert Haak.

29. On the context as a whole, see F. E. Guyer, "The Dwarf on the Giant's Shoulders," *Modern Language Notes* 45 (1930): 398–402; G. Sarton, "Standing on the Shoulders of Giants," *Isis* 24 (1935): 107–109; R. Klibansky, "Standing on the Shoulders of Giants," *Isis* 26 (1936): 147–149; J. de Ghellinck, "Nani et gigantes," *Archivium Latinatis medii aevi (Bulletin Du Cange)* 18 (1945): 25–29.

30. See Michel de Montaigne, *Complete Essays,* trans. Donald M. Frame (Stanford: Stanford University Press, 1958), 3:13; quoted in Buck, "Aus der Vorgeschichte der Querelle," 540.

31. See Lucretius, *On the Nature of Things,* Bk. II, 1150–1152; Bk. V, 826–827.

32. "Neque enim quasi vetula mulier, suis est viribus parens effocta natura, ut nostro scilicet hoc sacculo quasi nimio partu lassata defecerit. Nec deus optimus maximus nostrae aetati non est largitus ingenia. . . . Crescunt (ut mea fert opinio) verius quam decrescant ingenia. Multa enim quae ad rerum spectant notitiam, et nostrum sacculum, et huic proxima novere, quae docta illa ignoravit antiquitas." In Le Episole, *De Imitatione* di G. Pico della Mirandola e di Bembo, a cura di G. Santangelo (Florence, 1954), 31.

33. See as well the French humanist Loys Le Roy, who rejects the assertion contained in this image by referring to the power of the Renaissance epoch and thus postulating the superiority of the "moderns." See H. Baron, "The 'Querelle' of the Ancients and the Moderns as a Problem for Renaissance Scholarship," *Journal of the History of Ideas* 20 (1959):3–22.

34. Galileo, quoted from Buck, "Aus der Vorgeschichte der Querelle," 535.

35. G. Bruno, *La cena della ceneri I: Le opere italiane di G. Bruno,* ristampate da P. de Lagarde, I (Gottinga, 1888); quoted in Buck, "Aus der Vorgeschichte der Querelle," 536.

36. Bacon, "Novum organum" I, 84, *Opera omnia* (Frankfurt am Main, 1665), 302. Malebranche, "De la recherche de la vérité," livre II, IIe partie, chap. III, *Oeuvres complètes,* éd. crit. de D. Roustan en collaboration avec P. Schrecker (Paris, 1938), 284ff.

37. See Hans Blumenberg, *Lebenszeit und Weltzeit* (Frankfurt am Main: Suhrkamp, 1986), esp. chap. 7, "Die Wahrheit—Tochter der Zeit?" 153ff.

38. Luiz Costa Lima, "Die Kontrolle des Imaginären," in Gumbrecht and Pfeiffer, *Stil,* 16.

39. Ibid., 17.

40. Ibid., 21f.
41. Ibid., 24.
42. Ibid., 23.
43. Ibid., 33.
44. Ibid., 34. Emphasis in original.
45. Ibid., 35.
46. Ibid., 49f.
47. Marc Fumaroli, quoted in Costa Lima, "Die Kontrolle des Imaginären," 35.
48. Costa Lima, "Die Kontrolle des Imaginären," 36.
49. Ibid., 43.

Chapter 8. Intertextuality, Fragmentation, Desire

1. Thomas M. Green, "Erasmus's 'Festina lente': Vulnerabilities of the Humanist Text," in Lyons and Nichols, *Mimesis,* 132–148.

2. See Marc Fumaroli, *L'Âge de l'éloquence: Rhétorique et "res literaria" de la Renaissance au Secs fuil de l'époque classique* (Geneva, 1980), 81ff.; and especially Antoine Compagnon, *La seconde de main, où le travail de la citation* (Paris: Seuil, 1979), 235–327.

3. See J. D. Cave, "The Mimesis of Reading in the Renaissance," in Lyons and Nichols, *Mimesis,* esp. 157; see also L. Perpile, "Paper and Ink! The Structure of Unpredictability," in *"O, un Amy!" Essays on Montaigne in Honor of Donald M. Frame,* ed. Raymond C. La Charité (Lexington: French Forum, 1977), 190–218; and M. B. McKinley, *Words in a Corner: Studies in Montaigne's Latin Quotations* (Lexington: French Forum, 1981).

4. Montaigne, *Complete Essays,* 219.

5. Ibid., 537.

6. Jean Starobinski, *Montaigne in Motion,* trans. Arthur Goldhammer (Chicago: University of Chicago Press, 1985), 223.

7. Auerbach, *Mimesis,* 289.

8. Montaigne, *Complete Essays,* 244.

9. Starobinski, *Montaigne in Motion,* 226.

10. Auerbach, *Mimesis,* 291.

11. See John Doebler, *Shakespeare's Speaking Pictures: Studies in Iconic Imagery* (Albuquerque: University of New Mexico Press, 1974). This investigation uses a few Shakespeare plays as examples to explicate their Renaissance iconography. Key scenes are thereby cast in a new light; a specific symbolism of specific scenic arrangements and gestures becomes understandable; their mimetic character becomes clear.

12. Weimann, *Shakespeare,* 17.

13. David Scott Kastan has pointed out that Hamlet breaks with the tradition of revenge. What happens in the play is not a repetition of the *Ur-Hamlet* but a fresh imagining of Hamlet; it results in a humane, if not even humanistic, "act of imitation" (David Scott Kastan, "'His semblable is his mirror': Hamlet and the Imitation of Revenge,") *Shakespeare Studies* 19 (1987): 111–124.

14. Weimann, *Shakespeare,* 244.

15. Ibid., 247.

16. See Dietmar Kamper and Christoph Wulf, eds., *Lachen—Gelächter—Lächeln: Reflexionen in drei Spiegeln* (Frankfurt am Main: Syndikat, 1986).

17. Weimann, *Shakespeare,* 252.

18. J. W. von Goethe, "Zum Shakespeare-Tag (1771)," in *Werke,* Jubiläumsausgabe, vol. 36 (Stuttgart, 1902–1912), 6.

19. Weimann, *Shakespeare,* 290.

20. Ibid., 320.

21. Ibid.

22. Cf. René Girard, *A Theater of Envy: William Shakespeare* (New York: Oxford University Press, 1991). For a critical discussion of this theory of mimesis, see chapter 20, below.

23. Ibid., 17.

Chapter 9. The Conflict Over History

1. Thus Du Bellay in *La Défence et illustration de la langue française:* "Le tens viendra (peut-estre), . . . et je l'espère moyennant la bonne destinée Françoyse, que ce noble et puyssant Royaume obtiendra à son tour les resnes de la monarchie, et que nostre Langue . . . qui commence encore à jeter ses racines, sortira de terre, et s'élevera en telle hauteur et grosseur qu'elle se pourra égaler aux mesmes Grecz et Romains, produysant comme eux des Homères, Demosthènes, Virgiles et Cicérons, aussi bien que la France a quelques fois produit des Périclès, Nicies, Alcibaides, Themistocles, Césars et Scipions" (quoted from Gillot, *La Querelle,* 105).

2. Du Bellay at the end of *La Défence;* see also the epistle "Au Peuple François" at the beginning of the French edition of *L'Histoire* by Paul Aemile, "De rebus gestis Francorum libri IV Parisiis" (1500), trans. Jean Regnar (Paris, 1581).

3. Gillot recognized this when he wrote, "Une imitation scrupuleuse de l'Antique, non point cette imitation qui consiste à retrouver l'âme de l'Antiquité, mais une imitation superficielle et pédantesque qui borne ses efforts à reproduire les procédés des maîtres, non point l'imitation qui recrée, mais l'imitation qui copie, partant, l'abus de la règle et la manie du précepte" (Gillot, *La Querelle,* 105).

4. Roger de Piles, *Dialogue sur le coloris* (Paris: Chez Nicolas Langlois, 1688).

5. Nor were music and architecture excepted from these disputes. See François Blondel, *Cours d'architecture* (Paris, 1683); Claude Perrault, "De la musique des anciens," in *Essai de Physique,* vol. 2 (Paris, 1680–1688); Roland Fréart de Chambray, *Parallèle de l'architecture antique et de la moderne* (Paris, 1650); H. Jouin, *Conférences de l'Académie Royale de peinture et de sculpture* (Paris, 1883).

6. La belle antiquité fut toujours vénérable; / Mais je ne crus jamais qu'elle fut adorable. / Je vois les anciens, sans plier les genoux; / Ils sont grands, il est vrai, mais hommes comme nous. / Et l'on peut comparer, sans craindre d'être injuste, / La siècle de Louis au beau siècle d'Auguste.

7. See Auerbach, *Mimesis,* 371ff.

8. Ibid., 381f.

9. Ibid., 377.

10. Ibid.

11. Ibid., 387.

12. Ibid., 389.

13. See the chapter "De la Mode" in Jean de La Bruyère's *Caractères*.

14. See "The Faux Devot," in Auerbach, *Mimesis,* 359ff.

15. Etudiez la Cour, et connoissez la Ville; / L'une et l'autre est toûjours en modeles fertile. / C'est par là que Molière, illustrant ses écrits. / Peut-estre de son Art eus remporté le prix; / Si moins ami du peuple, en ses doctes peintures, / Il n'eus point fait souvent grimacer ses figures, / Quitté, pour le bouffon, l'agreable et le fin, / Et sans honte à Terence allié Tabarin. / Dans ce sac ridicule, où Scapin s'enveloppe, / Je ne reconnois plus l'auteur du Misanthrope. / Le Comique, ennemi des soupirs et des pleurs, / N'admet point en ses vers de tragiques douleurs: / Mais son employ n'est pas d'aller dans une place, / De mots sales et bas charmer la populace. / Il faut que ses Acteurs badinent noblement (Nicolas Boileau Despréaux, *Epîtres-art poétique-Lutrin* [Paris: Société les Belles Lettres, 1952], 108).

16. See Auerbach, *Mimesis,* 368.

17. See Jean-Baptiste Molière, "The Bourgeois Gentleman," in *Eight Plays by Molière* (Mattituck, N.Y.: Aeonian Press, 1957).

18. See Gadamer, *Truth and Method.*

19. See Hans-Georg Gadamer and Gottfried Böhm, *Seminar: Hermeneutik und die Wissenschaften* (Frankfurt am Main: Suhrkamp, 1978).

20. Perrault, first dialogue.

Chapter 10. Mimesis as the Self-Representation of Political Power

1. See the essay by Timothy Reiss, "Power, Poetry, and the Resemblance of Nature," in Lyons and Nichols, *Mimesis,* 215–247. The political theory and literature of absolutism, acting together, produce a concept of representation that itself rests on a concept of universal reason and nature and that is essential to the reordering of political power (215). The new concept of representation objectifies the subject by depicting its ability to create order as a general faculty of the vernacular language at the disposal of the linguistic community. "The relation of private to public will take on a variety of names: that of 'taste' in the area of aesthetics, of 'contract' in that of political and economic theory" (218). Language correctly used corresponds through its grammar to the universal, rational order of methodical common sense; the latter, in turn, corresponds to the natural order (224). The dominant understanding beginning in the middle of the seventeenth century is "that the syntax of a properly ordered language . . . automatically provides us with an analysis of the order of reason *and* the order of the material world" (225). Literature, in that it functions as nature does, manifests to the reader the order of things and nature (237).

2. What is unique in the concept of representation in French absolutism lies in the unified symbolic order constructed for all areas of public concern. A theatricalization of political life characterizes the seventeenth century in general, especially in Spain and England. "The dominant and characteristic metaphor of the baroque age can be everywhere identified by the topos of the *theatrum mundi,* of the *theatrum vitae humane.* Here the 'theater' and the 'world,' which is to say, 'human life,' appear as two

magnitudes which are in principle referred to each other and which can only be characterized and understood in their reciprocal reference in terms of the metaphor'' (Erika Fischer-Lichte, *Semiotik des Theaters: Eine Einführung* 2:11). [Tübingen: Gunter Narr, 1983], The representation of politics via the metaphors of theater is also among the essential characteristics of Shakespeare's dramatic work. Inversely, he regards the stage as a model of the universe that is to be subjected to rational control (see Stephen Orgel, *The Illusion of Power: Political Theater in the English Renaissance* [Berkeley, Los Angeles, and London: University of California Press, 1975] 26). Elizabeth and James I openly state the theatrical character of the rulers. They thus lend emphasis to the point that rulers, like actors, occupy center stage, that they represent, that they have a highly developed consciousness of their appearance, and that they have need of applause (T. Neumann). Reference must be made in this context to the theatrical masques at the English and French courts, which put the monarch at the center of everyone's attention.

3. See Kantorowicz, *King's Two Bodies.*

4. See Louis Marin, *Portrait of the King,* trans. Martha M. Houle (Minneapolis: University of Minnesota Press, 1988). This comprehensive analysis of the concept of representation under Louis XIV is the basis of our further discussion.

5. Plots are thus not immediately given in history writing but are first produced by means of an extensive symbolic apparatus. From this perspective, we see that there was in Louis's court a high degree of consciousness of the symbolically constructed character of plots. The conception present in modern language analysis of the linguistic impregnation of plots finds here an early political pendant.

6. See Norbert Elias's studies of the ceremonial at Versailles, the procedures of which Louis XIV, responsible in part for their invention, strictly observed; in *Court Society.*

7. Marin, *Portrait of the King,* 74.

8. Ibid., 83.

9. Ibid., 78ff.

10. Ibid., 80.

11. Ibid., 86.

12. Ibid., 87f.

13. Ibid., 195f.

14. Ibid., 197.

15. See the Jansenist-inspired critique of the concept of representation in Madame de Lafayette. Another critique, likewise influenced by Port-Royal, comes from Pascal: images, although they can contribute to genuine knowledge, betray in their figurative aspect a dangerous side. The figurative conceals something secret; it provokes interpretation, while the secret of the king's portrait is that it is empty: "The absolute monarch is an empty monument, a cenotaph, a tomb that shelters no body but that is royal body in its very vacuity" (Marin, *Portrait of the King,* 238 discussing Pascal's *Trois discours*). Pascal's insight into the simulation and imagination of the king's portrait is not meant to depreciate the monarchy, but it does allow him to recognize that precisely what the common people regard as the cause of absolutist representation is in fact its effect: the effect of representation is the assumption that the king is better born and possesses qualities that excel those of others; this presumed possession is regarded

as the cause of the king holding power. The advantage over which the king disposes is the effect of an institution, of power, and of belief. As institutionalized imagination, it has the same effect it would if it were real.

16. George Steiner, *The Death of Tragedy* (New York: Alfred A. Knopf, 1961), 53.

17. Auerbach, *Mimesis,* 370.

18. "All classic art strives," as Steiner remarks in *The Death of Tragedy,* "for [the] ideal of impersonality, for the severance of the work from the contingency of the artist" (139).

19. Auerbach, *Mimesis,* 382.

20. On the history of the rules of the unity of plot, place, and time, see René Bray, *La Formation de la doctrine classique en France* (Paris: Nizet, 1931). Aristotelianism in France at the beginning of the seventeenth century, represented in particular by Chapelain, Scudéry, and de la Mesnadièr, undertakes a determined codification of art. Aristotelianism and rationalism are postulated as coterminous; Aristotle is regarded as the interpreter of universal reason in matters of literature (59). The demand for the imitation of nature in literature expresses a striving toward "the conformity of the artwork with a model, which is customarily designated nature" (143). But the imitation of nature is joined early on in France with the demand that art should improve on the individual and embellish the model. Corneille does indeed express his respect for Aristotle, but he defends, in the name of progress, his own point of view (in the foreword to *Agésilas*). Saint-Evremond represents the same view; on this issue, see the *Querelle des Anciens et des Modernes.* In the course of the discussion, according to Bray, the unity of plot acquires meaning as the heart of the conception of theater in the *doctrine classique.* According to Manfred Fuhrmann, contemporary writers did not reflect on the reasons for the Aristotelian postulate of plot unity. They took it over "much more in the form given it by Italian commentators and French critics: as the settled dogma of the three unities" (*Einführung in die antike Dichtungstheorie* [Darmstadt, 1973], 247).

21. See Corneille's remark in the *Trois discours:* "It is necessary to observe the unity of plot, of place, and of time—no one doubts that; but it is no small matter to know what the unity of plot is and the extent to which it is possible to stretch the unity of time and place." Pierre Corneille, *Trois discours sur le poeme dramatique* (Paris: Société d'edition d'Enseignement Superieur, 1982).

22. On the development of the peep show theater and the loge theater, see Fischer-Lichte, *Semiotik des Theaters,* 2:69ff.

23. This theatrical perspective is, for one thing, a symbolic form (Panofsky); for another, it is the expression of the new physics of Descartes. Descartes fundamentally changed the concept of physical space by making it mathematical. From now on nature is represented in the three dimensions of geometry. "Nature is geometrical, and everything that happens in nature happens through figures and movements" (Fontenelle, quoted in Jean Ehrard, *L'Idée de nature en France à l'aube des lumières* [Paris: Flammarion, 1970], 46). Nature becomes a "spectacle" that corrupts through "the economy of devices." The "enormous multiplicity of effects that we see in the universe is referred back to a simple matter of mechanics" (Ehrard, *L'Idée de nature,* 47f).

24. See Fischer-Lichte, *Semiotik des Theaters,* 2:70: The place reserved for the prince was initially in front in the pit; then it was "shifted to the rear wall of the first loge and decorated especially splendidly as the counterpart to the stage." It "is possible

in principle to think of only one point in the theater toward which the perspective from the stage should be organized''; this ideal point ''was located at the prince's seat'' (ibid.). ''The prince represented . . . the ideal spectator'' (2:71).

25. On the connection between representation, theater, visibility, and power, see Apostolidès, *Le prince sacrifié*, 33.

26. See Jean-Marie Apostolidès, *Le prince sacrifié: Theatre et Politique au temps de Louis XIV* (Paris: Editions de Minuit, 1985). We rely on this study in what follows.

27. In this way a strict plot logic is created which makes the universal visible; see Fuhrmann, *Einführung in die antike Dichtungstheorie*: ''only that which is coherent and nonaccidental can present something universal and universally valid to the eye; only a course of action in which the phases are locked into each other according to the rules of necessity and probability has 'meaning' and may serve as a model'' (247).

28. Jean Racine, *Andromache, Britannicus, Berenice,* trans. John Cairncross (London: Penguin Books, 1967), 131.

29. In *L'Art poétique,* Boileau identifies the aspect of order in art but remains silent on the question of power. The latter, however, is introduced in a concealed fashion in the term ''bienséances.'' The given order and the bon sens are to dominate the whole of artistic production. Boileau establishes the rules of the fine arts suitable for the royal court and does so after the essential works of French classicism had already been composed (Nerlich). Within the strict confines of bienséances (''L'etroite beinséance veut être gardée,'' III, 122f.), differentiation and diversifications must be borne in mind. Thus does every passion speak a different language (III, 132); the play should be restrained, accomplished, solid, pleasant, and profound (III, 154f.). The poet should surprise the spectator with a thousand inventions; he should embellish, elevate, improve, and enlarge (III, 174f.). Lowly circumstances, in contrast, should never be presented (III, 260).

30. Apostolidès, *Le prince sacrifié,* 17. Here the connection to Girard's theory of violence, to which the author refers explicitly, becomes evident.

31. Ibid., 46.

32. The deployment of violence is represented in the ritual of the end of violence; Roland Barthes draws attention to this in his work on Racine: in Racine's tragedies he recognizes the ''dual function'' as the essential underlying structure (*On Racine,* 36). The fundamental pattern of tragic reversal is symmetry (43); the most important counterparts in the plots of Racine's dramas are symmetrically related to each other. ''Racinian theater is full of doubles, which continually raise division to the level of the play itself'' (37).

33. See Paul Bénichou, *Man and Ethics: Studies in French Classicism,* trans. Elizabeth Hughes (Garden City, N.Y.: Anchor Books, 1971): ''Indeed at the time of Louis XIV, the heroic sublime was in general disrepute, and all the great writers of the period—Racine, Molière, Boileau—were, each in his own way, the witnesses and the artisans of this fall from favor, the outcome of an irresistible evolution'' (116).

34. M. Prigent, *Le héros et l'état dans la tragédie de Pierre Corneille* (Paris: PUF, 1986), 1.

35. Ibid., 351.

36. Ibid., 109.

37. Ibid., 29.

38. Ibid., 366.

39. Ibid., 545.

40. See Bénichou, *Man and Ethics,* 85, 101, 107.

41. See Lucien Goldmann, *The Hidden God: A Study of the Tragic Vision in the Penseés of Pascal and the Tragedies of Racine,* trans. Philip Thody (London: Routledge & Kegan Paul, 1964). In his tragedies Racine "was presenting the world with a universe where true greatness could be found only in a refusal of the world" (327). "Faced with the absolute purity of tragic man . . . the world which did not satisfy his ethical demands became a purely negative reality" (349).

42. See Benichou, *Man and Ethics:* "Racine shattered this tradition by introducing into tragedy a violent and murderous love, opposed in every respect to courtly custom" (143). The "brutal and possessive passion" is "powerless to find . . . its equilibrium. That is the main link between Racine's psychology and the inhuman views of Port-Royal" (146).

43. Ibid., 161.

44. Ibid., 165.

45. Roland Barthes, *On Racine,* trans. Richard Howard (New York: Hill and Wang, 1964). Racine's oeuvre is essentially paradoxical. It is the "sign of a story and at the same time resistance against this story" (123).

46. With *Nicomède,* Corneille intervenes directly, as Bénichou surmises, in the confrontation between the king and the Fronde (in *Man and Ethics,* 65f.).

47. M. Nerlich, "Essay über die Einheit des Ortes und Molière," *Lendimains* 22 (1981): 54.

48. Ibid.

49. Ibid.

50. Nerlich speaks of "Corneille's spatial survey of Paris" (ibid.).

51. Quoted by Nerlich, in "Difesa del Seicento: Note Sulla commedia francese dell'età 'classica,'" *Sigma* 12, nos. 2–3 (1979): 163–197. Taken here from Corneille, *Oeuvres complètes,* ed. G. Couton (Paris 1980, 1984), 2:551.

52. See note 28, above.

53. Nerlich, "Difesa del Seicento," 184.

54. Ibid., 190.

55. M. Nerlich, "Notizen zum politischen Theater von Molière," *Lendemains* 22 (1981): 37. Nerlich's interpretation cited here offers good arguments against the usual view, supported, for example, by Bénichou and Apostolidès, that Molière's bourgeois characters appear only as comic types.

56. Ibid., 41.

57. Ibid., 56.

58. Ibid., 59.

59. Molière, *Eight Plays by Molière* (Mattituck, N.Y.: Aeonian Press, 1957), 115. H. Stenzel refers to this statement in his essay, "Molière und der Funktionswandel der Komödie im 17. Jahrhundert," *Lendemains* 22 (1981): 67. Stenzel continues as follows:

> The argument by which the superiority of the comedy over the tragedy is justified here thus declares the tragedy a pure product of the imagination, alien to the lived reality of the public. Audiences were more able to find their own sphere of experience reflected in the comedy.

Interesting in this context are the results of an investigation by Karolyn Waterson, which depicts the transmutation of the *valeurs héroiques corneilliennes dans le théâtre de Molière*. In contrast to Corneille's protagonists, whose action is marked by the conflict of abstract values, the characteristics of the comic characters is realized in their confrontation with concrete problems. All of these elements of Molière's conception of comedy already point to essential features of the eighteenth-century *drame bourgeois*.

(67f)

Chapter 11. Against Mimesis as Self-Representation

1. Michel Foucault, *The Order of Things: An Archaeology of the Human Sciences* (New York: Vintage Books, 1970), 61. Foucault provides a detailed analysis of the classical theory of signification (58ff.). According to the Port-Royal theory of signification, the signifying element is conceived as a "signifying idea." It "becomes double, since superimposed upon the idea that is replacing another there is also the idea of its representative power" (64). Port-Royal offers as an example a map or an image. The image represents its contents; thus a portrait represents the person of whom the portrait is made. But the idea of the representative power of the image supplements the contents. It is this that forges the connection, so to speak, between the portrait and the real person.

2. Quotations taken from Madame de Lafayette, *The Princess of Cleves*, trans. Nancy Mitford (Westport, Conn.: Greenwood Press, 1977).

3. In the novel *Zaide* of 1670–1671. *The Princess of Cleves* was the next of Lafayette's works (published in 1678).

4. This idea is presented in detail in John D. Lyons, "Speaking in Pictures, Speaking of Pictures: Problems of Representation in the Seventeenth Century," in Lyons and Nichols, *Mimesis*, 166–187.

5. Ibid., 179.

6. Ibid., 180.

7. Ibid., 184.

8. Ibid., 187.

9. W. Matzat pursues his interpretation of the *Princess of Cleves* in a somewhat different direction. "Not only the power, but also the impotence of signs in classical discourse results from their tie to the discursive practice of the court: their power to mobilize passions in court society corresponds to their impotence to represent emotions independently of the court's discursive practice and thus lend them a certain stability.... All possibility of representing emotions outside the discursive practice of the court is forbidden, and emotional life necessarily atrophies" ("Affektrepräsentation im klassischen Diskurs: *La Princesse de Clèves*," in F. Nies and K. Stierle, eds., *Französische Klassik: Theorie, Literatur, Malerei* (Munich: W. Fink, 1985), 231–266).

10. As it is put at the beginning of the novel, "every form of pleasure was to be found at . . . Court" (4).

11. Foucault, *Order of Things*, 15.

12. *The Princess of Cleves*, 202.

13. Karlheinz Stierle, "Die Modernität der französischen Klassik: Negative Anthropologie und funktionaler Stil," in Nies and Stierle, *Französische Klassik*, 83.

14. Ibid., 87.

15. Ibid., 89.

16. Ibid., 93.

17. Ibid.

18. Ibid., 101.

19. Ibid., 107.

20. Ibid., 108.

21. Ibid., 114.

22. Ibid., 88f.

23. Regarding the vernacular in his discussion of Pascal, Stierle writes, "It is representation that reflects what is represented in the gesturality of the linguistic act" (ibid., 91).

24. Ibid., 98. Stierle is referring to the essay by Jean Starobinski, "La Rochefoucauld et les morales substitutives," *La Nouvelle Revue Française* 14 (1966): 16–34, 211–229.

25. Tzvetan Todorov, *Theories of the Symbol,* trans. Catherine Porter (Ithaca: Cornell University Press, 1982). As a second reason for the disappearance of rhetoric, Todorov offers the rise of empiricism and historical thinking.

26. Ibid., 79.

27. Ibid., 80.

28. Ibid., 111. Todorov accentuates his discussion of the end of rhetoric by quoting Kant's *Critique of Judgment* as follows (ibid., 81):

> I must confess to the pure delight which I have ever been afforded by a beautiful poem; whereas the reading of the best speech of a Roman forensic orator, a modern parliamentary debater, or a preacher, has invariably been mingled with an unpleasant sense of disapproval of an insidious art that knows how, in matters of moment, to move men like machines to a judgement that must lose all its weight with them upon calm reflection. Force and elegance of speech (which together constitute rhetoric) belong to fine art; but oratory (*ars oratoria*), being the art of playing for one's own purpose upon the weaknesses of men (let this purpose be ever so good in intention or even in fact) merits no *respect* whatever. Besides, both at Athens and at Rome, it only attained its greatest height at a time when the state was hastening to its decay, and genuine patriotic sentiment was a thing of the past [I, ii, 53].

29. Svetlana Alpers, *The Art of Describing: Dutch Art in the Seventeenth Century* (Chicago: University of Chicago Press, 1983).

30. This is the thesis of Judovitz, *Subjectivity and Representation in Descartes.*

31. Ibid., 34.

32. Ibid., 38.

33. Ibid., 47.

34. Admittedly, this argument no longer applies as an interpretation of the final certainty to which Descartes arrives, characterizing it with the words, "Je suis, j'existe." Does Descartes refer to an ego that designates itself with this statement according to Judovitz's interpretation? One can alter the accents in the interpretation of this formula by shifting the critical turn of Cartesian philosophy into the center. Thinking substance is supposed to be distinguished as fundamentally indubitable and certainly existing. The formula is not a possible statement of such an abstract construction of a person, but an impersonal res cogitans, which is characterized as subjective, as not belonging to the

object world, by means of the first-person narrative form. This thought does not necessarily require the involvement of literary or rhetorical forms in order to be thought. The narrative of the conversion is nothing more than a didactic aid and—despite all the efforts at "neutralization"—an exploitation of the suggestive effect of the literary medium.

Descartes demonstrates that thinking can never be reduced to nothing. Even in the case of the strongest possible doubt, there always remains a something, a *quelque chose,* leftover. It is a pure substratum of thought, which, "whenever I say it or apprehend [*conçois*] it in my mind, is necessarily true." According to Descartes's presuppositions, the formula requires no linguistic performance, but has an immaterial existence, something like a pure signification, which he imagines as having been freed of verbal symbols. Is it not possible for Descartes, once he has arrived at the final certainty, to discard the device that got him there? This would be like Wittgenstein's ladder: "Anyone who understands me . . . must, so to speak, throw away the ladder after he has climbed up it. . . . He must transcend these propositions, and then he will see the world aright" (*Tractatus,* 6.54).

35. Judovitz, *Subjectivity and Representation in Descartes,* 182.

36. Ibid., 190.

37. Against Judovitz's critique of Descartes, the following argument can be made: The fact that literary forms are constitutive of philosophical discourse in Cartesian texts does not mean that the forms are necessary for the philosophy. The contrary can be maintained only if one takes the "philosophical discourse" to be identical with the "philosophical argument" and the "philosophical construction."

38. Our discussion essentially follows the investigation by Alpers, *The Art of Describing.* This work is controversial, to be sure, but it appears to us quite tenable on the point that interests us, namely, the antimimetic tendencies of Dutch art.

39. Alpers, *The Art of Describing,* xix.

40. Ibid., xxi.

41. Ibid., 27.

42. Ibid., 40.

43. Ibid., 48.

44. Ibid., 136.

45. Ibid., 37.

46. According to a quotation from Kepler in Alpers, *The Art of Describing,* 36. Kepler wrote in Latin.

47. Alpers, *The Art of Describing,* 38, including quotation from Kepler's *Dioptrice* of 1611.

48. Ibid., 37.

49. Ibid., 36.

50. Ibid.

51. Ibid., 39.

Chapter 12. Problems in the Imitation of Nature in the Eighteenth Century

1. See John D. Boyd, *The Function of Mimesis and Its Decline* (New York: Fordham University Press, 1980). Boyd identifies four major developments characterizing the change in the concept of mimesis.

The first of these was the attenuation or thinning out of the concept of imitation. This means that form in the cognitive element was thought of as derived from a very superficial level of nature, and hence could hardly be called the probable. The visible and audible aspects of life drew more critical attention as the fit object of poetic imitation. Secondly, as a result, we find attention drawn to formalistic elements rather than to a viable sense of form. . . . A third tendency was to deny that the arts, especially painting and music, were imitative at all; or if they were so only in a superficial way. This, finally, parallels the fourth tendency, that of thinking of the arts as subjectively oriented, as self-expressive, rather than as imitative, or if still considered imitative, as a kind of transfer of an emotive state from author to audience, rather than as the intelligible structuring of emotion's meaning. . . . Part of this stress comes from the influence of Associationism, and part from such reactions to its mechanical barrenness as the Platonist interest in beauty and sublimity of Shaftesbury and the schools of ''taste'' and ''common sense.''

(98f.)

2. Hilary Putnam, *Reason, Truth and History* (Cambridge: Cambridge University Press, 1981). Putnam discusses these issues in chapter 3, ''Two Philosophical Perspectives,'' 49–74.

3. Ibid., 57.

4. See Ulrich Hohner, *Zur Problematik der Naturnachahmung in der Ästhetik des 18. Jahrhunderts* (Erlangen: Palm & Enke, 1976): ''Interiority as 'evidence of truth' becomes a central category of modern aesthetics; yet, while this truth is of an individual nature in Shaftesbury . . . , it is not the product of the subjective elevation of autonomous imagination over reality'' (134f.). Imagination as the ''organ of the poetic representation of reality'' develops ''the subjective artistic responses to empirically recognized reality''; it is the ''medium of the subjective mastering of these phenomena'' (104–107).

5. Karl Philipp Moritz, *Über die bildende Nachahmung des Schönen* (1788).

6. Putnam, *Reason, Truth and History,* 61.

7. Ibid.

8. Ibid., 64.

9. Rose A. Zimbardo, *A Mirror to Nature: Transformations in Drama and Aesthetics, 1660–1732* (Lexington: University Press of Kentucky, 1986).

10. Ibid., 59.

11. Ibid., 80.

12. Ibid., 85.

13. Ibid., 51.

14. Ibid., 57.

15. Ibid.

16. Ibid., 96.

17. Ibid., 123.

18. Ibid., 132.

19. Ibid., 168.

20. Ibid., 129.

21. Ibid., 130.

22. Ibid., 166f.

23. Ibid., 207ff.

24. H. P. Herrmann, *Naturnachahmung und Einbildungskraft: Zur Entwicklung der deutschen Poetik von 1670 bis 1740* (Bad Homburg, 1970), 276.

25. Ibid., 277.

26. Ibid.

27. Hohner, *Problematik der Naturnachahmung,* 144.

28. Ibid. See also Susi Bing, "Die Naturnachahmungstheorie bei Gottsched und den Schweizern und ihre Beziehung zu der Dichtungstheorie der Zeit" (Ph.D. diss., Wurzburg, 1934), 67.

29. Hohner, *Problematik der Naturnachahmung,* 104.

30. Herrmann, *Naturnachahmung und Einbildungskraft.*

31. Ibid., 77.

32. Ibid., 91.

33. Ibid., 279.

34. Ibid.

35. Ibid., 144.

36. Ibid., 276. See also A. Huyssen, "Das Versprechen der Natur. Alternative Naturkonzepte im 18. Jahrhundert," in R. Grimm and J. Hermand, eds., *Natur und Natürlichkert: Stationen des Grünen in der deutschen Literatur* (Königstein: Athenäum, 1981): "The reason-nature-virtue synthesis defined by Gottsched's *Versuch einer Critischen Dichtkunst,* as well as the categorizing and totalizing tendency of his formal poetics, correspond to Christian Wolff's enlightened absolutist concept of natural law, in which the subordination of subjects and the obligation of the authorities in regard to the general welfare are contractually regulated. In both cases nature is a concept of rules and domination" (8).

37. Herrmann, *Naturnachahmung und Einbildungskraft,* 181f.

38. Ibid., 276.

39. According to Boyd, a new epistemological mode had taken the place of the old one. Following Hamilton, he characterizes this new epistemological mode as one in which knowledge proceeds from things, while words are no more than a vehicle to transport it. In the old epistemological mode, all knowledge comes from words and language; this conception unifies all humanistic undertakings: philosophy, literature, and rhetoric (*The Function of Mimesis and Its Decline,* 206).

40. Herrmann, *Naturnachahmung und Einbildungskraft,* 275.

41. Of decisive significance for this development was the concept of the miraculous. On this, see Hans Otto Horrig and Georg-Michael Schulz, *Das Wunderbare und die Poetik der Frühaufklärung. Gottsched und die Schweizer* (Darmstadt: Wissenschaftliche Buchgesellschaft, 1988), which offers the only detailed overview of the state of research. See, in particular, J. Bruck, "Der aristotelischen Mimesisbegriff und die Nachahmungstheorie Gottscheds und der Schweizer" (Ph.D. diss., Erlangen-Nürnberg, 1972): "The first point of attack against the theory of mimesis is . . . the impossible and the miraculous; the more they were freed from hypothetical conditions of probability, the more the principle of the 'imitation of nature' lost in validity" (104).

42. J. J. Winckelmann is of the same opinion, in *Gedanken über die Nachahmung.* (n.p.) According to his view, to be sure, the Greek-oriented artistic imitation of nature must first be learned (16). The reason for this is the "perfect nature of the Greeks" (104), which is manifest, in particular, in the sensuousness of the Greek language and the physicality of Greek art (108f.).

43. Moritz, *Über die bildende Nachahmung des Schönen,* 258f. Emphasis in original.

44. Ibid., 266–269.

45. Ibid. Emphasis in original.

46. Ibid., 269.

47. Ibid., 272. Emphasis in original.

48. Ibid., 276.

49. Ibid., 282.

50. Ibid., 283.

51. Ibid., 288.

52. See, for a contrasting view, François Hemsterhuis, *Lettre sur la sculpture* (1769), who maintains that "the beautiful" possesses "no reality whatever of its own" (31). The attribution of beauty or ugliness to specific things is founded only in the soul (see the argument on p. 32).

53. S. Sting, "Der Mythos des Fortschreitens: Zur Geschichte dur Subjekt-Bildung" (Ph.D. diss., Freie Universität Berlin, 1990), 291. In the Reveries, Rousseau writes, "I assimilated all these lovely objects to my fictions; and finally finding myself brought back by degrees to myself and to what surrounded me, I could not mark out the point separating the fictions from the realities; it was this thorough conjunction of everything which made the absorbed and solitary life I led during this beautiful sojourn so dear to me" (*The Reveries of a Solitary Walker,* 70). This quotation makes clear how unconcerned Rousseau was with an exact representation of nature. Of moment to him are the psychological effects and interior bearing that are occasioned by the beautiful. In this way nature is transformed into a matter of aesthetics.

54. On the rise of a literary and political public sphere, see Jürgen Habermas, *The Structural Transformation of the Public Sphere: An Inquiry into a Category of Bourgeois Society,* trans. Thomas Berger (Cambridge: MIT Press, 1989); and Richard Sennett, *The Fall of Public Man* (New York: Alfred A. Knopf, 1977).

55. Cf. Pierre Bourdieu, "The Historical Genesis of a Pure Aesthetic," in Richard Shusterman, ed., *Analytic Aesthetics* (Oxford: Oxford University Press, 1989), 147–160.

Chapter 13. Mimesis in the Theater of the Enlightenment

1. The theme of artistic mimesis under absolutism is power. The various arts take part in its representation; power, however, is produced in the sphere of politics.

2. On this, see Michel Foucault, *Discipline and Punish: The Birth of the Prison,* trans. Alan Sheridan (New York: Vintage Books, 1979).

3. Peter Szondi, *Die Theorie des bürgerlichen Trauerspiel im 18. Jahrhundert: Der Kaufmann, der Hausvater und der Hofmeister,* ed. Gert Mattenklott (Frankfurt am Main: Suhrkamp, 1979).

4. The concept of the doux commerce designates the sphere of the private, which is not shaped by economic thinking and is juxtaposed to the life of gainful activity.

5. Denis Diderot, *Le père de famille.*

6. Denis Diderot, *Entretiens sur le fils naturel,* in *Oeuvres esthétiques* (Paris: Editions Garnier Freres, 1965), 154.

7. Gotthold Ephraim Lessing, *Hamburgische Dramaturgie* (Stuttgart: Reclam, 1981).

8. Szondi, *Theorie des Bürgerlichen Trauerspiel,* 166.

9. Diderot, *Entretiens sur le fils naturel,* 154.

10. Szondi, *Theorie des bürgerlichen Trauerspiel,* 61. Pierre Bourdieu, in his studies on the relationship between symbolic artifacts (e.g., of literary, artistic, and philosophical works) and the social world, refers to the autonomy of the "literary field." The political positions of an author are expressed in this field as literary positions; political struggles brought into the literary field from outside take the form of conflicts over literary problems. "External determinants, whether those that are inscribed in the producers' dispositions or those that stem from directly affected groups never exercise their effects directly; they come to expression solely through the mediation of the forces and specific forms of the field, that is, after they have undergone a *restructuring,* which is more significant the more autonomous the field, the more the latter is capable of successfully asserting its specific logic" (Bourdieu, "Le champ littéraire," 16). Literary works are not reflections of economic and social processes, nor does their history follow any system of laws immanent in the literary field. If we continue in Part IV to place dramatic characters and spectators in the theater in relation to each other (and novelistic characters and readers in Part V), we do so in the presupposition that the literary field operates according to its own lawlike systematicities that are different from those in the social world. Moreover, it is assumed that reciprocal influences between the literary and social world are possible under the condition of restructuring.

11. Szondi, *Theorie des bürgerlichen Trauerspiel,* 61.

12. Ibid., 68.

13. The bourgeois conception of catharsis has, as Brecht remarked, a "culinary" side, in that the capacity to feel fear and compassion contributes to the self-presentation and the enjoyment of the self.

14. Erving Goffman, *The Presentation of the Self in Everyday Life* (New York: Doubleday, 1959).

15. Bernard Mandeville's *Fable of the Bees* (1705) is an attempt to interpret the meaning of and to justify the unbridled pursuit of gain.

16. The myths of which the French classicists made use, in contrast, are already fully codified.

17. See Michel Foucault, *Discipline and Punish* and *The History of Sexuality,* trans. Robert Hurley, 3 vols. (New York: Pantheon Books, 1978–1986).

18. *Figures II,* 72. Emphasis in original.

19. Ibid., 73.

20. See Kant's category of the sublime, in particular, the dynamically sublime in nature in *Critique of Judgment:*

> Bold, overhanging, and as it were threatening rocks; clouds piled up on the sky, moving with lightning flashes and thunder peals; volcanoes in all their violence of destruction; hurricanes with their track of devastation; the boundless ocean in a state of tumult; the lofty waterfall of a mighty river, and such like—these exhibit our faculty of resistance as insignificantly small in comparison with their might. But the sight of them is the more attractive, the more fearful it is, provided only that we are in security; and we willingly call these objects sublime, because they raise the energies of the soul above their accustomed height and discover in us a faculty of resistance of a quite different kind, which gives us courage to measure ourselves against the apparent almightiness of nature.

(Second Book, "Analytic of the Sublime," B, "Of the Dynamically Sublime in Nature," §28, "Of nature regarded as might," 100–101)

21. See, on the conception of play, Sigmund Freud, "Der Dichter und das Phantasieren," *Studienausgabe* 10 (Frankfurt am Main: S. Fischer Verlag, 1989), 169–179; and Gregory Bateson, "Eine Theorie des Spiels und der Phantasie," *Ökologie des Geisfes* (Frankfurt am Main, 1985): 241–261.

22. The idea that the play manifests the deeper strata of a society that do not appear on the surface is represented by Clifford Geertz in his essay, "Deep Play: Notes on the Balinese Cockfight," in Geertz, *The Interpretation of Cultures* (New York: Basic Books, 1973), 412–453.

23. The new class wants first of all to see itself represented. Such a desire is typical for the first phase of the appropriation process of an as yet new medium. The later phases are characterized by a superior and analytical manipulation of the verbal-theatrical medium. The phase of appropriation is that of naive usage, self-representation, and taking possession.

Symbolic interactionism makes use of theatrical metaphors to understand the working of society as an analogue to the course of action in the theater, in which approach is concealed the assumption that society functions as if it were composed of theatrical pieces. Our considerations provide the basis for raising the following objections to this view. First, the comparison between the theater and society is far too nonspecific. Comparability can be established, at most, for particular epochs, especially in the dramatic theory of the Enlightenment. Second, society functions differently than a play, namely, on a level the representation of which is precisely nonsymbolic. Third, on the level of symbolic representation, theatrical elements are employed in the constitutional phase of bourgeois society, and only in this phase, but not in a fashion as if the self-representation of bourgeois actors proceeded as if in a play, but in the sense that the medium of the theater is employed as a genuine modeling of representative ways of behaving.

24. The most conclusive answer to this problem is offered by the concept of habitus in the sociology of Bourdieu.

25. The concept of mimesis or of "imitation" remains—or recurs, as one will—in the center of the sociological work at the end of the nineteenth century by Gabriel de Tarde, *Les lois de l'imitation*. On this, see the essay by K. Thomas, "Von der Imitation zur Mimesis: Der vergessende Gabriel Tarde und der zu entdeckende René Girard," in *Kassler Philosophische Schriften*, vol. 9, *Drie Vorträge* (Kassel, 1983). The concept is taken up anew by S. Moscovici in more recent sociological research; cf. *L'Âge des foules: Un traité historique de psychologie des masses* (Paris: Fayard, 1981).

26. The mimetic is gradually rediscovered only in the nineteenth century, and then as social mimesis. But it no longer appears then as a combination of practical ability and knowledge, as knowledge bound in a special way to practice, but as imitation, as an inferior mode of action that is incapable of knowledge. This development is already secured in the eighteenth century on account of a change in the concept of reason, which results in a different conception of reality. The dichotomies of creative, original, and subjective, on the one hand, and duplicative, imitative, and copied, on the other, arise at this time.

27. Norbert Elias, *The Civilizing Process,* trans. Edmund Jephcott (New York: Urizon Books, 1978).

28. Foucault, *Discipline and Punish.*

29. The development of textualization becomes ever more rapid in the nineteenth century and incalculable in the present. This acceleration stands in contrast to the all but static situation of rhetoric, which has created only minor possibilities for movement since antiquity. Confined to small pedagogical circles of a Latin-speaking male elite, rhetoric is cultivated artificially, without any reference to the experience of daily life (see Ong, *Orality and Literacy*).

Chapter 14. Diderot's *Paradox of Acting*

1. References in the following are to the text from the *Oeuvres esthétiques,* ed. P. Vernière (Paris: Editions Garnier Freres, 1965).

2. Diderot, *Oeuvres esthétiques,* 292.

3. Ibid., 22.

4. Yvon Belaval, *L'Esthétique sans paradoxe de Diderot* (Paris: Gallimard, 1950), 97.

5. Ibid., 83.

6. On this, see in particular, the chapter "L'imitation de la nature," in Belaval, *L'Esthétique,* 93–136.

7. Ibid., 206.

8. Ibid., 110.

9. Ibid., 181.

10. Ibid., 177.

11. Ibid., 195.

12. Ibid., 188.

13. What offends Rousseau is the paradoxical nature of the theatrical play; in *Politics and the Arts: Letter to M. d'Alembert on the Theatre,* trans. Allen Bloom (Ithaca: Cornell University Press, 1960), Rousseau writes, "What is the talent of the actor? It is the art of counterfeiting himself, of putting on another character than his own, of appearing different than he is, of becoming passionate in cold blood, of saying what he does not think as naturally as if he really did think it, and, finally, of forgetting his own place by dint of taking another's" (79).

14. Belaval, *L'Esthétique,* 211.

15. Denis Diderot, *The Paradox of Acting,* trans. Walter Herries Pollock (New York: Hill and Wang, 1957), 13.

16. Ibid., 76f.

17. Ibid., 81.

18. Ibid., 44.

19. Ibid., 22.

20. Ibid., 85.

21. Ibid.

22. Ibid., 74.

23. One could name as examples Lacan, Wittgenstein, symbolic interactionism (especially Goffman), and the study of biography by literary criticism (see, in particular,

Manfred Schneider, *Die erkältete Herzensschrift: Der autobiographische Text im 20. Jahrhundert* [Munich: C. Hanser, 1986]).

24. Diderot, *Paradox of Acting.*

25. Philippe Lacoue-Labarthe, "Diderot: Paradox and Mimesis," in Christopher Fynsk, ed., *Typography: Mimesis, Philosophy, Politics* (Cambridge: Harvard University Press, 1989), 248–266.

26. Ibid., 260. Emphasis in original.

27. Bourdieu, quoted in Lacoue-Labarthe, "Diderot," 264.

28. Lacoue-Labarthe, "Diderot," 265. Emphasis in original.

29. In conclusion, it can be said of Lacoue-Labarthe's interpretation that it is valid only if it can be definitively demonstrated that the point for Diderot was to transcend the distance separating the stage from the audience. In favor of his interpretation, Lacoue-Labarthe ("Diderot," 264) quotes a passage from Diderot's *Paradox of Acting:* "In the great play, the play of the world to which I am constantly returning, the stage is held by the fiery souls and the pit is filled with men of genius. The actors are in other words madmen; the spectators, whose business it is to copy their madness, are sages."

30. Diderot, *Paradox of Acting,* 53.

31. Ibid., 68.

32. Ibid., 95.

Chapter 15. The Transformation of Mimesis in Lessing

1. The following citations are to Gotthold Ephraim Lessing, *Laocoön: An Essay on the Limits of Painting and Poetry,* trans. Edward Allen McCormick (Indianapolis: Bobbs-Merrill Educational, 1962).

2. Karlheinz Stierle, "Das bequeme Verhältnis," in Gunter Gebauer, ed., *Das Laokoön-Projekt: Pläne einer semiotischen Ästhetik* (Stuttgart: Metzler, 1984), 25.

3. Ibid., 27.

4. This section is based on the preliminary work published in Gunter Gebauer, "Die Beziehungen von Bild und Text in Lessings *Laokoön,*" in S. Dümchen and M. Nerlich, *Texte-Image, Bild-Text* (Berlin: Technische Universität Berlin, Institute für Romanische Literaturwissenschaft, 1990), 17–27.

5. Lessing, *Laocoön,* 126.

6. J. Vuillemin, "Bemerkungen über Lessings *Laokoon,*" in Gebauer, *Das Laokoön-Projekt,* 167–182.

7. Authors can also become the recipient of their own works: in reading their own writing, they find themselves in the role of the re-producer.

8. See Ricoeur's conception of Mimesis$_3$, in *Time and Narrative.*

9. See Vuillemin, "Bemerkungen."

10. Lessing directs his argument against Johann Winckelmann's text, *Gedanken über die Nachahmung;* see pp. 21–24. It is, admittedly, possible to doubt that Lessing does Winckelmann justice. See also in Winckelmann the interesting considerations on the material (28f.) and on the mimesis of space (32ff.).

11. Goodman, *Languages of Art.* This work discusses, although without any reference to Lessing, problems that are quite similar to those treated in *Laocoön.* We shall make use of Goodman's conceptual instruments in our further argumentation.

12. Lessing, *Laocoön,* 78.

13. Tzvetan Todorov, ''Poiétique et poétique selon Lessing,'' in *Recherches poi-étiques,* vol. 1, *Collection d'esthetique* 22 (Paris, 1975): 25–41.

14. This becomes clear in Lessing's *Hamburgische Dramaturgie:* ''The unity of plot was the first dramatic law of the ancients; the unity of time and the unity of place were simply the consequence of the former'' (*Gesammelte Werke,* 6:237).

15. Goodman, *Languages of Art,* 135.

16. Ibid., 136.

17. Ibid., 136.

18. See the chapter on Madame de Lafayette, above.

19. See Foucault, *The Order of Things.*

20. Ibid., 311.

21. Ibid., 367ff.

22. Ibid., 369.

23. On the following, see Tzvetan Todorov, ''Ästhetik und Semiotik im 18. Jahrhundert. G. E. Lessing: *Laokoon,*'' in Gebauer, *Das Laokoön Projekt,* 9–22.

24. G. E. Lessing, *Briefe von Lessing,* in *Sämtliche Schriften,* vol. 17, ed. K. Lachmann (Leipzig, 1904).

25. See Svenbro, *Phrasikleia.* This work is also the basis of our following discussion of the history of the interrelations between reading and time.

26. Ibid., 68.

27. Ibid., 68–69.

28. Lessing, *Briefe von Lessing,* 291. Emphasis in original.

29. H. Blumenberg develops the concept of lived time in detail in his *Lebenszeit und Weltzeit.*

30. This consideration is based on the argument advanced by Ivan Illich and Barry Sanders in their book, *A B C: The Alphabetization of the Popular Mind* (San Francisco: North Point Press, 1988).

31. It is not important for this idea that the intervals of time spent by author and readers correspond; the critical point is that a text costs time both in the writing and the reading and that this time is represented in its syntactic dimension.

32. Svenbro, *Phrasikleia,* 2.

33. Ibid., 28.

34. Ibid., 30.

35. Ibid.

36. Ibid., 44.

37. Ibid., 46.

38. Ibid., 156.

39. Ibid., 60.

40. Ibid., 168. Emphasis in original.

41. Ibid., 169.

42. Ibid., 171.

43. Ibid., 174.

44. Ibid., 180. The relationship between the text as externality and the inscribing of it in the mind is demonstrated by the Athenian poet Callias in the *ABC Show* (*Grammatikē theōria*). It is performed by twenty-four women, representing the Ionian

alphabet. It is a play with the *grámmata,* letters, offering definitive proof here of their autonomy (Svenbro, *Phrasikleia,* 186).

45. See G. E. Lessing, *Gesammelte Werke,* vol. 6. In his critique of Voltaire, Lessing writes, "Did [Voltaire] observe the unity of time? The letter of this rule he fulfilled, but not the spirit. For what he has happen in *one* day can indeed be done in *one* day, but no reasonable person would do it in *one* day. The physical unity of time is not enough; to it must be added the moral unity" (233f.).

46. Since the time of the Italian commentaries on Aristotle's *Poetics,* the duration of a stage performance had been measured as physical time. The rule of the unity of time was interpreted from that standpoint insofar as the duration of the performance was understood as measurable time.

47. Illich and Sanders, *A B C,* 72.

48. Ibid., 71. "Where there is no alphabet, there can neither be a memory conceived as a storehouse nor the '1' as its appointed watchman. With the alphabet both text and self became possible, but only slowly, and they became the social construct on which we found all our perceptions as a literate people" (72).

49. On Augustine's philosophy of time, see Ricoeur, *Time and Narrative.*

50. Fuhrmann, *Einführung in die antike Dichtungstheorie,* 232f.

51. Jean Starobinski, *Jean-Jacques Rousseau: Transparency and Obstruction,* trans. Arthur Goldhammer (Chicago: University of Chicago Press, 1988), 198.

52. Ibid., 199.

Chapter 16. Self-Mimesis (Rousseau)

1. Confessional literature existed long before Rousseau: see Schneider, *Die erkaltete Herzensschrift.* Also see *Actes de la recherche,* nos. 62–63, in particular the contribution of Bourdieu, "L'illusion biographique."

2. Christopher Lasch, *The Culture of Narcissism: American Life in an Age of Diminishing Expectations* (New York: W. W. Norton, 1979).

3. Lionel Trilling, *Sincerity and Authenticity* (Cambridge: Harvard University Press, 1972), 93.

4. Starobinski, *Jean-Jacques Rousseau,* 195.

5. Ibid., 198. Emphasis in original.

6. "Voici le seul portrait d'homme, peint exactement d'après nature et dans toute sa vérité" (Rousseau, in the foreword to the *Confessions*). Subsequent quotations will be taken from *The Confessions,* trans. J. M. Cohen (London: Penguin Books, 1953).

7. Rousseau, *Confessions,* 17.

8. Rousseau, "Ebauches des Confessions," In *Oeuvres complète,* 1:1150.

9. Ibid., 1153.

10. Rousseau "must cast about for a style suited to its object" (Starobinski, *Jean-Jacques Rousseau,* 191), a style that represents and exhibits a searching *I,* including all the errors it is bound to make. This idea, which unifies in a new way poetic style and authenticity, simultaneously displacing onto literature philosophy's claim to seek the truth, has been of great significance in the history of the novel. It can be said that it achieved its highest—and probably final—form in Proust; see Gunter Gebauer, *Der Einzelne und sein gesellschaftliches Wissen* (Berlin: Walter de Gruyter, 1981).

11. Language can be such a medium. But there are many other possibilities for the ego's expression. The defenders of the idea of authenticity postulate the existence of a medium the characteristics of which do not influence the expressed ego. Our further argumentation is directed against this idea.

12. Jacques Lacan, "The Mirror Stage as Formative of the Function of the I," in *Écrits: A Selection,* trans. Alan Sheridan (New York: W. W. Norton, 1977), 1–7.

13. One mirror medium the importance of which is impossible to overestimate is photography. Roland Barthes, in *Camera Lucida: Reflections on Photography,* trans. Richard Howard (New York: Hill and Wang, 1981), argues that its defining characteristic is that "the power of authenticiation exceeds the power of representation" (89). Against Barthes's interpretation it can be said that photography produces authenticity only in the imagination of the recipient. The medium itself offers no guarantee of authenticity. For a number of modern photographic artists (e.g., Gerz, Le Gac, Kuppel, Boltanski), the appeal of their works derives precisely from the illusory authenticity of photography.

14. This is the point at which a critique of the identity theory of symbolic inter-actionism becomes possible. This theory fails to reflect in any fundamental fashion on the identity-forming characteristics of expressive and representational media. Erving Goffman et al. assume as self-evident that people make use of representational forms suggestive of the theater. They offer no indication as to how we are to resolve the conflict between the fact that people experience themselves as real in their self-representations and the fact that they are clearly only playing the part of themselves. We might ask whether symbolic interactionists are aware of the influence exercised over mirror media by their own theories.

15. The *Confessions* admittedly fails to exhibit one important feature of the drama, namely, a textual organization characteristic of stageplays: the text is not distributed among various characters. Nevertheless, it was read aloud by Rousseau, and it has also been performed dramatically (*Oeuvres complètes,* 1:1611, notes).

16. Rousseau implicitly assumes that his life can be differentiated into a series of relatively self-enclosed, distinct events and that each of these acquires a meaning in connection with the other events of his life. These events are at the same time the basic units of biographical meaning.

17. In the drama of Rousseau's autobiography the final and most extreme instance of *I*-formation is that of a self totally cut off from the human world, a self that is neither understood nor loved. The intention is to make contact with the public, to break through the walls of isolation. But the actual effect Rousseau achieves, at least in his reading at the castle of Braisne, is precisely the opposite: "Thus I concluded my reading, and everyone was silent. Mme d'Egmont was the only person who seemed moved. She trembled visibly but quickly controlled herself, and remained quiet, as did the rest of the company. Such was the advantage I derived from my reading and my declaration" (*Confessions,* 606).

18. See Trilling's critique of the idea that aesthetic products foster "personal autonomy" (*Sincerity and Authenticity,* 73f.).

19. See Part V, below.

20. The following discussion takes up certain ideas that have already been formulated in Gunter Gebauer, "Die arme Seele des Athleten," in Dietmar Kamper and Christoph Wulf, *Die erloschene Seele: Disziplin, Geschichte, Kunst, Mythos* (Berlin, 1988), 89–116.

21. Choderlos de Laclos, *Les Liaisons dangereuses,* trans. P. W. K. Stone (Harmondsworth: Penguin Books, 1961).

22. See Laclos's astonishing prize essay for the Academy of Châlons-sur-Marne, "De l'éducation des femmes" ("Happiness consists, not in desiring nothing, but in obtaining what one desires"; *Oeuvres complètes,* 425).

23. Affection for other persons and the desire to possess them can take many forms. Rousseau depicts himself as a person who is markedly uninterested in the actual performance of physical love. He is conspicuous in his pursuit of relationships with women whom, on the one hand, enable him to have continual intimate contact, to describe and treat it without inhibition as a literary theme, while, on the other, forbidding him the sexual act. The sole exceptions are the maternal figures of "Mamma" and his wife, Thérèse.

24. Søren Kierkegaard, "Diary of a Seducer," in *Either/Or,* 1:297–440.

25. Ibid., 303.

26. Ibid., 308.

27. Ibid., 331.

28. Ibid., 384.

29. Ibid.

30. Ibid., 437.

31. Ibid., 439.

32. Ibid.

33. See Kierkegaard, *Either/Or,* vol. 1, part 1: "The Immediate Stages of the Erotic or the Musical Erotic" and "Shadowgraphs."

34. The following descriptions are influenced by René Girard's *Deceit, Desire, and the Novel: Self and Other in Literary Structure,* trans. Yvonne Freccero (Baltimore: Johns Hopkins University Press, 1965). It, however, does not address directly the issues discussed here.

35. Valmont's intimate confidante and later antagonist in *Dangerous Liaisons.*

36. Madame de Merteuil to Valmont (*Les Liaisons dangereuses,* 321).

37. Thus Julie's letter to Saint-Preux: "and I'd rather see you gentle and vulnerable at the bottom of my heart, than strained and distracted in company" (*Oeuvres complètes,* II:105).

38. Ibid., II:204.

39. Ibid., II:508.

40. Ibid., II:487.

**Chapter 17. The Mimetic Constitution
of Social Reality**

1. See Honoré de Balzac, *La Comédie humaine,* ed. P.-G. Castex (Paris: Gallimard, 1976–1977), Vol. I.

2. Balzac, *Traité de la vie élégante,* 251.

3. Ibid. See J. Grange on how close Balzac comes to physiognomy: "For Balzac the whole world is legible according to the criteria established by Lavater or Gall; everything is an indication and a sign. Arranged in a series of reciprocal references, the real is rational or, at least, ordered and therefore subject to description" (*Balzac:*

L'Argent, la prose, les anges [Paris: La Differánce, 1990], 50). "A forgotten hat summarizes its owner" (60).

4. Lavater, quoted in G. Böhme, "Der sprechende Leib: Die Semiotiken des Körpers am Ende des 18. Jahrhunderts und ihre hermetische Tradition," in Dietmar Kamper and Christopher Wulf, eds., *Transfigurationen des Körpers: Spuren der Gewalt in der Geschichte* (Berlin: D. Reimer, 1989), 144–181.

5. On the concept of the image and its role in knowledge, see Jean-Pierre Vernant, *Religions, histoires, raisons* (Paris: F. Maspero, 1979).

6. The doxa makes up a field of knowledge to which the episteme is juxtaposed. In distinction to the sciences, the doxa is a simple opinion; it is uncertain and fluid for the objects to which it refers (see Vernant, *Religions,* 129f.). The doxa applies to the visible aspect of objects. Up until the separation of being and appearance, which begins to arise, according to Vernant, in the fifth century B.C., the doxa constitutes valid intellectual acts that make use of similarities, comparisons, and analogies as well as indexes used to comprehend objects that are concealed or invisible.

7. B. Krais, "Soziales Feld, Macht und kulturelle Praxis: Die Untersuchungen Bourdieus über die verschiedenen Fraktionen der 'herrschenden Klasse' in Frankreich," in Klaus Eder ed., *Klassenlage, Lebenstel und kulturelle Praxis: Beiträge zur Ausein-andersetzung mit Pierre Bourdieus Klassentheorie* (Frankfurt am Main: Suhrkamp, 1989), 47.

8. See Klaus Eder, "Klassentheorie als Gesellschaftstheorie. Bourdieu's dreifache kulturtheoretische Brechung der traditionellen Klassentheorie," in Klaus Eder, ed., *Klassenlage, Lebenstil und kuturelle Praxis* (Frankfurt am Main, 1989), 15–43.

9. Pierre Bourdieu, *Zur Soziologie der symbolischen Formen,* 60.

10. Pierre Bourdieu, *Distinction: A Social Critique of the Judgment of Taste,* trans. Richard Nice (Cambridge: Harvard University Press, 1984), 55.

11. Bourdieu, *Zur Soziologie der symbolischen Formen* (Frankfurt am Main: Suhrkamp, 1989), 61.

12. Ibid., 69, with a quote from the *Littré* on the category "distinction."

13. Balzac, *Traité de la vie élégante,* 254.

14. Ibid., 239.

15. See Grange: the characters are "subject to description as objects and are described in terms of the objects that surround them" (*Balzac,* 53). Auerbach had already emphasized the predominant role of signs and the legibility in the terms of the worlds of Balzac's creation (*Mimesis,* 468ff.). "The motif of the unity of a milieu has taken hold of him so powerfully that the things and the persons composing a milieu often acquire for him a sort of second significance which, though different from that which reason can comprehend, is far more essential—a significance which can best be defined by the adjective demonic" (ibid., 472).

16. Friedrich Nietzsche, *The Will to Power,* trans. Walter Kaufmann and R. J. Hollingdale (New York: Vintage Books, 1968), 496.

17. See Gilles Deleuze, *Proust and Signs,* trans. Richard Howard (New York: G. Braziller, 1972), which analyzes Proustian disenchantments.

18. Balzac maintains that the world represented in the novel is a reality that works to destroy illusions.

19. In the following, the two novels, *Lost Illusions* and *A Harlot High and Low,* will be treated as a single interrelated work.

20. See Balzac, *Comédie humaine,* Vol. I.

21. "'J'ai l'air du fils d'un apothicaire,' se dit-il à lui-même" (*Comédie humaine,* V:269; *Lost Illusions,* 165).

22. "les gracieux, les coquets, les élégants jeunes gens des familiies du faubourg Saint-Germain, qui tous avaient une maniére à eux qui les rendait tous semblables par la finesse des contours, par la noblesse de la tenue, par l'air du visage; et tous différents par le cadre que chacun s'était choisi pour se faire valoir. Tous faisaient ressortir leurs avantages par un espèce de mise en scène. . . . Lucien tenait de sa mère les précieuses distinctions physiques dont les privilèges éclataient à ses yeux; mais cet or était dans sa gangue, et non mis en oeuvre" (*Comédic humaine,* 270; *Lost Illusions,* 165).

23. ". . . par quels moyens il pouvait le [l'abîme] franchir, car il voulait être semblable à cette svelte et délicate jeunesse parisienne" (*Comédie humaine,* 270f.; *Lost Illusions,* 166).

24. See Georg Lukács, "Balzac: Lost Illusions," in *Studies in European Realism* (1935): "Balzac wrote this novel in the fullness of his maturity as a writer [1843]; with it he created a new type of novel which was destined to influence decisively the literary development of the nineteenth century. This new type of novel was the novel of disillusionment, which shows how the conception of life of those living in a *bourgeois* society—a conception which, although false, is yet necessarily what it is—is shattered by the brute forces of capitalism" (47). Proust saw this even more clearly: "To read through that wonderful book called *Les Illusions perdues,* clips the wings, rather than not, of that lovely title, *Lost Illusions,* and brings it to earth. The title means, that on going to Paris, Lucien de Rubempré discovered that Mme de Bargeton was absurd and provincial, that journalists were rascals, that life was hard" (Marcel Proust, *By Way of Sainte-Beuve,* 126f.). The illusions the novel is concerned with are of a quite personal, arbitrary type (126).

25. "Louise était restèe la même. Le voisinage d'une femme à la mode, de la marquise d'Espard, cette Mme de Bargeton de Paris, lui nuisait tant, la brillante Parisienne faisait si bien ressortir les imperfections de la femme de province, que Lucien vit enfin dans la pauvre Anais de Nègrepelisse la femme réelle, la femme que les gens de Paris voyaient" (*Comédie humaine,* V:273; *Lost Illusions,* 169).

26. "Mme de Bargeton surprit un des regards pétillants de Lucien; elle l'observa et le vit plus occupé de la marquise que du spectacle" (*Comédie humaine,* V:282; *Lost Illusions,* 179).

27. "Elle devint jalouse, mais moins pour l'avenir que pour le passé. 'Il ne m'a jamais regardé ainsi' pensa-t-elle" (Comédie humaine, V:282; *Los Illusions,* 179).

28. "En perdant ses illusions sur Mme de Bargeton, comme Mme de Bargeton perdait les siennes sur lui, le pauvre enfant, de qui la destinée ressemblait un peu à celle de J.-J. Rousseau, l'imita en ce point qu'il s'amouracha d'elle aussitôt" (*Comédie humaine,* V:281; *Lost Illusions,* 178).

29. "Elle avait pris les gestes et les façons de sa cousine; assise comme elle, elle jouait avec une élégante cassolette attachée à l'un des doigts de sa main droite par une petite chaîne, et montrait ainsi sa main fine et bien gantée sans avoir l'air de vouloir

la montrer. Enfin ell s'était faite sembable à Mme d'Espard sans la singer; elle était la digne cousine de la marquise, qui paraissait être fière de son élève'' (*Comédie humaine,* 286; *Lost Illusions,* 184).

30. Christopher Prendergast, *The Order of Mimesis: Balzac, Stendhal, Nerval, Flaubert* (Cambridge: Cambridge University Press, 1986), 87.

31. ''C'était horrible et gai. La chair éclatante des épaules et des gorges étincelait au milieu des vêtements d'hommes presque toujours sombres, et produisait les plus magnifiques oppositions . . . les hommes les plus insensible étaient émus'' (*Comédie humaine,* V:360; *Lost Illusions,* 265).

32. Prendergast, *Order of Mimesis,* 92. Emphasis in original.

33. Balzac, *Physiologie de la toilette,* quoted in Prendergast, *Order of Mimesis,* 94.

34. ''Je veux aimer ma créature, la façonner, la pétrir à mon usage, afin de l'aimer comme un père aime son enfant . . . je dirai: 'Ce beau jeune homme, c'est moi! ce marquis de Rubempré, je l'ai crée et mis au monde aristocratique; sa grandeur est mon oeuvre, il se tait ou parle à ma voix, il me consulte en tout' '' (*Comédie humaine,* V:708; *Lost Illusions,* 655).

35. Prendergast, *Order of Mimesis,* 108.

36. Ibid., 111.

37. Balzac, *Comédie humaine,* VI:918; *A Harlot High and Low,* 536.

38. At the end, Balzac has Vautrin say, ''I shall always reign over this world, in which, for twenty-five years, I have been obeyed'' (*Comédie humaine,* 934; *Harlot,* 553).

39. In *By Way of Sainte-Beuve,* Proust draws attention to the fact that Balzac himself shares the attitudes, wishes, and ambitions that are described in his novels. He quotes a letter of Balzac to his sister, as he was contemplating marriage to Madame Hanska: ''in Paris it means something to be able, when one wants to, to throw open one's house and entertain the cream of society, who will meet a woman there who is polished, stately as a queen, of high descent, related to the grandest families, witty, well-educated and handsome. That's a great step toward becoming a power in the land. . . . Heart, soul, ambition, everything about me is set on just this one thing that I've been in pursuit of the last sixteen years; if this stupendous happiness slips through my fingers, there's nothing else I want. Don't suppose that I love luxury. It's the luxury of the rue Fortunée that I love, and all that goes with it: a beautiful woman, well-born, comfortably off, and knowing all the best people'' (118). Balzac writes further to his sister (quoted from *Sainte-Beuve*): ''If the *Comédie humaine* does not make a great man of me . . . this achievement will'' (119f.). What he means is his marriage to Madame Hanska. But precisely this openly expressed mix of ambition, desire for recognition, wealth, and love and the fact that Balzac pronounces all of this with extreme clarity and naïveté are the reasons, in Proust's mind, for the literary success of *Comédie humaine:* ''the verisimilitude of some of his pictures [*peintures*] may be due to that same vulgarity'' (120). Balzac, according to Proust, is able ''to show that the most romantic feelings may be no more than a play of refracted light transfiguringly directed on his ambitions by the ambitious man himself, and to show this, consciously or unconsciously, in the most compelling way: that is, by showing objectively, as the bleakest of adventurers the man who himself, subjectively, sees himself in his own eyes as a romantic wooer'' (120). Proust recognizes that Balzac describes his own life in the same way that he describes

the lives of his fictional characters: "one can say that his life was a novel which he set about in exactly the same spirit. There was no dividing line between real life . . . and the life of his novels (which for the writer is the only true life). In his letters to his sister where he talks about the possibility of this marriage to Mme Hanska, not only is everything built up like a novel, but those involved are placed, analyzed, described, seen as factors in the development of the plot, as if in one of his books" (121). Proust describes the effect on the reader of Balzac's works as follows: "So in reading Balzac we can still feel and almost gratify those cravings which great literature ought to allay in us" (126). A soirée described by a great writer should purge us of our worldliness, in the sense of Aristotelian catharsis; but with Balzac, Proust claims, "we feel almost a worldly satisfaction at taking part in it" (126).

Chapter 18. "Mimetic Desire" in the Work of Girard

1. We shall split our discussion of Girard's work into two parts; here we deal with his strictly literary critical examination of nineteenth- and twentieth-century novels. His interpretive hypothesis has a clearly delimited field and can therefore be responsibly passed over. The comprehensive theory of mimesis of his later works will be described and criticized on its own; while it is true that the foundation for this theory is laid in *Deceit, Desire, and the Novel,* it only takes on the character of a general anthropological hypothesis in later publications. We are of the opinion that Girard's theory of mimesis, as restricted to the novel, can be more easily justified and accepted than his later, comprehensive theory of culture. In the end, *Deceit, Desire, and the Novel* seems to us an essential contribution to the history of mimesis in the nineteenth century.

2. Girard, *Deceit, Desire, and the Novel,* 7.

3. Ibid. Emphasis in original.

4. On the mimetic structure of *Remembrance of Things Past,* see Gunter Gebauer, "Überwindung des verinnerlichten Dialogs: Die Mimesis des Schönen und die Proustschen Enttäuschungen," in Hans Lenk, ed., *Zur Kritik der Wissenschaftlichen Rationalität* (Freiburg: K. Alber, 1986), 543–552; on the aspect of truth in *Remembrance,* see Gebauer, *Der Einzelne und sein gesellschaftliches Wissen: Untersuchungen zum Symbolischen Wissen* (Berlin, 1981).

5. Girard, *Deceit, Desire, and the Novel,* 233.

6. In the nineteenth century, the exposure of social mimesis combined with the protest against the mimetic worldmaking of art. The two defensive postures, while distinct, are closely connected; this is what distinguishes the rejection of mimesis in the nineteenth century from the critique of mimesis that we identified in the seventeenth.

7. It becomes evident that the achievements attributed to the modern means of mass communications were already recognizable in the first half of the nineteenth century. In the twentieth century, new technical means have been added which perfect and extend the achievements.

8. At issue here in principle are the same problems treated in the modern discussion of media, which culminate in the question of the reality of the world mediated or produced by the media.

9. New in the nineteenth- and twentieth-century development is the attempt to overcome artistic mimesis by means of art, that is, once again by means of mimetic procedures. In this way, art becomes antimimetic only in the sense that it distances itself from artistically produced worlds. The protest against mimesis in art is finally not capable of getting free of mimetic procedures.

10. The internal medium is reproduced most effectively by the modern mass media, which produce a "secondary orality" (Walter Ong). This is particularly the case with television, but radio and newspapers are also capable, to a considerable degree, of simulating oral or quasi-oral addressive speech situations.

11. See Nietzsche, *Will to Power.* See also our further critique of Girard in chapter 20, "The Mimesis of Violence." A few of the critical points elaborated there also apply to *Deceit, Desire, and the Novel;* the points at issue are more clearly and comprehensively formulated only in Girard's later work.

Chapter 19. Violence in Antiromantic Literature

1. Quoted by Marthe Robert, *En haine du roman: Étude sur Flaubert* (Paris: Balland, 1982), 144.

2. It is also possible to formulate these thoughts as follows: In investigating literature we have to do with at least two different worlds—the world of the novel with its constellation of characters and the empirical world of the author with his or her relationships to other empirical persons. A series of objects have to remain the same through these two types of worlds; they are the fixed elements in the transworld comparison (Hilary Putnam), which are responsible for making a comparison possible in the first place. Traditional literary criticism naively assumes that the verbal expressions used are these fixed elements. But it has long since become the dominant conviction that language is used in literature in a different way than in the context of daily speech. For this reason its intraliterary meaning differs from its extraliterary meaning. Our concern here is to point out that an essential fixed element, which appears as the same in the empirical world of the author and in his or her literary worldmaking, is the relationship between *I* and Others.

3. See Goodman, *Ways of Worldmaking.*

4. Ibid., 104: "Fiction operates in the actual world in much the same way as nonfiction."

5. See Gebauer, *Das Laokoön-Projekt.*

6. Goodman, *Ways of Worldmaking,* 124.

7. "quand elle aperçut près de la porte d'entrée la figure d'un jeune paysan presque encore enfant, extrêmement pâle et qui venait de pleurer" (Stendhal, *Le Rouge et le noir,* in *Romans et nouvelles,* I:241). In English: *Scarlet and Black: A Chronicle of the Nineteenth Century,* trans. Margaret R. B. Shaw (Harmondsworth: Penguin Books, 1953), 46.

8. "... quand une voix douce dit tout prés de son oreille: 'Que voulez-vous ici, mon enfant?' Julien se tourna vivement, et, frappé du regard si rempli de grâce de Madame de Rênal, il oublia une partie de sa timidité. Beintôt, étonné de sa beauté, il oublia tout, même ce qu'il venait faire" (*Le Rouge et le noir,* I:241; *Scarlet and Black,* 46).

9. "Il y aurait de la lâcheté à moi de ne pas exécuter une action qui peut m'être utile, et diminuer le mépris que cette belle dame a probablement pour un pauvre ouvrier" (*Le Rouge et le noir*, 244; *Scarlet and Black*, 49).

10. "Enfin Julien parut. C'était un autre homme. C'eût été mal parler que de dire qu'il était grave; c'était la gravité incarné" (*Le Rouge et le noir*, 247; *Scarlet and Black*, 51).

11. Béatrice Didier, in the foreword to *Vie de Henry Brulard* (Paris: Garnier, 1973), 13.

12. "Laissez-moi, vilain laid!" (*Vie de Henry Brulard*, 138; *Life of Henry Brulard* [New York: Noonday Press, 1958], 96).

13. "La superficie de mon corps est de femme. De là puet-être une horreur insurmontable pour ce qui a l'air *sale*, ou humide, ou noirâtre" (*Vie*, 168; *Life*, 123; emphasis in original).

14. "Mais au fond, cher lecteur, je ne sais pas ce que je suis: bon, méchant, spirituel, sot" (*Vie*, 280; *Life*, 216).

15. *Vie*, 201; *Life*, 149. Emphasis in original.

16. Ibid., 372/292.

17. Ibid.

18. Ibid., 424/337.

19. Ibid., 246/188. Emphasis in original.

20. Ibid., 412/327.

21. "Grand Dieu! quel mécompte! mais que dois-je donc désirer?" (ibid., 352/276).

22. Marthe Robert, "Flaubert écrit pour ne pas vivre" (72). See, as well, the work by Rainer Wannicke, *Sartres Flaubert: Zur Misanthropie der Einbildungskraft* (Berlin: D. Reimer, 1990).

23. See the works of René Girard on this and the following considerations.

24. On this assumption, see the developmental psychology of Jean Piaget.

25. Stendhal, *Lucien Leuwen*, in *Romans et nouvelles*, Vol. I; English: *Lucien Leuwen*, trans. Louise Varèse (New York: New Directions, 1950). Gustave Flaubert, *L'Éducation sentimentale*, in *Oeuvres*, Vol. II, ed. A. Thibaudet and R. Dumesnil (Paris: Gallimard, 1952); English: *The Sentimental Education*, trans. Perdita Burlingame (New York: New American Library, 1972).

26. Stendhal, *Lucíen Leuwen*, 931; English, 194.

27. "Dans l'obscurité profonde, Madame de Chasteller dinstinguait quelquefois le feu du cigare de Leuwen. Elle l'aimait à la folie en ce moment" (ibid., 951/212).

28. Flaubert, *L'Éducation sentimentale*, 36; English, 10.

29. "il sentait quelque chose d'inexprimable, une répulsion, et comme l'effroi d'un inceste" (ibid., 452/415).

30. Ibid., 453/416.

31. On this problematic, see Tzvetan Todorov, *The Conquest of America: The Problem of the Other*, trans. Richard Howard (New York: Harper & Row, 1984).

32. Ludwig Wittgenstein, *Philosophical Investigations*, trans. G. E. M. Anscombe (New York: Macmillan, 1968), §495.

33. See Konrad Wünsche, *Der Volksschullehrer Ludwig Wittgenstein* (Frankfurt am Main: Suhrkamp, 1985).

34. Fyodor Dostoyevsky, *Notes from Underground*, trans. Serge Shishkoff (New York: Thomas Y. Crowell, 1969).

35. Ibid., 67.
36. Ibid., 120.
37. Ibid.
38. Ibid., 36.

Chapter 20. The Mimesis of Violence (Girard)

1. René Girard, *Violence and the Sacred,* trans. Patrick Gregory (Baltimore: Johns Hopkins University Press, 1977; orig. 1972); *Things Hidden since the Foundation of the World,* trans. Stephen Bann and Michael Metteer (Stanford: Stanford University Press, 1978); *The Scapegoat,* trans. Yvonne Freccero (Baltimore: Johns Hopkins University Press, 1986); *Job: The Victim of His People,* trans. Yvonne Freccero (Stanford: Stanford University Press, 1987). On Girard's work, see J. M. Oughourlian, *The Puppet Desire: The Psychology of Hysteric, Possession, and Hypnosis* (Stanford: Stanford University Press, 1991). P. Dumouchel and J.-P. Dupuy, *L'Enfer des choses: René Girard et la logique de l'economie* (Paris: Seuil, 1979); Konrad Thomas, *Rivalität: Sozialwissenschaftliche Variationen zu einem alten Thema* (Frankfurt: P. Lang, 1990).

2. Girard is able to illustrate his thesis especially well in cases of struggles over prestige, duels, and agons, in which nothing is at issue but reputation or honor, except, that is, intangible imaginary objects that are rendered valuable because of rivalries. In the case of other sorts of conflicts, it is clearly more difficult to demonstrate the plausibility of Girard's thesis.

3. See Girard, *Violence and the Sacred,* 155.

4. Ibid., 31. It is important that the violence deployed to counter other violence seem to those involved to come from an external source.

5. Girard, *The Scapegoat,* 39.

6. Girard is influenced in this interpretation by James George Frazer and Sigmund Freud. On this, see Carsten Colpe, *Über das Heilige: Versuch, seiner Verkennung kritisch vorzubeugen* (Frankfurt am Main: A. Hain, 1990): "Girard's thesis offers probably the most realistic incorporation of the nature and socialization of the individual into the primary character of the victim—insofar as it exists. But it nevertheless will not do as a reliable prehistorical reconstruction" (63f.).

7. Girard, *Violence and the Sacred,* 20.

8. Ibid., 18.

9. Ibid., 266.

10. Girard, *Things Hidden,* 32. Emphasis in original.

11. Girard, *Violence and the Sacred,* 31.

12. Ibid., 36.

13. Jean-Pierre Vernant, "Ambiguity and Reversal: On the Enigmatic Structure of *Oedipus Rex,*" in *Myth and Tragedy in Ancient Greece,* trans. Janet Lloyd (New York: Zone Books, 1990), 113–140.

14. Girard, *Violence and the Sacred,* 107.

15. Ibid., 99, 118, 273.

16. Ibid., 167.

17. Ibid., 287.

18. Ibid. On the pharmakon, see Derrida, "Plato's Pharmacy."

19. Girard, *Violence and the Sacred,* 92.

20. Girard, *Things Hidden,* 78.

21. Girard, *The Scapegoat,* 24.

22. Girard, *Violence and the Sacred,* esp. pp. 68–88.

23. Ibid., 290.

24. Ibid., 297.

25. See the discussion of the Christian religion in Girard, *Things Hidden,* Bk. II, esp. chaps. 2 and 3.

26. See the interpretation of the Book of Job in Girard, *Job.*

27. Girard, *Things Hidden,* 149.

28. Ibid., 167.

29. Ibid., 180.

30. Ibid., 183.

31. Ibid., 210.

32. Ibid., 232.

33. Ibid., 197.

34. Girard, *The Scapegoat,* 101.

35. The same applies with equal force to Freud's works of cultural-psychological interpretation, in particular, *Totem and Taboo,* trans. James Strachey (New York: W. W. Norton, 1950).

36. See Goodman, *Languages of Art.*

37. See Goodman, *Ways of Worldmaking.* For a critique, see also Colpe, *Über das Heilige:* "None of these origin theories can truly be verified. Yet even if one goes on from the beginnings further into human history, one never arrives at a history of the sacred, but only at individual aspects which are characteristic both of continuous developmental lines and also of fundamental historical givens. The latter, for their part, are just as constitutive of initial beginnings as of repeated new beginnings in the historical period." Aspects of the sort he is referring to, Colpe thinks, could be comprehended in a historical anthropology.

Chapter 21. Nonsensuous Similarity

1. See also Jürgen Habermas, "Bewußtmachende oder rettende Kritik: Die Aktualität Walter Benjamins," in *Zur Aktualität Walter Benjamins. Aus Anlass des 80. Geburtstags von Walter Benjamin,* ed. Siegfried Unseld (Frankfurt am Main: Suhrkamp, 1972), 173ff. On the points raised in what follows, see also Peter Gebhardt et al., eds., *Walter Benjamin Zeitgenosse der Moderne* (Krönberg: Scriptor, 1976); Anna Stüssi, *Erinnerung an die Zukunft: Walter Benjamins "Berliner Kindheit um Neunzehnhundert"* (Göttingen: Vandenhoeck & Ruprecht, 1977); J. Leineweber, *Mimetische Vermögen und allegorisches Verfahren. Studien zu Walter Benjamin und seiner Lehre vom Ähnlichen,* Ph.D. diss., Philips-Universität, Marburg, 1978; Werner Fuld, *Walter Benjamin: Zwischen den Stühlen, eine Biographie* (Munich: Hanser, 1979); Jean-Pierre Schobinger, *Variationen zu Walter Benjamins Sprachmeditationen* (Basel: Schwabe, 1979); Winfried Menninghaus, *Walter Benjamins Theorie der Sprachmagie* (Frankfurt am Main: Suhrkamp, 1980); Krista Greffrath, *Metaphorischer Materialismus: Untersuchungen zum Geschichtsbegriff Walter Benjamins* (Munich: W. Fink, 1981); Norbert W. Bolz and Richard Faber, eds., *Walter Benjamin: Profane Erleuchtung und rettende*

Kritik (Würzburg: Königshausen & Neumann, 1982); Marleen Stoessel, *Aura, das vergessene Menschliche: Zu Sprache und Erfahrung bei Walter Benjamin* (Munich: C. Hanser, 1983); Ullrich Schwarz, *Rettende Kritik und antizipierte Utopie: Zum geschichtlichen Gehalt asthetischer Erfahrung in den Theorien von Jan Mukarovsky, Walter Benjamin und Theodor W. Adorno* (Munich: W. Fink, 1981); Ullrich Schwarz, "Walter Benjamin: Mimesis und Erfahrung," in *Grundprobleme der großen Philosophen, Philosophie der Gegenwart* VI, ed. J. Speck (Göttingen, 1984), 43–78; Torsten Meiffert, *Die enteignete Erfahrung: Zu Walter Benjamins Konzept einer "Dialektik im Stillstand"* (Bielefeld: Aisthesis Verlag, 1986); Uwe Steiner, *Die Geburt der Kritik aus dem Geiste der Kunst: Untersuchungen zum Begriff der Kritik in den frühen Schriften Walter Benjamins* (Würzburg: Königshausen & Neumann, 1989).

2. See F. Cramer, *Chaos and Order: The Complex Structure of Living Systems,* trans. D. I. Loewus (New York: UCH, 1993).

3. Foucault, *The Order of Things.*

4. Ibid., 17ff.

5. Ibid., 42.

6. Schwarz, *Rettende Kritik und antizipierte Utopie,* 140.

7. Walter Benjamin, "Lehre vom Ähnlichen," *Gesammelte Schriften* (Frankfurt am Main: Suhrkamp: 1980), II:209.

8. Walter Benjamin, "On the Mimetic Faculty," in *Reflections: Essays, Aphorisms, Autobiographical Writings,* trans. Edmund Jephcott (New York: Harcourt Brace Jovanovich, 1978), 335.

9. Ibid.

10. Ibid.

11. Benjamin, "Probleme der Sprachsoziologie," *Gesammelte Schriften,* III:478.

12. Benjamin, "On the Mimetic Faculty," 335.

13. Schwarz, *Rettende Kritik,* 87.

14. Benjamin, "On the Mimetic Faculty," 336.

15. Ibid.

16. Walter Benjamin, "On Some Motifs in Baudelaire," in *Illuminations,* trans. Harry Zohn (New York: Schocken Books, 1969), 199.

17. See Johann Gottfried Herder, *Abhandlung über den Ursprung der Sprache,* ed. H. D. Irmscher (Stuttgart: Reclam, 1975).

18. Arnold Gehlen, *Man: His Nature and Place in the World,* trans. Clare McMillan and Karl Pillemer (New York: Columbia University Press, 1988).

19. Herder, *Abhandlung,* 5.

20. Ibid., 33.

21. Ibid., 47.

22. Schwarz, "Walter Benjamin," 56.

23. Benjamin, "Probleme der Sprachsoziologie," 480.

24. Gehlen, *Man,* 248.

25. On this, see Schneider, *Die erkaltete Herzensschrift,* 134ff.

26. Benjamin, *Berliner Kindheit um Neunzehnhundert,* in *Gesammelte Schriften,* IV:1, 262–263.

27. Ibid., 244.

28. Stüssi, *Erinnerung an die Zukunft,* 61.

29. Benjamin, *Gesammelte Schriften,* VI:1, 532.

30. Cf. Schneider, *Die erkältete Herzensschrift,* 125.

31. Benjamin, "A Small History of Photography," in *One-Way Street and Other Writings,* trans. Edmund Jephcott and Kingsley Shorter (London: New Left Books, 1979), 251.

32. Benjamin, "On Some Motifs in Baudelaire," 188.

33. Quoted according to Schwarz, *Rettende Kritik,* 100.

34. Benjamin, *Illuminationen, Schriften,* 1 (Frankfurt am Main, 1977), 303.

35. Benjamin, "On Language as Such and on the Language of Man," in *Reflections,* 319.

Chapter 22. Vital Experience (Adorno)

1. Max Horkheimer and Theodor Adorno, *Dialectic of Enlightenment,* trans. John Cumming (New York: Seabury Press, 1972). On this, see also Stefano Cochetti, *Mythos und "Dialektik der Aufklärung"* (Königstein: A. Hain, 1985); Josef Früchtl, *Mimesis: Konstellation eines Zentralbegriffs bei Adorno* (Würzburg: Königshausen & Neumann, 1986); Peter Bürger, *Prosa der Moderne* (Frankfurt am Main, 1988).

2. Horkheimer and Adorno, *Dialectic of Enlightenment,* 31.

3. Ibid., 180.

4. Roger Caillois, *Man and the Sacred,* trans. Meyer Barash (Westport, Conn.: Greenwood Press, 1980).

5. Sigmund Freud, *Beyond the Pleasure Principle,* trans. James Strachey (New York: W.W. Norton, 1961), 30.

6. Ibid., 32. Emphasis in original.

7. Horkheimer and Adorno, *Dialectic of Enlightenment,* 180.

8. See Marcel Mauss, *A General Theory of Magic,* trans. Robert Brian (London: Routledge & Kegan Paul, 1972), 63ff.

9. Horkheimer and Adorno, *Dialectic of Enlightenment,* 22.

10. Theodor Adorno, *Aesthetic Theory,* trans. C. Lenhardt (London: Routledge & Kegan Paul, 1984), 162.

11. Theodor Adorno, *Minima Moralia: Reflections from a Damaged Life,* trans. E. F. N. Jephcott (London: Verso, 1978), 222.

12. Adorno and Horkheimer, *Dialectic of Enlightenment,* 180.

13. Ibid., 3.

14. Ibid., 54–55.

15. Adorno, *Aesthetic Theory,* 162.

16. Horkheimer and Adorno, *Dialectic of Enlightenment,* 181.

17. Adorno, *Minima Moralia,* 154.

18. Horkheimer and Adorno, *Dialectic of Enlightenment,* 187.

19. Ibid., 189.

20. Adorno, *Minima Moralia,* 192.

21. Theodor Adorno, *Dissonanzen. Musik in der Verwaltete Welt* (Göttingen: Vandenhoeck & Ruprecht 1963), 124.

22. See H. H. Kappner, *Die Bildungstheorie Adornos als Theorie der Erfahrung von Kultur und Kunst* (Frankfurt am Main, 1984).

23. Adorno, *Minima Moralia,* 127–128.

24. Theodor Adorno, *Negative Dialectics,* trans E. B. Ashton (New York: Seabury Press, 1973), 203. On this, see also J. Naecker, *Die Negative Dialektik Adornos* (Oplanden, 1984); and Anne Thyen, *Negative Dialektik und Erfahrung: Zur Rationalität des Nichtidentischen bei Adorno* (Frankfurt am Main, 1989).

25. On this, see, among others, W. M. Lüdke, *Anmerkungen zu einer "Logik des Zerfalls": Adorno, Beckett* (Frankfurt am Main: Suhrkamp, 1981); B. Lindler and W. M. Lüdke, eds., *Materialien zur Ästhetischen Theorie Th. W. Adornos: Konstruktion der Moderne* (Frankfurt am Main: Suhrkamp, 1980); Schwarz, *Rettende Kritik;* W. Oelmüller, ed., *Colloquium Kunst und Philosophie 1: Ästhetische Erfahrung* (Paderborn: Schoningh, 1981); Bürger, *Prosa der Moderne;* Claudia Kalász, *Hölderlin: Die poetische Kritik Instrumenteller Rationalität* (Munich: Text & Kritik, 1988).

26. Adorno, *Minima Moralia,* 191.

27. Adorno, *Negative Dialectics,* 150.

28. Theodor Adorno, *Against Epistemology: A Metacritique. Studies in Husserl and the Phenomenological Antinomies,* trans. Willis Domingo (Oxford: Basil Blackwell, 1982), 143.

29. Theodor Adorno, *Der getreue Korrepetitor* (Frankfurt: Suhrkamp, 1963), 38.

30. Adorno, *Aesthetic Theory,* 236.

31. Ibid., 153.

32. Ibid., 114.

33. Ibid., 192.

34. Theodor Adorno, *Gesammelte Schriften* (Frankfurt am Main: Suhrkamp, 1970–1986), II:230.

35. Adorno, *Aesthetic Theory,* 80.

36. Ibid., 79.

37. Ibid., 162.

38. Schwarz, *Rettende Kritik,* 192.

39. Adorno, *Aesthetic Theory,* 474.

40. Ibid., 394.

41. Ibid., 178.

42. Ibid., 181.

43. Ibid., 185.

44. Ibid., 470.

45. See Dietmar Kamper and Christoph Wulf, eds., *Die Sterbende Zeit* (Darmstadt, 1987).

46. See Kamper and Wulf, *Der Schein des Schönen.*

Chapter 23. The Between-Character of Mimesis (Derrida)

1. See Mark Krupnick, ed., *Displacement: Derrida and After* (Bloomington: Indiana University Press, 1982), in which the problem of displacement and the new constitution of meaning is given a detailed treatment against the background of Derrida's positions.

2. Jacques Derrida et al., *Mimésis des articulations* (Paris: Aubier-Flammarion, 1964), 6.

3. Ibid., 7.

4. Ibid., 6.

5. Derrida, "Plato's Pharmacy," 127.

6. Ibid., 129.

7. Ibid., 145.

8. Ibid., 168.

9. Ibid., 169.

10. Derrida, "Economimesis," in Derrida et al., *Mimésis des articulations,* 55–93.

11. Derrida, "The Double Session," in *Dissemination,* trans. Barbara Johnson (Chicago: University of Chicago Press, 1981), 186 n. 14.

12. Ibid., 198. Emphasis in original.

13. Ibid., 209. Emphasis in original.

14. Ibid., 213. Emphasis in original.

15. Ibid., 209.

16. Derrida, "Economimesis," 67.

17. Ibid., 68.

18. Kant, *Critique of Judgment,* §46, 150. Emphasis in original.

19. Derrida, "Economimesis," 75.

20. Ibid., 74.

21. Kant, *Critique of Judgment,* §23, 83.

22. Derrida, "Economimesis," 92.

23. See Philippe Lacoue-Labarthe, "Typographie," in Derrida et al., *Mimésis des articulations,* 165–270; and "L'Imitation des modernes," *Typographies 2* (Paris, 1986).

24. Lacoue-Labarthe, "Diderot: Paradox and Mimesis."

25. Ibid., 259.

26. Ibid., 260.

27. Ibid.

28. On this, see Geoffrey Hartmann, *Saving the Text* (Baltimore: Johns Hopkins University Press, 1981); and Krupnick, *Displacement.*

Results

1. On this, see the fundamental work by Pierre Bourdieu, *Outline of a Theory of Practice,* trans. Richard Nice (Cambridge: Cambridge University Press, 1977).

2. The modern position of Marxist-influenced reflection theory has meanwhile developed similar ideas. See D. Schlenstedt, ed. *Literarische Widerspiegelung: Geschichtliche und theoretische Dimensionen eines Problems* (Berlin: Aufbau, 1981) and Weimann, *Shakespeare und die Macht der Mimesis.*

3. See F. Burwick and W. Pape, eds., *Aesthetic Illusion: Theoretical and Historical Approaches* (Berlin: Walter de Gruyter, 1990).

4. See S. C. H. Barrett, "Mimikry bei Pflanzen," *Spektrum der Wissenschaft* 11(1987): 100–107. The animals and plants that are imitated in the processes of mimicry are always clearly distinguished from the imitators; they belong to another species. In mimicry, characteristics, precisely those the imitator does not possess, are—apparently—appropriated for purposes of deception. In this way, an animal or a plant gains an advantage that it does not have in its own constitution. A plant organism, for example, imitates an animal model: an orchid deceives a dagger wasp by means of the lower lip

of its blossom, which in size, shape, and pilose approximately coincides with the female wasp. Males eager to mate are signal receivers; they cannot distinguish precisely between the model and the imitation. In their search for a mate, they are attracted by the orchids, pick up nectar and pollen, and spread the latter among individuals of the same species. In mimicry the relations are clear. The plant's external characteristics deceive the animal, and the plant thus attains an adaptive advantage; but neither does the plant become animal nor vice versa.

5. Analytic philosophy contents itself with the statement that symbols are (also) material things and that empirical reality is shaped by language. It is not interested in the genesis and development of symbolic systems. But only through observation of historical processes is it possible to assess the convergent development of symbolic systems and empirical reality.

6. This point of view is elaborated by G. Grossklaus, "Das technische Bild der Wirklichkeit: Von der Nachahmung (Mimesis) zur Erzeugung (Simulation)," *Friedericiana* (1991): 39–57.

Bibliography

Abrams, M. H. *The Mirror and the Lamp.* New York: W. W. Norton, 1953.

Adam J. *The Republic of Plato.* With Critical Notes, Commentary, and Appendices. Cambridge: Cambridge University Press, 1963.

Adorno, Theodor. *Against Epistemology: A Metacritique. Studies in Husserl and the Phenomenological Antinomies.* Trans. Willis Domingo. Oxford: Basil Blackwell, 1982.

―――. *Aesthetic Theory.* Trans. C. Lenhardt. London: Routledge & Kegan Paul, 1984.

―――. *Dissonanzen. Musik in der Verwaltete Welt.* Göttingen: Vandenhoeck & Ruprecht 1963.

―――. *Gesammelte Schriften.* Frankfurt am Main: Suhrkamp, 1970–1986.

―――. *Der getreue Korrepetitor.* Frankfurt: Suhrkamp, 1963.

―――. *Minima Moralia: Reflections from a Damaged Life.* Trans. E. F. N. Jephcott. London: Verso, 1978.

―――. *Negative Dialectics.* Trans. E. B. Ashton. New York: Seabury Press, 1973.

Aemile, Paul. *De rebus geshis Francorum libri IV Parisiis.* Trans. Jean Regnar. Paris, 1581.

Alpers, Svetlana. *The Art of Describing: Dutch Art in the Seventeenth Century.* Chicago: University of Chicago Press, 1983.

Alter, Robert. *Motives for Fiction.* Cambridge: Harvard University Press, 1984.

Altrichter, V. "Konstruktion und Dekonstruktion des manieristischen Genies im Cinquecento." Ph.D. dissertation, Freie Universität Berlin, 1987.

d'Andeli, Henri. *The Battle of the Seven Arts; French Poem.* Ed and trans. Louis John Paetow. Berkeley: University of California Press, 1914.

Apostolidès, Jean-Marie. *Le prince sacrifice: Theatre et politique au temps de Louis XIV.* Paris: Editions de Minuit, 1985.

Aquinas, Thomas. *The Summa Theologica.* Trans. Fathers of the English Domincan Province. Rev. Daniel J. Sullivan. 2 vols. Chicago: Encyclopaedia Britannica, 1952.

————. *Truth.* Trans. Robert W. Schmidt. 3 vols. Chicago: Henry Regnery, 1954.

Aristotle. *Poetics.* Trans. Stephen Halliwell. Chapel Hill: University of North Carolina Press, 1987.

————. *Rhetoric.* Trans. Rhys Roberts. New York: Modern Library, 1954.

————. *The Politics of Aristotle.* Ed. and trans. Ernest Barker. London: Oxford University Press, 1958.

Assmann, Alaida, and Jan Assmann, eds. *Schrift und Gedächtnis.* Munich: W. Fink, 1983.

————. "Kulturgesellschaft." *Ästhetik und Kommunikation,* nos. 67/68 (Berlin, 1987).

Atkins J. W. H. *Literary Criticism in Antiquity.* 2 vols. London: Methuen, 1934.

Auerbach, Erich. "Epilogomena zu *Mimesis.*" *Romische Forschungen* 65 (1954): 1–17.

————. *Gesammelte Aufsätze zur romanischen Philologie.* Ed. F. Schalk. Bern, 1982.

————. *Literatursprache und Publikum in der lateinischen Spätantike und im Mittelalter.* Bern, 1958.

————. *Mimesis: The Representation of Reality in Western Literature.* Trans. Willard R. Trask. Princeton: Princeton University Press, 1953.

Bakhtin, Mikhail. "Epos und Roman." *Kunst und Literatur* 18, no. 2 (1970): 918–942.

Balzac, Honoré de. *La Comédie humaine.* Ed. P.-G. Castex. Vols. I, II, V, VI. Paris: Gallimard, 1976–1977.

————. *A Harlot High and Low.* Trans. Rayner Heppenstall. Harmondsworth: Penguin Books, 1970.

————. *Lost Illusions.* Trans. Herbert J. Hunt. Harmondsworth: Penguin Books, 1971.

Bandera, C. *Mimesis conflictiva: Ficción literaria y violenca en Cervantes y Calderón.* Madrid, 1975.

Barrett, S. C. H. "Mimikry bei Pflanzen." *Spektrum der Wissenschaft* 11 (1987): 100–107.

Baron, Hans. "The 'Querelle' of the Ancients and the Moderns as a Problem for Renaissance Scholarship." *Journal of the History of Ideas* 20 (1959): 3–22.

Bartetzko, Dieter. *Zwischen Zucht und Ekstase: Zur Theatralik von NS-Architektur.* Berlin: Mann, 1985.

Barthes, Roland. *Camera Lucida: Reflections on Photography.* Trans. Richard Howard. New York: Hill and Wang, 1981.

————. *The Pleasure of the Text.* Trans. Richard Miller. New York: Hill and Wang, 1975.

————. *On Racine.* Trans. Richard Howard. New York: Hill and Wang, 1964.

Bateson, Gregory. "Eine Theorie des Spiels und der Phantasie," *Ökologie des Geistes* (Frankfurt am Main, 1985): 241–261.

Baudrillard, Jean. *L'autre par lui-même.* Paris, 1987.

Bäuml, F. *From Symbol to Mimesis.* Göttingen, 1984.

Beck, H., et al. *Ideal und Wirklichkeit der bildenden Kunst im späten 18. Jahrhundert.* Berlin, 1984.

Belaval, Y. *L'Esthétique sans paradoxe de Diderot.* Paris: Gallimard, 1950.

Benichou, Paul. *Man and Ethics: Studies in French Classicism.* Trans. Elizabeth Hughes. Garden City, N.Y.: Anchor Books, 1971.

Benjamin, Walter. *Gesammelte Schriften.* Frankfurt am Main: Suhrkamp, 1980.

————. *Illuminationen, Schriften 1.* Frankfurt am Main: Suhrkamp, 1977.

————. "On Language as Such and on the Language of Man." In *Reflections: Essays, Aphorisms, Autobiographical Writings.* Trans. Edmund Jephcott. New York: Harcourt Brace Jovanovich, 1978.

————. "A Small History of Photography." In *One-Way Street and Other Writings.* Trans. Edmund Jephcott and Kingsley Shorter. London: New Left Books, 1979. 240–258.

————. "On Some Motifs in Baudelaire." In *Illuminations.* Trans. Harry Zohn. New York: Schocken Books, 1969. 155–200.

————. "The Storyteller." In *Illuminations.* Trans. Harry Zohn. New York: Schocken Books, 1969. 83–110.

————. "On the Mimetic Faculty." In *Reflections: Essays, Aphorisms, Autobiographical Writings.* Trans. Edmund Jephcott. New York: Harcourt Brace Jovanovich, 1978. 333–336.

Benz, E. *Akzeleration der Zeit als geschichtliches und heilgeschichtliches Problem.* Mainz, 1977.

Bing, Susi. "*Die* Naturnachahmungstheorie bei Gottsched und den Schweizern und ihre Beziehung zu der Dichtungstheorie der Zeit." Ph.D. dissertation, Würzburg, 1934.

Black, Max. *Models and Metaphors: Studies in Language and Philosophy.* Ithaca: Cornell University Press, 1962.

Blanchard, M. E. *Description: Sign, Self, Desire. Critical Theory in the Wake of Semiotics.* Den Haag, 1980.

Blanshard, F. B. *Retreat from Likeness in the Theory of Painting.* New York: Columbia University Press, 1949.

Block, Ned. *Imagery.* Cambridge: MIT Press, 1982.

Blondel, François. *Cours d'architecture.* Paris: L. Roulland, 1683.

Blumenberg, Hans. "'Nachahmung der Natur': Zur Vorgeschichte der Idee des schöpferischen Menschen." In *Wirklichkeiten, in denen wir leben.* Stuttgart, 1981. 55–103.

————. *Lebenzeit und Weltzeit.* Frankfurt am Main: Suhrkamp, 1986.

Bodmer, J. J. *Critische Abhandlung von dem Wunderbaren in der Poesie.* Reprint of 1740 edition. Stuttgart, 1966.

Böhme, G. "Der offene Leib: Eine Interpretation der Mikrokosmos-Makrokosmos-Beziehung bei Paracelsus." In Dietmar Kamper and Christoph Wulf, eds., *Transfiguration des Körpers: Spuren der Gewalt in der Geschichte.* Berlin, 1989. 44–58.

————. "Der sprechende Leib: Die Semiotiken des Körpers am Ende des 18. Jahrhunderts und ihre hermetische Tradition." In Dietmar Kamper and Christoph Wulf, eds., *Transfiguration des Körpers: Spuren der Gewalt in der Geschichte.* Berlin, 1989. 144–181.

————. *Der Typ Sokrates.* Frankfurt am Main: Suhrkamp, 1988.

Bohn, V., ed. *Bildlichkeit.* Frankfurt am Main, 1990.

Boileau Despreaux, Nicolas. *L'Art poétique.* Ed. J.-C. Lambert and F. Mizrachi. Paris, 1966.

————. *Epîtres-art poétique-Lutrin.* Paris: Société les Belles Lettres, 1952.

Bolz, Norbert W., and Richard Faber, eds. *Walter Benjamin: Profane Erleuchtung und rettende Kritik.* Würzburg: Königshausen & Neumann, 1982.

Bourdieu, Pierre. "Le champ littéraire." In *Actes de la recherche en sciences sociales* 89 (1991): 4–46.

———. *Distinction: A Social Critique of the Judgment of Taste.* Trans. Richard Nice. Cambridge: Harvard University Press, 1984.

———. "The Historical Genesis of a Pure Aesthetic." In Richard Shusterman, ed., *Analytic Aesthetics.* Oxford: Oxford University Press, 1989.

———. "L'Illusion biographique." *Actes de la recherche en sciences sociales* 62/63 (1986): 69–72.

———. *Outline of a Theory of Practice.* Trans. Richard Nice. Cambridge: Cambridge University Press, 1977.

———. *Le Sens pratique.* Paris, 1981.

———. *Zur Soziologie der Symbolischen Formen.* Frankfurt am Main: Suhrkamp, 1979.

Bourdieu, Pierre, and L. Boltanski et al. *Photography: A Middle-Brow Art.* Trans. Shaun Whiteside. Stanford: Stanford University Press, 1990.

Bowra, C. M. *Heroic Poetry.* London: Macmillan, 1956.

———. *Poesie der Frühzeit.* Munich, 1967.

Boyd, John D. *The Function of Mimesis and Its Decline.* New York: Fordham University Press, 1980.

Bray, René. *La Formation de la doctrine classique en France.* Paris: Nizet, 1931.

Breitinger, J. J. *Critische Dichtkunst.* 2 vols. Reprint of 1840 edition. Stuttgart, 1966.

Brownlee, M. S. "Autobiography as Self-(Re)presentation." In John D. Lyons and Stephen G. Nichols, Jr., eds., *Mimesis: From Mirror to Method, Augustine to Descartes.* Hanover, N.H.: University Press of New England, 1982. 71–82.

Bruck, J. "Der aristotelische Mimesisbegriff und die Nachahmungstheorie Gottscheds und der Schweizer." Ph.D. dissertation, Erlangen-Nürnberg, 1972.

Bruck, J., et al. "Der Mimesisbegriff Gottscheds und der Schweizer." *Zeitschrift für deutsche Philologie* 90 (1971): 563–578.

Bruyne, E. de. *Etudes d'esthétique médiévale.* Vols. 1–3, *De Boèce à Jean Scot Erigène.* Brügge, 1946.

Buck, A. "Aus der Vorgeschichte der Querelle des Anciens et des Modernes." *Bibliothèque de l'Humanisme et de la Renaissance* 20. Geneva, 1958. 527–541.

Bürger, Peter. *Prosa der Moderne.* Frankfurt am Main: Suhrkamp, 1988.

Burke, Kenneth. *Language as Symbolic Action.* Berkeley, Los Angeles, and London: University of California Press, 1966.

Burkert, W. *Anthropologie des religiösen Opfers: Die Sakralisierung der Gewalt.* Munich: Veröffentlichung der C. F. von Siemens-Stiftung, 1984.

———. *Homo necans.* Berlin, 1972.

Burwick, F., and W. Pape, eds. *Aesthetic Illusion: Theoretical and Historical Approaches.* Berlin: Walter de Gruyter, 1990.

Butcher, S. H. *Aristotle's Theory of Poetry and Fine Art.* London: Macmillan, 1932.

Bywater, Ingram. *Aristotle on the Art of Poetry.* Oxford: Oxford University Press, 1909.

Caillois, Roger. *Man and the Sacred.* Trans. Meyer Barash. Westport, Conn.: Greenwood Press, 1980.

————. *Le Mythe et l'homme*. Paris, 1938.

Canetti, E. *Crowds and Power*. Trans. Carol Stewart. New York: Farrar, Straus, Giroux, 1984.

Cave, J. D. *The Cornucopian Text: Problems of Writing in the French Renaissance*. Oxford, 1979.

————. "The Mimesis of Reading in the Renaissance." In John D. Lyons and Stephen G. Nichols, Jr., eds., *Mimesis: From Mirror to Method, Augustine to Descartes*. Hanover, N.H.: University Press of New England, 1982. 149–153.

Cochetti, Stefano. *Mythos und "Dialectic der Aufklärung."* Königstein: A. Hain, 1985.

Colpe, Carsten. *Über das Heilige: Versuch, seiner Verkennung kritisch vorzubeugen*. Frankfurt am Main: A. Hain, 1990.

Compagnon, Antoine. *La seconde de main, où le travail de la citation*. Paris: Seuil, 1979.

Corneille, Pierre. *Oeuvres complètes*. Ed. G. Couton. 2 vols. Paris, 1980, 1984.

Costa Lima, Luiz. "Historie und Metahistorische Kategorien bei Erich Auerbach." In Hans Ulrich Gumbrecht and K. L. Pfeiffer, eds., *Stil: Geschichte und Funktion eines Kulturwissenschaftlichen Diskurselements*. Frankfurt am Main, 1986. 289–313.

————. "Die Kontrolle des Imaginären." in Hans Ulrich Gumbrecht and K. L. Pfeiffer, eds., *Stil: Geschichte und Funktion eines kulturwissenschaftlichen Diskurselements*. Frankfurt am Main, 1986.

Cramer, F. *Chaos and Order: The Complex Structure of Living Systems*. Trans. D. I. Loewus. New York: VCH, 1993.

Crane, R. S., ed. *Critics and Criticism, Ancient and Modern*. Chicago: University of Chicago Press, 1952.

Curtius, E. R. *Europäische Literatur und lateinisches Mittelalter*. Bern: Francke, 1954.

Dällenbach, L. *Le récit spéculaire*. Paris, 1977.

Danto, Arthur C. *The Transfiguration of the Commonplace*. Cambridge: Harvard University Press, 1981.

Dauk, E. *Denken als Ethos und Methode: Foucault lesen*. Berlin, 1989.

Davy, M. M. *Initiation à la symbolique romane*. Paris, 1964.

Deleuze, Gilles. *Proust and Signs*. Trans. Richard Howard. New York: G. Braziller, 1972.

Dennis, J. *The Comical Gallant,* Introduction. Facsimile. London, 1702.

Derrida, Jacques. "The Double Session." In *Dissemination*. Trans. Barbara Johnson. Chicago: University of Chicago Press, 1981. 173–286.

————. "Economimesis." In Jacques Derrida et al., *Mimésis des articulations*. Paris: Aubier-Flammarion, 1964.

————. *Of Grammatology*. Trans. Gayatri Chakavorty Spivak. Baltimore: Johns Hopkins University Press, 1976.

————. "Plato's Pharmacy." In *Dissemination*. Trans. Barbara Johnson. Chicago: University of Chicago Press, 1981. 173–286. Originally published 1968.

————. *The Post Card: From Socrates to Freud and Beyond*. Trans. Alan Bates. Chicago: University of Chicago Press, 1987.

Diderot, Denis. *Overview esthétiques*. Paris. Editions Garnier Freres, 1965.

————. *The Paradox of Acting*. Trans. Walter Herries Pollock. New York: Hill and Wang, 1957.

Dieckmann, H. "Die Wandlung des Nachahmungsbegriffes in der französischen Ästhetik des 18. Jahrhunderts." In H. R. Jauss, ed., *Nachahmung und Illusion.* Munich:
W. Fink, 1969. 28–59.

Doebler, John. *Shakespeare's Speaking Pictures: Studies in Iconic Imagery.* Albuquerque: University of New Mexico Press, 1974.

Dostoyevsky, Fyodor. *Notes from Underground.* Trans. Serge Shishkoff. New York:
Thomas Y. Crowell, 1969.

Douglas, Mary. *Ritual, Tabu und Körpersymbolik: Sozialanthropologische Studien in
Industriegesellschaft und Stammeskultur.* Frankfurt am Main, 1974.

Dumouchel, P., and J.-P. Dupuy. *L'Enfer des choses: René Girard et la logique de
l'économie.* Paris: Seuil, 1979.

Eco, Umberto. *The Aesthetics of Thomas Aquinas.* Cambridge: Harvard University
Press, 1988.

———. *The Open Work.* Trans. Anna Cancogni. Cambridge: Harvard University
Press, 1989.

———. *Über Spiegel und andere Phänomene.* Munich, 1988.

Eco, Umberto, and C. Marmo. *On the Medieval Theory of Signs.* Amsterdam, 1989.

Eder, K. "Klassentheorie als Gesellschaftstheorie: Bourdieus dreifache kulturtheoretische Brechung der traditionellen Klassentheorie." In Klaus Eder, ed., *Klassenlage,
Lebenstil und kulturelle Praxis: Beiträge zur Auseinandersetzung mit Pierre Bourdieus Klassentheorie.* Frankfurt am Main: Suhrkamp, 1989.

Ehrard, J. *L'Ideé de nature en France à l'aube des lumières.* Paris: Flammarion,
1970.

Elias, Norbert. *The Court Society.* Trans. Edmund Jephcott. New York: Pantheon Books,
1983.

———. *The Civilizing Process.* Trans. Edmund Jephcott. New York: Urizen Books,
1978.

Else, G. F. *Aristotle's Poetics: The Argument.* Cambridge: Harvard University Press,
1957.

———. "Imitation in the 5th Century." *Classical Philology* 53, no. 2 (April 1958):
73–90.

Feldmann, H. *Mimesis und Wirklichkeit.* Munich, 1988.

Finas, L., et al. *Ecarts.* Paris, 1973.

Fink, E. *Spiel als Weltsymbol.* Stuttgart, 1960.

Finsler, Georg. *Platon und die Aristotelische Poetik.* Leipzig, 1900.

Fischer-Lichte, Erika. *Semiotik des Theaters: Eine Einführung.* Vol. 2. *Vom "kunst-
lerischen" zum "natürlichen" Zeichen: Theater des Barock und der Aufklärung.*
Tübingen: Gunter Narr, 1983.

Fish, Stanley. *Is There a Text in this Class?* Cambridge: Harvard University Press,
1980.

Flasch, Kurt. "*Ars imitatur naturam:* Platonischer Naturbegriff und mittelalterliche
Philosophie der Kunst." In *Parusia, Festgabe für J. Hirschberger,* ed. Kurt Flasch.
Frankfurt am Main: Minerva, 1965. 265–306.

Flashar, H. *Der Dialog Ion als Zeugnis platonischer Philosophie.* Berlin, 1958.

Flaubert, Gustave. *Oeuvres.* Vol. II. Ed. A. Thibaudet and R. Dumesnil. Paris: Gallimard, 1952.

—————. *The Sentimental Education.* Trans. Perdita Burlingame. New York: New American Library, 1972.

Fontenelle, B. *Nouveaux dialogues des morts.* Chapel Hill: University of North Carolina Press, 1966.

Foucault, Michel. *The Archaeology of Knowledge.* Trans. Alan Sheridan Smith. New York: Pantheon Books, 1972.

—————. *Discipline and Punish: The Birth of the Prison.* Trans. Alan Sheridan. New York: Vintage Books, 1979.

—————. *The History of Sexuality.* Vol. 2: *The Use of Pleasure;* vol. 3: *The Care of the Self.* Trans. Robert Hurley. New York: Pantheon Books, 1978–1986.

—————. *The Order of Things: An Archaeology of the Human Sciences.* New York: Vintage Books, 1970.

Fozza, J.-C., et al. *Petite fabrique de l'image.* Paris, 1985.

Fréart de Chambray, Roland. *Parallèle de l'architecture antique et de la moderne.* Paris, 1650.

Freud, Sigmund. *Beyond the Pleasure Principle.* Trans. James Strachey. New York: W. W. Norton, 1961.

—————. "Der Dichter und das Phantasieren." *Studienausgabe* 10 (Frankfurt am Main, 1989): 169–179.

—————. *Totem and Taboo: Some Points of Agreement Between the Mental Lives of Savages and Neurotics.* Trans. James Strachey. New York: W. W. Norton, 1950.

Früchtl, Josef. *Mimesis: Konstellation eines Zentralbegriffs bei Adorno.* Würzburg: Konigshausen & Neumann, 1986.

Frye, Northrop. *Anatomy of Criticism.* Princeton: Princeton University Press, 1957.

Fuhrmann, Manfred. *Einführing in die antike Dichtungstheorie.* Darmstadt, 1973.

Fuld, Werner. *Walter Benjamin: Zwischen Stuhlen, eine Biographie.* Munich: Hanser, 1979.

Fumaroli, Marc. *L'Âge de l'éloquence: Rhétorique et "res literaria" de la Renaissance au Secs fuil de l'époque classique.* Geneva, 1980.

Gadamer, Hans-Georg. *Die Aktualität des Schönen.* Stuttgart, 1967.

—————. *Truth and Method.* Trans. Garrett Barden and John Cumming. New York: Seabury Press, 1975.

Gadamer, Hans-Georg, and Gottfried Böhm. *Seminar: Hermeneutik und die Wissenschaften.* Frankfurt am Main: Suhrkamp, 1978.

Galli, Uberto. *La Mimesis artistica secundo Aristotele: Studi Italiani di filologica classica.* Florence, 1925.

Ganthier, G. *Vengt et une leçons sur l'image et le sens.* Paris, 1989.

Gaster, Theodor Herzl. *Thespis, Ritual, Myth and Drama in the Ancient Near East.* Garden City, N.Y.: Doubleday, 1961.

Gebauer, Gunter. "Die Beziehungen von Bild und Text in Lessings *Laokoon.*" In S. Dümchen and M. Nerlich, *Texte-Image, Bild Text.* Berlin: Technische Universität Berlin, Institute für Romanische Literaturwissenschaft, 1990.

—————. *Der Einzelne und sein gesellschaftliches Wissen: Untersuchungen zum Symbolischen Wissen.* Berlin: Walter de Gruyter, 1981.

—————. *Das Laokoön-Projekt: Pläne einer semiotischen Ästhetik.* Stuttgart: Metzler, 1984.

————. "Die Unbegründbarkeit der Sprachtheorie und notwendige Erzählungen über die Sprache." In Gunter Gebauer et al., *Historische Anthropologie*. Reinbek: Rowohlt, 1989. 127–169.

————. "Überwindung des verinnerlichten Dialogs: Die Mimesis des Schönen und die Proustschen Enttäuschungen." In H. Lenk, *Zur Kritik der wissenschaftlichen Rationalität*. Freiburg: K. Alber, 1986. 543–552.

Gebhardt, Peter, et al. *Walter Benjamin: Zeitgenosse der Moderne*. Krönberg: Scriptor, 1976.

Geertz, Clifford. "Deep Play: Notes on the Balinese Cockfight." In Geertz, *The Interpretation of Cultures*. New York: Basic Books, 1973. 412–453.

Gehlen, Arnold. *Man: His Nature and Place in the World*. Trans. Clare McMillan and Karl Pillemer. New York: Columbia University Press, 1988.

Genette, Gerard. *Figures II*. Paris, 1969.

————. *Figures III*. Paris: Seuil, 1972.

————. *Mimologiques*. Paris: Seuil, 1976.

————. *Paratexte*. Frankfurt am Main, 1989.

Gessinger, J., and W. von Rahden, eds. *Theorien vom Ursprung der Sprache*. Vol. 1. Berlin, 1989.

Geulen, Dieter. *Das vergesellschaftete Subjekt: Zur Grundlegung der Sozialisationstheorie*. Frankfurt am Main: Suhrkamp, 1977.

Ghellinck, J. de. "Nani et gigantes." *Archivium Latinatis medii aevi (Bulletin Du Cange)* 18 (1945): 25–29.

Gilbert, K., and H. Kuhn. *A History of Esthetics*. New York: Macmillan, 1939.

Gillot, Hubert. *La Querelle des Anciens et des Modernes en France*. Geneva: Slatkine Reprints, 1968.

Girard, René. *Critique dans un souterrain*. Paris, 1976.

————. *Deceit, Desire, and the Novel: Self and Other in Literary Structure*. Trans. Yvonne Freccero. Baltimore: Johns Hopkins University Press, 1965.

————. "Der grundlegende Mord im Denken Nietzsche." In Dietmar Kamper and Christoph Wulf, eds., *Das Heilige: Seine Spur in der Moderne*. Frankfurt am Main, 1987. 255–274.

————. *Job: The Victim of his People*. Trans. Yvonne Freccero. Stanford: Stanford University Press, 1987.

————. *The Scapegoat*. Trans. Yvonne Freccero. Baltimore: Johns Hopkins University Press, 1986.

————. *A Theater of Envy: William Shakespeare*. New York: Oxford University Press, 1991.

————. *Things Hidden since the Foundation of the World*. Trans. Stephen Bann and Michael Metteer. Stanford: Stanford University Press, 1987.

————. *Violence and the Sacred*. Trans. Patrick Gregory. Baltimore: Johns Hopkins University Press, 1977.

Goethe, J. W. von. "Zum Shakespeare-Tag (1771)." In *Werke*, Jubiläumsausgabe, vol. 36. Stuttgart, 1902–1912.

Goffman, Erving. *The Presentation of the Self in Everyday Life*. New York: Doubleday, 1959.

Goldmann, Lucien. *The Hidden God: A Study of the Tragic Vision in the Pensées of Pascal and the Tragedies of Racine.* Trans. Philip Thody. London: Routledge & Kegan Paul, 1964.

Goldstein, H. D. "Mimesis and Catharsis Reexamined." *Journal of Aesthetics and Art Criticism* 24 (1965–1966): 567–578.

Goodman, Nelson. *Languages of Art: An Approach to a Theory of Symbols.* Indianapolis: Bobbs-Merrill, 1968.

———. *Ways of Worldmaking.* Indianapolis: Hackett, 1978.

Goodman, Nelson, and Catherine G. Elgin. *Reconceptions in Philosophy and other Arts and Sciences.* Indianapolis: Hackett, 1988.

Goody, Jack. *The Domestication of the Savage Mind.* Cambridge: Cambridge University Press, 1977.

———. *The Interface Between the Written and the Oral.* Cambridge: Cambridge University Press, 1987.

———. *Literacy in Traditional Society.* Cambridge: Cambridge University Press, 1968.

———. *The Logic of Writing and the Organization of Society.* Cambridge: Cambridge University Press, 1986.

Goody, Jack, Ian Watt, and Kathleen Gough. *Enstehung und Folgen der Schriftkultur.* Frankfurt am Main, 1986.

Gottsched, J. C. *Versuch einer Critischen Dichtkunst.* Darmstadt, 1962.

Grange, J. *Balzac: L'Argent, la prose, les anges.* Paris: La Differánce, 1990.

Green, Thomas M. "Erasmus's 'Festina lente': Vulnerabilities of the Humanist Text." In John D. Lyons and Stephen G. Nichols, Jr., eds., *Mimesis: From Mirror to Method, Augustine to Descartes.* Hanover, N.H.: University Press of New England, 1982.

Greenblatt, Stephen, ed. *Allegory and Representation.* Baltimore: Johns Hopkins University Press, 1981.

Greffrath, K. R. *Metaphorischer Materialismus: Untersuchungen zum Geschichtsbegriff Walter Benjamins.* Munich: W. Fink, 1981.

Grossklaus, G. "Das technische Bild der Wirklichkeit: Von der Nachahmung (Mimesis) zur Erzeugung (Simulation)." *Friedericiana* (1991): 39–57.

Guetzkow, Harold, ed. *Simulation in Social Science.* Englewood Cliffs, N.J.: Prentice-Hall, 1962.

Gumbrecht, Hans Ulrich, and K. L. Pfeiffer, eds. *Stil: Geschichten und Funktionen eines kulturwissenschaftlichen Diskurselements.* Frankfurt am Main: 1986.

Guyer, F. E. "The Dwarf on the Giant's Shoulders." *Modern Language Notes* 45 (1930): 398–402.

Haarman, Harald. *Universalgeschichte der Schrift.* Frankfurt: Campus, 1990.

Habermas, Jürgen. "Bewußtmachende oder rettende Kritik: Die Aktualität Walter Benjamins." In S. Unseld, ed., *Zur Aktualität Walter Benjamins. Aus Anlass des 80. Geburtstag von Walter Benjamin.,* ed. Siegfried Unseld. Frankfurt am Main: Suhrkamp, 1972. 173ff.

———. *The Structural Transformation of the Public Sphere: An Inquiry into a Category of Bourgeois Society.* Trans. Thomas Berger. Cambridge: MIT Press, 1989.

Hager, Fritz Peter. *Plato Paedagogus: Aufsätze zur Geschichte und Aktualität des pädagogischen Platonismus.* Vol. 1. Stuttgart, 1981.

Halliwell, Stephen. *Aristotle's Poetics.* London: Ducksworth, 1986.

Hans, James. *Imitation and the Image of Man.* Philadelphia: J. Benjamins, 1987.

————. *The Play of the World.* Amherst: University of Massachusetts Press, 1981.

Harari, Josue, ed. *Textual Strategies.* Ithaca: Cornell University Press, 1979.

Harth, H. "Dichtung und Arete." Ph.D. dissertation, Frankfurt am Main, 1965.

Hartmann, Geoffrey. *Saving the Text.* Baltimore: Johns Hopkins University Press, 1981.

Havelock, Eric A. *The Literate Revolution in Greece and Its Cultural Consequences.* Princeton: Princeton University Press, 1982.

————. *Origins of Western Literacy.* Toronto: Ontario Institute for Studies in Education, 1976.

————. *Preface to Plato.* Cambridge: Harvard University Press, 1963.

Herder, Johann Gottfried. *Abhandlung über den Ursprung der Sprache.* Ed. H. D. Irmscher. Stuttgart: Reclam, 1975.

Herrmann, H. P. *Naturnachahmung und Einbildungskraft: Zur Entwicklung der deutschen Poetik von 1670 bis 1740.* Bad Homburg, 1970.

Hohner, Ulrich. *Zur Problematik der Naturnachahmung in der Ästhetik des 18. Jahrhunderts.* Erlangen: Palm & Enke, 1976.

Hollander, Robert. "Imitative Distance." In John D. Lyons and Stephen G. Nichols, Jr., eds., *Mimesis: From Mirror to Method, Augustine to Descartes.* Hanover, N.H.: University Press of New England, 1982. 83–99.

Horace, *Collected Works.* Trans. Lord Dunsany and Michael Oakley. New York: Dutton, 1961.

Horkheimer, Max, and Theodor Adorno. *Dialectic of Enlightenment.* Trans. John Cumming. New York: Seabury Press, 1972.

Horrig, Hans Otto, and Georg-Michael Schulz. *Das Wunderbare und die Poetik der Frühaufklärung, Gottsched und die Schweizer.* Darmstadt: Wissenschaftliche Buchgesellschaft, 1988.

Hume, Kathryn. *Fantasy and Mimesis: Responses to Reality in Western Literature.* New York: Methuen, 1984.

Huyssen, A. "Das Versprechen der Natur: Alternative Naturkonzepte im 18. Jahrhundert." In R. Grimm and J. Hermand, eds., *Natur und Natürlichkeit: Stationen des Grünen in der deutschen Literatur.* Königstein: Athenäum, 1981. 1–18.

Illich, Ivan, and Barry Sanders. *A B C: The Alphabetization of the Popular Mind.* San Francisco: North Point Press, 1988.

Imdahl, Max, et al. *Theorie und Geschichte der Literatur und der schönen Künste.* Vol. 2. Munich, 1964.

————. *Theorie und Geschichte der Literatur und der schönen Künste.* Vol. 9. Munich, 1969.

Iser, Wolfgang. *The Act of Reading: A Theory of Aesthetic Response.* Baltimore: Johns Hopkins University Press, 1978.

————. *The Implied Reader: Patterns of Communication in Prose Fiction from Bunyan to Beckett.* Baltimore: Johns Hopkins University Press, 1974.

Jauss, Hans Robert. "Ästhetische Normen und geschichtliche Reflexion in der 'Querelle des Anciens et des Modernes.'" In Charles Perrault, ed., *Parallèle des Anciens et des Modernes.* Munich: Eidos Verlag, 1964. 8–64.

Jaynes, Julian. *The Origin of Consciousness in the Breakdown of the Bicameral Mind.* Boston: Houghton Mifflin, 1976.

Jouin, Henry. *Conférences de l'Académie Royale de peinture et de sculpture.* Paris: A. Quantin, 1883.

Jousse, Mathurin. *L'Anthropologie du geste.* Vol. 1. Paris, 1974. Vol. 2: *La manducation de la parole.* Paris, 1975. Vol. 3: *Le parlant, la parole et le souffle.* Paris: Gallimard, 1978.

Judovitz, Dalia. *Subjectivity and Representation in Descartes: The Origins of Modernity.* Cambridge: Cambridge University Press, 1988.

Jürgens, Martin. *Moderne und Mimesis: Vorschlag für eine Theorie der modernen Kunst.* Münster, 1988.

Kager, Reinhard. *Herrschaft und Versöhnung: Einfuhren in das Denken Theodor W. Adornos.* Frankfurt am Main: Suhrkamp, 1988.

Kalász, Claudia. *Hölderlin: Die poetische Kritik Instrumenteller Rationalität.* Munich: Text & Kritik, 1988.

Kamper, Dietmar. *Zur Geschichte der Einbildungskraft.* Munich, 1981.

———. *Zur Soziologie der Imagination.* Munich, 1986.

———. "Tod des Körpers—Leben der Sprache. Über die Intervention des Imaginären im Zivilisationsprozess." In Gunter Gebauer et al., *Historische Anthropologie.* Reinbek, 1989. 49–81.

Kamper, Dietmar, and Christoph Wulf, eds. *Die erloschene Seele: Disziplin, Geschichte, Kunst, Mythos.* Berlin, 1988.

———. *Das Heilige: Seine Spur in der Moderne.* Frankfurt am Main, 1987.

———. *Lachen—Gelächter—Lächeln: Reflexionen in drei Spiegeln.* Frankfurt am Main: Syndikat, 1986.

———. *Der Schein des Schönen.* Göttingen: Steidl, 1989.

———. *Die Sterbende Zeit.* Darmstadt: 1987.

Kant, Immanuel. *Critique of Judgement.* Trans. J. H. Bernard. New York: Hafner Press, 1951.

Kantorowicz, Ernst H. *The King's Two Bodies: A Study in Medieval Political Theology.* Princeton: Princeton University Press, 1957.

Kappner, H. H. *Die Bildungstheorie Adornos als Theorie der Erfahrung von Kultur und Kunst.* Frankfurt am Main, 1984.

Kastan, David Scott. "'His semblable is his mirror'": Hamlet and the Imitation of Revenge." *Shakespeare Studies* 19 (1987): 111–124.

Kierkegaard, Søren. "Diary of the Seducer." In *Either/Or.* Vol. 1. Trans. David F. Swenson and Lillian Marvin Swenson. Princeton: Princeton University Press, 1959.

Killy, W. *Wirklichkeit und Kunstcharakter.* Munich, 1963.

Kippenberg, H. G., and B. Luchesi, eds. *Magie: Die sozialwissenschaftliche Kontroverse über das Verstehen fremden Denkens.* Frankfurt am Main, 1978.

Klibansky, R. "Standing on the Shoulders of Giants." *Isis* 26 (1936): 147–149.

Kofman, S. *Derrida lesen.* Vienna, 1987.

Koller, Hermann. *Die Mimesis in der Antike: Nachahmung, Darstellung, Ausdruck.* Bern: A. Francke, 1954.

Kosellek, R. *Kritik und Krise: Eine Studie zur Pathogenese der Welt.* Frankfurt am Main, 1973.

————. *Vergangene Zukunft.* Frankfurt am Main, 1979.

Krais, B. "Soziales Feld, Macht und kulturelle Praxis: Die Untersuchungen Bourdieus über die verschiedenen Fraktionen der 'herrschenden Klasse' in Frankreich." In Klaus Eder, ed., *Klassenlage, Lebenstil und kulturelle Praxis.* Frankfurt am Main, 1989. 47–70.

Krauss, W. *Fontenelle und die Aufklärung.* Munich, 1969.

————. *Der Literatur der französischen Frühaufklärung.* Frankfurt am Main, 1971.

Kristeller, P. O. "The Modern System of the Arts: A Study in the History of Aesthetics." *Journal of the History of Ideas* (October 1951): 510ff.

Krupnick, Mark, ed. *Displacement: Derrida and After.* Bloomington: Indiana University Press, 1982.

La Bruyère, Jean de. *Oeuvres de Heab de la Bruyère.* Nouvelle édition. Rev. sur les plus Anciens, impr. et les autographes et augm. par Jean Servois. Parts I-IV. Paris, 1865–1882.

Lacan, Jacques. "The Mirror Stage as Formative of the Function of the I." In *Écrits: A Selection.* Trans. Alan Sheridan. New York: W. W. Norton, 1977. 1–7.

Laclos, Choderlos de. *Les Liaisons dangereuses.* Trans. P. W. K. Stone. Harmondsworth: Penguin Books, 1961.

Lacoue-Labarthe, Philippe. "Diderot: Paradox and Mimesis." In Christopher Fynsk, ed., *Typography: Mimesis, Philosophy, Politics.* Cambridge: Harvard University Press, 1989.

————. "L'Imitation des Modernes." In *Typographies 2.* Paris, 1986.

————. "Theatricum analyticum." *Glyph 2* (1977).

————. "Typographie." In Jacques Derrida et al., *Mimésis des articulations.* Paris, 1964. 165–270.

Lafayette, Marie Madeleine Pioche de La Vergne. *The Princess of Cleves.* Trans. Nancy Mitford. Westport, Conn.: Greenwood Press, 1977.

Lasch, Christopher. *The Culture of Narcissism: American Life in an Age of Diminishing Expectations.* New York: W. W. Norton, 1979.

Leineweber, J. *Mimetisches Vermögen und allegorisches Verfahren: Studien zu Walter Benjamin und seiner Lehre vom Ähnlichen.* Marburg, 1978.

Lenk, Hans, ed. *Zur Kritik der Wisssenschaftlichen Rationalität.* Freiburg: K. Alber, 1986.

Lenzen, D. *Mythologie der Kindheit.* Reinbek, 1985.

————, ed. *Kunst und Pädagogik.* Darmstadt, 1990.

Lesky, Albin. "A Review of Koller's *Mimesis.*" *Gymnasium* (1956): 442–444.

Lessing, Gotthold Ephraim. *Briefe von Lessing.* In *Sämtliche Schriften,* vol. 17, ed. K. Lachmann. Leipzig, 1904.

————. *Hamburgische Dramaturgie.* Stuttgart: Reclam, 1981.

————. *Laocoön: An Essay on the Limits of Painting and Poetry.* Trans. Edward Allen McCormick. Indianapolis: Bobbs-Merrill Educational, 1962.

Lindler, B., and W. M. Lüdke, eds. *Materialien zur Ästhetischen Theorie Th. W. Adornos: Konstruktion der Moderne.* Frankfurt am Main: Suhrkamp, 1980.

Lipp, W. "Institutions—Mimesis or Drama? Thoughts on the Reconstruction of a Theory." In *Gesichtspunkte zur Neufassung einer Theorie.* Bielefeld, 1976.

Lippe, R. zur. *Sinnenbewußtsein: Grundlegung einer anthropologischen Ästhetik.* Reinbek, 1987.

Lord, Albert B. *The Singer of Tales.* Cambridge: Harvard University Press, 1960.

Lüdke, W. M. *Anmerkungen zu einer "Logik des Zerfalls": Adorno, Beckett.* Frankfurt am Main: Suhrkamp, 1981.

Luehe, I. von der. *Natur und Nachahmung: Untersuchungen zur Batteux-Rezeption in Deutschland.* Bonn, 1979.

Lucretius. *Lucretius on the Nature of Things.* Trans. Cyril Bailey. Oxford: Clarendon Press, 1910.

Lukács, Georg. *Ästhetik.* In *Werke*, vols. 11–12. Darmstadt, 1961.

———. "Balzac: Lost Illusions." In *Studies in European Realism.* New York: Grosset & Dunlap, 1964. 47–64.

Lüsebrink, H.-J. "Schrift, Buch und Lektüre in der französischsprachigen Literatur Afrikas." In H.-J. Lüsebrink, ed., *Zur Wahrnehmung und Funktion von Schriftlichkeit und Buchlektüre in einem kulturellen Epochenumbruch der Neuzeit.* Tübingen, 1989.

Lyons, John D. "Speaking in Pictures, Speaking of Pictures: Problems of Representation in the Seventeenth Century." In John D. Lyons and Stephen G. Nichols, Jr., eds., *Mimesis: From Mirror to Method, Augustine to Descartes.* Hanover, N.H.: University Press of New England, 1982.

Lyons, John D., and Stephen G. Nichols, Jr., eds. *Mimesis: From Mirror to Method, Augustine to Descartes.* Hanover, N.H.: University Press of New England, 1982.

Lyotard, Jean-François. *The Postmodern Condition: A Report on Knowledge.* Trans. Geoff Bennington and Brian Massumi. Minneapolis: University of Minnesota Press, 1984.

McKinley, M. B. *Words in a Corner: Studies in Montaigne's Latin Quotations.* Lexington: French Forum, 1981.

Malinowski, B. *Magie: Wissenschaft und Religion und andere Schriften.* Frankfurt am Main, 1973.

Marin, Louis. *Détruire la peinture.* Paris, 1977.

———. *Portrait of the King.* Trans. Martha M. Houle. Minneapolis: University of Minnesota Press, 1988.

———. *Le Récit est un piège.* Paris, 1978.

Matthies, K. *Schönheit, Nachahmung, Läuterung: Drei Grundkategorien für ästhetische Erziehung.* Frankfurt, 1988.

Matzat, W. "Affektrepräsentation im klassischen Diskurs: *La Princesse de Clèves.*" In F. Nies and K. Stierle, eds., *Französische Klassik: Theorie, Literatur, Malerei.* Munich: W. Fink, 1985. 231–266.

Mauss, Marcel. *A General Theory of Magic.* Trans. Robert Brian. London: Routledge & Kegan Paul, 1972.

Meiffert, T. *Die enteignete Erfahrung: Zu Walter Benjamins Konzept einer "Dialektik im Stillstand."* Bielefeld: Aisthesis Verlag, 1986.

Menninghaus, Winfried. *Walter Benjamins Theorie der Sprachmagie.* Frankfurt am Main: Suhrkamp, 1980.

Menz, E. "Die Schrift Karl Philipp Moritzens *Über die bildende Nachahmung des Schönen.*" Ph.D. dissertation, Göttingen, 1968.

Merleau-Ponty, Maurice. *Phenomenology of Perception.* Trans. Colin Smith. New York: Humanities Press, 1962.

Metscher, Th. "Ästhetik als Abbildtheorie: Erkenntnistheoretische Grundlagen materialistischer Kunsttheorie und das Realismusproblem in den Literaturwissenschaften." *Das Argument* 11/12 (1972): 919–976.

Molière, Jean-Baptiste. *Eight Plays by Molière.* Mattituck, N.Y.: Aeonian Press, 1957.

———. *The School for Wives.* Trans. Richard Wilbur. New York: Harcourt Brace Jovanovich, 1971.

Montaigne, Michel de. *Complete Essays.* Trans. Donald M. Frame. Stanford: Stanford University Press, 1958.

Moraux, P. *Aristotoles in de neueren Forschung.* Darmstadt, 1968.

———. "La mimesis dans les théories anciennes de la danse, de la musique et de la poésie." *Les Etudes Classiques* 23 (1955): 3–13.

Moritz, Karl Philipp. *Über die bildende Nachahmung des Schönen.* Nendeln, Liechtenstein: Kraus Reprint, 1968.

———. *Werke.* Ed. J. Jahn. 2 vols. Berlin: Insel Verlag, 1981.

Moscovici, S. *L'Âge des foules: Un traité historique de psychologie des masses.* Paris: Fayard, 1981.

Mourier, M. *Comment vivre avec l'image.* Paris, 1989.

Naumann, M., ed. *Gesellschaft—Literatur—Lesen: Literaturrezeption in theoretischer Sicht.* Berlin, 1975.

Naecker, J. *Die Negative Dialektik Adornos.* Oplanden, 1984.

Neckam, Alexander. *De nahiris rerum.* Ed. T. Wright. London: Longman, 1863.

Nelson, Benjamin. "Die Anfänge der modernen Revolution in Wissenschaft und Philosophie: Fiktionalismus, Probabilismus, Fideismus und katholisches Prophetentum." In Benjamin Nelson, *Der Ursprung der Moderne.* Frankfurt am Main: Suhrkamp, 1977. 94–139.

Nerlich, Michael. *Apollon et Dionysos ou la science incertaine des signes: Montaigne, Stendhal, Robbe-Grillet.* Marburg: Hitzeroth, 1989.

———. "Difesa del Seicento: Note sulla commedia francese dell'età 'classica.'" *Sigma* 12, nos. 2–3 (1979): 163–197.

———. "Essay über die Einheit des Ortes und Molière." *Lendemains* 22 (1981): 49–62.

———. "Notizen zum politischen Theater von Molière." *Lendemains* 22 (1981): 27–61.

Nichols, Jr., Stephen G. "Romanesque Imitation or Imitating the Romans?" In John D. Lyons and Stephen G. Nichols, Jr., eds., *Mimesis: From Mirror to Method, Augustine to Descartes.* Hanover, N.H.: University Press of New England, 1982. 36–59.

Nietzsche, Friedrich. *The Will to Power.* Trans. Walter Kaufmann and R. J. Hollingdale. New York: Vintage Books, 1968.

Oelmüller, W., ed. *Colloquium Kunst und Philosophie 1: Ästhetische Erfahrung.* Paderborn: Schoningh, 1981.

Ong, Walter J. *Interfaces of the Word.* Ithaca: Cornell University Press, 1977.

———. *Orality and Literacy: The Technologizing of the Word.* London: Routledge, 1982.

————. *Rhetoric, Romance, and Technology.* Ithaca: Cornell University Press, 1971.

Orgel, Stephen. *The Illusion of Power: Political Theater in the English Renaissance.* Berkeley, Los Angeles, and London: University of California Press, 1975.

Oughourlian, J. M. *The Puppet of Desire: The Psychology of Hysteria, Possession, and Hypnosis.* Stanford: Stanford University Press, 1991.

Parry, Milman. "The Making of Homeric Verse." In *The Collected Papers of Milman Parry.* Ed. Adam Parry. Oxford: Clarendon Press, 1971.

Patrizi, Francesco. *Della poetica la deca disputata.* Ferrara: V. Baldini, 1586.

Perpile, L. "Paper and Ink! The Structure of Unpredictability." In *"O, un Amy!" Essays in Montaigne in Honor of Donald M. Frame,* ed. Raymond C. La Charité. Lexington: French Forum, 1977. 190–218.

Perrault, Charles. *Parallèle des anciens et des modernes.* Vol. 2. Munich: Eidos Verlag, 1964.

Perrault, Claude. "De la musique des anciens." In *Essai de Physique* 2. Paris, 1680–1688.

Piles, Roger de. *Dialogue sur le coloris.* Paris: Chez Nicolas Langlois, 1699.

Plato. *The Collected Dialogues of Plato.* Ed. Edith Hamilton and Huntington Cairns. Princeton: Princeton University Press, 1961.

Plessner, H. "Der imitatorische Akt." In *Gesammelte Werke,* vol. 7, *Ausdruck und Menschliche Natur.* Frankfurt am Main, 1982. 449–457.

————. "Zur Anthropologie der Nachahmung." In *Gesammelte Werke,* vol. 7, *Ausdruck und Menschliche Natur.* Frankfurt am Main, 1982. 391–398.

Preisendanz, W. "Mimesis und Poesis in der deutschen Dichtungstheorie des 18. Jahrhundert." In *Rezeption und Produktion zwischen 1570 und 1730: Festschrift für Gunther Weydt zum 65. Geburtstag.* Ed. W. D. Rasch et al. Bern, 1972. 537–552.

————. "Zur Poetik der deutschen Romantik I: Die Abkehr vom Grundsatz der Naturnachahmung." In H. Steffen, ed., *Die deutsche Romantik.* Göttingen, 1967. 54–74.

Prendergast, Christopher. *The Order of Mimesis: Balzac, Stendhal, Nerval, Flaubert.* Cambridge: Cambridge University Press, 1986.

Prigent, Michel. *Le héros et l'état dans la tragédie de Pierre Corneille.* Paris: PUF, 1986.

Proust, Marcel. *By Way of Sainte-Beuve.* Trans. Sylvia Townsend Warner. London: Chatto & Windus, 1958.

Putnam, Hilary. *Reason, Truth and History.* Cambridge: Cambridge University Press, 1981.

Racine, Jean. *Andromache, Britannicus, Berenice.* Trans. John Cairncross. London: Penguin Books, 1967.

Rapp, U. *Handeln und Zuschauen.* Darmstadt, 1973.

Reich, Hermann. *Der Mimus: Ein litterar- und entwicklungsgeschichtlicher Versuch.* Berlin, 1903.

Reina, L. *Romanzo e mimesis: Dal romanticismo al neorealismo. Aspetti della narrativa italiana.* Salerno, 1975.

Reiss, Timothy. "Power, Poetry, and the Resemblance of Nature." In John D. Lyons and Stephen G. Nichols, Jr., eds., *Mimesis: From Mirror to Method, Augustine to Descartes.* Hanover, N.H.: University Press of New England, 1982. 215–247.

Ricoeur, Paul. *Die lebendige Metapher.* Munich, 1986.

————. *Time and Narrative.* Trans. Kathleen McLaughlin and David Pellauer. 3 vols. Chicago: University of Chicago Press, 1984.

Riedel, R. J., and F. Kreuzer, eds. *Evolution und Menschenbild.* Hamburg, 1983.

Riffaterre, M. *Semiotics of Poetry.* Bloomington: Indiana University Press, 1978.

Rigault, Hippolyte. *Histoire de la Querelle des Anciens et des Modernes.* Paris: Hachette, 1856.

Robert, Marthe. *En haine du roman: Étude sur Flaubert.* Paris: Balland, 1982.

Rosenmeyer, T. G. "Antiquity." *Erasmus, Speculum Scientarium* 10 (1957): 293–296.

————. "A Review of Koller's *Mimesis.*" *Erasmus, Speculum Scientarium* 10 (1957): 293–296.

Rousseau, Jean-Jacques. *The Confessions.* Trans. J. M. Cohen. London: Penguin Books, 1953.

————. *On the Origin of Language.* Trans. John H. Moran and Alexander Gode. Chicago: University of Chicago Press, 1966.

————. *Politics and the Arts: Letter to M. d'Alembert on the Theatre.* Trans. Allan Bloom. Ithaca: Cornell University Press, 1960.

————. *The Reveries of a Solitary Walker.* Trans. Charles E. Butterworth. New York: New York University Press, 1979.

Ruh, K. *Geschichte der abendländischen Mystik.* Vol. 1, *Die Grundlegung durch die Kirchenväter und die Mönchstheologie des 12. Jahrhunderts.* Munich, 1990.

Sander, H. "Das Subjekt der Moderne." In *Mentalitätswandel und literarische Evolution zwischen Klassik und Aufklärung.* Tübingen, 1987.

Sarton, George. "Standing on the Shoulders of Giants." *Isis* 24 (1935): 107–109.

Scaliger, J. C. *Poetices libri septem, Faksimile: Neudrück der Ausgabe von Lyon 1561 mit einer Einleitung von A. Buck.* Stuttgart: F. Frommann, 1964.

Schaffnit, H. W. *Mimesis als Problem: Studien zu einem ästhetischen Begriff der Dichtung aus Anlass Robert Musils.* Berlin, 1971.

Scheler, M. *Wesen und Formen der Sympathie—Deutsche Philosophie der Gegenwart.* Ed. M. S. Frings. Bern, 1973.

Schenker, M. *Batteux und seine Nachahmungstheorie in Deutschland.* Berlin, 1909. Reprint, Hildesheim, 1977.

Schier, D., ed. *Bernard le Bovier de Fontenelle: Nouveaux dialogues des morts.* Chapel Hill: University of North Carolina Press, 1965.

Schipper, E. W. "Mimesis in the Arts in Plato's Laws." *Journal of Aesthetics* 22 (1963–1964): 199–202.

Schlaffer, H. "Einleitung." In Jack Goody, Ian Watt, and Kathleen Gough. *Entstehung und Folgen der Schriftkultur.* Frankfurt am Main, 1986.

Schlenstedt, D., ed. *Literarische Widerspiegelung: Geschichtliche und theoretische Dimensionen eines Problems.* Berlin: Aufbau, 1981.

Schlosser, I. "Die Kunstlehre des 17. und 18. Jahrhunderts." *Materialien zu Quellenkunde der Kunstgeschichte* 9 (Vienna, 1920).

Schneider, Manfred. *Die erkältete Herzensschrift: Der autobiographische Text im 20. Jahrhundert.* Munich: C. Hanser, 1986.

Schobinger, Jean-Pierre. *Variationen zu Walter Benjamins Sprachmeditationen.* Basel: Schwabe, 1979.

Schrader, M. *Mimesis und Poiesis: Poetologische Studien zum Bildungsroman.* Berlin, 1975.

Schramm, P. E. *Herrschaftszeichen und Staatssymobolik: Beiträge zu ihrer Geschichte vom 3. bis 16. Jahrhundert.* Vols. 1–3. Stuttgart: A. Hiersemann, 1954.

Schreckenberg, H. *Drama: Vom Werden der griechischen Tragödie aus dem Tanz.* Würzburg: K. Triltsch, 1960.

Schultz, Karla L. *Mimesis on the Move. Adorno, T. W.: Concept of Imitation.* New York: P. Lang, 1990.

Schwartz, Elias. *The Forms of Feeling: Toward a Mimetic Theory of Literature.* Port Washington, N.Y.: Kennikat Press, 1972.

Schwarz, Ullrich. *Rettende Kritik und antizipierte Utopie: Zum geschichtlichen Gehalt ästhetischer Erfahrung in den Theorien von Jan Mukarovsy, Walter Benjamin und Theodor W. Adorno.* Munich: W. Fink, 1981.

———. "Walter Benjamin: Mimesis und Erfahrung." In Josef Speck, ed., *Grundprobleme der großen Philosophen, Philosophie der Gegenwart* VI. Göttingen, 1984.

Schweiker, William. *Mimetic Reflections: A Study in Hermeneutics, Theology, and Ethics.* New York: Fordham University Press, 1990.

Schweitzer, B. "Mimesis und Phantasia." *Philologus* 89 (1943): 286–300.

———. "Platon und die bildende Kunst der Griechen." *Die Gestalt* 25 (Tübingen, 1953).

———. *Zur Kunst der Antike. Ausgewählte Schriften* 2 (Tübingen: E. Wasmuth, 1963).

Sennett, Richard. *The Fall of Public Man.* New York: Alfred A. Knopf, 1977.

Sidney, P. *The Defense of Poetry.* Ed. W. Clemen. Heidelberg, 1950.

Smith, B. H. *On the Margins of Discourse: The Relation of Literature to Language.* Chicago: University of Chicago Press, 1979.

Sörbom, Goran. *Mimesis and Art: Studies in the Origin and Early Development of an Aesthetic Vocabulary.* Stockholm: Svenska Bokforlaget, 1966.

Spariosu, M., ed. *Literature, Mimesis and Play: Essays in Literary Theory.* Tübingen, 1982.

———. "Six Authors in Search of a Shadow." In Spariosu, *Literature, Mimesis and Play: Essays in Literary Theory.* Tübingen, 1982. 53–73.

Starobinski, Jean. *Jean-Jacques Rousseau: Transparency and Obstruction.* Trans. Arthur Goldhammer. Chicago: University of Chicago Press, 1988.

———. *Montaigne in Motion.* Trans. Arthur Goldhammer. Chicago: University of Chicago Press, 1985.

Steiner, George. *The Death of Tragedy.* New York: Alfred A. Knopf, 1961.

Steiner, Uwe. *Die Geburt der Kritik aus dem Geiste der Kunst: Untersuchungen zum Begriff der Kritik in den frühen Schriften Walter Benjamins.* Würzburg: Königshausen & Neumann, 1989.

Stendhal. *The Life of Henry Brulard.* Trans. Jean Stewart and B. C. J. G. Knight. New York: Noonday Press, 1958.

———. *Lucien Leuwen.* Book One. Trans. Louise Varèse. New York: New Directions, 1950.

———. *Romans et Nouvelles.* Paris: Gallimard, 1952.

———. *Scarlet and Black: A Chronicle of the Nineteenth Century.* Trans. Margaret R. B. Shaw. Harmondsworth: Penguin Books, 1953.

————. *Vie de Henry Brulard*. Paris: Garnier, 1973.

Stenzel, H. "Molière und der Funktionswandel der Komödie im 17. Jahrhundert." *Lendemains* 22 (1981): 63–77.

Stierle, Karlheinz. "Das bequeme Verhältnis." In Gunter Gebauer, ed., *Das Laokoön-Projekt: Pläne einer semiotischen Asthetik*. Stuttgart: Metzler, 1984.

————. "Die Modernität der französischen Klassik. Negative Anthropologie und funktionaler Stil." In F. Nies and K. Stierle, eds., *Französische Klassik: Theorie, Literatur, Malerei*. Munich: W. Fink, 1985.

Sting, S. "Der Mythos des Fortschreitens: Zur Geschichte der Subjekt-Bildung." Ph.D. dissertation, Freie Universität Berlin, 1990.

Stoessel, Marlene. *Aura, das vergessene Menschliche: Zu Sprache und Erfahrung bei Walter Benjamin*. Munich: C. Hanser, 1983.

Stüssi, Anna. *Erinnerung an die Zukunft: Walter Benjamins "Berliner Kindheit um 1900."* Göttingen: Vanderhoeck & Ruprecht, 1977.

Svenbro, Jesper. *La parole et le marble aux origines de la poetique grecque*. Lund: [S. A.], 1976.

————. *Phrasikleia: An Anthropology of Reading in Ancient Greece*. Trans. Janet Lloyd. Ithaca: Cornell University Press, 1993.

Szondi, Peter. *Die Theorie des bürgerlichen Trauerspiel im 18. Jahrhundert: Der Kaufmann, der Hausvater und der Hofmeister*. Ed. Gert Mattenklott. Frankfurt am Main: Suhrkamp, 1979.

Szukala, R. *Philosophische Untersuchungen zur Theorie ästhetischer Erfahrung*. Stuttgart, 1988.

Taffanin, G. *Il secolo senza Romana*. Bologna, 1942.

Tarde, G. de. *Les lois de l'imitation*. 2d ed. Paris, 1895.

Tarot, R. "Mimesis und Imitatio." *Euphorion* 64 (1970): 125–142.

Tate, J. "Mimesis, a Review of Koller's *Mimesis*." *Classical Review* n.s. (1955): 258–260.

Teuber, B. "Sprache—Körper—Traum." In B. Teuber, ed., *Zur karnevalesken Tradition in der romantischen Literatur aus früher Neuzeit*. Tübingen, 1989.

Theissing, H. *Die Zeit im Bild*. Darmstadt, 1987.

Thomas, Konrad. "Von der Imitation zur Mimesis: Der vergessene Gabriel Tarde und der zu entdeckende René Girard." *Kassler Philosophische Schriften*, vol. 9, *Drei Vorträge*. Kassel, 1983.

————. *Rivalität: Sozialwissenschaftliche Variationen zu einem alten Thema*. Frankfurt: P. Lang, 1990.

Thyen, Anne. *Negative Dialektik und Erfahrung: Zur Rationalität des Nichtidentischen bei Adorno*. Frankfurt am Main, 1989.

Todorov, Tzvetan. "Ästhetik und Semiotik im 18. Jahrhundert. G. E. Lessing: *Laokoön*." In Gunter Gebauer, ed., *Das Laokoön Projekt: Pläne einer semiotischen Ästhetik*. Stuttgart, 1984. 9–22.

————. *The Conquest of America: The Problem of the Other*. Trans. Richard Howard. New York: Harper & Row, 1984.

————. "Poiétique et poétique selon Lessing." In *Recherches poiétiques*. vol. 1, *Collection d'esthétique* 22 (Paris, 1975): 25–41.

————. *Theories of the Symbol.* Trans. Catherine Porter. Ithaca: Cornell University Press, 1982.

Toffanin, Giuseppe. *Il secolo senza Roma.* Bologna: N. Zanichelli, 1943.

Tomberg, F. "Nachahmung als Prinzip der Kunst." Ph.D. dissertation, Berlin, 1963.

Trabant, J. *Apeliotes oder Der Sinn der Sprache: Wilhelm von Humboldts Sprach-Bild.* Munich, 1986.

Treusch-Dieter, G., et al., eds. *Denkzettel Antike: Texte zum kulterellen Vergessen.* Berlin: Reimer, 1989.

Trilling, Lionel. *Sincerity and Authenticity.* Cambridge: Harvard University Press, 1972.

Tubach, F. C. "Die Nachahmungstheorie: Batteux und die Berliner Rationalisten." *Germanisch-Romanische Monatsschriften* 44 (1963): 262–280.

Tumarkin, A. "Die Überwindung der Mimesislehre in der Kunsttheorie des 18. Jahrhunderts." *Festgabe für Samuel Singer* (Tübingen, 1930): 40–55.

Verdenius, W. J. "Mimesis: Plato's Doctrine of Artistic Imitation and Its Meaning to Us." *Philosophia Antiqua* 3 (Leiden, 1949).

————. "A Review of Koller's *Mimesis.*" *Mnemosyne,* 4th ser. (1957): 254–258.

Vernant, Jean-Pierre. "L'Individu dans la cité." In Jean-Pierre Vernant, *L'Individu, la mort, l'amour: Soi même et l'autre en Grèce ancienne.* Paris: Gallimard, 1989.

————. *Myth and Tragedy in Ancient Greece.* Trans. Janet Lloyd. New York: Zone Books, 1990.

————. "Naissance d'images." In Jean-Pierre Vernant, *Religions, histoires, raisons.* Paris: F. Maspero, 1979. 105–137.

Vuillemin, J. "Bermerkungen über Lessings *Laokoön.*" In Gunter Gebauer, ed., *Das Laokoön-Projekt: Pläne einer semiotischen Ästhetik.* Stuttgart, 1984. 167–182.

————. *Élements de poétique.* Paris, 1991.

Walter, J. *Die Geschichte der Ästhetik im Altertum ihrer begrifflichen Entwicklung nach.* Leipzig: Reisland, 1883.

Wannicke, Rainer. *Sartres Flaubert: Zur Misanthropie der Einbildungskraft.* Berlin: D. Reimer, 1990.

Wanning, F. *Diskursivität und Aphoristik.* Tübingen, 1989.

Weber, W. *Der mimetische Erzähler, James Joyces Ulyssees.* Bochum, 1982.

Weidle, W. "Der Sinn der Mimesis." *ERANOS-Jahrbuch* (Zurich, 1963): 249–273.

Weimann, Robert. *Shakespeare und die Macht der Mimesis: Authorität und Repräsentation im Elisabethanischen Theater.* Berlin: Aufbau-Verlag, 1988.

Weinberg, Bernard. *A History of Literary Criticism in the Italian Renaissance.* Chicago: University of Chicago Press, 1961.

Weiss, K. *Grundlegung einer puritanischen Mimesislehre. Einer literatur- und geistesgeschichtliche Studie der Schriften Edward Taylors und anderer puritanischer Autoren.* Paderborn, 1984.

Wellbery, David. *Lessing's Laocoön: Semiotics and Aesthetics in the Age of Reason.* Cambridge: Cambridge University Press, 1984.

Wellek, René. *A History of Modern Criticism: 1750–1950.* New Haven: Yale University Press, 1955.

Welsch, W. *Aisthesis: Grundzüge und Perspektiven der Aristotelischen Sinneslehre.* Stuttgart, 1987.

———. *Unsere postmoderne Moderne.* Weinheim, 1987.

Werhli, Beatrice. *Imitatio und Mimesis in der Geschichte der deutschen Erzähltheorie unter besonderer Berücksichtigung des 19. Jahrhunderts.* Göttingen: A. Kummerle, 1974.

Werner, H. *Metaphysik, Zeichen, Mimesis, Kastration: Möglichkeiten und Grenzen begrifflichen Philosophieverständnisses nach J. Derrida.* Pfaffenweiler, 1985.

Wilke, Sabine. *Zur Dialektik von Exposition und Darstellung. Ansätze zu einer Kritik der Arbeiten M. Heideggers, Th. W. Adorno und J. Derrida.* New York: P. Lang, 1988.

Willems, G. *Anschaulichkeit.* Tübingen, 1989.

Wimmer, K.-M. *Der Andere und die Sprache: Vernunftkritik und Verantwortung.* Berlin, 1988.

Wimsatt, William K., and Cleanth Brooks. *Literary Criticism: A Short History.* New York: Alfred A. Knopf, 1957.

Winckelmann, J. J. *Gedanken über die Nachahmung.* n.p.

Winter, H. ''Zur Entwicklung des Imitatio-Konzepts in der englischen Literaturtheorie des 16. und 17. Jahrhunderts.'' *Zeitschrift für Literaturwissenschaft und Linguistic* 8 (1978): 35–47.

Wittgenstein, Ludwig. *Philosophical Investigations.* Trans. G. E. M. Anscombe. New York: Macmillan, 1968.

———. *Tractatus Logico-Philosophicus.* Trans. D. F. Pears and B. F. M. Guinness. London: Routledge & Kegan Paul, 1974.

Wolbert, K. *Die Nackten und die Toten des ''Dritten Reichs'': Folgen einer politischen Geschichte des Körpers in der Plastik des deutschen Faschismus.* Giessen: Anabas, 1982.

Wulf, Christoph. ''Ästhetische Wege zur Welt: Über das Verhältnis von Mimesis und Erziehung.'' In D. Lenzen, ed., *Kunst und Pädagogik: Erziehungswissenschaft auf dem Weg zur Ästhetik.* Darmstadt, 1990.

———. ''Der Körper der Götter.'' In Dietmar Kamper and Christoph Wulf, eds., *Transfigurationen des Körpers: Spuren der Gewalt in der Geschichte.* Berlin: D. Reimer, 1989. 11–22.

———. ''Lebenszeit—Zeit zu leben? Chronokratie versus Pluralität der Zeiten.'' In Dietmar Kamper and Christoph Wulf, eds., *Die Sterbende Zeit, 20 Diagnosen.* Darmstadt: Luchterhand, 1987. 266–275.

———. ''Die Liebesflamme.'' In Dietmar Kamper and Christoph Wulf, eds., *Das Heilige: Seine Spur in der Moderne.* Frankfurt am Main: Althenaum, 1987.

———. ''Mimesis.'' In Gunter Gebauer et al., *Historische Anthropologie.* Reinbek: Rowohlt, 1989. 83–125.

———. ''Mimesis und Ästhetik: Zur Entstehung der Ästhetik bei Platon und Aristoteles.'' In G. Treusch-Dieter et al., eds., *Denkzettel Antike.* Berlin: Reimer, 1989.

———. ''Mimesis und der Schein des Schönen.'' In Dietmar Kamper and Christoph Wulf, eds., *Der Schein des Schönen.* Göttingen, 1989.

Wünsche, Konrad. *Der Volksschullehrer Ludwig Wittgenstein.* Frankfurt am Main, 1985.

Ziegler, L. "Von der Ahmung." In L. Ziegler, ed., *Spätlese eigener Hand*. Munich, 1953. 93–106.

Zimbardo, Rose A. *A Mirror to Nature: Transformations in Drama and Aesthetics, 1660–1732*. Lexington: University Press of Kentucky, 1986.

Zimbrich, Ulrike. *Mimesis bei Platon. Untersuchungen zu Wortgebrauch, Theorie der dictherischen Darstellung und zur dialogischen Gestaltung bis zur Politeia*. Frankfurt: P. Lang, 1984.

Zuckerkandl, V. "Mimesis." *Merkur* 12 (1958): 225–240.

Zumthor, Paul. *Oral Poetry: An Introduction*. Trans. Kathryn Murphy-Judy. Minneapolis: University of Minnesota Press, 1990.

Index

Designer: UC Press Staff
Compositor: Braun-Brumfield, Inc.
Text: 10/12 Times Roman
Display: Helvetica
Printer: Braun-Brumfield, Inc.
Binder: Braun-Brumfield, Inc.